Alexander and Cleopatra, first and last of the Hellenistic monarchs.
Left: head of Alexander. (*British Museum*). Right: head of Cleopatra VII. (*Altes Museum, Berlin*)

Hellenistic Naval Warfare and Warships 336-30 BC

War at Sea from Alexander to Actium

Michael Pitassi

Pen & Sword
MILITARY

For Ann

First published in Great Britain in 2023 by
Pen & Sword Military
An imprint of Pen & Sword Books Limited
Yorkshire – Philadelphia

ISBN 973 1 39909 760 4

A CIP catalogue record for this book is
available from the British Library

Typeset by Mac Style
Printed and bound in India by Replika Press Pvt. Ltd.

Pen & Sword Books Limited incorporates the imprints of After the Battle,
Atlas, Archaeology, Aviation, Discovery, Family History, Fiction, History,
Maritime, Military, Military Classics, Politics, Select, Transport, True Crime,
Air World, Frontline Publishing, Leo Cooper, Remember When, Seaforth
Publishing, The Praetorian Press, Wharncliffe Local History, Wharncliffe
Transport, Wharncliffe True Crime and White Owl.

For a complete list of Pen & Sword titles please contact

PEN & SWORD BOOKS LIMITED
47 Church Street, Barnsley, South Yorkshire, S70 2AS, England
E-mail: enquiries@pen-and-sword.co.uk
Website: www.pen-and-sword.co.uk
or
PEN AND SWORD BOOKS
1950 Lawrence Rd, Havertown, PA 19083, USA
E-mail: Uspen-and-sword@casematepublishers.com
Website: www.penandswordbooks.com

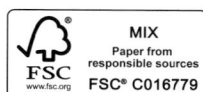

FSC — MIX — Paper from responsible sources — FSC® C016779 — www.fsc.org

Contents

Maps

Illustrations

All photographs, plans, drawings, maps and models © the author except where stated

Introduction

Since before the dawn of recorded history, the eastern Mediterranean basin has been an arena for naval warfare, the earliest recorded naval battle (although undoubtedly not the first) that we know of having been in 1210, when a Hittite fleet defeated one from Cyprus, allied to the 'Sea Peoples.'

What differentiates the Hellenistic Era however (the three centuries following the death of Alexander the Great in 323) is the veritable explosion of naval technology and warfare that took place as the players who sought to succeed him and acquire his empire fought for position in a bewildering succession of manoeuvrings and campaigns. That comparatively short period saw a naval arms race the like of which had never been seen before and only rarely since. It also gave rise to the development of ever-greater and more sophisticated ships and to the oar-powered warship reaching perhaps its ultimate expression, echoed in the great fleets of these ships that battled for maritime supremacy. It is with these ships and their activities that this book is concerned.

With the ending of that era in the universal supremacy of Rome, the technology became redundant, disused and eventually so completely forgotten that in the next (nearly as) great period of oar-powered fleets, the Renaissance and after, ancient terms, such as 'trireme', were resurrected for ships unrecognisable from those for which the terms had been coined and which owed nothing to them.

In an attempt to bring some semblance of logical order to this confusing melee of events, I have divided the period into six parts that seem to lend themselves to such treatment. They are somewhat arbitrary but, it is hoped, will help to put the developing events into a context. Each part has been divided into firstly a chapter dealing with the historical narrative, the background against which the drama was played out. To each part, save the first, an Appendix is added to enable a more detailed examination of a specimen battle of that period, without an overlong interruption of the overall narrative. Other chapters seek to define, examine and reconstruct the ship types involved and the new types as they were introduced. The attempted reconstructions are based on the scant available evidence and try to keep within what is known of the technology of the time and yet be workable in practice, as the originals of course, were.

The interpretation of the all-too-limited references in ancient literature can understandably only be subjective; after all, if I wrote 'he got into the car and drove away', I would not go on to give a detailed explanation of what a car is – you all know. So it was with the ancient author who might write 'he went aboard the *hepteres* and sailed away', he was writing for an audience who knew what a *hepteres* was. Until the fifteenth century AD and the invention of printing, books were disseminated by successive copying by hand; despite all the care, editing and re-reading that has gone into producing this very book, you will doubtless find a typographical error or two, so imagine what a couple of thousand years of copying and translation can do. Add misguided attempts to substitute ancient terms with modern 'equivalents' for whatever reason and the problems are compounded. For example, in otherwise very good translations, one has seen the substitution of 'company commander' for a centurion and, even worse, 'sloop' for one of Alexander's *hemioliae*. I have tried to adhere to what is believed to be the original terminology wherever possible but feel that it does not detract from such purity to use such terms as 'trireme' where appropriate.

This leads to the problem of spelling of names of people and places, particularly the former, most of which are, of course, Greek. I have sought to use the familiar, common renditions of names and, whereas I have tried to avoid inconsistencies, any anomalies or peculiarities are down to me.

Alexander's untimely death and his failure to nominate a clear successor left a vacuum in which his generals, although at first nominally propounding unity, were in fact, from the start, jostling for power. The machinations and wars of these *diadochoi* or successors provided a most confusing and constantly changing kaleidoscope of personalities, many sharing the same name. Basic genealogical tables are included in the Appendices, together with an index of the characters appearing in the text. Characters of the same name have their respective number included and where rulers are named, regnal years are given.

All dates given are of course, BC, any exceptions being so noted.

The term 'bulwark' has been used throughout for the topmost edge of a ship hull, rather than the more usual modern term 'gunwale', which seems inappropriate in an age before the invention of the gun which gave rise to it.

Another clarification is needed in the matter of a commonly used term to describe rowing arrangements, that is the word 'bank'; thus it is commonly said that a trireme had three 'banks' of oars – it did not; it had three horizontal layers of oars, each of which was single-banked, i.e. one rower per oar. The term 'bank' refers to the *banco* or bench upon which the rowers sit, thus one rower sitting rowing is single-banked; add another pulling the same oar or a separate oar but sat on the same bench and they are double-banked and so on. If we add a second horizontal layer of rowers (a bireme), who sit on their own benches, each layer can be single or double-banked and so on. As in my previous books, I shall refer to a horizontal layer of rowers as a 'reme' and will seek to avoid the term 'bank' altogether. This fits nicely with the ship types, mono-, bi- and triremes, which are of course, hybridised modern terms but simple and convenient.

All interpretations, reconstructions and hypotheses as to the ships are those of the author, intended as his attempt at finding solutions to the problem of ascertaining what those ships of yore were actually like and how they worked. At no point am I suggesting that this is definitive, but only, hopefully, that it will provide food for further thought and in the hope that one day, hard evidence will be unearthed to give an unequivocal description of them.

'… they moved along like castles and cities, while the sea groaned and the winds were fatigued.'

Florus, LV.11

Chronology

Part I

359 Philip II succeeds to Macedonian throne.

357 Athenian fleet fails to prevent secession of Chios from its maritime league.

356 Allies attack Athenian possessions; Athenian fleet beaten. Piracy grows again.

355 Final dissolution of maritime league.

352 First Macedonian fleet in Aegean, extends Philip's power.

351 Macedonians raid Attica; undeclared sea war in effect.

340 Athenian grain fleet attacked in Propontis.

339 Athenian fleet relieves Philip's siege of Byzantion.

338 Battle of Chaeronea, Philip gains hegemony over Greece.

Part II

336 October. Assassination of Philip II, Alexander succeeds.

334 Invasion of Asia; June: Battle of Granicus. Late Summer: sieges of Miletus and Halikarnassos.

333 November: Battle of Issus.

332 January to July: siege of Tyre. Siege of Gaza; Alexander in Egypt, founds Alexandria.

331 July, Alexander sets off for Persia.

326 Hephaestion reaches the River Indus. May: Battle of Hydaspes.

325 Alexander prepares to return. June: Craterus marches west with part of the army. Late August: Alexander marches with the rest of the army. October: Nearchos sails with his fleet. December: Nearchos' rendezvous with Alexander in Carmania.

324 January to February: Nearchos sails to the head of the Persian Gulf, returns to Carmania to meet Alexander, then returns to River Tigris.

323 Alexander in Babylon, plans naval expansion. 10 June, death of Alexander the Great. Generals meet. Philip Arrhideios named Philip III. Regents appointed and provinces allotted. Alexander's son born (Alexander IV).

Part III

Part IV

301 Demetrios in Greece. Ptolemy expands his influence. Independent states in Asia Minor.

297 Death of Cassander. Demetrios attacks Athens.

296 Demetrios takes Athens but loses his remaining possessions in Asia Minor to Lysimachus, Seleucos and Ptolemy; extends his power in Greece.

289 Lysimachus and Pyrrhus invade Macedon.

287 Demetrios invades Asia Minor.

285 Demetrios captured. Antigonos II succeeds in Greece. Ptolemy dominates at sea; Lysimachus makes himself King of Macedon.

282 Death of Ptolemy I, Ptolemy II succeeds.

281 Battle of Corupedion, Lysimachus killed. Seleucos dies, succeeded by Antiochus I.

277 Antigonos II king in Macedon.

275 Ptolemy's fleet in Red Sea. Pyrrhus invades Macedon.

270 Hieron of Syracuse gives two great ships to Ptolemy.

264 Start of First Punic War.

262 Antigonos II captures Athens.

261 Antiochus I dies; Antiochus II succeeds and makes accord with Antigonos II against Ptolemy. Start of naval arms race.

258 Sea battle off Cos. Antigonos II defeats Ptolemy II's fleet.

256 Antigonos II defeats Ptolemy's fleet at Andros. Ptolemy increases his fleet.

255 Ptolemy's fleet beaten at Ephesos; sues for peace.

246 Death of Ptolemy II and Antiochus II, Ptolemy III and Seleucos II succeed. Ptolemy occupies Antioch and wins naval victory off Andros.

241 First Punic War ends with Roman naval victory.

239 Death of Antigonos II, succeeded by Demetrios II.

233 Rivalry between Aetolian and Achaean Leagues of Greece.

229 Illyrians defeat a Greek fleet. Roman fleet and troops seize Corcyra, defeat Illyrians and form protectorate. Demetrios II killed, succeeded by Philip V.

225 Seleucos II dies, succeeded by Seleucos III and then, in 223, by Antiochus III.

222 Death of Ptolemy III, Ptolemy IV succeeds.

219 Demetrios of Pharos invades Roman protectorate (220). Roman fleet and troops sent and beat him. Antiochus III takes Phoenicia and Palestine from Ptolemy III.

218 Start of Second Punic War. Roman squadron thwarts Philip V attempt to gain in Illyria.

216 Attempted pact between Philip V and Hannibal thwarted.

214 Philip's foray into Illyria defeated by Romans. Macedonian war in Greece.

212   Siege and fall of Syracuse.
210   Roman fleet in Ionian sea and then the Aegean.
209   Roman and Pergamene fleets operate in Aegean.
205   End of Macedonian War. . Death of Ptolemy IV, infant Ptolemy V succeeds.
202   Defeat of Hannibal at Zama ends Second Punic War. Antiochus III and Philip
        V ally against Ptolemy. Philip advances into Aegean and Asia Minor; defeats
        Rhodian fleet off Lade.
201   Philip attacks Chios; loses naval battle against Pergamene and Rhodian fleets.
        Allies appeal to Rome.

Part V

200   Philip attacks Athens and Hellespont; Antiochus seizes Sidon and Phoenicia
        from Ptolemy. Romans send fleet and army; start of Macedonian War.
199   Roman and allied fleet operate in Aegean.
198   Philip attempts peace talks.
197   Battle of Cynoscephalae; Philip defeated, war ends. Antiochus extending into
        Asia Minor, builds fleet.
196   Antiochus takes Cilicia, Ephesus, invades Thrace.
194   Roman and allies campaign against Sparta.
192   Antiochus invades Greece; Roman troops attacked, start of war.
191   Romans and allies drive Antiochus from Greece. Antiochus' fleet defeated at
        Battle of Cape Corycus.
190   Romans invade Asia Minor. Rhodian fleet defeated at Panormus. Rhodians
        defeat Hannibal's fleet off Side. Roman and Rhodian fleet defeat Antiochus'
        fleet off Cape Myonnesus.
189   Antiochus' army defeated at Battle of Magnesia, end of war.
188   Romans withdraw. Rhodes, Pergamum expand.
183   Rome brokers peace between Pergamum and Bithynia.
172   Third Macedonian War; Roman fleet supreme in Aegean.
168   Romans seize Illyria, defeat Macedon at Battle of Pydna, end of war.
        Antiochus invades Egypt, seizes Cyprus; withdraws under Roman pressure.
167   Romans hand Delos to Athens as a free port; decline of Rhodes; Jewish revolt.
163   Rhodian fleet in Lycia.
162   Octavius burns Seleucid fleet.
161   Jewish revolt crushed by Seleucids.
155   Crete revolts against Rhodes.
154   Fleet action between Pergamum and Bithynia.
149   Attempted usurpation of Macedonian throne.

148 Romans re-invade Macedon.

146 Final war between Rome and Carthage. Romans sack Corinth, withdraw fleet from Aegean.

133 Death of Attalus II, bequeaths Pergamum to Rome.

130 Pergamum becomes Roman province.

102 After prolonged increase in piracy, Romans send fleet on anti-piracy operation.

Part VI

100 Marcus Antonius (snr.) concludes anti-piracy operations.

96 Cyrene bequeathed to Rome. Social unrest in Italy.

89 Mithridates VI of Pontus expands his power. Rome distracted by civil war and conflict in Africa and central Europe.

88 Mithridates invades Greece. Sulla defeats him twice and drives him out.

83 Lucullus gathers fleet to support Sulla; beats Mithridates' fleet twice. Sulla in Asia Minor, peace with Mithridates. Caesar in Bithynia. Lesbos revolt suppressed.

79 Vatia campaigns against pirates.

77 Vatia defeats pirate fleet.

75 Second Mithridatic War, Vatia withdrawn.

74 Romans in Black Sea. Cyrene annexed. Bithynia bequeathed to Rome, invaded by Mithridates.

73 Lucullus and Cotta attack Mithridates, who is eventually beaten and flees to Armenia.

72 Piracy rampant.

69 Pirates sack Delos. Metellus invades Crete.

67 Pirates raid Ostia. *Lex Gabinia*. Pompeius commands anti-pirate campaigns in the West and the East Mediterranean, eradicating pirates.

66 Mithridates attempts return to power. Pompeius occupies Pontus, marches to Armenia; establishes naval squadrons.

64 Pompeius in Syria. Civil war in Judaea.

63 Phoenicia comes under Roman hegemony.

62 Crete annexed; Syria annexed.

49 Civil war between Caesar and Pompeius.

48 Caesar confronts Pompeius in Illyria. Naval activity in Adriatic. Battle of Pharsalus (Aug) Pompeius defeated, flees to Egypt and murdered there. Caesar in Alexandria.

47 'Alexandrian War' Caesar besieged there.

44 Caesar assassinated.

PART I

BEFORE ALEXANDER –
SETTING THE SCENE

Bronze ram recovered from Piraeus harbour, thought to be from a trireme. (*Piraeus Archeological Museum*)

MACEDONIA

PELLA

VERGINA

HALKIDIKI

THESSALY

EPIRUS

N. SPORADES

LEUCTRA

ACARNANIA

AETOLIA

BATTLE OF
CHAERONEA 338

THEBES

ACHAEA

ISTHMUS

ATTICA

ATHENS
PIRAEUS

CORINTH

AEGINA

ARGOS

ARCADIA

GULF OF NAFPLION

SPARTA

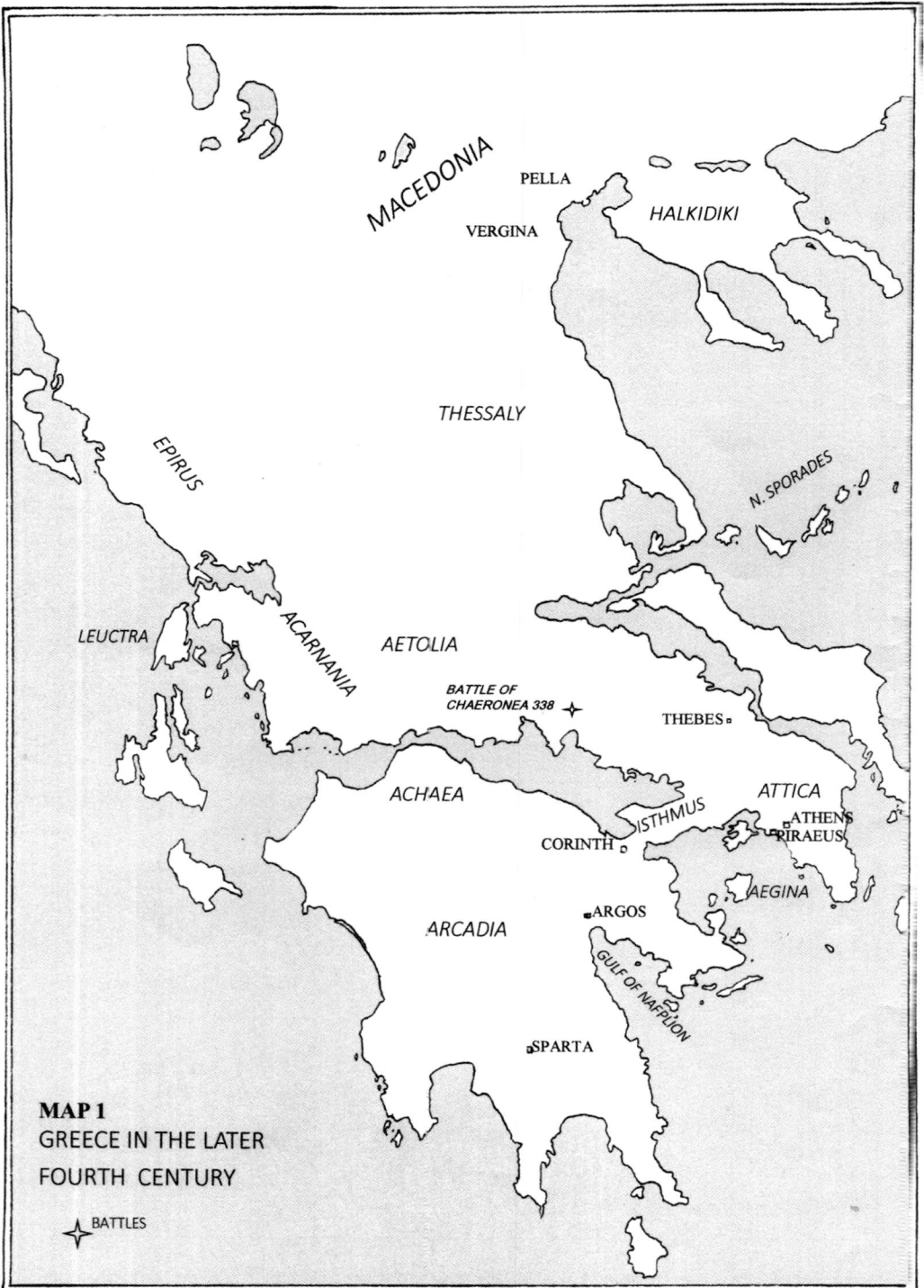

MAP 1
GREECE IN THE LATER
FOURTH CENTURY

BATTLES

Chapter 1

Philip II and the Rise of Macedon

359 In 359, Philip II succeeded to the throne of the Kingdom of Macedonia, a kingdom centred on the fertile plains and valleys of the Rivers Vandar and Aliakmon in what is now north-east Greece, 'a land of stalwart peasants and horse-riding squires'.[1] Bounded by the Rhodope mountains to the north and east and the Pindos mountains to the north and west, its people spoke a dialect of Greek barely understandable to the Greeks 'proper' to their south, who regarded them as semi-barbarous. Philip was a warrior king and an excellent general who fought off challenges to his throne, formed a formidable army and campaigned to turn his country into a dominant power. From 358, his campaigns extended his realms to the north of Macedonia proper, followed by his overrunning of Thessaly to the south in 352. Annexation of Halkidiki in 349 was followed by the conquest of southern Thrace in 342. Philip's conquests gave him an extended coastline and possession of many of the ports around the northern Aegean. He had started to

Figure 1. Philip II (359 to 336). King of Macedon, Father of Alexander the Great. Modern statue in a park in Thessaloniki; the armour reproduces Philip's own armour found in his tomb at Verghina.

acquire warships from 352 and these took to raiding and extending his power over the islands of the northern Aegean. The principal Greek naval power, Athens, was unable to prevent this as its fleet was at that time in a poor state of repair and funding, as well as lacking clear leadership. Philip nevertheless remained unable to challenge the Athenians for dominance at sea, which

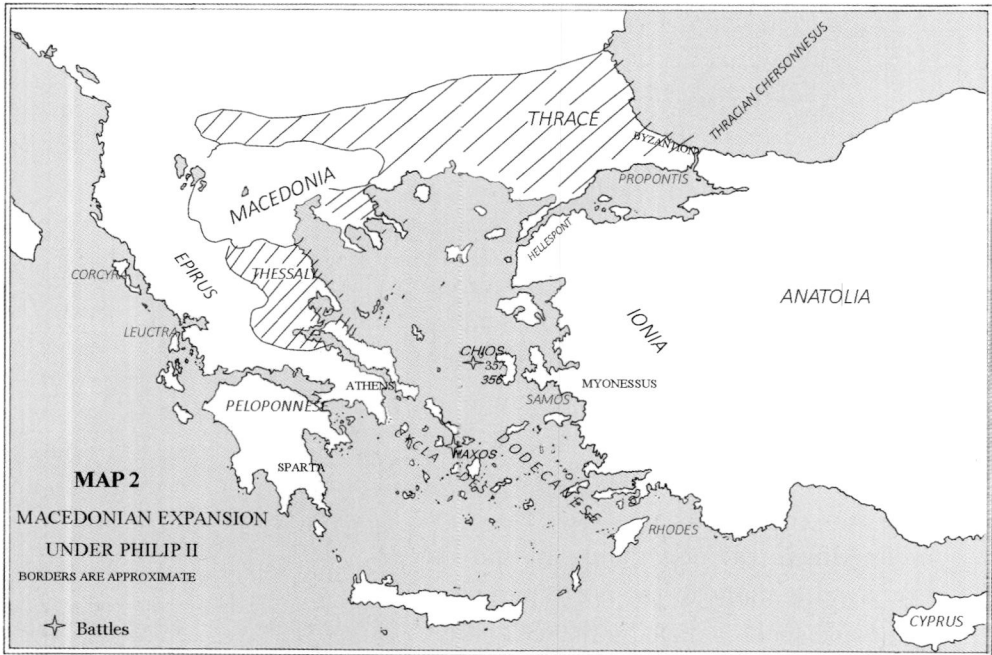

MAP 2

MACEDONIAN EXPANSION

UNDER PHILIP II

BORDERS ARE APPROXIMATE

⚓ Battles

enabled them to retain their hold on the Hellespont, ensuring their trade routes to the Black Sea.

For Athens, it was not just a matter of trade, important though that was; the city was unable to feed its people from the produce of Attica, which had also been vulnerable to invasion. Grain, that basic foodstuff, had to be imported and the most reliable source of adequate supplies was the lands of the Crimea and northern areas of the Black Sea. For this reason, it was essential for the Athenians to safeguard, preferably by dominating it, the route through the Bosporus, Propontis (Sea of Marmara) and Hellespont (Dardanelles, see Map 8). It was towards this route that Philip's power increasingly encroached and his expansionist aims meant that he needed access across it. Philip's ambition was to invade the Persian Empire and to free the Greek Ionian cities from them, doubtless to add them to his own realms.

Athenian dominance thwarted Philip's ambitions to invade Asia, but his occupation of the northern Aegean coast closed its ports to Athenian shipping. In a virtually undeclared war he made extensive use of privateers and pirates to raid Athenian possessions who, for their part were as bad and, apart from 'their' pirates, some of their own warships undertook similar operations.[2]

357   Since her defeat in the Peloponnesian Wars of the previous century, Athens had recovered and once more became the pre-eminent naval power among the Greeks and had formed a maritime league to unite the Greek islands and

city-states. By 360, disenchantment with that league was growing. Spartan sea power, the original reason for the league's existence, had been greatly reduced as a result of battles and natural disasters which led to the effective dissolution of the league by the secession of various states. In 357, Chios, Kos, Rhodes and Byzantion seceded, followed shortly by most of the other allies and subject territories; attempts at re-conquest failed. Although Athens continued to have numerically the largest navy in Greece, the other (now independent) states also built or acquired warships. As will be seen later, most of these fleets tended to be small, of between five and twenty ships on average; their strength lay in joint operations. Athens sent a fleet of sixty ships to recover rebellious Chios in 357, but the islanders (presumably with the help of their allies) could muster 100 ships in their harbour and repulsed the Athenians who lost one ship. Another Athenian fleet of sixty ships was sent to confront its former allies but a storm prevented any decisive encounter.

Piracy was (and will continue to be) a recurrent theme and always quickly became endemic in the absence of policing. Having long been regarded as 'trade by other means', roving seafarers voyaged for trade or plunder, depending upon the strength of the places or ships that they encountered. The growth of the Athenian Empire in the fifth century[3] with its dependency on the seas, required protection by its navy, which had extended to the policing of them, ending piracy in the Aegean and around the Peloponnese as far as Epirus.[4] Policing of the seas had to be progressively abandoned during the Peloponnesian War (431 to 404). Much of the naval activity of the war consisted of raids by both sides on the coasts of the other, aided by privateering, i.e. little more than state-sanctioned piracy.[5] These 'privateers' were indiscriminate in their choice of prey, so that neutral shipping also suffered their depredations, encouraging those neutrals to seek retribution, adding in turn to the problem.[6] The deployment of fleets during the various wars of that century had continued to require the drafting of large numbers of seamen but, with occasional peace and reduction in warships, many men who had known no trade other than that of arms and unequipped for a civilian life that had by-passed them, were redundant and free to pursue less legitimate careers. Several of the characters herein actually encouraged and, indeed, employed pirates to exploit opportunities for plunder and profit to further their own ends or to augment their strength, the lure of booty taking the place of wages.

As an example, despite their naval strength, the Athenians were unable to prevent the privateers of one Alexander of Pherae, in 362 and 361, from ravaging the Cyclades, raiding the Sporades and even entering Piraeus and looting the money-changers there (the bankers of the day).[7]

Philip's ships raided Athenian islands and the coasts of Attica (351) while, for their part, Athenian privateers operated widely, even when 'peace' was supposed to be in force.[8] Athenian captains took and enslaved people from Macedonian coasts and seized merchant ships sailing to and from Macedonian ports.[9] Overall however, Athenian trade suffered greatly and her economic situation deteriorated and with it, her ability to pay her ship crews; merchant captains could literally hire Athenian warships to escort them to ensure safe passage.[10] Piracy thrived, encouraged rather than openly supported by both sides and became a permanent feature with pirates ready to be hired as mercenary naval forces or to operate *ex officio* alongside regular naval ships for a share of the loot. Philip continued his relentless advance into the northern hinterland of the Hellespont, further threatening the grain route from the Black Sea.

356   In 356, a Macedonian and allied fleet of 100 ships raided Athenian islands and laid siege to Samos. The Athenians sent sixty ships to the Hellespont to threaten Byzantion; the allies sailed to protect it and managed to intercept and beat the Athenian fleet near to Chios.[11] Athenian sea-power had been disrupted and without her former 'associates' and their manpower, became even less able to police the seas, further encouraging piracy.[12] Some of the smaller islands became pirate lairs, as did Myonnesus and the Thracian Chersonesus.[13] An Athenian attempt to eradicate this last-named nest of pirates failed.[14] Finally, in 355, Athens was forced by the threat of a massive Persian fleet, backed by an army, to conclude a peace with her former league members and recognise their independence,[15] although some, notably Rhodes, fell under Persian domination

Over all of these events loomed the shadow of the vast Persian Empire and its domination of the Levant, Egypt and Anatolia, including the western part, Ionia, with its Greek population; it also held suzerainty over Cyprus and many of the Greek islands. Although its hold on the cities of the Ionian Greeks of

Figure 2. Themistocles (c. 527 to 460). 'Father' of the Athenian Navy, he persuaded the Athenians to invest a windfall from the silver mines at Larium in building triremes. Commanded the Greek Fleet in its victory against the Persian Fleet at Salamis in 480. (*Vatican Museum*)

the Aegean littoral and some of the islands of that sea waxed and waned, it remained by far the dominant power. The Empire was always able to, and did, take advantage of the internecine quarrels of the mainland and island Greeks to play off, or sometimes pay off, one against the other, ensuring thereby that no single Greek entity would be strong enough to seriously challenge them. This situation changed when Philip established hegemony and placed some semblance of unity upon the Greeks.

Although having no navy as such, the Persians' hold of the Levant and Egypt and their wealth, enabled them to levy ships and crews from their tributary seafaring peoples and to hire mercenary ships and crews from among the Greeks, allowing a potential total of about 400 warships. As an example, in 394 they had levied 100 triremes from Ionia, the Levant and Egypt; due to poor communications and inefficiency however, this fleet took months to organise and assemble. The century had however been marked by serious rebellions in Egypt in 361 which spread, and the Egyptians briefly held the southern coast of Syria. Phoenicia revolted by 351 and defeated a Persian army. Spartan and Athenian expeditions had helped the Egyptians throw off Persian rule in the mid-360s, but in 348, the Persian King Artaxerxes III recovered Phoenicia and by 343 had re-conquered Egypt and re-established Persian rule.

341   Athens and Philip were by now at open war for control of the Hellespont and Gallipoli Peninsula, the former with help from some of the local cities (some with Persian help) who were wary of Philip. Athens sent a fleet of 100 ships there, which the outnumbered Macedonian fleet only narrowly managed to evade. In 340, the annual Athenian grain fleet of 230 ships was moored in the Propontis at Hieron Oros, awaiting their escort of forty Athenian triremes. Philip's fleet could not capture the convoy so he sent part of his army, who attacked from the land and captured and destroyed between 170 and 180 of the ships. In 339, in retaliation, Athens again sent a warfleet, which was joined by allied ships from Rhodes, Chios and Cos, all apprehensive of Philip's ambitions. The fleet sailed to Byzantion, then under siege by Philip, relieving the city and forcing him to abandon his siege and return home.[16]

338   In the face of the threat posed by Philip and his ships' interference with Athenian commerce, Athen's navy was increased to some 300 ships. Philip could not compete and returned to a land campaign, culminating in his crushing defeat of Athens, Thebes and their allies at the Battle of Chaeronea in the late summer of 338,[17] which gave him effective hegemony over all of Greece. This he secured by the creation of a Hellenic League, the League of Corinth, to unite the Greeks and direct its focus against Persia. In 337, the League voted for war against Persia.

336   Philip now had at his disposal all of the naval forces of Greece, grudgingly including that of Athens, in addition to his own Macedonian fleet, enough to provide a challenge to the Persians. Their empire had been weakened by various revolts, followed by a period of court intrigue and the murder of three kings, leaving Darius III, who ascended the throne in 336. With command of the Athenian forces, Philip also had access to the Hellespont and the crossing to Asia.

In 336, a Macedonian army under Philip's general Parmenion and backed by a fleet, crossed into Asia and advanced as far south as Ephesus. The islands of Tenedos, Lesbos and Chios were also taken; the naval forces available to Philip that supported these operations, included ships from Macedon and those levied from Athens and other Greek states. There seems to have been no Persian naval opposition to Parmenion's crossing and operations. Philip's plans for the further invasion of the Persian Empire and liberation of the Ionian Greeks were brought to a sudden end by his assassination at the hands of one Pausanias in 336.

To the west the city-state of Syracuse on Sicily would fundamentally influence Hellenistic naval warfare. Founded by settlers from Corinth in about 733, the city possesses Sicily's best natural harbour and it prospered and grew in territory and power to become the pre-eminent Greek city on the island. For centuries, Greeks and Carthaginians had been vying for dominance of Sicily, with successive wars which saw one side then the other expand across the island.[18] Having defeated the Athenian invasion and siege of the city in 415 to 413, Syracusan focus had to return to Carthage, who maintained a large and formidable navy with which they dominated the western Mediterranean and jealously guarded their trade. Carthage was able to deploy fleets of up to 200 warships, with ships and well-trained crews of the highest quality. Although Syracuse could never expect to be able to overcome the Carthaginian Navy completely, it did have to maintain a fleet to ensure its independence and, from time to time, gained local superiority.[19] Their fleet was also used, wholly or in part, when Syracuse became involved in matters on the Italian mainland, Epirus and even North Africa; it was more effective in restricting piracy in the Ionian Sea and Southern Adriatic and thus protecting Syracusan trade.

The constant threat from Carthage, together with the expansionist plans of the tyrant Dionysius I, led, by the end of the fifth century, to the development of new types of warship and weapons that would revolutionise battlefleets and stimulate naval developments that followed. To counter the recent Carthaginian invention and introduction of the 'four', *tetrereis* or quadrireme (see Chapter 2) he recruited military engineers and ship designers to produce new weapons

Figure 3. Syracuse. Top: view south from seaward of the island of Ortygia. The Great Harbour lies beyond the point. The land in the distance to the right is Achradina, a mainland district of the city. Bottom: the site of the former small harbour between Ortygia (on the right) and the mainland (left); this was the military harbour and gave access either side, to the sea (beyond, to the left of the large, square building) and the Great Harbour (foreground). It is now closed by a causeway.

and ships to further his own ambitions. The result would be the invention and introduction of new artillery weapons and the emergence of the 'five', *pentereis* or quinquereme (see Chapter 2).[20] Dionysius expanded his navy to nearly 200 warships,[21] including both fours and fives,[22] to equal the Carthaginians, who also now built fours and fives for their fleet.

With one exception, the numbers and composition of the fleets of this period are difficult to gauge, the available information being scant. An occasionally mentioned number, together with an assessment of the particular polity, its size, population and relative wealth, together with the rare indication of ship type (all too often simply referred to with the omnibus term 'triremes') is all the evidence available to attempt a determination of fleets. One common matter of all the fleets that will be examined in the pages following was that they were all crewed by free men. The 'galley slave', in common usage and practice from the mid-sixteenth century AD onward,[23] has led to a popular modern misconception and was a state unknown in the Ancient World; true, some men may have been conscripted for military service, or even been prisoners of war pressed into service, but they were all free-born, a status not altered by their service aboard the ships.

The Athenian Navy of the fourth century is the best known as records survive in the form of inventories incised on marble tablets, created by the Navy Commissioners upon the expiry of their one-year term of office, to pass on to their successors.[24] From the twelve ships allowed by the peace after Aegospotami in 405, the Athenians had rebuilt their navy, so that by 394 they counted forty triremes and 106 by 379. There would have been additional numbers of smaller ships, conters and the like but these were never included in the Navy Lists, although their existence is attested in the literary record.[25] The Lists and their totals were deceptive as they seem to have included worn-out, unseaworthy and even ships that had been lost; neither did Athens have the manpower to crew all of them at one time; losses of ships could always be replaced however. Even if only half the number listed could be counted as fit for active service, Athens was still the largest naval power after Persia.

Due to reforms in 375, the Athenian citizen body that provided the ships was organised into sixty 'wards,' each supplying a trireme[26] and giving rise to the deployment of fleets of this number in 357 and 356 (despite the official lists containing no less than 283 triremes). Although Athens was reasonably wealthy, the cost of building and operating a fleet was a burden[27] and a severely limiting factor for the smaller states. It cost two talents of silver to build and fit out a trireme and another half to one talent a year to maintain it. There were six *obols* to a *drachma*, one hundred *drachmai* to a *mina* and sixty *minae* to one talent. A *mina* was equivalent to one pound (454g) of silver. The crew received three *obols* a day per man, from which they had to buy their food; shipwrights were paid twice this and officers received more; a trireme crew cost four talents per annum in wages.[28]

Challenges to Athenian naval superiority by its old enemy, Sparta and later by Thebes had disappeared and towards the end of the period, the Athenians, although having some 300 ships of all types, sent only 100 ships in the largest fleet they actually deployed. Athenians themselves were becoming less enamoured of overseas adventures and, to make up crews, manpower had to be sought from allies and many foreign mercenaries had to be recruited for larger fleet operations.

Worthy of mention is the island of Rhodes, which will play an increasing role in the period to come. Having been subject to Persia, by the early fourth century it had detached itself and had been contested between an oligarchic faction, supported by Sparta and democrats who founded a republic, supported by Athens. The island's autonomy was finally recognised by the Persian 'King's Peace' of 385. With this came the founding of a navy to protect the island's interests.[29]

Rhodes, after ten years, had joined the second Athenian League, having built up her navy so that it was now considered to be a naval power by the 360s.[30] Their fleet formed part of the allied fleet that then fought the Athenians to free the members of the League from their domination. After this however, the island fell back under Persian domination once more. It still maintained its navy, lending and even hiring ships (it cost 10,000 drachmae per month for a trireme) to various ventures in a limited way but always with their own narrow interest at heart.

The Republic of Rome had been steadily spreading across the Italian Peninsula and possessed a few, probably small, warships to cover its limited shores. The first surviving reference to a Roman warship dates from 394 and the first action by a Roman fleet was in winning an action off Antium (Anzio) in 338.[31]

Although Diodorus[32] says that the Phoenicians had 'many' fives by 351, there was a general hesitation in the Eastern Mediterranean over the adoption of the new larger types. Possibly the extremely heavy investment already made in triremes, especially by Athens, together with a mindset that had grown around the long-standing assumption that it was the supreme oared warship, as it had been for so long, together with the huge numbers that had been built and still existed, precluded the contemplation of something different.

The predominant warship type was thus still the trireme but the new, larger types had gradually started to be introduced; Sidon had fives by 351[33] and it is reasonable that the larger contributors to Persian sea-power also had a sprinkling of fours and fives. Athens seems to have been slower to introduce larger vessels and the earliest mention (so far found) of a ship larger than a trireme at Athens is of fours in 330, eighteen being included in the lists for that year. Other Greek cities would have a few warships for local policing, which for larger operations would be used in conjunction with the fleets of whichever larger power or league they belonged to. As has been seen, in 357, Chios mustered 100 ships to oppose the Athenians, a total that must have included allies, and in the following year, Chios, Rhodes, Cos and Byzantion, between them, fielded 100 triremes. Macedon had traditionally been a land power but Philip had founded a navy in 352 which was still small with, perhaps, no more than a dozen triremes by the time of his death.

When attempting to assess naval strengths, there must be included that amorphous group, the pirates and privateers, many often indistinguishable from more formal navies, in which many of their ships and crews would serve from time to time. They made use of a large variety of craft, including the smaller warship types, often massing to predate on larger or stronger victims. Although scattered *ad hoc* around the coasts and islands, their presence and preparedness to exploit opportunity, together with an ability to organise, was a constant.

Chapter 2

The Ships of Philip's Era

The evolution of the warship had been long, the earliest naval encounters having been an extension of warfare on land with boats, ships, even rafts used solely to enable the warring sides to come into contact and join battle.[1] At some point very early on, a distinction[2] was made between a narrow boat which was fast and manoeuvrable and a wide, deeper one which could carry a great deal more cargo, but was slower. The former performed better under oars and the latter, under sail.

A familiar concept is of a ship's hull being breached and the ship sinking, and indeed, many sunken ancient merchant shipwrecks have been located.[3] Ancient ships were made from wood, which obviously floats; the wrecks, holed or swamped had been dragged to the bottom by the weight of their cargoes. The heaviest thing in an ancient warship however was the crew, who, we can assume, would have wasted no time in abandoning a stricken ship. The weight of the bronze ram (if it did not fall off) was insufficient to overcome the latent buoyancy of the wooden hull which floated, unusable and in a swamped state, until it could be towed to shore for repair. Ships lost to storms broke up and those which were old or too badly damaged were burned or broken up. Thus, with a couple of exceptions only, no examples of sunken ancient seagoing warships have been found. It is convenient nevertheless, subject to this caveat, to refer to ships as 'sunk' in battle when damaged beyond any possibility of further action or even movement and effectively lost.

Early oar-powered ships[4] had grown and Homer listed ships of twenty, thirty and fifty oars in use for the Trojan War.[5] The invention of the ram in the ninth century[6] had changed the function of a ship intended for war, from simply being a transport and fighting platform for the warriors on board, to becoming the weapon itself, a guided missile no less. The challenge then became to maximise the effect of the weapon by making the ship upon which it was mounted faster and more powerful for ramming. The only way to do this was to increase the motive power of the ship by increasing the number of oars and rowers.

Warships became progressively longer to accommodate more rowers, each oarsman sitting (some at least on cushions[7]) one behind the other on each side of the ship in a single file, at the same horizontal level, tier or reme. The ships grew through twenty oars (ten per side)[8] through thirty[9] and up to fifty.[10] These single,

Figure 4. Top: monoreme conter showing twelve oars per side. Corinthian dish circa 500. (*Altes Museum, Berlin*) Lower: Conters under sail. Athenian but found at Vulci in Italy. Mid sixth century. (*Louvre*)

or monoreme ships were known as *kontoros,* or 'conters'[11] and further classified as triaconters (thirty oars), thiaconters (forty oars) and up to pentecontors (fifty oars) (there is no Greek word for a ship of more than fifty oars). Illustrations of these ships, predominantly on pottery, rarely depict such convenient round numbers and it would seem more logical therefore, to regard the designations as referring to ships with 'up to twenty oars' and 'between twenty and thirty oars' and so on. It was of course, possible to have two men at an oar, but the ship was still rated according to the number of oars in the water.

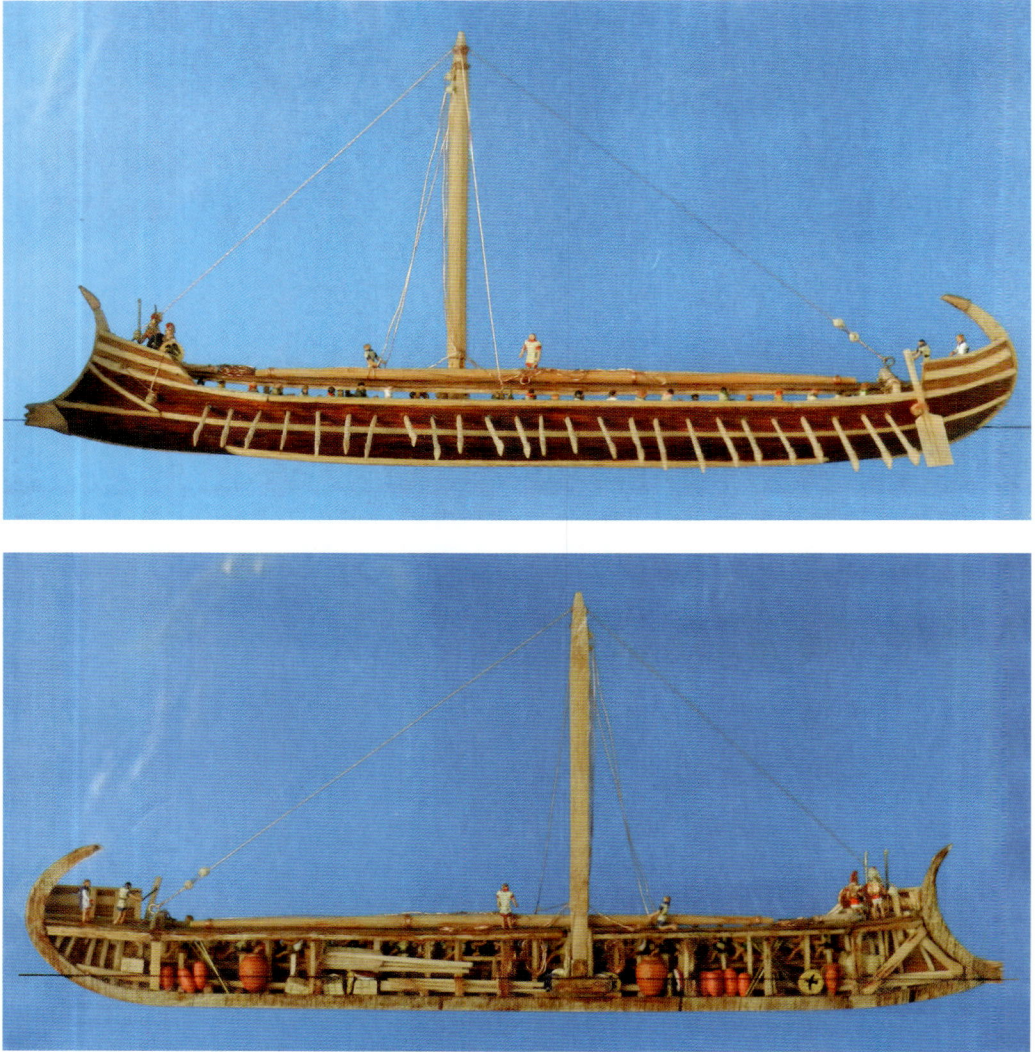

Figure 5. Author's half-model of a monoreme penteconter. The ship has a flying deck amidships for access between bow and stern and to enable the deck crew to handle the rig, which they are doing on the model. The space below is used for stowage, including two large water jars. Note: although Figure 4 shows vessels earlier than our period, the basic form of a monoreme conter was well established and would remain reasonably constant until they were superseded.

With the penteconter and its twenty-five men per side, the maximum was reached to which this formula could be stretched. Any longer and the ship hull became too long and narrow and lacked structural strength, causing the hull to flex, hog and sag; the long, narrow hull also required a large turning circle, which meant that shorter ships could turn inside it and ram. A rowing crew had of course, to be trained to row together and to synchronise their oar-strokes for maximum power, especially as ships continued to grow in size and complexity and in numbers of rowers.[12]

The second way in which the Greeks classified their warships was by a system of numbers, starting with *trieres* (literally, 'three–fitted') and so on in succession. Ships became rowed by men in arranged horizontal layers or *remes*, up to a maximum of three, thus *monoreme*, *bireme* and *trireme* (in their Anglicised versions); the first two of these terms are modern and unknown in the ancient world, but convenient for our use, as also is referring to a single 'layer' as a *reme*, again an Anglicised usage of the Latin word for an oar (*reme*, in Greek, *kope*).

The Bireme

The need for greater power could only be achieved by increasing the number or oars per given length of hull side and this was accomplished by building a slightly broader hull and installing a second horizontal tier or reme of rowers, sat a little above and outboard of the lower reme, taking advantage of the spaces between them to ply their oars. The same fifty rowers could now be accommodated in a shorter, broader and more seaworthy craft which can be classified as a bireme. The Greeks, confusingly, referred to both mono and bireme ships of about fifty oars as penteconters;[13] the Romans used the term, at least by the first century. The bireme arrangement dates

Figure 6. Bireme warship under oar and sail. Drinking cup circa 500, found at Vulci but probably made in Athens. (*British Museum*)

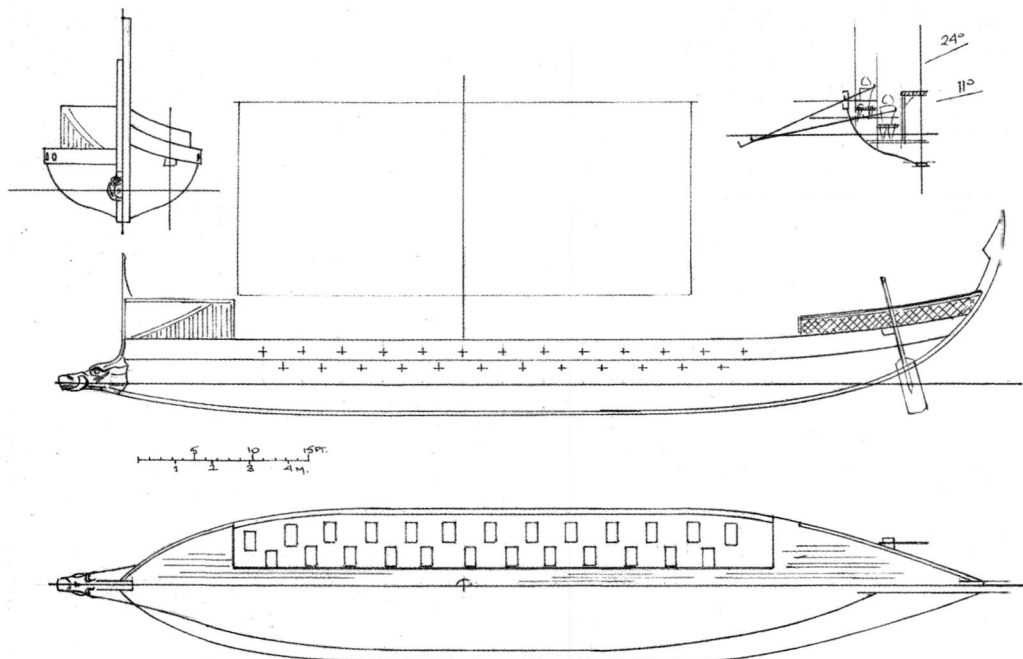

Figure 7. Author's reconstruction of a bireme penteconter in the Greek style, based on vase paintings.

from circa the late eighth century, the earliest depiction of it found so far being from Phoenicia.[14] It also enabled ships to become larger and able to accommodate more rowers, growing to sixty or more oars.[15] The two-level or bireme ship would remain, in various different guises, a popular arrangement to the end of 'antiquity' with its final incarnation as the Dromon of the Byzantines, over a millennium later.

The Trireme

From its introduction in the mid-sixth century, the trireme dominated naval warfare and would continue to do so for a good half of the fourth century, after which the introduction of new, larger types in increasing numbers would signal the end of its reign. The trireme had been perfected at Corinth in the mid-sixth century.[16] It had an impact on all preceding warship types, analogous to that of HMS *Dreadnought* in AD 1905 on its predecessors. In the trireme, a third reme of oarsmen was added who sat higher and outboard of the other two and in a ship not a lot bigger than the largest biremes. The best surviving contemporary details of a trireme are those from Athenian Navy inventories that have been recovered, confirming that the Athenian trireme was powered by 170 oars, resulting in a huge leap in propulsive power.[17] The ship was faster than all of the other types and immediately outclassed them. This, the 'classic' trireme, became the standard warship and was built in hundreds; it was the mainstay of the fleets that fought the Greek-Persian Wars and the Peloponnesian War of the fifth century. So many were built that most of southern Greece was denuded of timber and suffered consequent erosion, the results of which can still be seen.[18]

At this point, the classification system has changed as *tri*, of course, means three and no longer refers to the total number of oars in use. The trireme was a ship approximately 125 feet/38m in length and 16 feet/4.7m beam overall. These measurements are deduced from the size of the sheds built specifically at Athens and other locations, such as Carthage, to house the ships.[19] The topmost reme was of thirty-one oars per side, these rowers being called thranites after the *thranos* or topwale upon which they were positioned; the middle reme was of twenty-seven oars per side and their rowers were called zygites, after the *zygos* or thwart upon which they sat; the lowest reme, also of twenty-seven oars per side, were called thalamites, after the *thalamos* or hold in which they were installed. The zygite and thalamite remes rowed through oarports in the hull sides, as had their bireme predecessors but, to obtain the right spacing of their tholepins and the right gearing for their oars, the thranites rowed over an outrigger which extended beyond the hull sides. It was this innovation that enabled the Greeks to perfect their light, fast and deadly triremes.[20] It remained the most numerous class of ship in the fleets of both the Greeks and Persians throughout the fourth century and even though, during that time, other larger and more powerful types of warship were developed and came into service to displace the trireme's primacy, it would, in various iterations, continue to remain an important warship type until the fourth century AD.[21]

Of all the ancient warship types, the trireme has received the most attention and inspired the greatest academic debate (often heated) and a large number of attempted reconstructions. Morrison[22] very reasonably explains the numbers as referring to the number of files of rowers stretching along each side of a ship but Tilley, perhaps not unreasonably, suggests it was per cross-section of a hull.[23] The trireme is no help because the name refers to the number of horizontal rowing 'layers', not the number of rowers. The form of the ship was largely settled[24] by the eventual building of a full-size, working reproduction, the *Olympias*, in 1987, which was taken to sea and put through extensive sea trials under both oar and sail.[25]

Probably the best contemporary illustration of a trireme is the 'Lenormant Relief', which shows a section of the side of such a ship (Figure 8) and which led to the construction of the *Olympias* (Figure 9).

Figure 8. Some of the evidence for the layout of a trireme, the Lenormant Relief. Copy of the original, in the Acropolis Museum, Athens. (*Author's collection*)

No ancient ship is known with more than three horizontal levels of rowers and indeed, the geometry of rowing would militate against any greater number.[26] The larger ships were henceforth classified or rated by a number, 'five', 'six' etc., which has been generally assumed to have referred to the number of men rowing in a group on each side, whether in two (bireme) or three (trireme) level ships. For the larger ships we can only presume that the numbering continued to refer to such a group. The confirmation lies perhaps in the Greek's own word for a trireme, *triereis*, which means 'three-fitted'[27] i.e. a group comprising a thranite, a zygite and a thalamite, the only classes of rower noted in the sources and for which the Greeks had a name. If there were, for example, a trireme 'six' the group could comprise two of each. Unfortunately, the ancients left no detailed plans as to how this was achieved and thus any attempts to understand the rowing systems that they employed have tended to start with the group. This works reasonably well with numbers up to say seven, but becomes progressively more problematic the greater the number, as will be seen.

Neither the earlier dominance of the trireme, or the introduction of larger types entirely displaced the older, monoreme and bireme types, some of which continued

Figure 9. The *Olympias*, the full-size reproduction of a sixth century BC Athenian trireme. Top is an overall view of the ship. The lower view is of the starboard side oar ports, showing the three distinct levels of oars. together with the *ascomata*, the leather 'gloves' for the lowest (thalamite) reme as well as the outrigger to carry the top (thranite) oar tholes. The ship is housed at the Naval Museum at Nea Falero, near Piraeus.

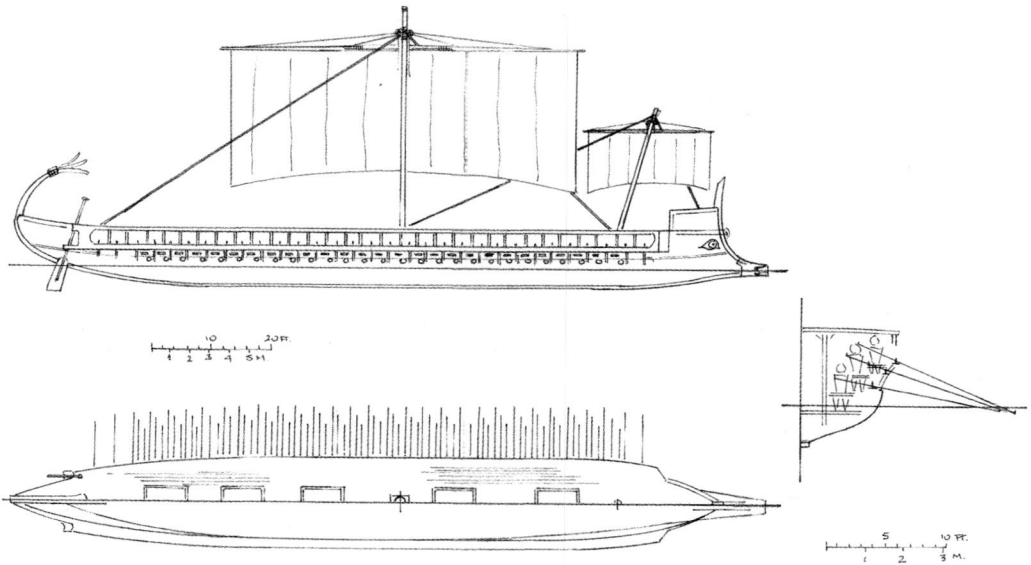

Figure 10. Author's reconstruction of a 'classic' trireme of the type used throughout the Persian and Peloponnesian Wars.

in service with all of the naval powers. These ships, although unable to stand in the line of battle, remained valuable for scouting, communication and reconnaissance, raiding, the carrying of despatches and all of the duties for which a larger ship would have been unsuitable or an unwarranted expense. Many of these small ship types evolved or were adapted from local, native types of boats, an obvious example being the Roman Liburnian, evolved from an Illyrian native craft, the *lembus* (see post Chapter 11).

The Four

At the end of the fifth century or very early fourth century, the Carthaginians developed an enlarged form of bireme with each oar manned by two rowers (i.e. double-banked) namely a 'four'[28] (*tetreres* in Greek, *quadrireme*, Latin).[29] Broader and more massive than a trireme, but (the early examples at least) capable of being stowed in trireme ship sheds, it was not as fast but was a better seaboat and reportedly fast under sail.[30]

It proved to be less complex than a trireme and less 'tender' at sea; being robust, comparatively simple in construction and not making too heavy a demand on available manpower. It was economical to build and to operate and stable enough to carry some artillery and, in Roman service at least, to mount a tower.

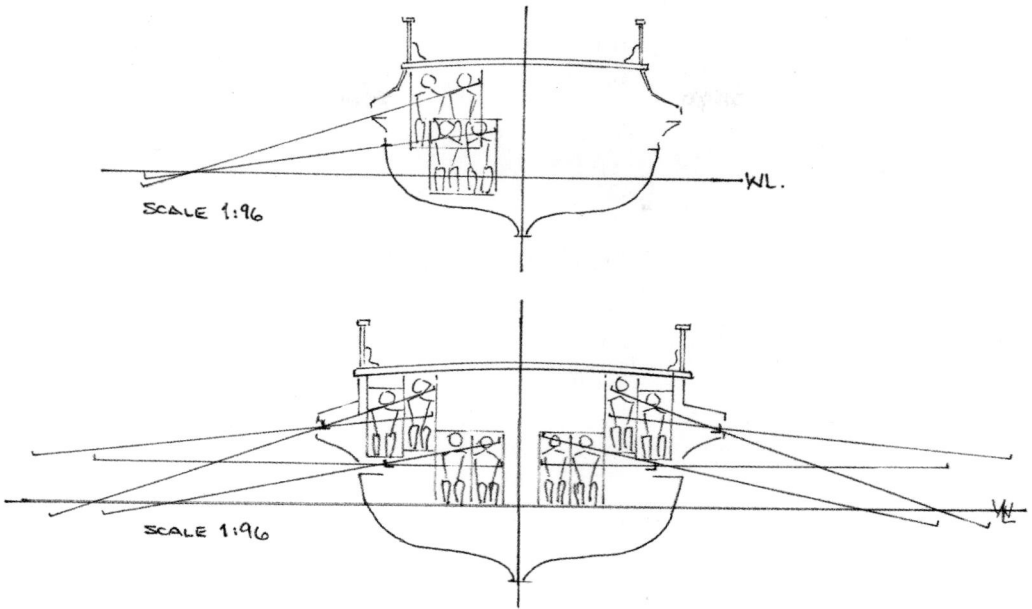

SCALE 1:96

WL.

SCALE 1:96

Figure 11. The Four, cross-sections. Top: it was known that (at least early) fours could be housed in the Piraeus ship sheds, this cross-section was scaled to fit. However, it is crowded below decks and the placing of the rowers must be carefully adjusted to enable them and their oars free movement without fouling. Lower: an enlarged, improved arrangement, with beam increased to 24 feet/7.3m overall, allowing the rowers plenty of room and a better proportioned hull. Figure 12 uses this section.

Figure 12. Author's reconstruction of a four based on wall paintings at Herculaneum.

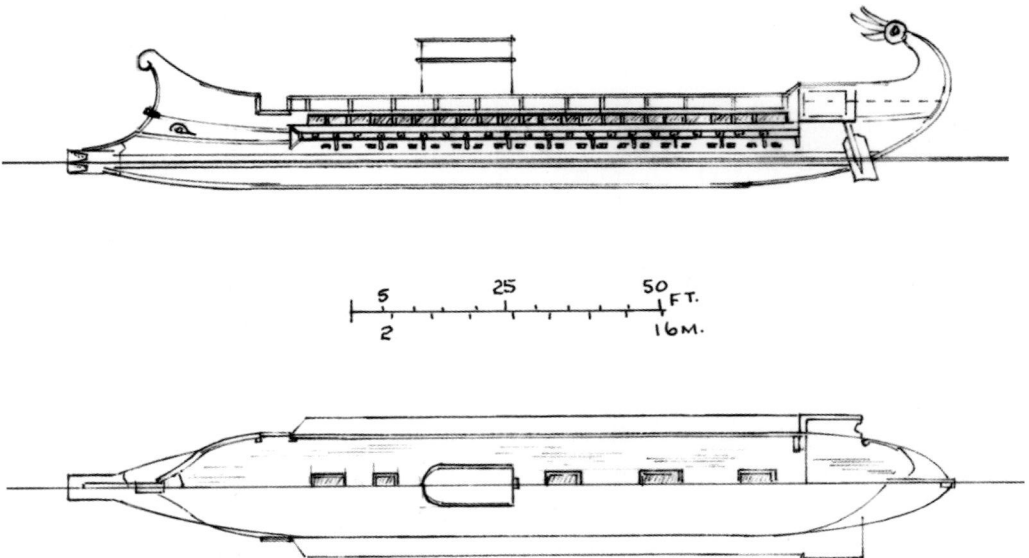

5   25   50 FT.

2   16M.

Figure 13. Author's model of a four fitting out at a shipyard. It is appreciated that, of necessity, the illustrations are of Roman fours, but, apart from details and of styling, the overall concept and sizes would have been fairly uniform.

As a type, it became extremely popular with many navies and will be found in the fleets of both antagonists at the siege of Tyre[31] (see Chapter 4) and thereafter spread throughout the fleets of the eastern Mediterranean. It became the type most widely used by Rhodes.

Internal arrangements are reasonably straightforward and variations are suggested in Figure 11.[32] There is a paucity of attributable illustrations but the 'Samothrace Prow' discussed later (see Chapter 9) may well represent one. A much later impression of Roman ships of the class at sea can be gathered from wall paintings at Herculaneum and finally, the author's own drawing (Figure 12) and models (Figure 13).

The Five

To counter this new type, the ship designers and builders of Dionysius of Syracuse (367 to 344) developed an even larger ship, the 'five' (*penteres*, Greek; *quinquereme*, (Anglicised) Latin) the first appearing in 398.[33] The Carthaginians soon followed suit in building a five, continuing to do so until, by the start of the Punic Wars against Rome (264), it was their principal combat type. To oppose Carthage, the Romans also built them and they became the predominant combat type in those wars; between them, the antagonists built and deployed over 1,300 of them.[34] It would remain the principal Roman combat type throughout the period covered in this book and the weapon by which the Romans became the dominant and ultimately, the only Mediterranean naval power.

The five was also adopted by other fleets of the eastern Mediterranean, Sidon in Phoenicia having them in its fleet by 351.[35] It was used by both sides at Alexander's siege of Tyre and would remain in widespread use with all of the various fleets, although not in the concentrations fielded by the Romans and Carthaginians.

Bigger and higher out of the water than all of the other types to date, the ship was rowed by between about 250 and 300 rowers, perhaps as a bireme with three men per oar in one reme and two per oar in the other;[36] the most likely arrangement, however, was as a trireme with both upper remes double-banked and a single man per oar in the thalamite reme. There is evidence that the upper deck of the five was higher than those of a four or trireme, which it would not necessarily have been if rigged as bireme.[37] Both Figure 15 and Coates' reconstruction[38] posit the ship as a trireme but, by definition, this will result in one oar (both have it as the thalamite) single-manned, while the other two in the group are double-manned. Obviously the

Figure 14. Roman coins of the third century, showing what are presumably the prows of fives (quinqueremes). Top left: *uncia*, mid-third century. (*Naples Archaeological Museum*) Top right: bronze *denarius*, second Punic War period. (*Naples Archaeological Museum*) Lower left: bronze *as*, circa 211. (*Altes Museum, Berlin*) Lower right: bronze *denarius*, second Punic War period. (*British Museum*)

one-man oar will be shorter than the others, which will result in a different stroke being delivered. The shorter oar could operate below and clear of the other two and perhaps the thalamite rower was trained to match his stroke to that of the others.[39] Since he could row independently of the others, perhaps the thalamite rowers were able to set their own striking rate.

As to representations of the five, only the Roman coin issues of the Punic Wars period (264 to 202) which show warship prows could be held, with some justification, to represent them (Figure 14). The author's drawing (Figure 15) was intended to show a Roman ship and from which the model was made (Figure 16). A more 'Hellenised' shape is proposed by Coates.[40]

It has been posited that both Carthage and Syracuse, depending to a large extent as they did on expensive mercenaries for their armies, had far less money available to pay or hire crews for triremes, where every rower had to be well-trained. If an oar could be manned by several men, however, only one of them need be an expensively trained man (the one on the inboard end of the oar), the rest, controlled by him, merely providing muscle, were cheap to employ.

The Hellenistic states and Romans, all with large reserves of citizen and allied manpower, did not have this problem but once bigger stronger ships had made an appearance, the others had to counter them.

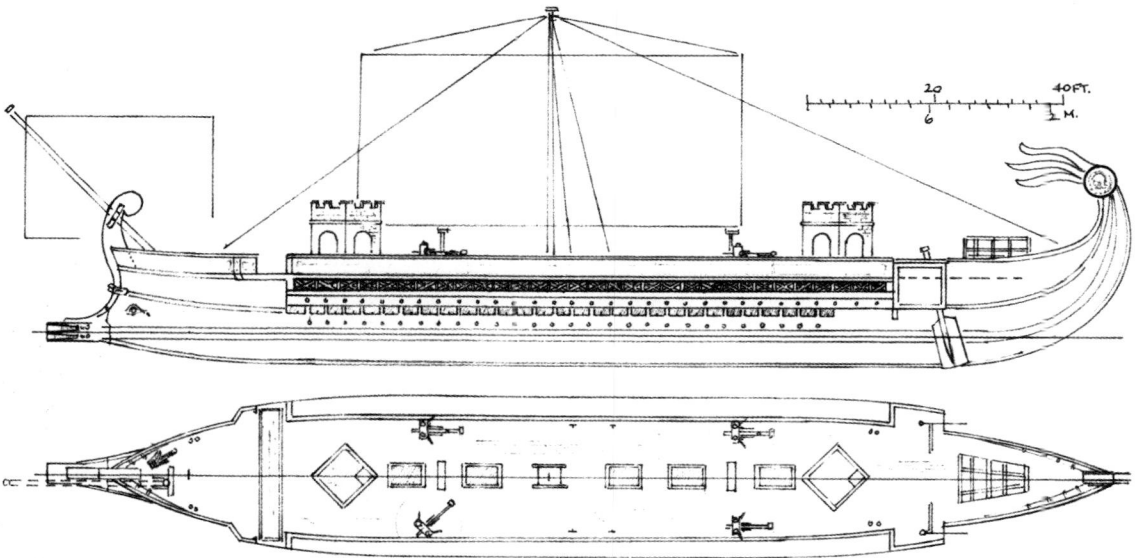

Figure 15. Reconstruction of a Roman quinquereme (five).

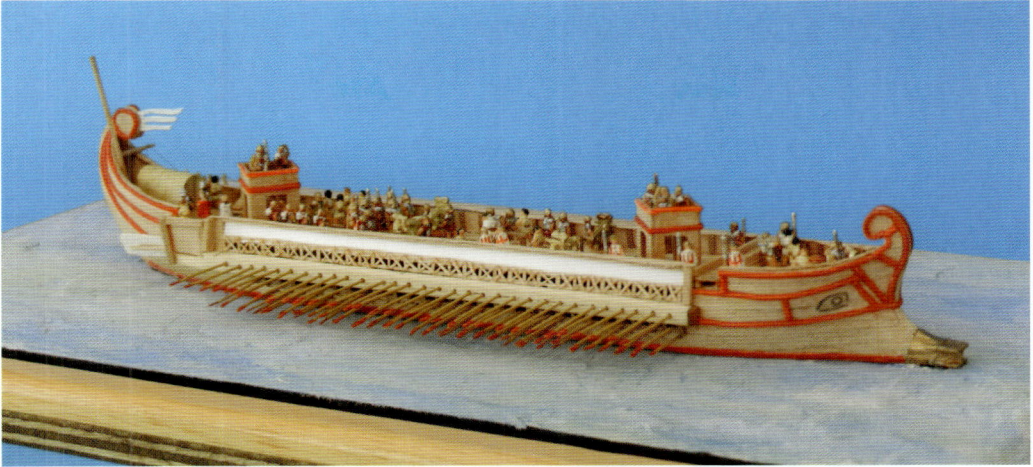

Figure 16. Author's model of the ship in Figure 15. The ship is hove-to and the 296 rowers have their oars raised, the rudders are also raised. There are four artillery pieces on deck, together with twenty sailors, the normal complement of forty marines and eight officers. For battle, the Romans would embark an extra century of eighty soldiers.

The Six

During his reign, Dionysius caused to be designed and constructed another new type, a six (*hexeres*)[41] the next stage of warship growth and presumably to give him a perceived advantage over the fives then being built by Carthage. The six was either an enlarged bireme with each oar triple-manned, or an enlarged trireme, with each oar double-manned (Figure 17).[42] In any event, it was a big ship, capable of carrying a large contingent of marines and of mounting up to a dozen artillery pieces. It would go into service with the fleets of the Hellenistic powers that succeeded Alexander and in small numbers with those of Rome and Carthage; the last of the type (in Roman service) finally going out of service in the early first century AD. With a group of six rowers at each section of oars, it is possible that the ship was rowed as a monoreme, with six rowers per oar, in a method known in Renaissance times as *a scaloccio*, but the existing technology and tradition of the Ancient World would suggest that it was more likely to have been a progression from the fours and fives and thus a multi-reme ship.

In attempting to reconstruct the ship, the author has previously preferred a bireme arrangement, sacrificing some performance for simplicity in internal arrangements, the possibility of gaining a higher freeboard and more modest operating angle for the upper oars.[43] The initial reconstruction (Figure 17 top) was for a very broad hull to afford stability for the large complement of marines, towers and artillery on deck. A re-working of the bireme (Figure 17 lower left) has produced a more compact

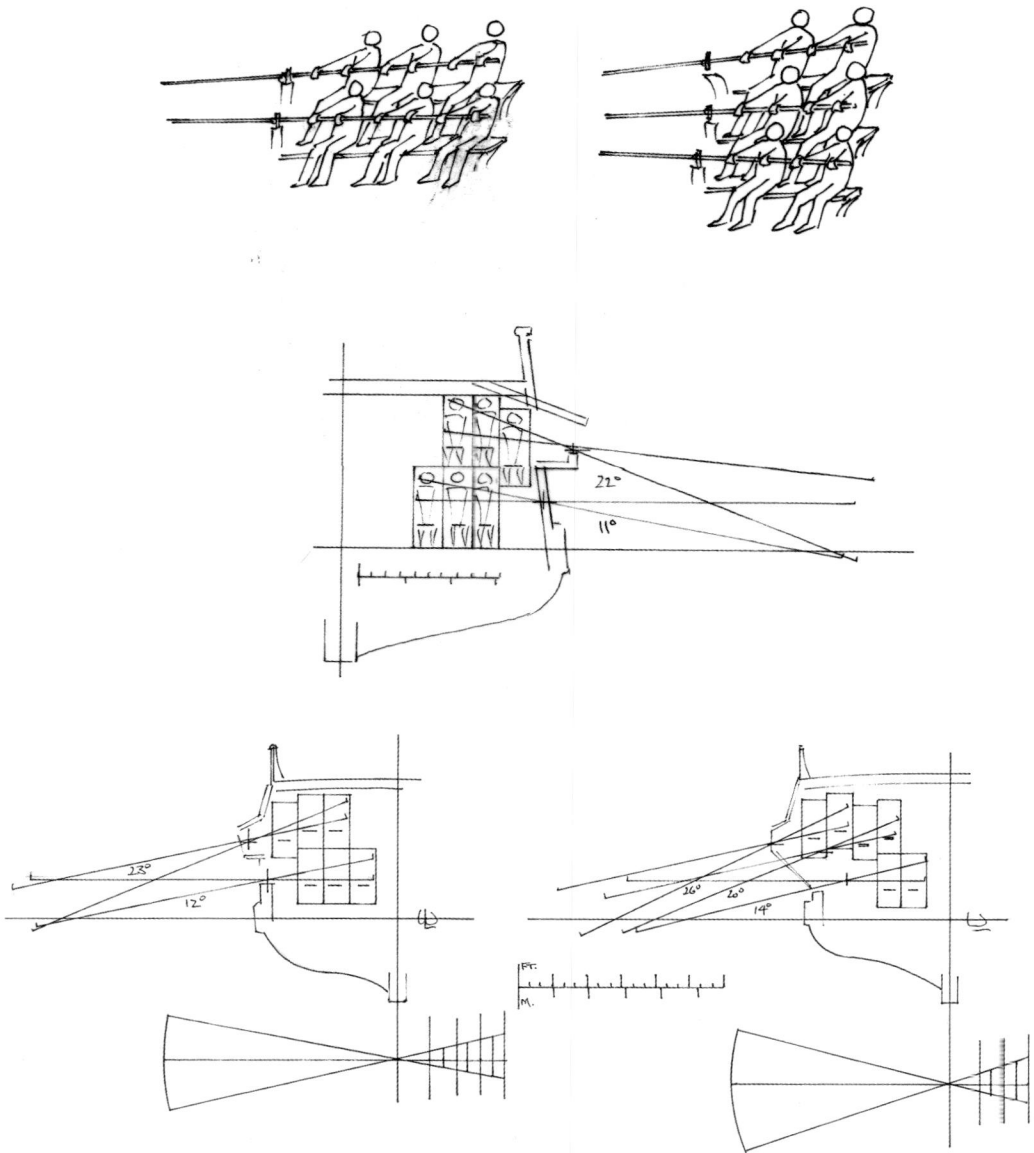

Figure 17. Top frame: general sketch to show the six configured as a bireme or a trireme. Centre: layout of the rowing crew upon which the model in Figure 19 is based. Lower frame, left: proposal for a bireme six in a more compact form. Beam overall 31ft. (9.4m), waterline beam 25ft. (7.6m); freeboard 2′6″ (0.76m); oars 30ft. (9.1m) gearing 3.1; deck height above waterline, 12.5ft. (3.8m). Right: proposal for a trireme six. Beam overall and waterline, freeboard and deck height the same. Oars 26ft. (7.9m.) gearing 2.8. Below each cross-section are diagrams to show the relative length of pull on the oar by each rower; thus the rowers of the three-man oar (from amidships) pull through 40 notes (1.01m) 31 inches (0.78m) and 24 inches (0.61m) respectively. The rowers of the two-man oar pull through 40 inches (1.01m) and 28 inches (0.71m) respectively.

hull section, whilst retaining the essential simplicity of the internal layout. But what would be the point of a compact ship, with the consequent reduction in fighting men, when surely the whole object was to build bigger to overawe and (hopefully) overpower the opposition.

As a trireme, the internal arrangements are more complex but the three double-manned oars will produce more power than the two triple-manned oars of the bireme version. A corollary however, is that the operating angle of the topmost (thranite) oars is greater and the available freeboard less.

Coates' reconstruction of a six[44] shows this and suffers only 2 feet/610mm freeboard, as well as having the zygite and thalamite rowers seemingly entangled. The author's further attempt at a reconstruction (Figure 17 lower right) has managed to give the rowers more room each, but in doing so, necessitated large oarports to allow for the arc of the zygite and thalamite oars (18 inches/460mm for the former and some 26 inches/635mm. for the latter) i.e. more holes for water to get in and more difficult to seal with the leather 'socks' (ascomata) used for this purpose on normal oarports.

Another problem with the trireme layout, and its consequent increased operating angle for upper oars, is that the angles change with any roll of the ship, not only making it more difficult to reach the water but also to raise the oars clear of it at the end of the stroke. In all of the reconstructions, all of the rowers are seated.

Perhaps shortcomings such as these are the reason why comparatively few of the type were built and Alexander, for one, opted to consider the seven for his projected fleet (see Chapter 4). As to performance, Polybius (Fragment 17) states that 'these vessels appear to be as swift sailers as penteconters, but to be much inferior to triremes (presumably also under sail) and their construction has been abandoned for many years past.'

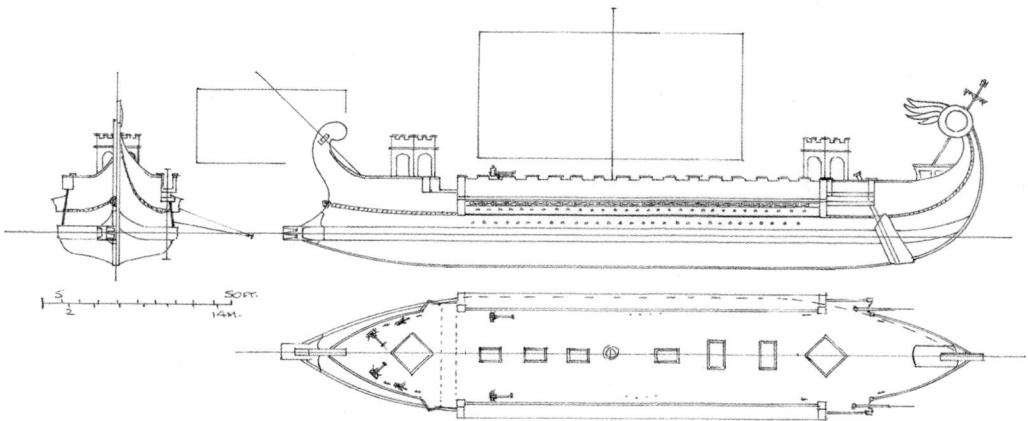

Figure 18. Reconstruction of a bireme six after the Praeneste Relief.

Figure 19. Model of a Roman six from the drawing in Figure 35. The ship is shown at sea in full combat mode, the decks packed with marines, deck crew and eight catapults, the towers are manned by archers. There are 178 figures on deck, with another 360 rowers and their officers, out of sight, below decks. The sailing rig has been lowered and stowed on crutches. Scale is 1:300.

He was also supposed to have laid down the measurements of such vessels 'which the Romans and Carthaginians appear to have often employed in their wars with (he means against) each other'.[45]

As Polybius most probably actually saw a six in the flesh as it were, his comments on its sailing ability must be accepted: interestingly, that it was better than the much smaller penteconter, presumably due to having greater stability, but not, as one would expect, a patch on the swift trireme. The other comment, that construction 'has been abandoned' perhaps confirms the arguments advanced above; how tantalisingly sad however that his account of their dimensions is lost.

The *Hemiolia*

A new type of light warship was first mentioned in about 350,[46] the *hemiolia* or 'one and a half'.[47] There are no surviving illustrations that can be said with authority to be of the type, leading therefore, from the scant references available, to much conjecture as to what a *hemiolia* actually was like. The term was used particularly to describe pirate ships and it may have been evolved by them; it was certainly very popular with them.[48] It may well be that the term referred to the rig and/or rowing method employed, rather than to a specific form of ship.[49]

Nevertheless, ships were built, used and recognised and named by the ancients as *hemioliai* and from the accounts, certain characteristics can be discerned. They seem to have originated with the pirates of the southern Anatolian coast.[50] To avoid pirates, a sail-powered merchant ship could stand out to sea, out of sight of land and of the pirates' lookouts and beyond the reach of their small, local coastal craft. The pirates seem to have therefore evolved a boat or ship with the ability to go further out to track their prey and with the speed to catch it, a vessel with sails for endurance and oars for speed.[51] In a warship, a sailing rig was an auxiliary to oar power and generally landed before action; the pirates did not, the ship being rowed and sailed at the same time.[52] To justify this view, Casson avers that the sixth century vase (Figure 6) shows a pirate ship overhauling a merchant ship, with the crew stowing the sailing rig before their attack.[53]

Figure 20. Greek seal ring showing what is possibly a *hemiolia* under sail and oar. Second century. (*British Museum*)

Good seakeeping would have been a prerequisite for these craft which voyaged far and wide, venturing to Italy,[54] the Aegean,[55] the Peloponnese[56] and Sicily.[57]

The ship would seem to have been smallish and comparatively beamy amidships, to accommodate the extra rowers;[58] Coates interprets the craft as 'having fine, lightly-built hulls' and with only a single file of rowers each side at the bow, which could be sharper, giving a fine entry and higher speed. He suggests a waterline length of 69 feet/21m and waterline beam of 8 feet 10 inches /2.7m. for a length to beam ratio of 7.7, which is reasonably fine but fits all the known parameters;[59] he also assumes fifty rowers.

The interpretation above depends, of course, on the premise that a *hemiolia* was a settled type, built to a defined pattern and not, as previously mooted, just any suitable hull adapted to meet the class of rig and/or oar system and function. In any event, the biggest problem in interpretation is the meaning of the term '*hemiolia*' (one and a half). Having met the *penteconter* in both mono- and bi-reme versions, it has been, not unreasonably, generally agreed that the type must fall somewhere between them and as with the former types, the term relates to the rowing system employed[60] and thus the number of fore and aft files of rowers on each side.

Accepting therefore a full line or file of rowers on each side, the problem becomes where, in relation to that file, to place the extra half-file; Torr[61] suggests that the extra 'half-bank' (he means file) be above the upper decking, but if not, 'then they would have to man half an ordinary 'bank' neither of which seems to make sense, especially as the existence of an 'upper deck' was highly unlikely. Casson posits that the pirates 're-modelled' a bireme to produce the *hemiolia* which enabled them to run under sails

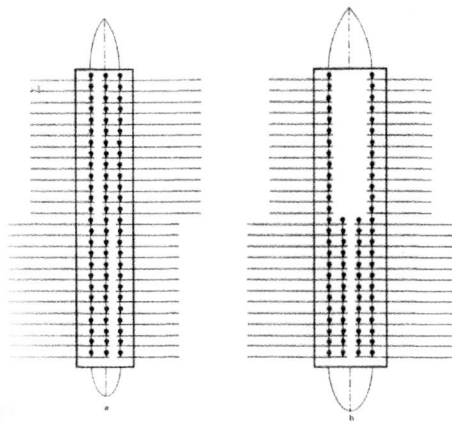

Figure 21. The *hemiolia*, rowing schemes. Top suggested schemes after Meijer; centre: extract from reconstruction by Coates. Lower left: midships sections: i. Single oar, double-manned; ii. 'semi-bireme' (per Coates) midships man has longer oar and thus normal order reversed in that he is pulling the lower oar, requiring a complicated support for the tholes; iii. as a bireme, complex in a small hull and fore and aft spacing of rowers needs careful working to give clearance between brackets for lower oars; iv. using Tilley's layout with each rower having an oar and thus more effective than i. Lower right: layout of double-banked rowers per Tilley.

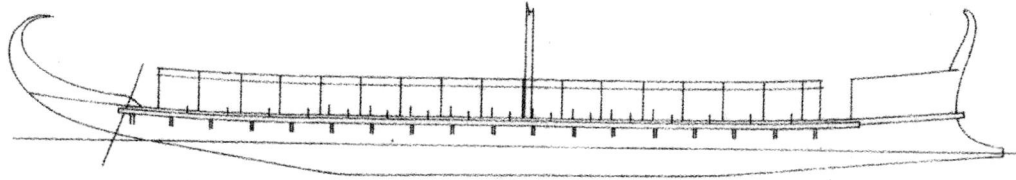

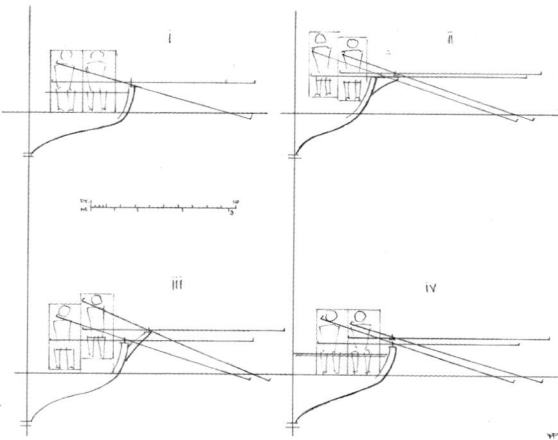

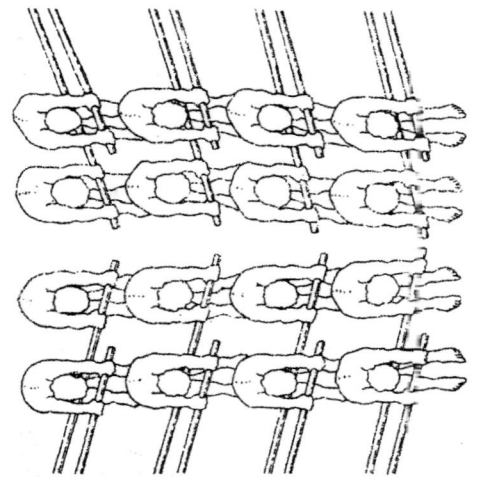

and oars at the same time.[62] This also makes little sense as a cut-down bireme with less oars becomes simply an underpowered bireme, possibly lighter but just as big.

Ormerod[63] also has an upper half-reme, allowing room at that level for extra fighting men. Casson[64] reverses the order, with the half-file below (zygites) the full file (thranites) so that half of the thranite rowers stopped rowing to stow the rig before attack, once more citing the sixth-century vase as showing this.

All of these interpretations envisage a bireme arrangement, but Morrison[65] suggests that all rowers were at the same level (monoreme), half the oars single-manned, the others with two men per oar;[66] in doing so, he largely follows Nelson,[67] who has inboard and outboard files of rowers staggered, with the inboard slightly ahead and lower, to give clearance and with one man per oar. He does however, have two full files per side rather than the one and a half of the name. Meijer follows this premise[68] with two suggested layouts (Figure 21) neither of which seems practical and both overlook Coates' logical contention (see later) that the ship's maximum beam, able to accommodate extra rowers, would be amidships.

Morrison also, more logically places the half-reme amidships,[69] interpreting Arrian's thirty-oar ship with three single-manned oars forward, five double-manned oars midships and two more single-manned oars aft, namely fifteen men per side. The double-manned oars, he avers, could be rowed *alla sensile* or *a scaloccio* (see

Figure 22. Model of a sixteenth century AD Venetian *Fusta* showing two rowers per bench, each with an oar; the angling of the benches allows each rower, although in close proximity, to operate clear of each other. The arrangement was then known as rowing *alla sensile*. Model by Admiral L. Fincanti, 1881. (*Museo Storico Navale, Venice*)

Chapter 3

Rams, Towers, Artillery and Tactics

Rams

It had been found very early on, perhaps in Mycenean times, that if the lower forefoot of the bow of a rowing vessel were extended ahead, the bow made a cleaner entry into the water and produced less spray to affect the foremost rowers. Whether by accident or design, it was found that hitting another boat with this forefoot could cause damage, perhaps fatal.

From this, the earliest rams, which emerged in the mid-ninth century, transformed warfare on water from an encounter between armed men on vessels, to a battle between the vessels themselves for the ram made the ship that mounted it into the weapon, a guided missile. The earliest rams were pointed and intended to make a hole in an enemy hull, at or below the waterline, and thereby cause it to become swamped and disabled. The 'ram' itself was a metal covering mounted upon the forefoot of the ship hull, to protect it when it came into contact with a target. The fore structure of the ship itself was designed with timbers projecting forward to carry the ram, strengthened to withstand the impact and to transmit and spread the shock of ramming back along the hull. The integrity of the hull was further protected, at least by the time of the Athenian trireme, by closing the bow of the hull behind the structure that carried the ram forming, in effect, a bulkhead. Ships were fitted with extra timbers along the waterline as protection against rams and to absorb blows and the very big ships became virtually impervious to ramming by smaller ships.

It was found that the early pointed rams had a tendency to become ensnared by the fibres of the edges of the timbers that they had pierced. This resulted in the attacker becoming trapped against its intended victim or in the ram being pulled off as the attacker tried to withdraw, leaving it probably as badly damaged as the victim. If it could not disengage, the attacker would in turn be assaulted by the crew of the stricken ship who had the ultimate motivation for a successful boarding counter-attack.

The ram evolved and by the sixth century had become blunted at the end, Greek pottery showing it shaped in the form of a boar's head or a ram's head (Figures 4 and 6). The purpose of this development was to push or stove in a section of enemy hull, rather than trying to make a hole, thereby disrupting the integrity of the hull and permitting the ingress of water. As ships grew in size and required larger castings for their rams, these also developed further, presumably also as a result of experience in battle. By the early fifth century the face of the ram had developed horizontal vanes, either side of a vertical central spine, designed to cut through the grain and joints of an enemy's hull timbers. This form of ram, of which examples have been found (see e.g. the frontispiece to this part) was a casting with a hollow socket at the rear shaped to fit over and be fixed to timbers projecting forward from the ship's hull proper, upward from the keel, downward from the stempost and on extended wales on either beam; together they formed a cruciform mounting frame (as seen in Figure 102). This was the weapon of the trireme age and obviously very effective. The form continued in use throughout the period covered herein with increasingly large castings to fit the larger ships.

As to the relative sizes of the rams fitted to warships, comparison can be made by comparing the size of their sockets; thus the ram fitted to the replica trireme *Olympias* had a socket 27.5 inches/700mm in width, while those taken from captured ships after the Battle of Actium and mounted on Octavius' victory monument at Nicopolis (Figure 102) range in size from 40 inches/1020mm to a massive 5 feet/1.51m in width, some of the mounting sockets being over 5 feet 6 inches/1.7m in height. The smallest of these is considered to be from a quinquereme, with the largest from a *dekares* or 'ten'.[1]

A ship was most vulnerable to ramming along its sides and stern. As long as an attacker had sufficient momentum *vis à vis* the target, the closing speed need not have been great. Just before impact, the attacker's rowers would back water to prevent their ram from penetrating too far into the enemy hull, to minimise the risk of it becoming stuck and torn off (which quite a few were) or caught and liable to boarding. The ram remained an effective weapon throughout the period and accounted for a great many ship losses.

Towers

The earliest surviving account of the mounting of a tower on a ship was by the Athenians who built one on a merchant hull to assist in their siege of Syracuse in 413.[2] Alexander the Great did the same for his siege of Tyre in 332 (see Chapter 4) as did Marcellus for his assault on Syracuse in 214.[3] In all of these cases, the ships were taken, rowed or towed, to their desired station and not intended to otherwise move (and see Figure 36). At the beginning of the First Punic War in 264, the Romans devised a form of tower with a timber frame, covered by canvas and which they mounted on the decks of their larger warships. Quadriremes were the smallest types to be so equipped;[4] They were first used in action by the Romans at the Battle of Mylae in 260; their use would not have gone unnoticed by the Hellenistic powers who doubtless added them to their own ships. Towers could be mounted forward, aft or amidships and even in pairs, one fore and one aft, on the biggest ships (see e.g. Figures 83 and 85). It may be that towers were also mounted on the very largest of ships, athwartships in pairs, jettied out beyond the hull on each side. The evidence for this, in the absence of extant illustrations, is in Polybius' account[5] of the Battle of Chios in 201 (see Chapter 9). At one stage in this battle, the ship of the Pergamene admiral Dionysodorus, a quinquereme, attacked a Macedonian 'seven', missed and brushed along the side of his intended victim. The latter had quickly withdrawn their oars but Dionysodorus' ship was not quick enough and had its starboard oars sheared off and also 'had the timbers supporting his towers smashed to pieces…' This was of course impossible for towers mounted amidships. Up to six archers, slingers or javelin men could be accommodated on each tower, able to shoot down on to an enemy deck.

As to height, the towers need not have been very tall; Athenaos' description[6] of Hierons' 'superfreighter' says that it had eight towers 'of the same height as the deck structures'. Assuming these to have been deck cabins of about 7 feet/2.13m overall, the tower, with a parapet would total about 10 feet /3m. There was also a 'raised battlemented fighting deck on pillars athwartship, with a large catapult', a feature very suitable for the largest of the ships reviewed. A fresco of this period from the Crimea, of a trireme warship bearing the name *Isis,* seems to show such raised decks

Figure 24. Silver tetradrachm from Messina, Sicily, showing the prow of a trireme. 493–488. Mounted in the prow on stanchions is a raised deck, bounded by a fence-like balustrade and possibly representing a raised platform for archers and javelin men. (*Altes Museum, Berlin*)

mounted on stanchions in both bow and stern of the ship, that of the stern being higher than the raised bow deck (and see Figure 24).[7]

The towers, as a permanent feature, were heavy and added to top-weight, wind-drag and thus to the instability of the ship and contributed to the loss of many ships in storms. They nevertheless continued in use until the thirties, by which time a new type was introduced by Agrippa. This was of lighter construction, collapsible and able to be stowed flat on deck when not in use, to reduce top-weight. The canvas coverings were often painted a distinguishing colour on all the ships of a squadron to aid in identification; by the later Roman civil war period, they were sometimes painted to resemble masonry.[8]

Artillery

Almost since its invention in the early fourth century, artillery was a feature of ancient warships. At that time the engineers of Dionysius of Syracuse made a large composite bow, larger and more powerful than could be drawn by a man; this they mounted on a timber stock, together with a winch and trigger mechanism to draw and release it. The whole was connected to a stand by a universal joint which enabled the machine to be elevated and traversed and thereby aimed. The stock to which the bow was fixed had a central channel along the top in which was fitted a slider with the trigger mechanism and a channel for the missile; this was locked to the bowstring and the whole slider pulled back by the winch, checked by a ratchet along the sides of the stock (Figure 25A). Upon release of the missile, the slider was pushed forward, to re-engage the bow string and winched back again to reload. These machines could hurl a large arrow or, with an adaptor, a stone shot, up to 300 yards/274m. Mounted on ships, they could cause devastation if shot among an enemy's rowers, easily piercing the leather screens which had been enough to protect them against javelins or arrows; the advent of artillery thus led to the progressive boxing in of the rowers, to provide them with better protection.

Reliable and simple to maintain, these machines were in use until about 240; before that, the engineers of Philip II of Macedon perfected a new type of propulsion system. The composite bow was replaced by two short bow staves, each inserted into a skein of animal sinew which had been woven into cords, stretched, oiled and twisted to form torsion springs which stored great power. These were mounted in special carriers and kept in tension by passing them through a hole and washer at the top and bottom and retained by a bar; they were mounted each side of a stock with slider and trigger, similar to their predecessors (Figure 25B). Being a good deal more powerful, range was increased to some 400 yards/366m and they could be made in ever

Figure 25. Artillery: A, earlier type powered by a large composite bow. B, similar machine but with sinew torsion springs.

increasing sizes. The springs were susceptible to damp and needed to be regularly removed and re-stretched and oiled, requiring in turn, specialised artillery artificers. As the pieces were made by estimation, with no set pattern of parts, performance could vary greatly, therefore the earlier form continued in parallel use.

From about 275, Ptolemy of Egypt's engineers had developed a formula for building torsion spring artillery pieces. Starting with the length of arrow that the intended machine was to shoot, the formula dictated the fraction of that length (it was one ninth) which was to be the diameter of the holes in the carrier through which the springs would pass. All dimensions of the components of the machine were then dictated by the formula, as multiples or fractions of that hole diameter. These 'formula machines' proved to be reliable, of known performance and could be mass produced in standard sizes.[9]

These machines supplanted the earlier types and became standard equipment aboard warships. The smallest type known to mount artillery was a triaconter; larger types could carry more and larger sizes of catapult (a quinquereme could carry up to ten). These weapons, although capable of inflicting damage to crew and ship, were not 'ship destroyers'[10] and the modestly-sized and well attested three-span (shooting an arrow 27 inches/685 mm in length, with a stock length of 4.5 feet/1.27m) and two-cubit (a 3 feet arrow/915mm, with a stock length of 6 feet/1.83m) machines would have been ideal as anti-personnel weapons.

Apart from shooting at each other,[11] warships could bring their artillery to bear in support of an opposed troop landing. As illustrations, during Alexander's journey

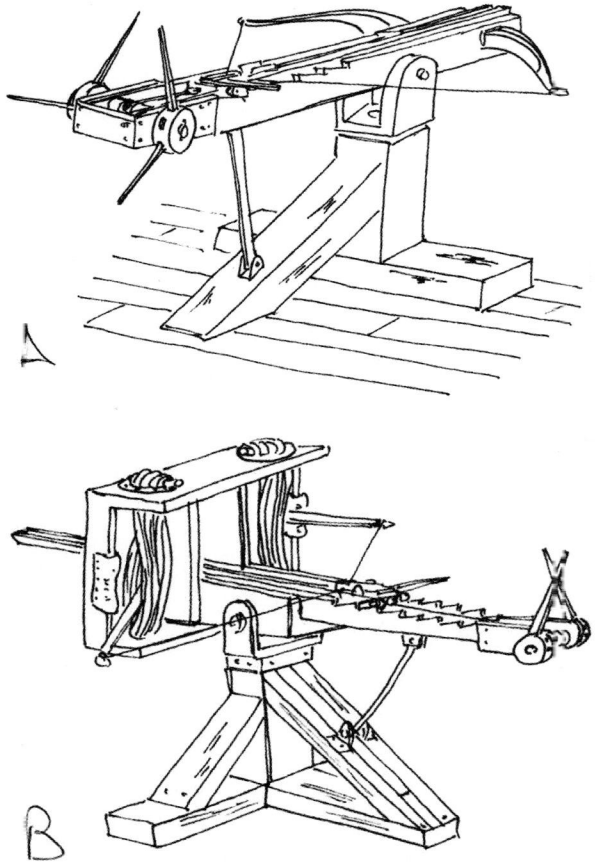

down the River Indus to the sea, to support an opposed landing 'the men on the ships took up the cry and loosed a barrage of bow and catapult fire on the natives';[12] as Caesar's ships did in his attack on the Heptastadion at Alexandria in 47.[13] Artillery on ships could also be used as floating batteries, as was done at the sieges of Tyre and Rhodes.

Apart from the normal complement of arrow and stone shooters, larger machines were on occasion mounted for siege or assault work. Siege artillery was substantially larger and predominantly stone throwers, the very biggest being capable of hurling a stone shot weighing an amazing 260 pounds/118kg. Although siege machines smaller than this were mounted, the additional weight of the machine and of its stone shot had to be considered. The weight of a three-span piece has been estimated at about a hundredweight (112 pounds/61.7kg) and a quinquereme could possibly carry ten, plus a couple of small stone throwers and still have its normal complement of forty marines.[14] For siege work, using larger machines, their installation had to be offset by weight savings, the marines being replaced by artillerymen and the rowing crew being reduced to just enough to manoeuvre the ship into position and all stores landed. As an example of this practice, in 210, the Roman fleet supported an assault upon Naupactus from seaward using siege artillery.[15]

Grapnels attached to a line and thrown had long been in use to ensnare and pull an enemy ship in so that it could be boarded[16] but for the 'War against Sextus' (38 to 36) Octavius' admiral Agrippa introduced the *harpax* (harpoon), a grapnel attached to the end of a shaft 7.5 feet/2.3m in length and lined with metal strips so that it could not easily be cut through.[17] It was shot from the larger onboard catapults and trailed a line which could be hauled in. Although the range of the machine was considerably reduced by the added weight of the missile and the drag of the line, it could still far outrange any hand-thrown grapnel.[18]

Artillery was not mounted on towers which, being comparatively flimsy, could not support the weight or the shock of discharge of the machines. Further, the position of the universal joint mounting, close behind the spring-carrier frame, prevented the piece from being depressed to shoot down on to an enemy deck. As mentioned earlier, low platforms for artillery were sometimes erected on decks of larger ships to give a slightly elevated position and enable them to shoot on either beam.

Tactics

Ancient warships were not very good seaboats; their very nature with multiple openings low in the hull for oars, shallow draft and hulls packed with men, largely precluded open sea voyages of any great duration and, in anything but reasonably calm conditions, many warships were lost through storms.[19] Ancient oar-powered warships were effectively boxes packed full of rowers with no living accommodation or facilities aboard and space enough to carry only a few days water and rations; the ship's crews had to be let ashore to rest and prepare their food, preferably each day, but at the most after no more than about three days.[20] They were essentially 'day boats' and could not stay at sea for extended periods and it is for the same reason that effective blockades proved impossible.[21]

On occasion it may seem obvious to the observer that an opportunity to defeat an enemy, or perhaps to seize an opportunity has been lost or simply ignored through a failure to effect what one might term 'command of the sea'. This more recent concept was impossible in the Ancient World simply because of the limitations of ancient warships.

Warships and fleets preferred to keep in sight of land and these considerations heavily influenced battle tactics. Nearly all of the battles related herein took place close to a shore, an admiral seeking to have one end of his line as close as possible to the shore, so that it could not be outflanked, while placing extra ships behind his offshore end to protect his open flank (as at Salamis in 306).

A warfleet was drawn up for battle in line abreast, with the rams pointed at the enemy and the ships spaced so that there was the minimum distance between the oars of each ship (just enough for them to be able to row) and so that there were no gaps for an enemy to exploit. Such a formation presented the smallest target to an enemy, while facing him with the rams and refusing the vulnerable sides and sterns of the ships. The oars were also vulnerable and a ship with a well-drilled crew would aim obliquely for the side of an enemy's ship, shipping their oars inboard at the last moment to slide along the beam, breaking off her oars. The result could be catastrophic, snapping the oars and forcing them back suddenly among the packed rowers, causing injury and death. Most of them could not see out and the disruption would come as a surprise; the ship would be rendered immobile and even if some oars could be rigged on the damaged side, the vessel would be much reduced in performance and in any case, open to further ramming attack.[22] To protect against damage to an outrigger or oarbox by such an attack, their forward ends (*epoteis*) were heavily constructed and reinforced.

At initial contact, each side would advance but trying to ram bow to bow could usually only result in the two ships sliding along each other (with possible damage to oars) and so a captain would seek to approach on a wider course and put his helm over at the last moment, to increase the angle for his ram to become more effective; his opponent would of course, be trying the same, resulting in damage to both ships. Nevertheless, fleets did engage by advancing into each other and, in the battles reviewed later, this is how the main part of the respective fleets initially came into contact.

Two manoeuvres were evolved to attempt to break an enemy line[23] whilst avoiding the head-on charge and to try and get behind an enemy. The first, called *periplous* or 'going around' was for a more numerous fleet to extend its line beyond that of the enemy and then advance beyond it and fall upon its rear, while they were engaged at the front, doubling the line (as at Corycus in 191).

The other was called *diekplous* or 'break through'. Here, several ships in very close order would aim straight for an enemy line and seek to force their way between two enemy ships, the lead ship putting its helm over at the last minute to ram, and seek, by sheer weight of attack, to force a breach; the lead ship would seek to shear the oars of an opponent to disable it. If its captain tried to put his helm over to avoid, he could be rammed by the next attacker in line. The lead ship would probably be badly damaged but if those following could take advantage of the gap caused and get through to the rear of the enemy line, they could turn and attack it in the rear (as at Myonnesus in 190).

The use of one of these tactics could leave an attacker open to counter-attack by the other. The counter to both was similar, if one had enough ships: to form a second line behind the first, at an open end of the line to counter a *periplous*, or simply behind the whole line to catch any ships breaking through in a *diekplous* attack.

As has been seen, despite these tactics most, sometimes all, of an ancient naval battle, after the initial advance to contact, developed into a general melee (as at Chios in 201) with each ship seeking opportunity to attack as it arose.

As the ships grew in size, they became less manoeuvrable and unable to make deliberate ramming attacks, except on their own kind; this did not prevent such attacks if opportunity presented itself and a blow from such a mass of ship would likely prove fatal to anything smaller. These ships were intended primarily to grapple and board a smaller ship and overwhelm it (Antonius' hope at Actium in 31). The Romans' best weapon was their superb infantry and thus boarding was their preferred tactic to which end they invented methods to get their marines on to an enemy deck, for example, the famous *corvus* (a 'bridge' with a spike at the end which, when dropped, pierced the enemy deck, locking the ships together and allowing the Roman marines to swarm across) and its developments. This did not preclude them from some very effective ramming attacks.

Another tactic was to employ a large number of *lemboi* or similar small craft alongside the more regular warships, the intent being that, although individually inferior, the small ships would swarm around and overwhelm a big ship, particularly by getting among and attacking the oars. Both Philip V and Mithridates VI adopted this tactic, employing pirate craft, but in practice (with the exception of Corcyra in 229) the small boats could not cause any but minor damage, more or less brushed aside by the mass of the bigger ships, and did not prove to be a battle-winning strategy.

Conversely, the Rhodians for example, with their swift, manoeuvrable ships, greatly preferred ramming attacks, at which they were very good (as demonstrated at Side in 190). With this notable exception, battles had passed from the heyday of the ramming attack in the sixth and fifth centuries, to once again become an extension of land warfare, i.e. a fight between troops rather than ships, only afloat.

The two approaches to a naval battle, the swift manoeuvrable ramming attack and the grapple and boarding attack finally came together when the Romans (boarding) operated with the Pergamenes and Rhodians (ramming) in the wars against Antiochus. There the two methods, working in tandem, rapidly overcame equally strong enemy fleets.

Even at Actium, the better performance at sea of Octavius' ships was needed to offset the superior strength of Antonius' big ships, while his more normal line of battle types, the fours and fives, could meet their own kind in a boarding melee.

Overall, tactics were fairly basic and, ultimately, it was the well-drilled, experienced and motivated rowing crews, with good sea officers, that prevailed and the ships so manned that dictated the tactics.

In all of this it is almost incredible to think that the ships and fleets of this period utilised, in all, hundreds of thousands of men, drawn from populations probably little more than a twentieth of those of today. The same populations were, at the same time, providing men for the large armies that were operating simultaneously and even allowing for some at least to be interchangeable, it must have meant that a large proportion, perhaps in some cases even the majority of able-bodied men were under arms.

PART II

ALEXANDER
336 TO 30 BC

Head of Alexander. Silver tetradrachm of Alexander from Babylon. (*Altes Museum, Berlin*)

Chapter 4

The Age of Alexander

In July 356 Philip II of Macedon's Queen, Olympias of Epirus presented him with a son, Alexander (he was in fact Philip's second son, he having an older but simple-minded son, Philip Arrhidaeus, Alexander's half-brother by a previous marriage).

After the assassination of his father, in 336, the twenty-year-old Alexander became King of Macedon and Hegemon of the Greeks. It took another two years for him to overcome insurrection and challenges and to secure his position in Greece, before he was able to set off for Asia and to pursue his father's war against the Persian Empire.

Alexander inherited Macedon's small navy of about a dozen triremes and a few smaller ships. Athens had about 300 ships but, as has been seen, the lists included old, worn-out, some rotten and many unseaworthy ships, so only about a third of them were effective. Additionally, Athens had a manpower shortage and the largest fleet that she managed to deploy in the period was of 100 ships and generally less. For the other Greek states, Sparta had some thirty-five or so triremes, not seaworthy and was finished as a naval power; the remaining city states had about 150 to 160 warships between them, mostly triremes and Rhodes had started to build her navy, having perhaps ten triremes and fours. Persia remained potentially the largest naval power, able to levy as many as 400 ships from its tributaries, mostly triremes and a few fours.

In the first campaign of his reign, Alexander took his army north against rebellious tribes as far as the Danube (which he briefly crossed). There he was met by warships (there are no details of types or numbers) that had sailed from Byzantion, via the Euxine (Black) Sea and up the Danube, to a point where the modern River Iskun joins it from the south. There, he 'filled (them) with archers and hoplites' and attacked the enemy gathered on an island; the ships were too few and the attack failed to dislodge them.[1] The Greeks had been navigating and planting colonies around the Euxine for centuries, but this demonstrates that they were also aware of the geography of the Balkans at least as far as the Danube (*Ister*) to be able to have the ships at a presumably pre-arranged time and place, after and despite a riverine passage between banks mostly hostile to them. This also indicates a force large enough to be able to land and fortify a riverbank camp for themselves every couple of days or so.

During this time, in 335 and in preparation, an Athenian squadron of twenty triremes was sent on Alexander's order on a policing and anti-piracy sweep.[2]

Figure 26. Portrait busts of Alexander. On the left he is wearing a lion's head as a helmet decoration, an allusion to his claimed descent from the hero demi-god Herakles, who wore the pelt of the Nemean Lion, slain by him. (*Metropolitan Museum, New York; right: Acropolis Museum, Athens*)

334   In the spring of 334, Alexander marched with his army, estimated at 30,000 infantry of all types and 5,000 cavalry, leaving Antipater to hold Greece. Also accompanying him was his half-brother Philip Arrhidaeus. They marched around the northern shore of the Aegean to the Hellespont, shadowed by a fleet of 160 triremes and some freighters,[3] commanded by Nicanor (son of the general Parmenion). Apart from the Macedonian ships and a squadron of twenty triremes from Athens, the remainder were levied from Thessaly, southern Thrace, Aetolia, Corinth, Arcadia and Euboia, the lands under Macedonian control. The fleet comprised mostly triremes, with perhaps a dozen conters and *hemioliae* and a few of the new fours and fives.[4]

They were at Abydos by April of 334 and while the fleet commander used warships to tow the transports to ferry the army across the narrows (only about a mile/1.7km)to the Asian shore, Alexander with the remaining warships sailed the 20 miles/32 km westward to the Dardanelles for a visit to the supposed tomb of Achilles at Troy, which is on the Asian side. This was not entirely for symbolic reasons as, with his ships there, patrols could be mounted to give early warning of the advance of any Persian fleet. No such threat in fact materialised, their fleet having been engaged at that time in helping to enforce Persian rule in Palestine and Egypt.

A Persian army had however, moved north to oppose Alexander, but was defeated by him in June 334 at the Battle of the Granicus, about 50 miles/80km from the Hellespont. Alexander was able to move south to Sardis and then down the Aegean coast, shadowed by his fleet. Save for the contingent of twenty ships, he did not rely on Athens' fleet, which remained inactive at home at this time.[5] There was a squadron of light Persian warships at Ephesus, which withdrew southward in the face of the Macedonian advance. The Persians were however amassing a fleet by levies from the Ionian Greeks, Cyprus, Phoenicia and Egypt and commanded by one Memnon of Rhodes[6] (he had in fact commanded the Greek mercenaries of the Persian Army at Granicus and had escaped after the battle). His strategy was to sail with such ships as he had so far gathered, to Piraeus, where he felt that he could persuade the Athenians to join him with what he believed were their 200 triremes. If he were successful, the resulting fleet could, apart from dominating the Aegean, probably foment a more general uprising in Greece against Macedonian rule and disrupt Alexander's supply lines.[7]

Before he could do this, Memnon's fleet had to set course for Miletos, where the Persian garrison felt well able to withstand a siege in the knowledge that a relief fleet was on its way to them. Before it could reach them however, Nicanor embarked 10,000 troops on his 160 warships and transports and managed to reach Miletos first, where he blocked the harbour with his ships and occupied the offshore island of Lade that dominated the approach to the port.[8] Thwarted, the Persians sought to put in at the port of Mycale, about 9 miles/14km to the north, but were again denied access by a flying column of Alexander's troops who got there first. Denied any port or safe landing place on the mainland, after anchoring off Mycale for a while, the Persian fleet withdrew to the island of Samos,[9] allowing Alexander's ships to keep blocking the harbour mouth by mooring the triremes side by side with their rams pointing out and preventing relief from reaching the garrison.[10]

With the opening of formal hostilities and the concentration of opposing naval forces, confusion reigned among the petty tyrants and rulers of the Greek towns and cities of the coasts of Asia Minor. With the lessening of any Persian control, especially after Granicus, many of them joined with pirates and took to plundering their citizens as well as preying upon any opportune target.[11]

Parmenion had previously urged a naval attack on the Persian fleet on the grounds that, if they won, they would wrest control of the Aegean and, if they lost, they would have damaged the Persians, leaving Alexander no worse off. This seems a somewhat strange recommendation from such an experienced

Agis III, remaining with the Persian fleet, sent a despatch to his brother, Agesilaos who was regent in his absence, to use the money to pay the ships' crews, then send the ships to establish an anti-Macedonian centre on Crete, which they duly did.

After some manoeuvring by both armies, Alexander heard that the Persians were behind (to the west) of him by the coast and he 'put some of his Companions (elite troops) aboard a thirty-oared ship' and sent them to confirm this.[17] As Alexander had sent his fleet home, this was presumably a local ship, found and pressed into service which he manned with his troops in the absence of its usual crew. He and Darius met at the Battle of Issus in October 333. The Persian army was shattered and some 8,000 of their mercenary Greek hoplites (heavy infantry) managed to retreat to Tripolis. There they boarded the ships that had brought them and escaped to Cyprus. Some

Figure 27. Coin of Sidon in Phoenicia. Gold double-shekel of about 400, showing a warship before the towers and walls of the city with two (possibly) lions below. The warship has a ram on a very extended forefoot and an upper overall deck, lined with shields; below this the ventilation course for the rowers can be clearly seen and what appears to be an outrigger below that. The stern is swept upwards; no side rudders are shown but there are two odd projections at the base of the sternpost, which unusually, is straight for the whole depth of the hull and suitable to hang a single stern rudder. The coin is only about an inch (25mm) in diameter and the accuracy of the depiction constrained accordingly. (*Altes Museum, Berlin*)

managed to join Agis in Sparta, the remainder went on to Egypt. Alexander meanwhile, marched south along the Levantine coast to Arados and Byblos, both of which surrendered to him. The kings of both cities were in fact away commanding their cities' respective squadrons forming part of the Persian fleet (Sidon providing fifty ships and Arados and Byblos another thirty). Sidon was the next of the Phoenician ports to come over to Alexander, despite (or perhaps because of) their king also being absent, commanding that cities' warships as part of the Persian fleet. This 100-ship fleet that had been stationed at Tenedos tried to recover command of the Hellespont but were met and beaten by a Macedonian and allied Greek fleet under Hegelodos and Amphecheros.

News of the defeat at Issos now reached the Persian fleet at Siphnos. Pharnabazos took half of the three thousand Greek mercenaries still with the

fleet and went to reinforce Chios, while Autophradates, with the rest of the fleet sailed for Halikarnassos. There, presumably finding the city in Macedonian hands, the fleet was dismissed into its various national contingents, who were sent home. The potential of Persian seapower had been progressively eroded by their loss of Ionian, Anatolian and Aegean island ports, each with its naval contingent, reducing it in a more finite way than any great naval victory over them.

In many cases, on both sides, the levy of contingents from various maritime states and islands depended for effectiveness on the loyalty of individual polities. This might depend upon who was most widely perceived to be in the ascendant, who was or might shortly be an occupying power and in many cases, where it was not so clear cut, whether a local tyrant could see a vacuum in which there might be opportunity for plunder. Thus, in the first case, the Cypriot kings threw in their lot with Alexander, in the second case, Arados and Byblos were occupied by his army, while the petty tyrants of some Ionian cities turned to buccaneering.

For the three Phoenician kings at least, return home brought the surprise that their cities were also now Alexander's and that they had, in effect, changed sides, certainly if they valued their positions. For Alexander, the acquisition of Sidon with its fifty warships, and then Arados and Byblos with their thirty, started to tip the balance in his favour. By the time of the siege of Tyre, he gathered, apart from his own Macedonian ships and twenty Athenian, the eighty Phoenicians, plus ten from Rhodes, ten from Lycia and three from Cilicia, seemingly all triremes and was joined by another 120 warships from Cyprus, including three fives, for a fleet totalling some 230 ships.[18] Persian strength had, of course, been reduced by the same amount and the balance of naval power thereby moved decisively in favour of Alexander.

332   In January of 332, Alexander led his forces to the ancient maritime city of Tyre (which had been an important trading centre for many centuries already, having been founded nearly two and a half millennia before).[19] The city refused to either accept Alexander's rule or to remain independent subject to a Macedonian garrison. There was little doubt about the vehemence of the Tyrian's rejection of Alexander's entreaties as they committed the ultimate diplomatic sin in throwing his emissaries from the city wall; after that, they could expect no quarter and he laid siege (see Appendix).

After the fall of Tyre, Alexander continued his march along the Phoenician and Palestinian coasts, accompanied by 200 warships and transports. He lay siege to Gaza, for which he had the ships bring the heavy siege equipment from Tyre. Gaza fell after a two month siege and Alexander continued to Pelusium, the border fortress of and entry to Egypt, still shadowed by his ships. The remainder of the fleet had been sent to eliminate the pockets of Persian power under the Persian admiral Pharnabazos; he had gone to Chios, which had gone over to Alexander and they took him prisoner. A pirate fleet of five *hemioliae* had sailed into the harbour there, expecting Pharnabazos to be in command, but the Chians sailed out, captured their leader and killed the pirate crews. Chios then sent sixty ships to secure the island of Cos for Alexander; as most of the big warships were with Alexander or hunting the Persian fleet, this fleet was most likely made up of smaller warship types, conters, *hemioliae* and the like.[20] Pharnabazos later escaped from Chios and joined his ships that were still holding out on the Aegean islands and along the South Anatolian coast. Alexander knew that before he could march into Persia proper to pursue Darius, he had to ensure that he did not leave a Persian presence and

MAP 3
ALEXANDER IN THE
EASTERN MEDITERRANEAN
334—331

✝ Battles

particularly a Persian fleet able to operate in his rear. By securing the coasts and littoral of the Mediterranean, he ensured that neither would be the case and he could march eastward with secure lines of communication and supply at his rear.[21] Alexander's advance and progressive acquisition of the Levantine coasts had denied the remaining Persian captains their home ports, reinforcements or communication with other Persian forces. Isolated, they finally had no option but to surrender and thus the 'Persian' navy ceased to exist.

The Persian Satrap of Egypt had died at Issos and his successor handed the country over to Alexander, who proceeded to march from Pelusium up the eastern, Pelusiac, branch of the Nile, accompanied still by his fleet, to the capital at Memphis. There he embarked on a ship and sailed down the western, Canopic, branch of the river to the sea and founded the city of Alexandria.[22] While there, he joined Phoenician ports and Alexandria into a 'maritime defensive network with Cos, for which sixty triremes were allocated; 110 other triremes were used to ship accumulated booty back to Macedon.[23]

Despite the Macedonians having cleared most of the Aegean and Asia Minor, the Persian commander Pharnabazos was still at large, with a few still-loyal ships. The 8,000 Greek mercenaries who had escaped to Egypt after Issos had left there and sailed to join King Agis in Sparta, who, thus reinforced attacked and seized Crete, declaring war against Macedon. Together, these forces under the Persian mercenary captain, Memnon, started an island-hopping campaign in the Aegean; they took Chios, Lesbos (where Memnon was killed) and Tenedos but were caught and destroyed by a Macedonian naval force off Euboea. The confused situation in the Aegean had also permitted an increase in the level of piracy. Reinforcements of 500 cavalry and 400 infantry arrived by sea and river to join Alexander at Memphis. Alexander organised his new province into the two traditional parts of Upper and Lower Egypt, leaving a garrison at Memphis for the former and at Pelusium for the latter and posted a naval squadron at Alexandria, all under Macedonian commanders. He next sent a force, conveyed by 100 warships and recovered Crete and then went on to help the Greeks oppose Sparta (May 332), which was later defeated. With the end of Persian seapower the maritime cities and their respective contingents of ships that could be levied now were all within the compass of Alexander's Macedonian-led world. As he set off in the early summer of 331, for the conquest of Persia, he left behind him a squadron of warships at Alexandria, the three allied Phoenician kings, each with their own fleets (Sidon, Arados and Byblos) three Cypriot allied kings with fleets and whatever Macedonian and allied Greek ships had been policing Greek home waters.

In the absence of any opposing power however it seems most likely that most of these fleets were disbanded and their ships laid up. Athens however, took advantage of Alexander's absence in the East to restore her navy, building new ships and naval installations and training crews. With a view to restoring her naval dominance, the new construction included fours and fives for the first time at Athens.[24] By 331, their naval lists included fifty fours and two fives together with 360 other ships, mostly triremes, some adapted as horse and personnel transports and also some triaconters.[25]

With the more secure establishment of Macedonian rule, Alexander was able to dispose of the various petty tyrants of the coastal towns and cities of Asia Minor. With their removal went their encouragement and provision of safe havens for pirates and, in 331, he appointed Amphoteros as admiral with orders to clear the seas of pirates.[26]

326   Alexander spent the next several years in the conquest and acquisition of the Persian Empire, proceeding beyond its borders into central Asia and on to India. Eventually, his advance column under Hephaestion reached the upper course of the River Indus by the Spring of 326.[27] There he bridged the river and collected and had built some 300 boats, including two triaconters (each of thirty oars). Alexander had brought large numbers of shipwrights and boatmen so that he could have boats built as needed.[28] This posits that he must have known before he left the Mediterranean that he would be faced with large rivers that would need them; alternatively, that enquiry before he left the cities of central Persia might have yielded such information, in which case he could then have sent for them. They were recruited from Phoenicia, Cyprus, Egypt and Caria (in Asia Minor). Alexander joined Hephaestion on the Indus, crossing it with the army and proceeding to the Hydaspes (Jhelum), which he found to be fast flowing and a half mile wide /805m. Alexander then had all of the boats brought the 100 miles /160km from the Indus, the smaller ones constructed so that they could be broken into two parts and the larger, into three parts to make them portable by ox wagons.[29] These he then used to cross the Hydaspes to meet the Indian King Poros in a great battle in May 326.

After his Indian campaign and with his army refusing to go further, Alexander had to organise the army's return to the west. More boats were built on the Hydaspes, so that a total of eighty warships, triaconters and *hemioliae*[30] with lighter types for scouting, horse transport and other lighters, as well as impressed local craft were gathered, a total of some 2,000 craft[31] of all types, commanded by Nearchos and crewed by the seamen. The warships were furnished with sails, dyed purple. The fleet sailed downstream in November

326 with army columns on each bank as escort and presumably with the fleet carrying their supplies. Rapids were encountered which caused the loss of some of the boats and damaged some others. When approaching the lands of the hostile Mallians, the admiral went three days ahead of the army with the ships, shadowing Hephaestion who was five days ahead with a flying column. The Mallians were defeated and the whole entourage continued downstream until the Hydaspes flowed into the Indus, when they continued together to the head of the river delta at Pattala. There, Alexander had facilities for the ships built where the ships (that were suitable) were prepared for sea. Scouting parties to the sea were surprised by the tides that they encountered as well as the south winds that would be against them. After repairs to the fleet, Alexander had to await the autumn's lighter breezes, to be able to sail.

325   The plan was that Craterus would proceed westward by a landward route with part of the army and baggage. As soon as the winds were favourable, Nearchos would sail with the fleet westward along the coast, shadowing Alexander with the rest of the army, who would follow the coast, digging wells for them both as they went. Craterus set off in June and Alexander in late August, but, delayed by the monsoon, it was October before Nearchos was able to sail. Alexander could only move with difficulty through the desert that girded the coast, the fleet following and putting down some unrest among the tribes that they encountered. The fleet also had a difficult and hazardous voyage along unknown coasts and some ships were lost. At one point, they attacked a school

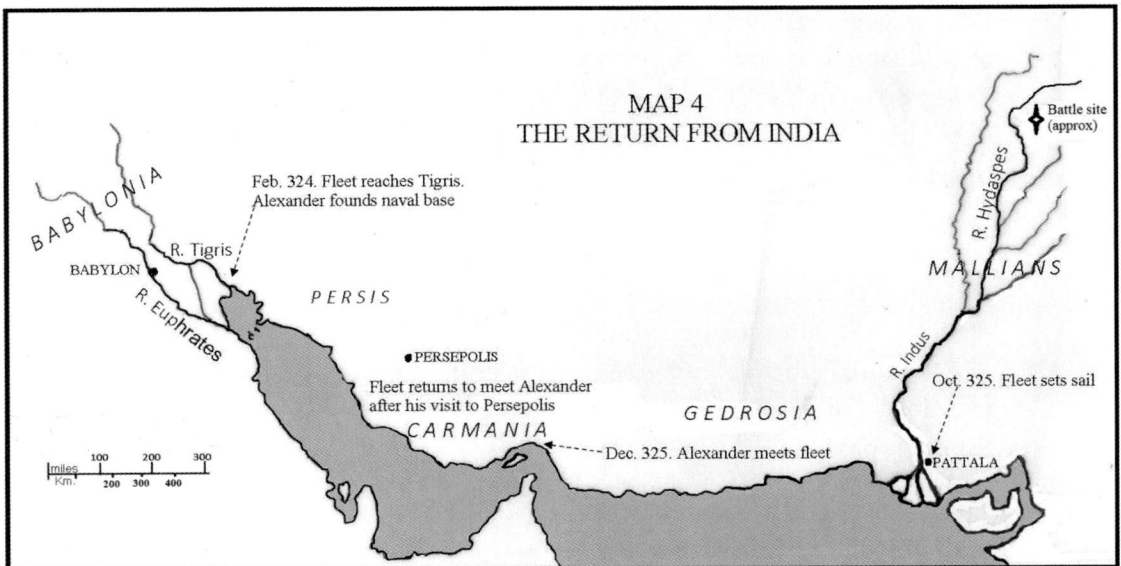

MAP 4
THE RETURN FROM INDIA

Feb. 324. Fleet reaches Tigris.
Alexander founds naval base

Battle site (approx)

BABYLONIA

R. Tigris
BABYLON
R. Euphrates

PERSIS

R. Hydaspes

MALLIANS

PERSEPOLIS

Fleet returns to meet Alexander
after his visit to Persepolis
CARMANIA

GEDROSIA

R. Indus

Oct. 325. Fleet sets sail

Dec. 325. Alexander meets fleet

PATTALA

miles   100   200   300
Km.   200   300   400

of whales, which had never before been seen by men from the Mediterranean. Nearchos had little in the way of supplies and had to put into shore to forage for what little was available; they subsisted mostly on fish and dates for the eighty-day voyage.[32] Eventually, Alexander crossed the desert and was joined by the fleet in Carmania in December, which he was able to re-provision.

324   The army and fleet continued their progress until they reached the mouth of the River Tigris at the head of the Persian Gulf in February of 324, sailing upriver a little way. Alexander went on to Persepolis and the fleet returned to a point on the north coast of the Persian Gulf nearest to it. Alexander rejoined the fleet there and sailed back to the mouth of the Tigris, where he founded a naval base, the Tigris having no delta. Alexander also sent an expedition to reconnoitre the Caspian Sea, intending to build a fleet there, for which he had ordered the building of 'Greek-style' vessels, both conters and decked ships,[33] orders which appear to have died with him. Alexander's cavalry commander and close friend, Hephaestion, died at Ecbatana and Alexander held a huge funeral for him; 'the bottom layer of the funeral pyre included the prows of 240 galleys (which presumably had to be transported from the coast) each with five 'banks' of oars, two kneeling archers and two hoplites with red felt banners between each.'[34]

Alexander finally went to Babylon, where he started to lay plans for vast war and merchant fleets both in Babylon and Alexandria and for great naval campaigns. He intended for this to start as early as June of 323, wishing to subdue Arabia by marching around its periphery and up the Red Sea,[35] accompanied by a large fleet. He had shipwrights brought from Greece and Phoenicia and timber and cordage brought also from Phoenicia, together with some dismantled warships overland to Thapsacus on the Euphrates (a distance of some 150 miles /240km), no less than two fives, three fours, twelve triremes and thirty triaconters.[36] Whereas the latter were in sections, the larger ships were more likely to have been transported as pre-cut timber and minor assemblies, rather than ship sections simply due to their complexity. Nothing further is heard of this fleet following Alexander's death. There, they were re-assembled and sailed down the river to Babylon to add to the surviving ships of Nearchos' fleet that had returned from India,

Additionally he planned to build a fleet of seven hundred sevens,[37] the first mention of such a type, together with other types of warship for a total of 1000 ships, an obvious exaggeration in numbers. The sevens had presumably been evolved to oppose the sixes recently introduced by Syracuse.

He planned to re-open the canal between the Nile and Red Sea[38] which had once more become silted and so that his proposed fleet could operate between the Persian Gulf, Arabian and Red Seas and into the Mediterranean, where the Carthaginians were the only major naval force. Having established bases at Pattala in the east and the Tigris' mouth in the west and dredged the Red Sea/Nile Canal, Alexander would appear to have envisaged a fleet that would shadow and support an army marching around the coast in a campaign to subdue the Arabian Peninsula, circumnavigate it and link all of the parts of his empire, from India to Macedon. Alexander caused some exploratory voyages to be undertaken to scout the coasts of Arabia for marching routes and staging places for the ships.[39] If these ships were to be built at Babylon, they would have to be taken along the connecting canals to the Tigris and then down that river to the sea. He ordered docks for his 1,000 ships to be built at Babylon (surely again, an exaggeration).

Clearly these plans have suffered in transliteration over the centuries as firstly and obviously, Babylon is far from the sea and its rivers unsuitable for large ships; secondly it has no easy or close access to the timber that would be needed, hence the need previously to bring dismantled ships overland; thirdly, there is no evidence of any naval opposition outside of the Mediterranean to Alexander, so who would such a fleet fight? Had a fleet been built at the head of the Persian Gulf however, sailing it the 'long way' down the Gulf and around Arabia, up the Red Sea and through the canal into the Mediterranean, would wear the ships out and those that survived the voyage would be in poor shape to face a determined opponent and all for no gain. We must assume that Alexander intended to rely on a levy of warships in the Eastern Mediterranean ports, where supplies of materials could be obtained and to support his intended advance to the West and for which the sevens, built there, would have been suitable. He could call upon about 400 warships of all types in the Mediterranean and had joined the Phoenician ports with the new Alexandria in Egypt to form a maritime network of bases for his fleets.[40] The strength of the fleet is not known but the island of Cos was allocated a squadron of sixty triremes to be permanently stationed there and no less than 110 warships were ordered to stand by to escort Alexander's body home to Macedon, a voyage that in the event, did not take place, but indicating that the overall estimate is not unreasonable. Of the huge fleets of great ships planned by Alexander, it is highly unlikely that any but a very few had commenced building; certainly there is no further mention of them in the record and the programme was cancelled by the army council following his death.[41] It may be that designs for the proposed sevens were in hand as they were to appear shortly after his death, in the wars of his successors.

323   Before all of these grandiose schemes could even start to come to fruition however, Alexander fell ill in April 323. Despite increasing illness, on the first of June, he ordered the army to be ready to march in three days and the fleet (or presumably so much of it as was built) to follow in four days. On the third of June he gave orders to Nearchos and other commanders and continued to oversee preparations over the next three days. His illness worsened however and he died at Babylon on the tenth of June 323, naming no heir, his alleged dying words when asked to whom he left his empire being 'to the strongest'. Before his body had cooled, Alexander's generals were all but fighting each other to succeed.

Appendix

The Siege of Tyre 332

332 In January of 332, Alexander laid siege to Tyre, which had refused to submit to him but was too valuable a naval base to be passed and left in the rear. The city would enable the Persian fleet, or what remained of it to have a secure base in which to re-form and reinforce itself and from which to operate along the Levantine coast and further afield thereby denying Alexander secure lines of communication, now even longer and more vulnerable, across the eastern Mediterranean.

At that time, the city of Tyre comprised a lightly protected suburb on the mainland, but the main, significant part of the city occupied an island, about a third of a mile /530m offshore. The island was about 3 miles /5km in circumference and shaped like a hammerhead, each (north and south) arm enclosing a sheltered anchorage and harbour between it and the mainland shore. The outline of the former island of Tyre and its surroundings have changed dramatically since the siege. Originally the island's harbours were built in stone blockwork, the foundations of which include gaps top allow the flow of sea water to keep them from silting. The southern (Egyptian) harbour also had moles placed *en échelon* at its south-west end, linking with offshore islets, to allow further flushing by the ocean swell, which prevails from that direction. Offshore to the south were two long moles, built into the tops of exposed reefs, to shelter ships waiting beyond the harbours (the reefs and moles have since sunk beneath the waves). The northern (Sidonian) harbour similarly had moles extended over foundations with gaps. The island is now a peninsula, Alexander's mole linking it permanently to the mainland having stopped the flow of the sea and allowing silting and is now nearly half a mile /800m in width in places. Much of the island's remaining coastal outline has been changed, especially on the west, by the effects of the sea swell and by the sinking of the land and/or reefs that maintained it.[1]

With a population of approximately 40,000, the island was encircled by strong walls, up to 150 feet /46m high above the water. It had only been captured once, by sea and between 580 and 572, had withstood a siege by Nebuchadnezzar of Babylon for twelve years without falling. The Tyrians had a

MAP 5
THE SIEGE OF TYRE

Ancient shoreline

Offshore reefs and shoals

Sidonian Harbour

TYRE

Alexander's mole

Egyptian Harbour

Prevailing winds
and sea swell

Anchorages behind
moles built on reefs

N

yards	220	440	660	1/2 mile		1 mile
metres	300		500		1 km.	

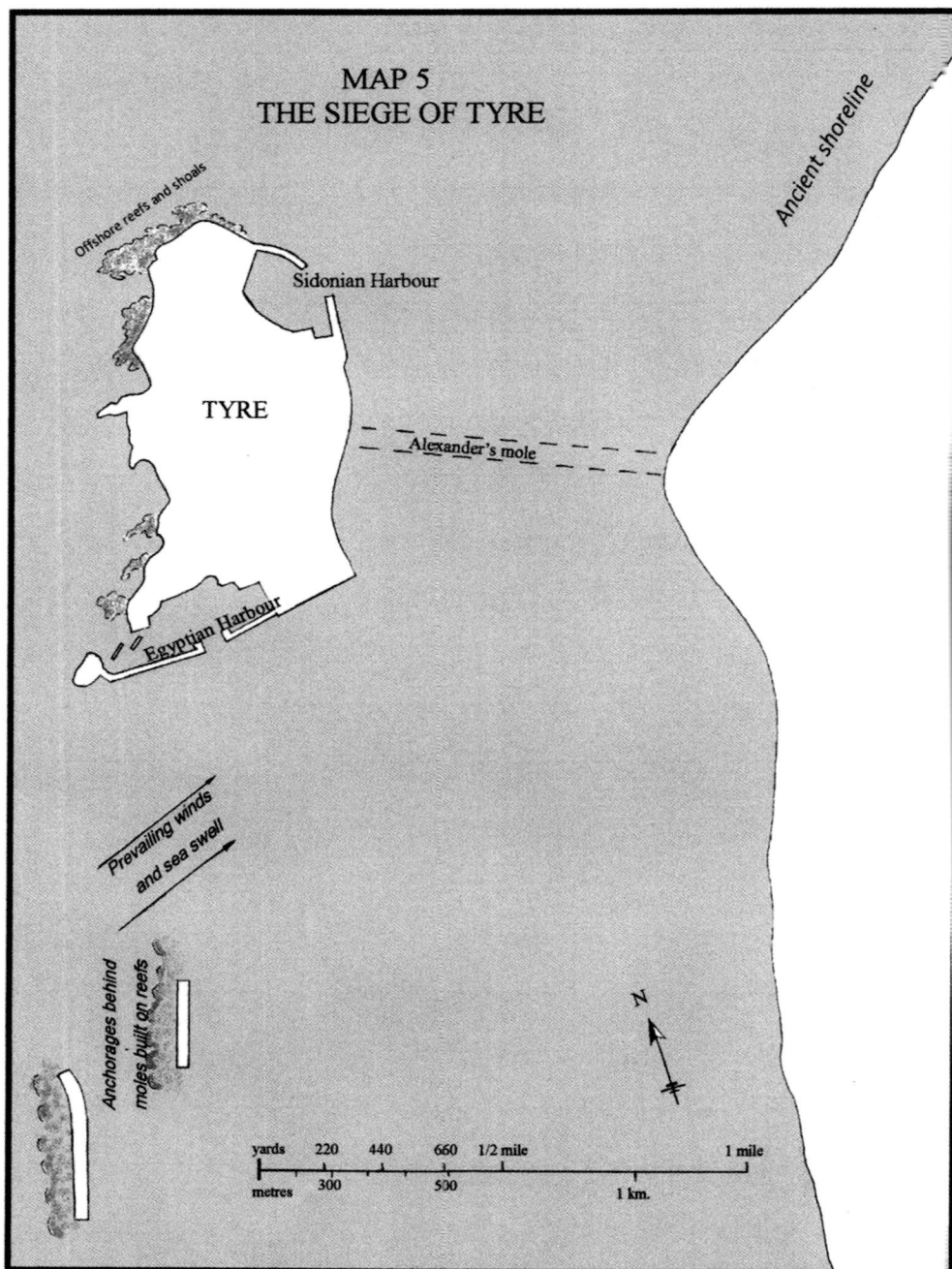

Note: the position of the reefs and shoals can only be approximate, as indeed can the
western side of the island. Apart from the remains of the masonry of the port installations, the position of the other features as they were at the time of the siege may
well have changed over the centuries since, particularly as virtually none of the forti-
fications have survived, to show their original extent.

navy based at home, of about a dozen triremes, together with at least three fours and three fives and many smaller, all in good fettle and with competent crews. Supplies had always reached the island city by sea and with the limitations of blockades in ancient times, could continue during a siege.

In opening the siege, Alexander set his army to work to construct a mole or causeway to link the mainland to the island and enable the walls to be directly assaulted. The Tyrians were very well supplied with artillery and as soon as the approaching end of Alexander's mole came within range (at about 400 paces) the men working on it were subjected to a barrage of arrows and stone shot from the walls of the city. The water, shallow at first, deepened to about 18 feet /5.5m and thus greater quantities of fill were required and the progress slowed. Even before they came within range of the defenders on the walls, Alexander's men were subject to harrying shooting from Tyrian ships sallying forth and even from raiding parties off the ships.

Alexander had two tall towers of wood, covered with green hides built and mounted his own artillery upon them to counter the enemy artillery. The Tyrians prepared a fireship in their north harbour, a horse transport which they filled with dry wood and any other flammable material that they had as fuel which also added buoyancy in case of holing by the rams of the Macedonian ships. Two masts were fitted forward each with double yards from which were hung cauldrons of flammable oil; high leeboards were placed around the deck to contain even more flammable material, as well as quantities of sulphur and pitch and to protect the crew. The stern was ballasted to counteract the added weight of the masts and to raise the bow so that it would ride up the side of the mole when it hit. Given a favourable wind which blew towards the enemy and to fan the flames, the ship was towed out of harbour by two triremes, one off each bow, with a cable forming a 'V' and so that the fireship could be aimed; when on course, the crew lit the fires, abandoned the fireship and swam back to the city and the triremes 'catapulted' the fireship at its target, dropped their cables and sheered away. The fireship, burning furiously, hit the mole and towers, which were soon burning beyond control; the triremes meanwhile, supported by other warships that had followed them, stood off and added their archery to the artillery shooting from the city picking off the men trying to combat the fires. Many of the Tyrians actually crossed in small boats onto the mole to inflict even more damage to the palisades and artillery pieces there, before eventually being driven off by the Macedonians.

The attack had been an outstanding success and Alexander had to re-think his strategy for the siege. Firstly, he ordered that the seaward end of the mole be widened, to increase the front facing the city, to accommodate more towers. He appreciated that this method of attack however, would always give a certain amount of advantage to the defenders in that, by definition, it concentrated the attack on a very narrow front, the width of the mole, enabling the defenders to know exactly where the greatest threat was and concentrate their own efforts and artillery against it. Alexander therefore had to add a naval element to his siege, firstly to prevent a repetition of the recent attack by keeping the Tyrian ships locked in their harbours and secondly to enable him to attack the other, seaward sides of the city.

Alexander took some infantry and light troops and went to Sidon, where the local fleet of fifty ships were complemented by the addition of another thirty from Arados and Byblos, thirteen from Lycia and Cilicia and ten from Rhodes[2] (which, although independent, had decided to join him); finally the large Cypriot fleet of 120 ships arrived, with one Macedonian penteconter. Alexander now had some 224 triremes and a total of 230 warships of all types, plus his original twenty Athenian triremes and had now therefore almost instantly become the pre-eminent naval power in the Eastern Mediterranean. Not so long before, most of these same ships had been levied to form the greater part of the Persian fleet, the rump of which was still spread in pockets around the Aegean or in Egypt, having now been denied any bases in Anatolia or Phoenicia. Four thousand reinforcements arrived at Sidon from Greece and Alexander put them and his infantry aboard the fleet and sailed, having taken only ten days to prepare the fleet. One could assume that orders for the massing of the ships at Sidon and for their victuals had been sent out prior to Alexander's visit.

The Tyrian navy, although a not inconsiderable force, found any further thought of offensive action to fight the besiegers at sea thwarted, now being totally outmatched by Alexander's new fleet. The Tyrians, having evacuated their women and children, kept within their harbours, blocking the entrances with triremes moored beam to beam with their rams pointed outward. Alexander's fleet immediately attacked the harbour mouths, ramming bow-to-bow, and sank three of the Tyrian ships; they could not follow into the harbour however as they would themselves have been trapped and so retired, the Cypriot contingent (commanded by Andromachos) to the beaches on the north and Phoenicians and others to the south side of the mole, each thereby guarding that respective enemy harbour. With a sufficient naval force so close to the enemy harbours, a more complete blockade could now be maintained.

Work to repair and continue the progress of the mole went on and in addition, Alexander's engineers also constructed more siege engines, battering rams, towers and catapults on some of the transports and older warships which could be moored at will to assault any part of the defences.[3] For stability, two ships were fixed together side-by-side to provide broad platforms for large stone-throwing catapults; these were supplemented by wooden housings on the ship's bows, housing bolt-shooting weapons. The enemy had concentrated on reinforcing their defences opposite the mole, the expected point of assault. To discourage Alexander's ships from using their artillery to bombard the other, weaker parts of the walls, the defenders shot fire missiles at them and lobbed rocks into the water to become underwater obstructions to hinder their approach. The ships tried to remove these obstacles but were in turn attacked by heavily armoured Tyrian ships sallying from their harbours, before the blockade ships could intercept. Alexander's men then rigged some small craft with catapults and protection for their crews and stationed them close to the harbour entrances as picket boats, the Tyrians sent swimmers to cut their anchor ropes, which had to be replaced with chains. Obviously sufficient obstacles could not be placed to deny the besieger's ships from the entire circuit of the defences and they remained largely able to pick their point of attack.

The Tyrians resolved to attempt to weaken the enemy's naval capabilities by a surprise attack on the Cypriot ships while they were still beached. They stretched sails across their north harbour mouth, to mask what was happening inside and waited. After some time, the blockaders relaxed, assuming from the inactivity that the Tyrians were exhausted. As the crews went ashore for their midday meal, the Tyrians raised the sails and their ships issued from the harbour in single file, seven triremes, three fives and three fours; starting silently and gently, they deployed into battle order and increased speed as soon as they were spotted. Taking the Cypriot ships completely unprepared and mostly unmanned, they rammed and sank the three fives (the flagships of the three Cypriot kings) and carried along the shore, cutting the cables of the other ships, which were moored with their sterns hauled up on the beach, so that the waves and surf caused them to tumble, broach and be damaged. The attack lasted over half an hour and the attackers added to their victims' discomfiture by hurling flaming missiles onto the enemy ships. News of the attack reached Alexander, who was on the south side of the mole, with the Phoenician part of his fleet; he immediately managed to have a five and five triremes manned and started to row around the island to counter-attack the Tyrian ships; the other Phoenician ships were ordered to block the southern harbour as soon as they could be manned, to prevent another sortie. Seeing this, the Tyrians signalled to recall their ships, who were so intent upon their business that despite it taking Alexander three quarters of an hour to row around the island, he still managed to catch a five and a four just before they could gain the safety of their harbour, the others having already scrambled inside, the crews of the lost ships managing to escape and swim home.

The defenders could not hope to repeat this success and their defences were increasingly subject to battering by large stone-throwing catapults, both from the mole and from the artillery ships all around the island. They made little impression where the walls were strong, but in the southern seaward sector they found a weaker part and managed to partly bring it down. An immediate assault was however, thrown back by the well-prepared defenders. Three days later, a full-scale assault was launched, not against the same breach where they were expected, but against a similarly weak stretch of wall nearby, part of which was brought down by a concentrated barrage. The breach was enlarged by further bombardment, then the artillery ships were withdrawn and two ships modified with ramps brought up, packed with assault troops. Other ships came up with them, shooting to keep the defenders down. As a further distraction, two squadrons of triremes attempted to rush the two harbour mouths. The main assault was successful and the Macedonians quickly extended along the walls to either side of the breach as more assault troops poured into the city; the attacks on the harbours were also successful and after a brief final stand, Tyre fell in July 332, after a seven-month siege. Alexander held a grand victory parade and also a naval review; he enslaved most of the population and garrisoned the city.[4] The Tyrians casualties were said to be 8,000 killed, while the Macedonians lost only twenty in the assault and 400 throughout the siege, figures which seem a little optimistic, considering the spirited defence and the successful offensive.

Chapter 5

The Ships of Alexander's Period

With the four and five, the trend had started toward bigger ships and would continue to extraordinary lengths. Bigger ships could carry more armour to protect against ram attack and cladding against artillery projectiles; they could in turn carry more and bigger artillery pieces themselves, to give cover for their larger contingents of marines for boarding. The trade-off was in slower speed and less handiness as well as an increased cost in manpower.

With the introduction of larger warships, boarding tactics tended to replace the ramming tactics perfected by the Athenians.[1] Athenian triremes originally carried only four archers and ten hoplite marines in battle, but their opponents increased those numbers to as many as forty per trireme; although the ram was to remain an important weapon, an opportunity to board a (preferably smaller) enemy would allow the larger contingents of marines to overwhelm it.

The Seven

When at Babylon and considering what were to be his last plans, Alexander was intending, as mentioned, to build the only completely new type apparently envisaged in his time, sevens (*hepteres*). Pliny[2] writing very much later, claimed that Alexander had built a ten (*dekeres*) but this is not reliable and despite apparently planning his sevens, the contemporary authors make no reference to anything bigger than a five being in service anywhere during Alexander's lifetime. The first reference to a seven actually in use, was in the fleet of Demetrios I Poliorcetes at Cyprus in 306, some seventeen years after Alexander's death.

Pre-existing types had proved more than sufficient for Alexander up to that point, at which he had no remaining naval opposition in the Eastern Mediterranean, or in any other part of his empire. To be able to advance into the Central Mediterranean however, Alexander presumably felt the need for an even larger and more powerful ship and thus intended to build sevens, presumably believing this to be a more powerful type than the six, which already existed (in extremely small numbers in the west and which he ignored). His death prevented this but, if the report is right, and Alexander did contemplate using this class of ship, the design of it must have been well advanced and the working system and disposition of the oarcrew more or less settled. The type would in fact go on to be built and used in reasonable numbers, probably more than any of the other larger rates (six and upwards), and so must have been successful in operation.

Arrian, in his *Anabasis*, otherwise all too specific about naming various classes of warship, nowhere mentions a seven, as neither does his near contemporary Plutarch in his *Life of Alexander*. The source is another near contemporary C. Rufus Curtius who specifies[3] that Alexander ordered the building of no less that 700 of these ships (surely an exaggeration) at Thapsakos (presumably nearer to the available timber; could there ever have been enough?) and to be sent downriver to him at Babylon.

The seven was presumably a logical next step in increasing propulsive power and could be accomplished by adding an extra rower to an existing rowing group. Thus it could have been a trireme with one reme of oars triple-manned and the other two remes double-manned; alternatively, a bireme with the one reme of triple-manned oars and the other reme, quadruple-manned (Figure 28).

Possibly there was enough room in the hull of a six to accommodate the extra man without needing extensive redesign of the internal architecture of the ship, which would add extra oar-power (for the cost of the weight of the extra rower). On the face of it, there would seem to be little advantage, but as mentioned, the type did become popular later, with many examples being built and used in battle; it is probably better to assume that a new, slightly broader hull was introduced. In any event, one oar had an extra man and so would have to be minimally longer, the width of a rower, about 2 feet /610mm and the same as the difference between the first and third oars of a Renaissance galley rowed *alla sensile*[4] (Figure 38).[5] In trying to envisage these schemes, it should be borne in mind that a rower will occupy a certain volume of space in a hull, a 'room' as it were. Thus, a sitting rower, of average height (for the time) would need a space approximately 4.5 feet /1.37m high, by 3 feet /910mm long, by 2 feet /610mm(minimum) wide; a standing rower would need a 'room' the same width but about 5.5 feet /1.7m high and 4.5 feet /1.37m long. When rowing they all move back and forth in concert, so the basic 'room' requirement remains the same. It is this concept that has been used in the various reconstructions and will become more pertinent as the ships become more complex.

It is known that rowers in ancient warships, at least up to now, sat to row[6] and the six is probably the last and biggest type where it is comparatively simple to have the groups of rowers so arranged. Ships would however continue to grow in rower numbers and perhaps the seven was that point beyond which adding more men per group obliged some at least of them to rise to deliver their stroke, in the manner of

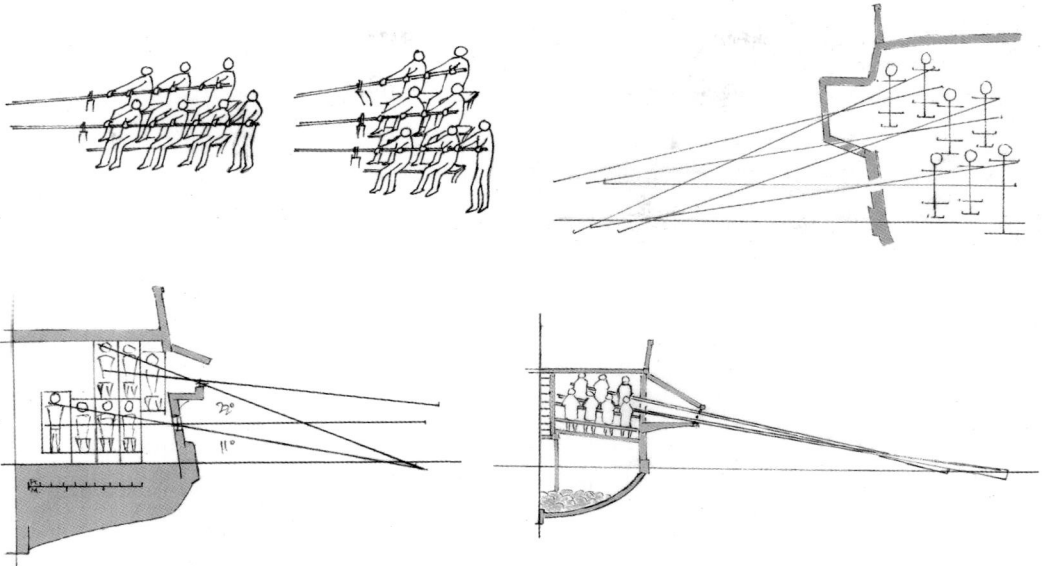

Figure 28. Possible rowing arrangements for a seven. Top: left, as a bireme, right, as a trireme. In each case it is a logical extension of the six, with the extra rower standing at the lowest level. The lower oar must be a little longer to accommodate the extra man, but not so much so as to cause a disruptive difference in the gearing of each. Top, far right: as a trireme after Coates (*GROW* p.306); note that both thranites are outboard of the zygites and that the thalamite oar is only two feet/610mm longer than the other two. Centre left: as a bireme, an extension of the author's layout for a six (see Chapter 3). Once again, the lower oar is two feet/610mm longer. Centre right: as a bireme, after Warry (*Warfare in the Ancient World* p.98) but with all of the rowers sitting and the oars worked *en échelon* (discussed in Chapter 12). Apart from the obvious lack of headroom (easily solved by a higher deck) the difference between the length of the two oars (six feet/1.8m) could prevent them from being worked in concert; the result is a gearing of 3 for the upper and 3.3 for the lower. It is not clear why such a large difference has been posited. The principal of sloping the benches downward does not work and they should be staggered horizontally. It seems that as shown, the lower rowers will foul the bench of the upper and be unable to deliver their stroke. Bottom: as a bireme also rowed *en échelon* after Nelson (*Warfleets of Antiquity* p.25). All rowers are again seated but the lower set are smaller than the others; the oars are of very different lengths (and do not reach the water). Assuming that both tholes are at the point where the oars emerge from the oarbox, then the difference in gearing, in addition to the different lengths, between the two (approximately 2.2 for the upper and 3.8 for the lower) is so great that it is impossible for them to work together.

the rowers of the later Renaissance galleys. The method was known in antiquity, appearing in Egyptian tomb paintings as early as the third millennium.[7]

In attempting to envisage a seven, Polybius[8] tells us that the Carthaginian flagship at the Battle of Mylae in 260, was a seven 'rowed by seven men to an oar' i.e. a monoreme. Silius Italicus[9] however, relates that the Carthaginian ship stood higher than all others and was the largest ever built by them, surely the same ship. It was rowed by about 400 men. The great height could have been due to towers on deck, but that device was only on the Roman ships[10] at that time and the size of a seven alone should have been enough without them, to overawe the other ships.

Polybius' alleged description of course, suits a Renaissance galley and there is no reason why it should not have been so, but the account could well have suffered variations and transliterations in the millennia since it was written[11] (as mentioned in the Introduction). Following the development from the trireme to the six, it seems logical to suppose that the principle of the multi-reme ship was continued into the seven, especially considering that it was higher than other ships.

If we interpret the seven as a bireme, a direct follow-on from the bireme six, it will have one reme of oars triple-manned and the other quadruple-manned. The reach of a man of average height at the time, sitting on a fixed seat was about 40 inches /1m and as each rower outboard of him will pull through a fifth less of that arc, so the fourth and furthest outboard can only pull the oar two fifths as much, a mere 16 inches or so /405mm and thus is hardly worth having him aboard. This will however, increase significantly if the inboard man adopts a rising stroke, increasing his reach to about 54 inches /1.37m, in which case the stroke of each man outboard of him will in turn increase by a proportionate amount. With an oar triple-manned, as has been seen with the six, all three can be seated, the outboard rower still contributing a useful three fifths of the inboard rower's arc (the inboard man will pull through 40 inches /1m, the middle man through 32 inches /810mm and the outboard man through 26 inches /660mm). It seems best to incorporate the standing rower at the lower level, to keep his weight as low as possible to minimise topweight and also, as that oar operated at the lowest angle and to which the extra man could be fitted more readily, whereas at the upper level the angle would have to become more, perhaps too, acute in operation; also the deckhead might have to be raised to allow him room to stand. There is a further point in that, at the lower level, the oar need be only 2 feet /610mm longer to accommodate the fourth rower, whereas in the upper level, it must be twice that length longer and thus have a very different gearing to the other oar in the group.

Alternatively, Morrison and Coates[12] propose the ship as a trireme with the thalamite oars triple-manned, the additional man standing to deliver his stroke. This

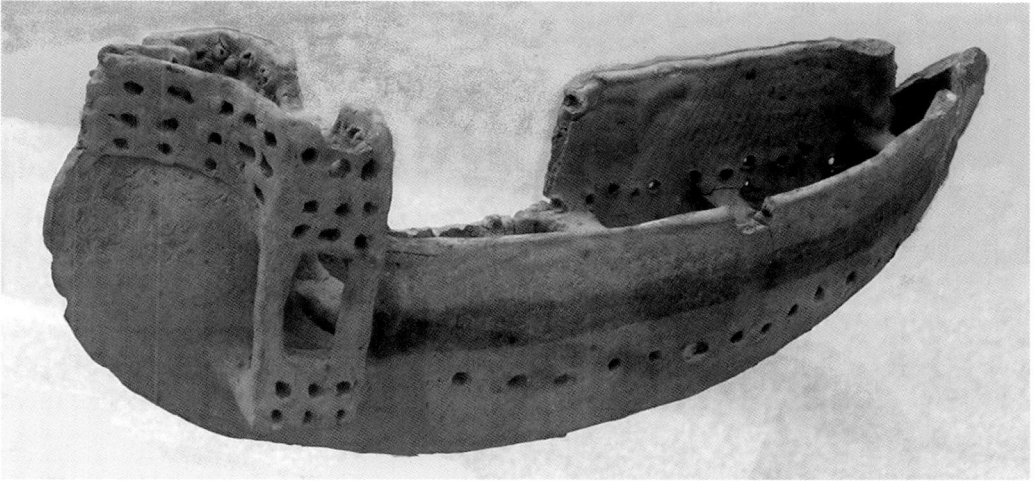

Figure 29: Two views of a terracotta model of a merchant ship from Cyprus, believed to be sixth century. Note that the steering oar positions are in enclosed sponsons, with a deck above, raised above the main deck level and enclosed by rails or screens. It is easy to envisage such an arrangement on larger warships to protect the steering positions and provide a raised fighting and command deck aft. As will be seen (see Chapter 7, Appendix) Demetrios' flagship may well have had a raised poop. (*British Museum*)

reconstruction also specifies a slightly longer thalamite oar (again, two feet /610mm) yielding little difference in gearing from the (double-manned) thranite and zygite oars above it, which are operating in the same space; the small difference in oar length should, with minor adjustment to the positioning of the thole pins, enable the oars to be worked together.

As to the number of oars: as a bireme, there could be two remes, each of twenty-eight oars per side, employing 196 rowers per side, the odd four men (if the figure of 400 total is literal) being perhaps overseers, reserves or water carriers; with remes of thirty oars, the total would of course rise to 260 per side, 520 in all. As a trireme, it has been posited[13] that by using the same number of oars as a classic trireme, namely thirty-one thranite, twenty-six zygite and twenty-six thalamite per side, requiring 199 men per side, the ship would have a power and small speed advantage over the very similar-size six, suggesting therefore, a reason for its adoption in preference to the six.

As to size, it is felt that with 400 or so men below decks in a wooden box (need one add in a Mediterranean Summer) that a much more roomy hull could have been developed, so the men were not so crammed together as in the smaller ships. An interscalmium of perhaps as much as 4.5 feet /1.37m would allow 'breathing room' between the men and still fit into a hull little different to that of a six.[14] Barker[15] suggests 140 feet in length and 23 feet beam (30 feet across the outrigger) but the author has suggested that the six could be 186 feet /57m overall, at which size there would be room in an existing hull to adapt it to include a seventh rower.

As to performance, it has been estimated that the seven could achieve eight to nine knots for ten minutes, four to five knots cruising for up to three hours and two to three knots all day, rowing by sections; a 360 degree turn could (optimistically) be done in about twice its length and take a minute[16] and that under sail, it could maintain six to seven knots, given a fair wind.[17]

Although it seems that a few triremes were built,[18] there is no evidence to suggest that the sevens that Alexander ordered, or indeed any others of the enormous fleets that he planned, were ever built. As mentioned, even the six, although already a proven type in the west, does not appear in the record for the east until well after Alexander's demise.

Figure 30. Sketch elevation of Demetrios I Poliorcetes' seven (not to scale). The bow is fashioned after the silver tetradrachm (Part III post) and the stern takes in the raised poop and protected steering positions in Fig. 29. Ventilation slots have been introduced between the top of the oar box and the main deck. The ship is a trireme, with thirty thranite and zygite oars and twenty-nine thalamite oars on each side, for a total of 178; there are two men to each of the upper two remes and three to the lowest, for a total of 360 rowers. Overall length is approximately 180 feet/55m.

The Triaconter

Although not new types, there was certainly novelty in the ships that Alexander had built on the River Jhelum when he started to turn for home. Apart from impressing local craft and fabricating lighters and rafts, light warships were built and Arrian[19] is particular in specifying that they were triaconters and *hemioliai*. As they were built by craftsmen brought from the Mediterranean, they were presumably built in the same way and similar in size and design to those in use there. The triaconter or ship of thirty oars, was presumably a continuation of the type that had been built for centuries. Clearly the type was found to be reasonably easy to build, especially in what must have been limited circumstances on the rivers of India. Further, it must have been considered most suitable for the many tasks entrusted to it, anything smaller lacking robustness and anything bigger requiring more complex building abilities and bigger, trained crews.

As a type, it had long been in use, Herodotus mentioning it as existing in what we know as the Bronze Age.[20] The Athenians, for their part, had used them extensively for raiding and scouting,[21] obviously an ideal size of light yet seaworthy warship, which would last into the first century before being superseded.[22]

Assuming a monoreme of thirty oars exactly and allowing a minimal enough interscalmium of 3.25 feet /1m and say 6.5 feet /2m each for bow and stern, a not unreasonable ship of about 60 feet /18.3m in length results.[23] As a comparison, the

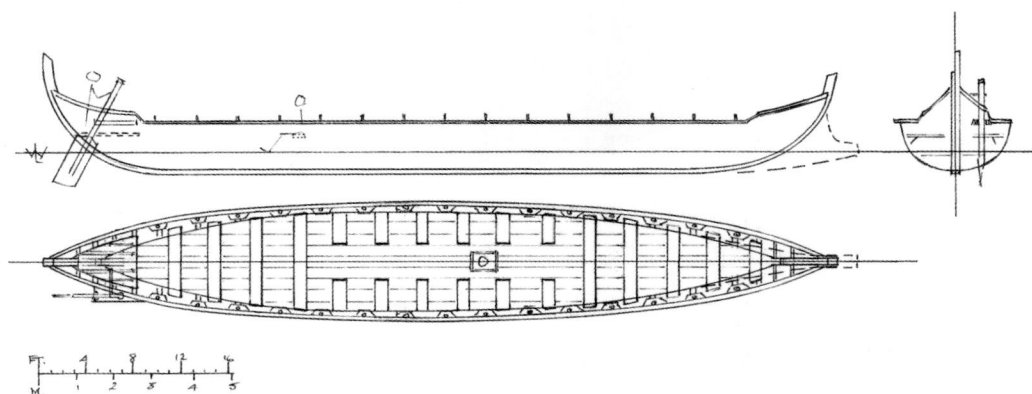

Figure 31. Suggested reconstruction of a triaconter of Alexander. A thirty-oar, open monoreme of straightforward build, of seagoing form. A well has been left amidships between the thwarts for a mast tabernacle and for the stowage of stores and tackle. Crew personal items could be stowed under their respective benches. An amended form with a reshaped lower forward hull could provide the extended forefoot to allow the mounting of a small ram. Length overall: 67 feet/ 20.4m; waterline: 59 feet/18m. Beam overall: 10feet/3m; waterline: 8 feet/2.4m. Draft: 1.75 feet/530mm. Freeboard 2.5 feet/762mm; interscalmium: 3.25 feet/990mm.

Chapter 6

The Empire Divided

323   The two decades following the death of Alexander were to be a period of intense political and military activity which would shatter his Empire into a number of rival parts, dominated by his former generals, the *Diadochoi* or Successors, all constantly jostling for advantage against each other, interspersed by periods of precarious balances of power. Within weeks of his death in the Summer of 323 the manoeuvring for a position from which to assume his mantle was well under way.

   On his deathbed, Alexander had given his ring, a symbol of authority, to his senior general, Perdiccas who called a meeting of the generals at Babylon. An agreement was reached by which Alexander's child, shortly to be born to his wife Roxana, if a son, would be joint king with his half-brother Philip Arrhideios, who was also at Babylon and was there proclaimed as Philip III. Perdiccas and Antipater (who had been left by Alexander in charge in Macedon) would be regents, the former in Asia and the latter in Europe. They were to appoint the others to be satraps or governors of the various parts of the Empire; in private however, the rest of the generals were already jockeying to grab as much of the Empire for themselves as they could. Ptolemy was granted the Satrapy of Egypt, enabling him to fulfil his secret ambition to have it for himself. Antigonos had Lycia, Pamphylia and Phrygia in Asia Minor; Eumenes received Cappadocia, Paphlagonia and Pontus, also in Asia Minor; Thrace went to Lysimachus; Seleucos became cavalry commander and Antipater remained in Macedon and Greece. Without Alexander to control them, the arrangement was doomed to failure, notwithstanding the birth of a son to Roxana, Alexander's widow and who was named Alexander IV.

   At his death, all of the naval forces in the Eastern Mediterranean (excepting those of Athens and Rhodes) were 'Alexander's' and merged into his Macedonian Fleet. There were nearly 400 ships in all, of which 110 had been assigned to Antipater as a 'home fleet'; another sixty had been based at Alexandria and the bulk of the remainder were in the Levant. With no opposition, apart from the occasional anti-piracy patrol, there was little for them to do and most were probably laid up.

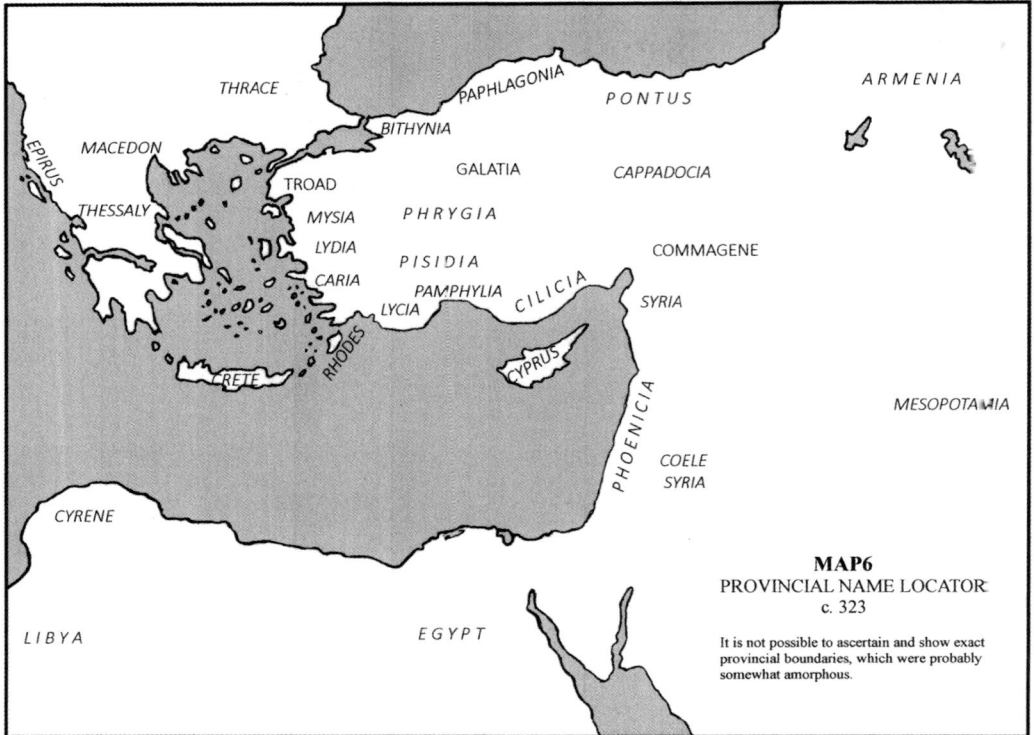

MAP6
PROVINCIAL NAME LOCATOR
c. 323

It is not possible to ascertain and show exact
provincial boundaries, which were probably
somewhat amorphous.

At first, the so-called successors of Alexander used whatever ships and crews that they found or could purloin in the territories that they managed to occupy from the break-up of the Empire. As circumstances started to develop and change however, it became more necessary to keep or acquire lands that had shipbuilding materials and abilities. Phoenicia was probably the biggest prize, having materials, the shipyards and expertise to build advanced warships; many of the large ships were in fact built there.

The island of Rhodes had submitted to Alexander in 332 and after over half a century of political instability, his influence had imposed stability (underwritten of course, by a garrison). Largely left to their own devices, the island had prospered gaining growing trade and economic strength. As soon as they heard of his death the Rhodians ejected the Macedonian garrison and asserted their independence.[1] Rhodes proceeded to build up her navy, probably at least doubling its number of ships. With limited numbers but highly skilled seamen, they preferred the smaller ships (requiring smaller crews) concentrating on having them extremely well handled. To their triremes they added fours, which would be their most numerous type and also evolved their own design, the *trihemiolia*, which probably replaced the triremes in due course.

Upon learning of the death of Alexander, Athens sought to lead the Greeks in a war of independence from Macedonian hegemony and formed a Hellenic League. Greece had suffered several bad harvests and with Macedonian control of the routes to the wheatfields of the Black Sea and Egypt, Athens looked to secure an alternate supply route. Using her burgeoning seapower, Athens sought to obtain a colony and trading station in the Adriatic. An expedition was therefore prepared with a fleet of fourteen triremes and fours, together with two horse transports and four triaconters,[2] to protect the new colony against Etruscan raiders. The expedition sailed in 324 but had to be recalled before it could achieve anything as Alexander had decreed that all Greek exiles be reinstated, which threatened Athens' sole remaining possession, the strategic island of Samos. Her active fleet at this time was about 170 ships, at least forty-three of which were fours, together with at least seven fives; the rest were triremes.[3]

Athens managed to recommission enough ships to make up a fleet of 240[4] which she sent against Antipater. This was still enough to vastly outnumber the 110 ships available to him and having been repulsed at Thermopylae, he was forced to withdraw to Lamia in Thessaly, where he was blockaded. To prevent reinforcements from reaching Antipater, in the Spring of 322, the Athenians sent 170 of their triremes and fours, commanded by Euetion, to the Hellespont. Reinforcements under Alexander's former general Cleitus arrived there, escorted by (curiously, the same number) no less than 240 ships, mostly triremes but with many fours and fives. Cleitus' fleet met and defeated the Athenians off Abydos, possibly in June of 322; although most of the Athenian fleet managed to escape, it was a severe set-back. Cleitus next attacked the blockading squadron at Lamia (presumably rejoined by the survivors of Abydos) where his ships combined with Antipater's fleet there, to give them overwhelming naval superiority and break the blockade. The Athenians withdrew and re-formed a fleet of 170 ships which sailed for Amorgos, where Cleitus' vastly bigger fleet met them again. The Macedonians rammed three of the Athenian ships before breaking through their line (presumably in a *diekplous* attack) and then proceeded to surround the Athenians. Seeing his position to be hopeless, Euetion signalled surrender. On their oath not to oppose the Macedonians again, the Athenian fleet, with its damaged ships in tow, was allowed to go home.

322   With the Athenian defeat, a Macedonian army under Craterus and Leonnatus, was able to cross the Hellespont into Europe and march to relieve Antipater. With Antipater's garrison at the isthmus isolating the Peloponnese and Cleitus blockading Athens, the Greeks were defeated at the Battle of Crannon and

MAP 7—CHANGING FORTUNES 323—301

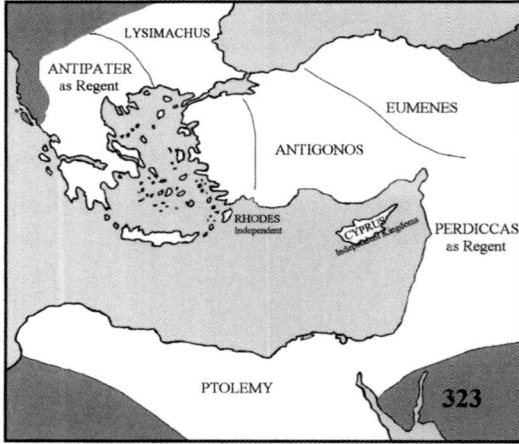

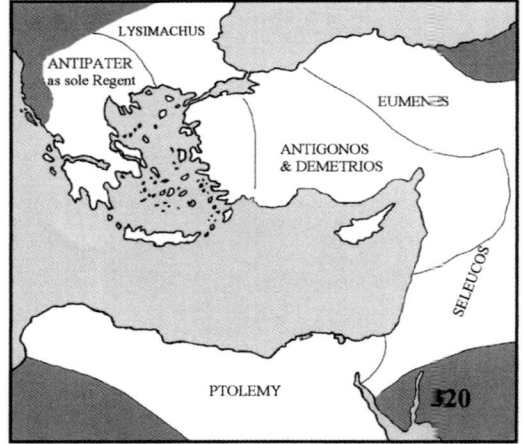

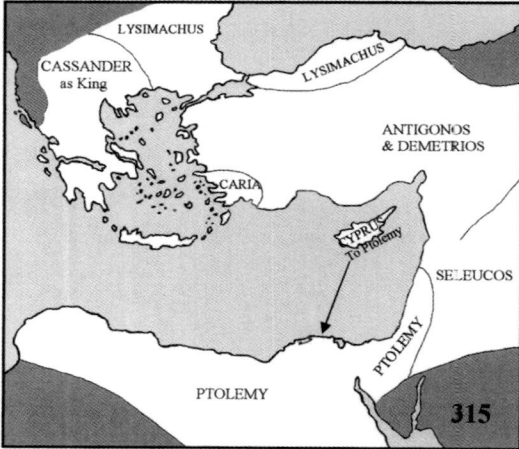

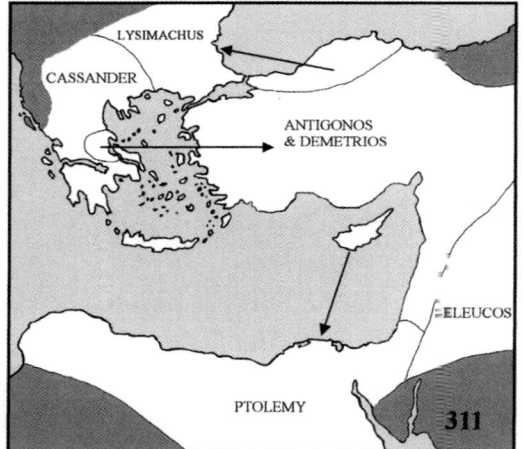

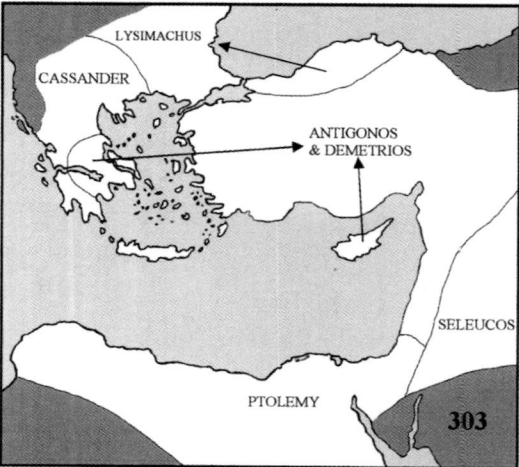

the insurrection ended. Cleitus then sailed on and destroyed an Athenian squadron at the Echinades Islands, near the mouth of the Gulf of Patras. Leonnatus was killed in battle and Antipater garrisoned Athens and Piraeus and consolidated his hold over the Aegean. He then joined with Antigonos to put down a revolt in Syria. With the defeats, loss of independence and the exile of many of its citizens, the Athenians' will had been broken and with it Athenian sea-power had been destroyed, never to recover, the warships in the harbour just so many lifeless hulks.[5]

Figure 32. Gold pentadrachm of Ptolemy I Soter. (*Metropolitan Museum, New York*)

Alexander had expressed a wish to be buried at the Temple of Ammon in Egypt. His brother took over a year preparing a splendid catafalque and it had carried his body as far as Syria by the winter of 322. It seems that Perdiccas and the other Macedonians wanted to bury Alexander near his father in the Macedonian Royal Tombs at Aegai (Verghina) in Macedon. Ptolemy intercepted the catafalque in Syria and made his way with it towards Egypt.[6]

Perdiccas, on hearing this, sent a force to recover it but Ptolemy sent a decoy catafalque (or perhaps the real one minus Alexander's golden sarcophagus containing his body) which diverted Perdiccas' force and enabled Ptolemy to take Alexander to Egypt. There, he could use its presence to legitimise his rule as Alexander's successor and Pharaoh, which he proclaimed himself in 305.

321   Antigonos, the governor of Phrygia, met Ptolemy and the local kings in Cyprus, to secure for themselves the sea trade of the Levant. Ptolemy used the opportunity to conclude treaties with the kings of Cyprus, increasing his influence there and giving him access to the island's forests and timber with which to build himself a fleet. Feeling under threat, Perdiccas, as regent, sent Eumenes to form an army to keep Antipater out of Asia and himself marched to attack Ptolemy in Egypt, accompanied by a Macedonian fleet. Perdiccas was killed in a mutiny and Eumenes killed Craterus in battle. The fleet sailed and was rebuffed at Rhodes, whereupon it was seized by Antigonos. Antipater crossed into Asia, and in Syria joined with the armies of Asia and Egypt and was declared sole regent (320). Antipater then returned to Macedon and assumed

sovereignty there, leaving Antigonos and his son Demetrios in Asia Minor as de facto rulers. Ptolemy I was meanwhile, securing his position in Egypt and had annexed Cyrene. The ex-cavalry commander, Seleucos was allotted the satrapy of Babylon, from which he assumed power over the former Asian domains to the east.

319   Antipater, the only one remaining legitimate regent appointed by Alexander, died in 319 and with him, any lingering claim to Alexandrian succession, unity or legitimacy of rule. The various claimants sought to consolidate their own power bases centred on various parts of the short-lived empire and from which to extend their rule and hope to become paramount. Antipater was succeeded by his son, Cassander; Antigonos and his son Demetrios became established in Asia Minor, while another general, Lysimachus held Thrace. Seleucos retained the main Asian parts of Syria, Mesopotamia and Persia with the lands to the east, with his capital at Babylon; finally, Ptolemy held Egypt.

With the initial exception of Seleucos, all turned their attentions and the focus of their desire for power, back to their Aegean and Eastern Mediterranean origins. These seas became the focus around which their power struggles were to revolve for well over a century and naval warfare was to be the main means by which they sought to resolve them. Ptolemy invaded Palestine and Phoenicia, while Antigonos, in alliance with Cassander, opposed the new regent, Polyperchon in Macedon and Eumenes in Asia Minor.

318   Cleitus, on behalf of Polyperchon and still in command of that part of the Macedonian fleet not controlled by Antigonos, went to the Hellespont to block Antigonos and to oppose any attempt by Ptolemy to control the straits. Antigonos turned his attentions instead against the Aegean seaboard of Asia Minor, taking Ephesus and Priene. In 317, Antigonos and Cassander gathered a fleet under Nicanor, from the ships at Athens (presumably repaired survivors of their previous fleet and new construction) and Greece. With this fleet, the allies entered the Bosporos and there engaged Cleitus, losing half of their ships. In a second naval battle they caught Cleitus' ships on the shore, near to Byzantion, killing him and destroying his fleet.[7] Now with no opposition in the Northern Aegean, Nicanor sailed south with the allied fleet and attacked and destroyed a fleet being built in Phoenician ports for Eumenes, forcing him to flee to Babylon. In the meantime, Alexander's half-brother, Philip Arrhidaeos had in the spring, besieged Cyzicus using arrow and stone-throwing artillery. The town was on an offshore islet and as he had no naval support, he failed to take it.[8] Later he made his way back to Macedonia, where he fell into the hands of and was killed by Alexander's mother, Olympias (in 317). Now unopposed,

Cassander occupied Athens, drove out Polyperchon, had Nicanor killed and formally assumed the crown of Macedon; he also captured Roxana, Alexander's widow and her son, Alexander IV. Antigonos meanwhile allied himself with the independent states of Rhodes and Cyprus.

316   In 316, Antigonos sent a force down the Euphrates, defeated and killed Eumenes and captured Babylon. There, he drove out the satrap, Seleucos (who fled to Ptolemy) and claimed to rule the Empire. Ptolemy and Seleucos, now anxious over Antigonos, allied themselves with Cassander and Lysimachus of Thrace. In the Levant, Ptolemy wanted to extend his realm from Egypt to encompass the Palestinian and Phoenician coasts, an ambition to gain territory that had belonged to his claimed pharaonic predecessors which would also give him access to extra supplies of timber needed to build his ships; such a move could also serve to contain Antigonos, as the new alliance would help to encircle him.

315   The new allies sent an ultimatum to Antigonos, which he rejected and striking first, invaded Syria and Phoenicia by land, leaving Ptolemy holding Tyre as an isolated enclave that he had to supply by sea. He next sent a squadron of warships to the Hellespont to prevent a crossing by Cassander, who in the meantime, had taken the Peloponnese. Now holding the maritime cities of Phoenicia, as well as the ports and towns and the all-important forests of Asia Minor, Antigonos and his son, Demetrios, set up shipyards at Tripolis, Byblos and Sidon and proceeded with the building up of a powerful navy with which,

Figure 33. Seleucos I. Silver tetradrachm issued at Susa in Persia circa 300, showing him offering a trophy of arms possibly following victory at Issos in 301. (*Altes Museum, Berlin*)

together with their ally Rhodes (from whom they also ordered ships to be built) they could oppose the naval supremacy of Ptolemy and his allies. With his growing fleet Antigonos was able to blockade Tyre, which he besieged. He could also expand his power into the Aegean, driving out the Athenians and garrisoning the islands; he also successfully turned the loyalties of some of the Greek mainland to his favour.

Ptolemy, starting with the sixty ships based at Alexandria, had built up his own fleet to over 100 ships and with it, took Cyprus. The kingdoms that ruled the island had divided and weakened, giving Ptolemy his opportunity to intervene and then progressively expand his power there. The appeal of the island, apart from its valuable timber, is of course, its strategic placement between Asia Minor and the Levant and thus across the coastal sea routes between them. The distance between Alexandria and say Paphos in Western Cyprus is 284 miles /456km; a trireme could travel 120 miles in a 'long' day, given reasonable sea and wind conditions,[9] placing the island within two and a half days' direct sailing. There was a brief re-emergence of Athenian seapower in 315/314, when the city sent some ships to Siphnos to suppress pirates operating from there.[10]

314   Antigonos had built up his naval strength to a total of 240 ships of all types (same total yet again!) namely ninety-seven triremes, ninety fours, ten fives, three sevens, ten tens and thirty light ships built in Phoenicia, Cilicia and Rhodes.[11] Fifty of these he sent to support the insurrections in Greece. He also formed an island league in the Cyclades and garrisoned them.[12] From Cyprus, Ptolemy and Seleucos sent a squadron of forty ships to help Cassander suppress the Antigonos-inspired insurrections in Greece. The rest of the Ptolemaic fleet based itself on Cyprus, across Antigonos' trade routes. Antigonos' son Demetrios had meanwhile advanced with an army and occupied Gaza on the border with Egypt, giving him control of the whole Levantine coast.

313   The next spring (313) Antigonos sent a maritime force into the Euxine Sea to attack Lysimachus, another to occupy Caria and a third to Greece against Cassander, where they captured thirty-six of his ships.[13] Antigonos took Tyre after a fifteen-month siege (June 313) and although Ptolemy had to withdraw to counter an uprising in Cyprus, his forces there caught one of Antigonos' armies and fleets by ambush on the South Anatolian Coast. Cassander was doing badly in Greece and sought peace but also invaded Euboea, forcing Antigonos to send his main fleet with 150 ships and troops to protect it. Antigonos next withdrew his fleet to the Hellespont but Lysimachus got there first and prevented a crossing to Thrace by his reinforcements. Antigonos had

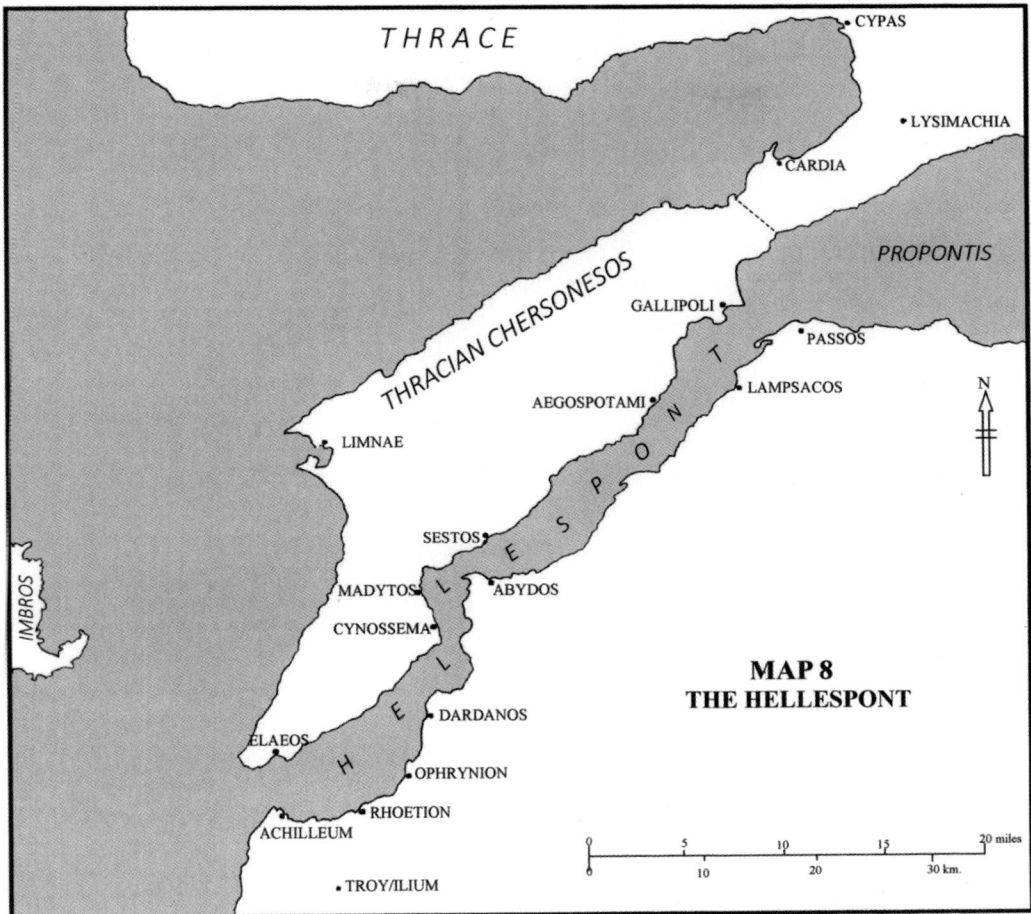

MAP 8
THE HELLESPONT

nevertheless managed to force Cassander from Central Greece and his sea power made him dominant in the Central Aegean. He was not totally successful however, losing four ships to an attack by Cassander's ships.

312   In the spring of 312, Ptolemy advanced with a large army against Gaza and soundly defeated Demetrios who had to retreat as far as Cilicia, where the coast was ravaged by Ptolemy's ships operating from Cyprus. Seleucos, who had been with Ptolemy, then hurried to Babylon where he made himself ruler of the eastern part of the Empire, in October 312.

311   In the next year, 311, Antigonos recovered most of Syria and Phoenicia[14] and made an unsuccessful attempt to break through to Petra and the Red Sea, but lost his initiative in Europe. He next attacked Seleucos in Asia Minor and whilst thus distracted, Ptolemy attempted to regain Phoenicia. Antigonos managed to stop Ptolemy's thrust but, exhausted, sued for peace in 311. Despite the loss

of Cyprus, Antigonos and Demetrios had established their naval power and used it to maintain command over the Ionian and Phoenician coasts and in so doing, reversed the tables and isolated Ptolemy from his erstwhile allies. Conversely, Ptolemy, by holding Cyprus, kept Antigonos' possessions in the Aegean and Syria separated. This first round of power struggles had nevertheless confirmed the antagonists in their respective power bases and at sea, left the Antagonids and Ptolemy in a stalemate. Antigonos held Syria, Caria and Phoenicia; Ptolemy had gained Cyprus; Cassander had lost most of Greece but held Athens and Lysimachus was secure in Thrace. Seleucos held the East and had founded his dynasty. Rhodes remained independent.

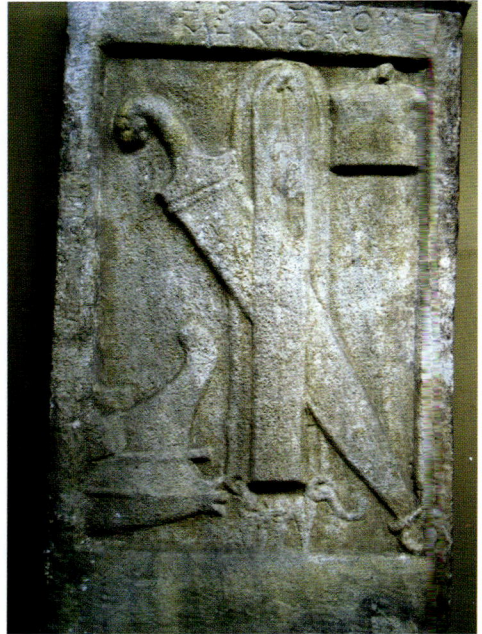

Figure 34. Grave stela of the third century showing the prow of a warship as well as the sword and other equipment of the deceased. (*Archaeological Museum, Istanbul*)

310   Alexander's posthumous son had been declared King Alexander IV of Macedon to support Antipater and Cassander's claims to be the regents/successors of his father. With the extinction of the Empire and of any possibility of being accepted as a paramount king, poor Alexander had outlived his usefulness and was killed by Cassander in 310. Antigonos again attacked Seleucos in 310 and 309 but without success[15] and Ptolemy finally took direct control of Cyprus, appointing his brother, Menelaos as governor.[16]

308   Peace was to be short-lived as the aggressive Antigonos and his equally motivated son, Demetrios next turned their attentions once more to the Greek mainland in a challenge to Cassander. Ptolemy, perhaps seeing an opportunity, backed their move by sending a fleet in 308 to occupy Andros and then to Corinth, taking that city. The Antagonids, with a fleet of 250 ships,[17] both warships and transports, captured Athens and Megara in 307, honing their siege techniques in the process. Holding Athens gave Demetrios access to its shipyards and he promised to order the building of warships there with timber to be sent by his father.[18] This policy resulted in the building of at least thirty fours, ships which were included in the fleet that Demetrios took with him against Cyprus.

The unnatural alliance of Ptolemy and Antigonos did not last long, the latter planning to seek maritime dominance in 306, by attacking Ptolemy's forces in Cyprus and Egypt in two operations. Rhodes had recently entered into a treaty with Rome and refused to lend assistance to the Antigonids, as they had previously done and who thus felt they could not leave such a potentially hostile entity across their lines of communication; Rhodes was thus added to their list of targets.

306   Demetrios, commanding a fleet of 118 warships, blockaded a Ptolemaic squadron of sixty ships under Menelaos, in the harbour of Salamis in eastern Cyprus, which he proceeded to besiege. Ptolemy came with reinforcements and 140 warships, landing at Paphos at the west of the island. He marched and sailed to break the siege, accompanied by his fleet, along the south coast and ordering the ships at Salamis to break out to join him. Demetrios sailed to intercept, leaving ships to prevent Menelaos from sallying to join Ptolemy. In the ensuing hard-fought battle, Ptolemy's fleet was heavily defeated (see Appendix); Demetrios' fleet suffered only twenty ships badly damaged. For Ptolemy it was a disaster and without the relieving force, his garrison in Cyprus could not hold out and the island fell to Demetrios. Ptolemy's brother Menelaos did eventually manage to break out of the harbour of Salamis but arrived after the battle to find Demetrios' victorious fleet and had to hastily retrace his steps to the safety of the harbour and later to surrender. Unable to maintain his presence there, Ptolemy also had to cede Corinth to Cassander and also abandon his bases in Asia Minor. Antigonos promptly declared himself to be king in succession to Alexander; the others did the same respectively, formally ending any pretence of a continuing empire.

306   In the October of 306, Demetrios with a fleet of 150 warships and 100 transports (his fleet augmented by ships captured from Ptolemy) attacked the Nile Delta while Antigonos, with a massive army, marched westward from Gaza. They had left it late in the year for campaigning and weather played a large part in frustrating the invasion. The fleet and army had to advance together along the coast but the fleet was at first becalmed and the warships had to tow the transports. A gale then drove some

Figure 35. Silver tetradrachm of (a young) Demetrios I Poliorcetes. (*Metropolitan Museum, New York*)

fours ashore and some transports were lost in the coastal marshes; the fleet had to retire to Gaza. Some of the bigger ships did advance but were again caught by a storm offshore and, with no good anchorage and in trying to ride out the storm, three fives were lost and foundered. Antigonos came up with the army but Ptolemy had fortified and held all the strong points to oppose the advance. Demetrios then returned with the rest of his fleet but his attempts to outflank Ptolemy by landing troops in his rear were foiled. A second attempt to land even further to the west was delayed by some of the ships having fallen behind, allowing Ptolemy time to bring up troops to thwart any landing. More transports were lost in yet another storm and with Demetrios' ships having to operate on an exposed coast with no havens and with supplies running low, increasing disaffection among the troops and having been thwarted by Ptolemy and the weather, Antigonos abandoned the enterprise.

305   Antigonos and Demetrios returned to the offensive in 305 with an attack on Rhodes. Rhodes had continued to assert its independence as an island trading nation with great success, growing wealthy from its position as a trading entrepot. To safeguard its position, it had built up a highly trained and efficient navy which, apart from ensuring the free passage of trade, operated as an effective counter to piracy.

    Rhodes had sought to remain neutral but, forced eventually to take sides, had thought its best opportunity lay in siding with Ptolemy. Although Rhodes would not have instigated an attack on him, Antigonos would not permit what he saw as a potential enemy so close to his coasts and dominating the seas around them. To support his attack on Ptolemy, Antigonos had sought to block all shipping between Rhodes and Egypt and to seize any Rhodian ships; the Rhodians had responded by sending their fleet which had defeated Antigonos' blockading squadron, giving him the pretext for his attack. Although Rhodes posed no threat to Antigonos, seeking only to remain neutral so that it could continue to trade, having failed against Ptolemy, it seemed to him that the lure of a quick but useful conquest of the island would remove them from his rear and restore his reputation.[19]

    Demetrios amassed a huge fleet of some 200 warships and 170 transports to carry his army of 40,000 men. There were also many hundreds of small craft including some local pirates seeking to take advantage of the absence of the Rhodian Navy.[20] The Rhodians fortified themselves in their city while Demetrios' irregulars ravaged the island. He extended siege lines around the city and fortified his landing place to secure a beach upon which to draw up his ships and land supplies. He caused a mole to be built to enable the heavy siege equipment to be landed. The besiegers went on to refit some small ships with shielding to carry small catapults and archers and also fixed pairs of larger ships together and on some of the resulting platforms, mounted stone-throwing artillery, protected by tortoises to give cover against enemy missiles and on others, up to four-storey towers with battering rams and artillery (Figure 36).

The assault commenced from seaward, Demetrios getting 400 men onto the east mole of Rhodes outer harbour, where they built a rampart across it. The next day, the floating assault towers were able to enter the main harbour itself, their flank being covered by the occupied mole. There, they managed to drive the defenders from their walls with artillery and actually make a small breach in the seaward walls. After a day's hard fighting, the 'tower ships' were towed out of range but the Rhodians sallied in a night attack in small boats and set them afire, destroying most of the special siege ships.

Figure 36. Siege tower. A beautifully modelled pair of fives, which have been linked to provide a platform for a large siege tower and artillery, such as used by Demetrios at his siege of Rhodes. The port side of the tower has been hung with hides, which were kept wet as a defence against fire arrows. (*Archaeological Museum, Thessaloniki*)

For the next week, Demetrios maintained a fierce bombardment with heavy siege engines, each throwing a one talent stone (57 lb./ 26 kg) but a further assault by troops in small boats against the sea walls was beaten off and some of their boats burned; a land assault was also beaten off.

After a lull, Demetrios renewed his attack on the harbour with fire-ships; three of the best Rhodian warships counter-attacked, breaking through Demetrios' protective boom and sinking two of his artillery ships, towing a third away. The Rhodians ventured too far however and two were rammed by enemy warships, the third being captured. Most of the crews managed to escape by swimming home. Demetrios had an even larger catapult mounted on a large raft but which was disabled and its tugs swamped by a squall. In the worsening weather, the Rhodians attacked Demetrios' men on the harbour mole; he was unable to reinforce them and they had to surrender. Demetrios' blockade could not stop Rhodian warships from slipping in and out of harbour and they successfully attacked Demetrios' supply ships, while maintaining their own lines of supply to Thrace, Macedonia and Egypt.[21]

Reinforcements for the hard-pressed Rhodians finally arrived in the form of 500 troops sent by Ptolemy, with some more from Knossos (on Crete). Demetrios turned his focus to a land assault and had his huge 'helopolis' built, a tower on wheels, nine storeys (150 feet /45.7m) high covered in sheet iron armour and mounting many catapults. It took 3,000 men to move it and ships' crews were landed and employed to level the ground for it. While the preparation of this and many other siege machines were under way, the Rhodians sent out three marauding squadrons, each of three warships, to attack Demetrios' ships and supplies, which they did with great success. Ptolemy had sent many ships with grain and other foods for the garrison, as did Cassander and Lysimachus. The blockade was not very effective and the Rhodians were never in danger of being short of supplies, let alone in danger of starvation. The Ptolemaic and other ships would suddenly appear, concentrate, then attack a small segment of the blockaders, forcing a way through them and into the harbour; they did the same on leaving and even on occasion, synchronised attacks from both seaward and the harbour.

The land assault progressed with mining and counter-mining by both sides, but for the main attack when the machines were brought up, Demetrios stationed his fleet off the harbour mouth as a diversion, to weaken the seaward defences and to be able to take advantage of any success by the land attack. Despite suffering serious damage in the land attack, the Rhodians mounted a night attack, destroyed a lot of the siege engines and caused many casualties;

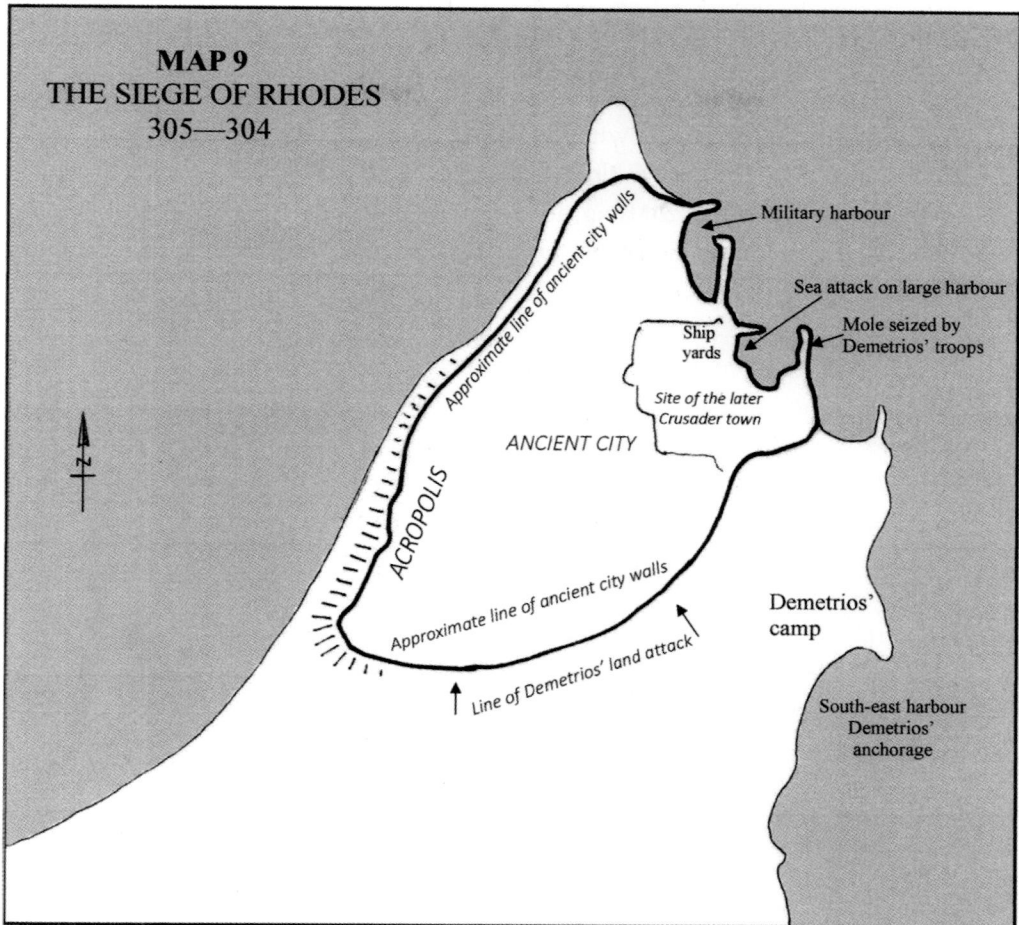

MAP 9
THE SIEGE OF RHODES
305—304

Military harbour

Sea attack on large harbour

Mole seized by
Demetrios' troops

Approximate line of ancient city walls

Ship
yards

Site of the later
Crusader town

ANCIENT CITY

ACROPOLIS

Approximate line of ancient city walls

Demetrios'
camp

Line of Demetrios' land attack

South-east harbour
Demetrios'
anchorage

the great heliopolis was only just saved from being burned down and had to be towed away.

The Rhodian admiral Amytas led his ships out to attack the pirates on the nearby mainland, who had been helping Demetrios and brought back a number of captured ships and even more supplies. Demetrios renewed his land attack, causing many casualties among the garrison, which managed to hold on until another 1,500 troops sent by Ptolemy arrived. A delegation from Greece arrived and asked Demetrios to make peace with Rhodes and instead help them against Cassander. Demetrios planned a final night attack and his men successfully broke into the city through a breach but were eventually driven out again by Ptolemy's fresh troops.

As Cassander was besieging Athens and with Demetrios (despite his nickname of Poliorcetes, the Besieger) having no successful resolution at Rhodes in sight, Antigonos ordered his son to abandon the siege and make peace. The great siege had failed; Demetrios' huge fleet, his 40,000 men and wealth of ingenious machines had been thwarted by a garrison of, initially only 8,000 men, who, notwithstanding being outnumbered five to one, had resisted for a whole year. With all of the metal salvaged from the machines and equipment abandoned by Demetrios, the Rhodians made and erected their famed Colossus, known as one of the seven wonders of the Ancient World.

304   In Greece, the ejection of Cassander from Athens in 307 had been followed by more general resistance across Greece against Macedonian overlordship. The resistance had not been going well and Demetrios arrived in 304 from Rhodes with his fleet and army. His fleet took position between Euboea and the mainland at Aulis. Cassander's forces on Euboea were thus separated from his forces at Athens (which he had taken earlier in the year) and to avoid being defeated in detail and with no fleet of his own to oppose Demetrios, Cassander withdrew from Athens and Euboea to concentrate his forces. Demetrios sent ships to Corcyra and Leucas to ensure co-operation from the Ionian Islands (at the same time, Roman forces were occupying the south-east of Italy, only some 60 miles /100 km away). Demetrios reoccupied Athens in 303; with his fleet there, he could maintain contact with his father in Asia Minor. Demetrios' campaign in 303, bolstered by his naval dominance, meant that he was able to take much of the Peloponnese and garrison Corinth, giving him control of much of Greece, from the Peloponnese to Thessaly. In the following year (302) he invaded Thessaly in pursuit of Cassander.

302   In 302, Mithridates I separated his province of Pontus from its nominal Seleucid control and declared himself king.

301   Tired of the aggressive policies of Antigonos and his son and fearful of their ambitions to eliminate them all, Ptolemy, Cassander, Seleucos and Lysimachos formed a grand alliance in 301 to close the net around the Antigonids. Cassander re-entered Thessaly to block Demetrios, while part of his army joined that of Lysimachus to attack Antigonos in Asia Minor. Demetrios' fleet proved unable to prevent Lysimachus from crossing the Hellespont and the latter's army proceeded to advance along the Ionian Coast, taking the cities there, with their ships and thus denying those harbours to Demetrios. Seleucos meanwhile, advanced from the East into Anatolia. Antigonos attempted to bring Lysimachus to battle before he could join with Seleucos but failed to do so and frantically sent for Demetrios to join him. Demetrios managed to make a hurried peace with Cassander in Greece, left part of his fleet at Athens and with

the rest, sailed and recovered Ephesus. His fleet also successfully intercepted one of three troop convoys sent by Cassander to Lysimachus, sinking some of the ships, with their troops and also the flagship, a six with 500 men aboard.

301   In the Spring, Antigonos and Demetrios met the combined armies of Lysimachus and Seleucos at Ipsos in Phrygia. It was a massive battle in which Antigonos was killed, his army routed and Demetrios fled with only 9,000 of the 80,000 men of their army, to join his fleet, still laying at Ephesus.[22] Once at sea, there was no-one to pursue him and he could retreat to Corinth. Cassander took Athens and part of southern Asia Minor, Lysimachus annexed most of western Asia Minor and Seleucos took most of Antigonos' other lands in eastern Anatolia and Syria. Ptolemy already held the southern part of Syria and, although Demetrios had been allowed to retain Phoenicia, when he left and was busily trying to re-establish himself in Macedonia, Ptolemy annexed it.

300   After Ipsos, the naval situation had changed completely; following the initial winnowing of the contenders, naval forces had become much more concentrated into the hands of the five remaining antagonists (plus of course, Rhodes). The two biggest naval powers were still Ptolemy and Demetrios, the latter had probably been able to replace his ship losses at Rhodes and could still muster about 150 warships of all rates from *hemioliai* up to tens. Ptolemy had achieved naval dominance and his fleet, again including all rates by now, probably mustered well over 200 ships. Unlike Demetrios, Ptolemy had access to almost unlimited manpower with which to crew his ships, augmented by having gained the shipbuilding resources of Phoenicia. Seleucos, for his part entered the naval scene by his acquisition of coastal Syria, where he would start to build up naval forces. Cassander still held Macedon with its navy, including the seaworthy ships taken from Athens. His strength was quite large, perhaps as many as 150 ships, but composed of triremes, fours and fives and not a match for Demetrios. Lysimachos, with Thrace and Pontus also had naval forces and importantly, access to shipbuilding and materials on the Black Sea Coast, free from interference by the others. His naval forces do not appear to have been great at this time and probably counted a few triremes and some *hemioliai* or other light types, sufficient to patrol his coasts but not enough to constitute a battle-worthy fleet.

Ipsos brought to an end the turbulent aftermath of Alexander's early and sudden demise and from the wreckage of his empire, the successors, or those who survived, now ruled over a totally different political landscape of separate, powerful kingdoms. The focus of these states remained the eastern Mediterranean, domination of which would give any one of them not only control of trade but the ability to direct a threat or even an attack against any of the others.

Appendix

The Battle of Cyprian Salamis 306

Ptolemy's brother Menelaos was holding Salamis on the eastern shore of Cyprus (North of modern Famagusta) where he had a fleet of sixty warships (triremes, fours and fives) in the harbour when he became besieged and blockaded by Demetrios. The topography of the area has changed greatly since ancient times (Map 10) and although extensive archaeological excavation has revealed large parts of the ancient city, the site of its harbour is not discernible. There must have been a natural harbour, as the town had been an important sea port and continued to be so for centuries to come; this also implies a sheltered harbour. The fact that Menelaos' sixty ships could be 'bottled up' in the harbour and restrained by a few guardships, also implies that the harbour mouth was reasonably narrow, indeed, Plutarch says so.[1] Perhaps the small river Pediaios that once flowed here emptied into the natural harbour, flushing it and preventing silting. Silting and probably land movement in this highly active tectonic region has now moved the coastline away from and made the former harbour into dry land.

Ptolemy came from Egypt to relieve Menelaos with 200 transports, carrying 10,000 troops and supplies and escorted by a fleet of 140 warships. They landed at Paphos, at the west end of the island. Ptolemy and his fleet, with the transport fleet following, then advanced to Kition on the south coast in Larnaca Bay. His fleet was composed of fours and a lesser number of fives (the largest rate that he had). Ptolemy sent word to his brother to break out from Salamis and join him; the antagonists also exchanged missives offering each other terms, which were unacceptable by either. Ptolemy, a somewhat more cautious man than the more hot-headed Demetrios, must have known of the latter's strength from his brother's reports. He must have been confident that his fleet of 140, especially if augmented by Menelaos' sixty ships, would give him a sufficient superiority in numbers, despite Demetrios' bigger ships, to overwhelm his fleet of 118 warships. To this end, Ptolemy sailed with his transports behind the warships, fully expecting to be able to land their troops and relieve the siege once he had seen off Demetrios' fleet.

Demetrios' fleet included seven Phoenician sevens, ten sixes, twenty fives and thirty fours and the rest smaller, probably triremes.[2] There is no mention of the nines and tens that he and his father had built being at Salamis and presumably they were with the fleet retained by Antigonos. By taking nothing bigger than the seven, which was faster, Demetrios could get to Cyprus in time to intercept Ptolemy before he could unite with his brother when he would have been faced with an overpowering fleet of 200 ships; he must also have known that Ptolemy had nothing bigger than a five, which his sevens would be able to overawe.

To prevent Menelaos from joining his brother, Demetrios stationed ten fives at the harbour mouth, while he loaded the rest of his fleet with extra troops and artillery and sailed south to take up a position to confront Ptolemy. He in turn must have been aware of the strength of Ptolemy's fleet and the lack of numbers of his own, demonstrated perhaps, by the fact that he could only spare ten ships to try to contain Menelaos' sixty. If Ptolemy's fleet advanced in a double line (which it did) it would have a frontage of seventy ships and would extend beyond Demetrios' seaward flank, assuming that he would also form a double line (of fifty-four) leaving it open to a *periplous* attack. Demetrios had to augment his fleet; he did have other ships that had been used to transport his invasion force to Cyprus, including 'threes'[3] which could have been old triremes, converted as fast transports, or another type of oar-powered transport, or a mixture of both. In any event, Demetrios had about fifty of these ships loaded with troops and artillery and rowed out to form the centre of his battle-line; his fleet thus formed now totalled about 170 ships.[4]

The fleet spent the night (obviously a calm one) at anchor there. Ptolemy meanwhile, had left Kition and had rounded the cape at the south-east of the island, into Famagusta Bay.

The two fleets each formed a line with one flank resting by the shore.[5] Demetrios deployed his cavalry along the shore, to help any of his own men struggling ashore and to round up any of his opponent's. Demetrios' dispositions were to strengthen his left (offshore) wing, where he commanded, with his seven sevens and thirty fours, with a second line behind him of the ten sixes and ten fives, to prevent a *periplous* attack (57 in all). Interestingly, apart from the sevens, the front line was of fours, opposed by fours and (bigger) fives; the mass of fives and sixes, his strongest squadron (apart from the few sevens) were kept in the second line. Perhaps he calculated that his augmented fours would be enough to stop Ptolemy's opposing ships, leaving the powerful second line free to tip the balance and round Ptolemy's flank and rear, which of course, they did.

Demetrios' armed transports made up the centre and the smaller warships made up the right (inshore) sections of the line. By placing his older and smaller warships in the centre, reinforced with extra troops on board, he was able to extend his battle line to seaward to counter Ptolemy's greater numbers and indeed, beyond the latter's

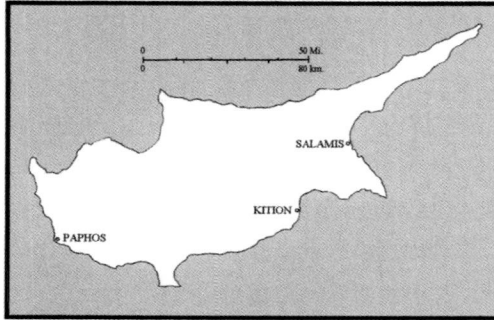

**MAP 10
THE BATTLE
OF SALAMIS
306**

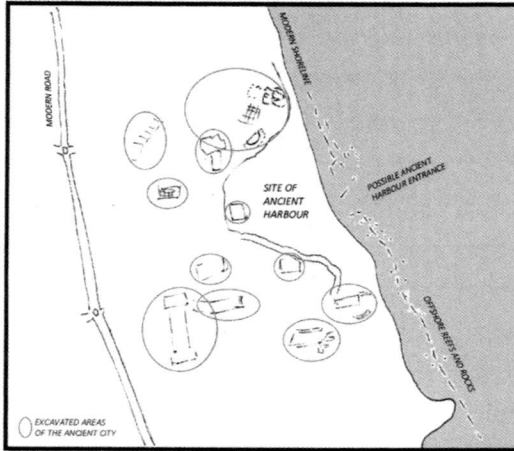

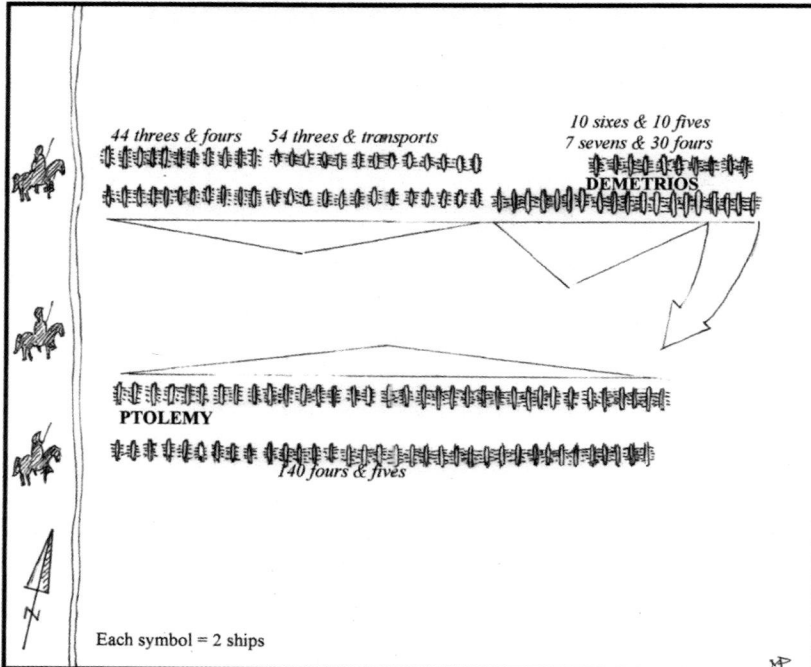

44 threes & fours   54 threes & transports

10 sixes & 10 fives
7 sevens & 30 fours

DEMETRIOS

PTOLEMY

140 fours & fives

Each symbol = 2 ships

flank; the line stretched nearly two miles offshore.[6] Just after dawn, Ptolemy saw the enemy approaching and ordered his transports to the rear, forming line of battle with himself and his heaviest ships, the fives, on the left, inshore. Demetrios intended for his smaller ships in his centre and inshore to fight a delaying action while he used his heavy ships to smash Ptolemy's offshore wing and envelop it.

Diodorus describes the action:[7]

The fleets being deployed, the boatswains accordingly made the signal for prayers to the gods and the crews made the invocations aloud. The two fleets being then about 600 yards apart, Demetrios gave the signal to engage by hoisting a golden shield which was seen by all. Ptolemy did the same and the two fleets closed quickly with each other, as the trumpets sounded the charge and the crews cheered. The engagement opened with archery and stones and darts from the catapults and many were wounded during the approach. The contact was made, the rowers being incited by the boatswains to make their greatest exertions and the men on deck fell on the enemy with spears. The first shock was violent, some ships had their oars swept from their sides and remained motionless with their soldiers out of action. Others, after striking, rowed astern to ram again and in the meantime the soldiers attacked each other hand to hand. Some captains struck their opponents broadside to broadside and the ships being held in contact became so many fields of battle with the boarders leaping onto the enemy's deck. In some cases these missed their footing and falling overboard were drowned, while others making good their foothold killed the enemy or drove them overboard. Many and varied were the fortunes of the ships. In one case a weaker crew was victorious owing to its higher deck and in another case the better crew lost because its decks were low. For luck has much to do in naval actions. On shore valour is pre-eminent, whereas at sea many accidents occur which bring ruin to those whose valour deserves success.

Among all the rest, Demetrios standing on the poop of a heptere showed brilliant courage. Surrounded by enemies, he struck them down with his own lance and avoided the missiles showered upon him, some by dodging and some by his defensive arms. Three bodyguards stood by him, one was killed with a lance thrust and the other two were wounded. At last Demetrios broke the wing opposite him and turned on the centre. In the meantime, Ptolemy with his heaviest ships and best crews had been successful on his flank, sinking some, taking others with their crews and putting the rest to flight. On turning back from pursuit to finish the battle he found the rest of his fleet defeated and he returned to Kition.

mostly to a lack of skilled rowers and the increased use of convicts and slaves as only the inboard-most men had to be trained, the others simply adding muscle; it was also simpler to install. One disadvantage was that the bigger the oar, the slower the striking rate, so that the 36 feet/11m oar of a fourteenth century AD galley had a striking rate of twenty-six per minute,[3] whereas the trireme *Olympias* with its 14 foot /4.2m oars, had a striking rate of forty-six per minute, for a maximum dash at nine knots.[4]

The next consideration is the maximum number of rowers that can operate one oar. If all the men rowing an oar are sitting, the arc described by the oar loom is of course, dictated by the reach of the man at the end or butt; for a man of 5 feet 4 inches /1.63m[5] this is about 40 inches/1m[6] and as has been seen (ante Chapter 5) each man outboard of him will pull through a progressively lesser proportion of that. Thus, the maximum number of sitting men who can usefully use an oar is limited to say four. The inboard man contributes 'one manpower' and the other three, just under two additional manpower between them. The outboard rower will be doing the least work and was, in later times, said to have been in the 'resting position' when rowers were rotated. In the later galleys, this could be done by every rower moving outboard by one place (without breaking stroke) and the displaced inboard man simply moving to the other end of the row, crossing outboard to the *telaro*, or outboard walkway and jumping down at his bench, to fill the, now vacant, outboard position. Most ancient galleys however, were fully decked and it is difficult to envisage how, without interrupting the oar-stroke, the rower could get from inboard to the outboard position and vice versa of his bench, especially when more than one reme is involved (unless each man swapped one place in turn).

To increase the number of rowers per oar beyond this requires the extra rowers to use a rising or walking stroke; as Morrison says 'though the work which it is possible to do in this stroke is rather less than sitting, its greater length allows the other (sitting) men on the oar to do more work',[7] the inboard rower by using the rising stroke, increases his reach to about 54 inches /1.37m[8], the arcs of pull by the other rowers of the same oar increasing accordingly.

Opposite: **Figure 37.** Rowing systems. Top: from an Egyptian tomb painting c.2330, showing the rowers rising to deliver their stroke and below, the stages of the stroke from Renaissance times. Below that: the two Renaissance rowing systems, that on upper being *alla sensile*, where each man has his own oar; note that the rowing bench is canted from the hull side to allow each man clearance; the oars are all the same length. On the lower, rowing *a scaloccio*, the three men rowing one large oar. At the bottom is a contemporary illustration, of the rowers manoeuvring by rowing in a 'push-pull' manner. There are only single rowing benches shown, the men pulling sitting on the upper foot rest of the bench astern (Rodgers, from Vice-Admiral Paris, *Souvenirs de Marine* 1691).

flank; the line stretched nearly two miles offshore.[6] Just after dawn, Ptolemy saw the enemy approaching and ordered his transports to the rear, forming line of battle with himself and his heaviest ships, the fives, on the left, inshore. Demetrios intended for his smaller ships in his centre and inshore to fight a delaying action while he used his heavy ships to smash Ptolemy's offshore wing and envelop it.

Diodorus describes the action:[7]

> The fleets being deployed, the boatswains accordingly made the signal for prayers to the gods and the crews made the invocations aloud. The two fleets being then about 600 yards apart, Demetrios gave the signal to engage by hoisting a golden shield which was seen by all. Ptolemy did the same and the two fleets closed quickly with each other, as the trumpets sounded the charge and the crews cheered. The engagement opened with archery and stones and darts from the catapults and many were wounded during the approach. The contact was made, the rowers being incited by the boatswains to make their greatest exertions and the men on deck fell on the enemy with spears. The first shock was violent, some ships had their oars swept from their sides and remained motionless with their soldiers out of action. Others, after striking, rowed astern to ram again and in the meantime the soldiers attacked each other hand to hand. Some captains struck their opponents broadside to broadside and the ships being held in contact became so many fields of battle with the boarders leaping onto the enemy's deck. In some cases these missed their footing and falling overboard were drowned, while others making good their foothold killed the enemy or drove them overboard. Many and varied were the fortunes of the ships. In one case a weaker crew was victorious owing to its higher deck and in another case the better crew lost because its decks were low. For luck has much to do in naval actions. On shore valour is pre-eminent, whereas at sea many accidents occur which bring ruin to those whose valour deserves success.
>
> Among all the rest, Demetrios standing on the poop of a heptere showed brilliant courage. Surrounded by enemies, he struck them down with his own lance and avoided the missiles showered upon him, some by dodging and some by his defensive arms. Three bodyguards stood by him, one was killed with a lance thrust and the other two were wounded. At last Demetrios broke the wing opposite him and turned on the centre. In the meantime, Ptolemy with his heaviest ships and best crews had been successful on his flank, sinking some, taking others with their crews and putting the rest to flight. On turning back from pursuit to finish the battle he found the rest of his fleet defeated and he returned to Kition.

Apart from the initial discharge of artillery there is, surprisingly perhaps, no mention of archery; fighting seems to have been at very close quarters, hand-to-hand and conducted with javelins and spears. After the initial impact, the fight turned into a general melee of ramming and boarding. Presumably the larger complement of troops on Demetrios' heavier ships, together with their higher decks, gave an advantage once in contact. While there are differences in translations,[8] they all seem to agree that Demetrios fought from the 'poop' of a seven, that he was in an open, unprotected space is demonstrated by the presence of three bodyguards (shieldbearers) close by him and that they fought with spears dictates either that his ship was boarded or in extremely close contact with an enemy ship. In any event, that he was on a 'poop', the stern-most and highest deck, indicates perhaps that the ship had a raised deck right aft. The idea of such a deck was known, as can be seen from the sixth century model merchant ship from Cyprus (Figure 29).

As can be seen, Demetrios' deployment enabled him to fall with his heaviest and best-armed ships and greatly superior force, upon Ptolemy's open, seaward flank, round it and roll up the line in a classic *periplous* attack. Ptolemy himself was with his inshore wing and successfully broke through his opponents'; however, with the defeat of the rest of his fleet, he had no option but to flee, saving only twenty of his warships.

Menelaos at Salamis directed his squadron of sixty ships to force its way out and join the fight down the coast. This it did, driving the blockading ships back to the support of their army on shore, but when Melelaos' ships arrived in the neighbourhood of the battle, Demetrios had already been successful and he could do nothing but return to Salamis. Demetrios sent a part of his fleet to continue in pursuit and pick up swimmers and with the rest, decorated with booty and towing the prizes, he returned to his camp and the port which he had left. The prizes were 100 transports with 8,000 soldiers, forty warships with their crews and eighty other seriously damaged and towed ashore. Of the victorious fleet, twenty were badly damaged but all were repaired and returned to service.[9]

Chapter 7

Rowing Systems

The progressive growth of warships beyond the four and five, to the six and seven (the first built in 315[1]) now to the nine and ten and the continued growth of the rowing 'groups' requires consideration of the manner in which these were employed to row the ships in either monoreme, bireme or trireme layouts. No class of rower other than the three already mentioned (thranite, zygite and thalamite) is known; further, there is no depiction in any of the iconography of more than three horizontal strata (remes) of oars; thus it can be said with some certainty that three remes are the maximum. Another limit is that at an operating angle of more than thirty degrees, an oar becomes unworkable: the geometry also therefore rules against any greater number of remes.

With the progressive increase in the rating of new types, it is desirable perhaps to revisit the 'group of rowers' definition. It has been seen that the trireme was, to its inventors, known as *triereis* or 'three-fitted' and a five was *pentereis*, or five-fitted. To the Romans, a five was a *quinquereme* or (literally) 'five-oars' *(remis)* rather than five rowers *(remiges)*.

We are sure that 'three-fitted' refers to being fitted for three oars and three rowers in three horizontal levels, conversely that 'five-fitted' does not relate to any more than the same three levels. Logically, it would mean a trireme with two extra fittings of some sort, which has been assumed to refer to extra rowers. The problem increases when considering the higher ratings and trying to fit the resultant numbers, presumably of rowers, into some form of effective working arrangement.

In later Medieval and Renaissance times, two methods of rowing were evolved. Firstly, the number of oars at each position was multiplied, and two or more oars were operated, each by a rower on the same bench, their oars pivoted against closely-spaced tholes, a system known as rowing *alla sensile* (Figures 22 and 38). The Venetians found by experimentation that the maximum number that could row together in this fashion was five, the advantage being that each man/oar contributed the maximum effort.[2] Obviously a very high degree of training and practice was needed to ensure that they rowed in concert.

The other rowing system was where several rowers at the same bench operated one big oar which was known as rowing *a scaloccio*. This method became prevalent due mostly to a lack of skilled rowers and the increased use of convicts and slaves as only the inboard-most men had to be trained, the others simply adding muscle; it was also simpler to install. One disadvantage was that the bigger the oar, the slower the striking rate, so that the 36 feet/11m oar of a fourteenth century AD galley had a striking rate of twenty-six per minute,[3] whereas the trireme *Olympias* with its 14 foot /4.2m oars, had a striking rate of forty-six per minute, for a maximum dash at nine knots.[4]

The next consideration is the maximum number of rowers that can operate one oar. If all the men rowing an oar are sitting, the arc described by the oar loom is of course, dictated by the reach of the man at the end or butt; for a man of 5 feet 4 inches /1.63m[5] this is about 40 inches/1m[6] and as has been seen (ante Chapter 5) each man outboard of him will pull through a progressively lesser proportion of that. Thus, the maximum number of sitting men who can usefully use an oar is limited to say four. The inboard man contributes 'one manpower' and the other three, just under two additional manpower between them. The outboard rower will be doing the least work and was, in later times, said to have been in the 'resting position' when rowers were rotated. In the later galleys, this could be done by every rower moving outboard by one place (without breaking stroke) and the displaced inboard man simply moving to the other end of the row, crossing outboard to the *telaro*, or outboard walkway and jumping down at his bench, to fill the, now vacant, outboard position. Most ancient galleys however, were fully decked and it is difficult to envisage how, without interrupting the oar-stroke, the rower could get from inboard to the outboard position and vice versa of his bench, especially when more than one reme is involved (unless each man swapped one place in turn).

To increase the number of rowers per oar beyond this requires the extra rowers to use a rising or walking stroke; as Morrison says 'though the work which it is possible to do in this stroke is rather less than sitting, its greater length allows the other (sitting) men on the oar to do more work',[7] the inboard rower by using the rising stroke, increases his reach to about 54 inches /1.37m[8], the arcs of pull by the other rowers of the same oar increasing accordingly.

Opposite: **Figure 37.** Rowing systems. Top: from an Egyptian tomb painting c.2330, showing the rowers rising to deliver their stroke and below, the stages of the stroke from Renaissance times. Below that: the two Renaissance rowing systems, that on upper being *alla sensile*, where each man has his own oar; note that the rowing bench is canted from the hull side to allow each man clearance; the oars are all the same length. On the lower, rowing *a scaloccio*, the three men rowing one large oar. At the bottom is a contemporary illustration, of the rowers manoeuvring by rowing in a 'push-pull' manner. There are only single rowing benches shown, the men pulling sitting on the upper foot rest of the bench astern (Rodgers, from Vice-Admiral Paris, *Souvenirs de Marine* 1691).

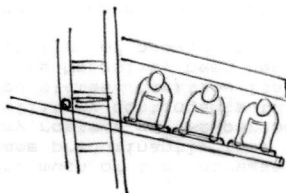

Pulling a simple great oar, eight men was found to be the practicable maximum number.[9] There is also the possibility of adding extra rowers to push the oar, i.e. facing the 'regular' rowers and so that it is operated from both sides; pushing is less efficient than pulling an oar, being only about three quarters as effective.[10] There is no evidence of such a 'push-pull' arrangement in any of the Renaissance ships,[11] other than when manoeuvring e.g. in harbour and then only as a temporary measure (Figure 37). In any arrangement, power and speed ultimately depend on the number of oars in the water per given length of hull[12] and although the ships did grow in length, the number of oars in the same length of hull in a push-pull system must thus be less than in a pulling-only one. Even more space is needed if there are men pushing and pulling as the distance between oars must be even greater to allow for double, opposed rowing benches at each oar.[13] The close spacing of oarports on ancient representations also seems to therefore preclude such a system.

The ships became big and bulky and probably slower but needed more power to just move them at all, without adding the effects of wind and current. It can therefore be said that, in the absence, although not impossibility of a 'push-pull' system, any car rating higher than an eight, must be a multi-reme ship.

In all but the smallest Medieval and Renaissance galleys, the rowing bench was canted aft from the bulwark to amidships, so that each man could deliver his maximum effort, the rowers having to rise to deliver the stroke, returning to the sitting position at the end of each stroke,[14] a more tiring method than sitting to row. That this method was also known in ancient times is evidenced by Egyptian tomb paintings[15] and an account by Lucan (AD 39 to 65): '(The rowers) sweep the blue sea and fall back on the benches and bring the oar (loom) against their breast.'[16]

It will be useful to refer to the later systems as the exact particulars of them are well known and documented.[17] One can rely on the experience of those later systems and contemporary accounts, as well as on the parameters that had to be adopted, as extra tools in any attempt to visualise the ancient warships. That those similar systems were known to the ancients must be assumed as they were capable of, and did, produce even more complicated systems of their own.

Two further problems now arise, however. Firstly, men rising to row require extra deck height above them, at least 6 to 9 inches/150 to 230mm. Secondly, extra space fore and aft will be needed as the rising rower's movement backwards and forwards is greater. A further parameter is that all of the oars should be more or less the same length[18] and gearing, so that the stroke of all of the rowers can be synchronised for maximum power and more obviously, so the oars will not clash. Many attempts at reconstruction of ancient rowing systems have assumed the use of oars of different lengths for each reme but, unless the strokes of all of the oars can be synchronised, the ship will not work.

In Renaissance and later galleys, which were all monoremes, all the oars of each ship could be and were of the same length; the same applies to ancient monoremes. It is known that the oars of a trireme were the same length[19] and that the oars of a trireme could be used in a four, so they also were of the same length throughout the ship; some at least were also useable on a five[20] but in both cases, this probably only worked in the early examples of the types. It has been seen (ante Chapter 5 when examining the seven) that a difference of 2 feet /610mm to allow for the extra rower, should be small enough not to affect the ability of both oars to work in concert. The gearing of the oars also favours them all being the same (or very nearly so), for the same reasons (gearing being the ratio of the length of the oar outboard of the thole (the sweep) to the length of it inboard (the loom) held by the rower). Four to one is the practicable limit and just under three to one gives a balanced oar, capable of prolonged use. As a guide the thranite oar of Ptolemy's forty, the biggest rowing warship of the ancient world (post Chapter 13) was 57 feet (17.4 m) in length;[21] however, there is nothing to say that it was the longest oar of the ancient world.[22] Theoretically therefore, it should be possible, given a maximum of three remes and eight men to an oar, to build any multiple of ship up to a twenty-four.

Another point, when installing multi-reme systems, must be to balance the crews of each oar of a group so that as far as possible, every oar has nearly the same number of rowers; obviously, having a five-man oar linked with a one-man oar in the same group would hardly make for smooth, synchronised rowing. As an example, in the case that Casson puts for the forty his proposal for a group of eight, seven and five (see later) offers a large discrepancy between thranites and thalamites; surely seven, seven and six, would yield a more even balance and distribution of muscle-power between the three oars.

To sum up the parameters therefore, we have maxima of three remes, eight men to an oar, a rowing angle of thirty degrees from the horizontal and a minimum interscalmium of 39 inches /1m and the overall ultimate limiting factor, the human body. Within that framework, any reasonable reconstruction should be valid; that is not to say that it can be definitive, but can at least adhere to known facts, proven in practice rather than theory.

Another matter to be considered is the size of these ships. Whereas the trireme was a modest 124 feet /37.8m long and 16 feet /4.9m beam overall, it is suggested that the four was a little larger at about 145 feet/(43.3m by 24 feet/(7.3m), the five grew to 169 feet /51.5m by 26 feet /8m and the six, to 186 feet/(56.7m by 34 feet/10.4m).[23]

Figure 38. Model of a sixteenth century AD Venetian 'trireme' used to prove the system of rowing *alla sensile* where several rowers, each with an oar, occupy the same bench and row on concert. (*Model by Admiral L. Fincanti. Museo StoricoNavale, Venice*)

Although this latter was probably large enough to include a seven, the continuing trend to fit ever more rowers into a hull necessitated larger ships again.

The question becomes therefore, could the ancients build bigger ships? The longest known was the incredible forty of Ptolemy Philopator (post Chapter 11) reported to have been 420 feet/128m long; it also appears to have been a freak that never went to sea, but there are other examples of very large ships built by the ancients that would make the dimensions of the proposed reconstructions seem reasonable and within their building capabilities.

There are five such ships so far known to us. Firstly the huge merchant ship built by Hieron of Syracuse c.270 to 265 which was over 200 feet/62m long.[24] Admittedly much later (but the point remains valid) are the actual remains of the two great pleasure barges built for the Roman Emperor Gaius (Caligula AD 37 to 41) on Lake Nemi in Italy; the first was 234 feet by 65 feet/71.3 by 20m and the second 213 feet by 77 feet/65 by 23.5m. Caligula also had a ship built to transport a huge obelisk from Egypt, reported to have been 320 feet by 65 feet/97.5 by 20m. This ship was sunk by Emperor Claudius as part of the breakwater for his extension to the harbour at Ostia (Portus); the remains of a vessel approximately 311 feet (95m) long and 70 feet wide/95 by 21m were more recently discovered at the ancient port, with hull planking 4 inches/100mm thick in places, which could well have been Caligula's ship.[25] Discounting the freak forty, therefore, the ancients were capable of building wooden ships over 300 feet /91m long.

The length of the ships was determined largely by the number of oars in the longest reme, multiplied by the interscalmium and adding bow and stern sections. Thus, for a multi-manned oar, if we allow the Renaissance interscalmium of 4 feet /1.24m[26] and a reme of thirty oars, the rowing section of the ship is 120 feet/36.5m long, plus say 30 feet/9.1m each for the bow and stern. The result is a ship of 180 feet/54.8m or so, per the six proposed above.

Concerning the progressive growth of these ships by increments, both odd and even (assumed to be the numbers making up a rowing 'group') from the two (bireme with each oar single-manned) to the four and six (and beyond) and from the three (trireme with each oar single-manned) to the five, then the seven and now the nine, could this also mean that even numbers referred to biremes and odd numbers to triremes? As has been seen already however, many of the numbers can be arranged as either biremes or triremes. Nevertheless, the logical progression suggested by the numbers, although there is no evidence to confirm it, could suggest two lines of progressive development which becomes relevant when considering reconstructions.

Although this book will continue to use what has become a conventional path in attempting interpretations and reconstructions, it must be borne in mind that this path is based solely on modern assumptions. To the shipbuilders of the Ancient World, the numbers might have indicated something totally different and which we have yet to discern.

Relative lengths of multi-manned oars, fifteenth to sixteenth centuries AD.

No. of rowers	Oar length, Feet/metres	Loom to thole length	Source
3	32/9.75		Anderson p.68
3	31/9.44 to 36.5/11.12	1/3rd.	Rodgers *Naval Warfare under oars* p.230
5	38.5/11.7	4/1.2	Anderson p.68
5	40/12.25	11.75/3.76	*Age of the Galley* p.196
7	47/14.31	14/4.25	*Age of the Galley* p.196

Note: Oars used by single rowers rowing *alla sensile* were (from the same sources) between 31.5 feet/9.6m and 36.5 feet/11.1m in length.

With the arrival of the nine-man rowing group, the numbers have risen to a point where a further examination must be made to establish an arrangement that could actually work in full size and three dimensions, before being able to move on to a consideration of the larger ships to follow, namely to produce a working arrangement whereby nine rowers can operate three oars. There have been many illustrations suggesting how multiple rowers can be installed in a hull, extracts from several being reproduced herein. They all show either side or (mostly) end elevations, but it is when trying to make these arrangements work in three dimensions that they seem to fall short for one reason or another.

In considering the nine as a trireme, Figure 39C would appear to work except that the layout has a gap between rowers in each reme to allow the next reme, up or down, to be interleaved and to work without fouling each other, desirable to reduce the height and weight above water. However, the gaps mean that as each man outboard will pull through one fifth less arc, instead of the three rowers pulling through one, four and three fifths of the arc respectively (total, two and two fifths manpower), they will in fact pull through one, three and one fifth only; if the inboard man pulls through 40 inches/1m, the outboard man will only pull through 8 inches /203mm and it is hardly worth him being there. Gaps therefore cannot be allowed between rowers of the same level (compare in Figure 39D).

Returning therefore to Figure 39A, can the nine men be so arranged to actually work? The exercise illustrated in Figure 40A, borrowed from the trireme, shows that with careful spacing, the rowers can work together but although the thalamite rowers and oars are simple enough to install and work, the zygite and thranite remes being so close, no vertical supports can be installed that will not inhibit the sweep of the oars. The thwarts on which they sit and their footrests, if sturdy enough, could span the 9 feet/3m plus between the centre stanchions and hull sides, but there remains the potential weakness of a large hull without bracing to be overcome, yet having to withstand the stress of rowing. Secondly and even more fatal to this arrangement is the geometry of the oars; even by lowering the outboard thranite and zygite rowers a little, they need impossibly long oars to even reach the water (attempts at such a rig using figurines produced the same result).[3] Such oars would be unusable by the thalamites as the angle of use would be so low as to have it incapable of making a clean entry and exit from the water.

A design with some of the rowers standing to deliver a 'walking stroke' allows them to be repositioned per Figures 40B and 40C. Here, two each of the thranite and zygite rowers have to stand, but the result is that they can all use a standard oar of 38 feet /11.6m with the same gearing of 2.9. The thalamite oar will move through a smaller arc (as they are all sitting) but this should not cause a problem. A criticism is

The length of the ships was determined largely by the number of oars in the longest reme, multiplied by the interscalmium and adding bow and stern sections. Thus, for a multi-manned oar, if we allow the Renaissance interscalmium of 4 feet /1.24m[26] and a reme of thirty oars, the rowing section of the ship is 120 feet/36.5m long, plus say 30 feet/9.1m each for the bow and stern. The result is a ship of 180 feet/54.8m or so, per the six proposed above.

Concerning the progressive growth of these ships by increments, both odd and even (assumed to be the numbers making up a rowing 'group') from the two (bireme with each oar single-manned) to the four and six (and beyond) and from the three (trireme with each oar single-manned) to the five, then the seven and now the nine, could this also mean that even numbers referred to biremes and odd numbers to triremes? As has been seen already however, many of the numbers can be arranged as either biremes or triremes. Nevertheless, the logical progression suggested by the numbers, although there is no evidence to confirm it, could suggest two lines of progressive development which becomes relevant when considering reconstructions.

Although this book will continue to use what has become a conventional path in attempting interpretations and reconstructions, it must be borne in mind that this path is based solely on modern assumptions. To the shipbuilders of the Ancient World, the numbers might have indicated something totally different and which we have yet to discern.

Relative lengths of multi-manned oars, fifteenth to sixteenth centuries AD.

No. of rowers	Oar length, Feet/metres	Loom to thole length	Source
3	32/9.75		Anderson p.68
3	31/9.44 to 36.5/11.12	1/3rd.	Rodgers *Naval Warfare under oars* p.230
5	38.5/11.7	4/1.2	Anderson p.68
5	40/12.25	11.75/3.76	*Age of the Galley* p.196
7	47/14.31	14/4.25	*Age of the Galley* p.196

Note: Oars used by single rowers rowing *alla sensile* were (from the same sources) between 31.5 feet/9.6m and 36.5 feet/11.1m in length.

Chapter 8

Bigger Ships

The Nine

First built by Antigonus I and his son Demetrios Poliorcetes in about 315 in Phoenicia, the type remained in use, in small numbers, for the remainder of the period covered by this book.[1] Following the logical stages of growth of ancient warships, this next development could be either a bireme with each upper and lower oar manned by four and five men,[2] or a trireme with each oar triple-manned. In any event, the length of the ship need not be appreciably greater than its predecessors, but the beam and depth of the hull, its massiveness, would have grown to accommodate the increased number of rowers and in turn result in a more stable platform for an increased number of marines and artillery pieces. As a bireme (Figure 39B) adopting two remes of say twenty-five oars (with a much larger interscalmium to allow better spacing and ventilation) at four men per oar (100 rowers) in the upper reme and five per oar in the lower reme (125 rowers) per side, there results a total of 450 rowers, manning 100 oars. This seems not unreasonable when compared to the 370 or so rowers of the seven.

As a trireme (Figures 39A and C) with the same twenty-five thranite and zygite oars plus say twenty thalamite oars per side, the result is a total rowing crew of 420 men, pulling 140 oars. All of these formulae are speculative but do conform to the known parameters that have been considered and once again, when considering the respective layouts, the difference in the number of oars in the water is relevant. The bireme is simpler but slower, the trireme is more complex and powerful. As to the relative 'manpower' provided by the rowers in each scheme, it has been seen that with sitting rowers, if the inboard man, with the longest pull, contributes 'one manpower', the men outboard of him will pull through an arc one fifth less and so on. Therefore as a bireme (Figure 39B) with two men standing in each reme, each group will total ten manpower with two oars; as a trireme (Figure 40B) with thalamites sitting and two standing in the other remes, the same group will provide ten and one fifth manpower, slightly more but with three oars. The oars in both versions can be the same length and, in the trireme, of greater number and more efficient in their use of the available muscle-power, all of which would logically suggest that, despite the added complexity, the nine was likely to have been a trireme.

**Figures 39A, 39B, 39C and
39D.** A: Schematic of a nine as
a trireme. B and C: As a bireme
and a trireme. Both versions have
a similar hull; draft 8 feet /2.4m
beam overall 42 feet /12.8m beam
waterline 34 feet /10.4m freeboard
3.5 feet /1.06m and deck height
above waterline 13 feet (4m). The
interscalmium is 4.5 feet /1.37m,
needed for the standing rowers.
Both utilise a 40 feet /12.2m oar.
D: Illustrates the respective length
of pull of the crew of a five-man
oar (in inches). In the trireme
above, the equivalent is that the
first, third and fifth man only
operates each oar and although
the gearing and operating angles
are reasonable, only three men are
using an oar suitable for a five-man
crew. In both cases, with all the
rowers well above the waterline,
ballasting would be needed, adding
to the ship's mass and load for the
rowers.

A

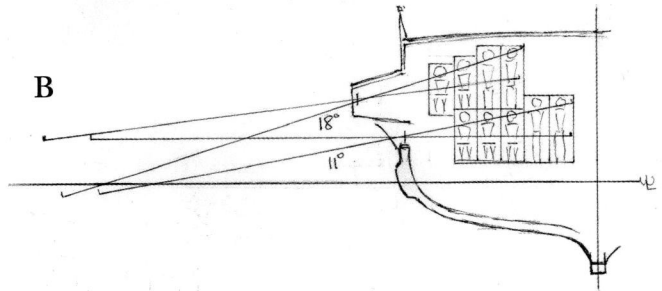

B

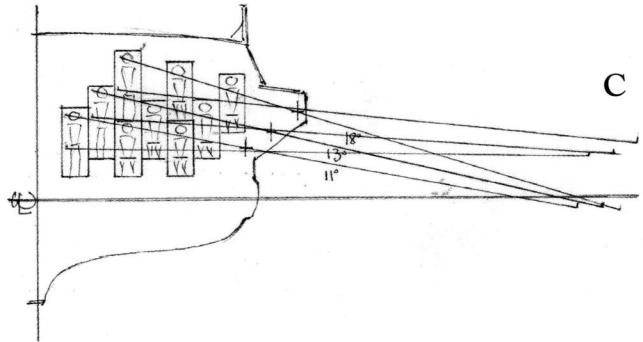

C

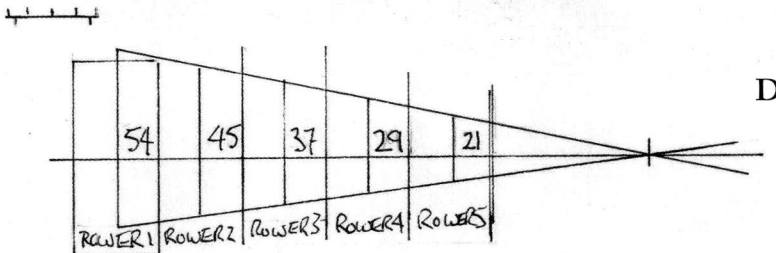

D

With the arrival of the nine-man rowing group, the numbers have risen to a point where a further examination must be made to establish an arrangement that could actually work in full size and three dimensions, before being able to move on to a consideration of the larger ships to follow, namely to produce a working arrangement whereby nine rowers can operate three oars. There have been many illustrations suggesting how multiple rowers can be installed in a hull, extracts from several being reproduced herein. They all show either side or (mostly) end elevations, but it is when trying to make these arrangements work in three dimensions that they seem to fall short for one reason or another.

In considering the nine as a trireme, Figure 39C would appear to work except that the layout has a gap between rowers in each reme to allow the next reme, up or down to be interleaved and to work without fouling each other, desirable to reduce the height and weight above water. However, the gaps mean that as each man outboard will pull through one fifth less arc, instead of the three rowers pulling through one four and three fifths of the arc respectively (total, two and two fifths manpower) they will in fact pull through one, three and one fifth only; if the inboard man pulls through 40 inches/1m, the outboard man will only pull through 8 inches /203mm and it is hardly worth him being there. Gaps therefore cannot be allowed between rowers of the same level (compare in Figure 39D).

Returning therefore to Figure 39A, can the nine men be so arranged to actually work? The exercise illustrated in Figure 40A, borrowed from the trireme, shows that with careful spacing, the rowers can work together but although the thalamite rowers and oars are simple enough to install and work, the zygite and thranite remes being so close, no vertical supports can be installed that will not inhibit the sweep of the oars. The thwarts on which they sit and their footrests, if sturdy enough, could span the 9 feet/3m plus between the centre stanchions and hull sides, but there remains the potential weakness of a large hull without bracing to be overcome, yet having to withstand the stress of rowing. Secondly and even more fatal to this arrangement is the geometry of the oars; even by lowering the outboard thranite and zygite rowers a little, they need impossibly long oars to even reach the water (attempts at such a rig using figurines produced the same result).[3] Such oars would be unusable by the thalamites as the angle of use would be so low as to have it incapable of making a clean entry and exit from the water.

A design with some of the rowers standing to deliver a 'walking stroke' allows them to be repositioned per Figures 40B and 40C. Here, two each of the thranite and zygite rowers have to stand, but the result is that they can all use a standard oar of 38 feet /11.6m with the same gearing of 2.9. The thalamite oar will move through a smaller arc (as they are all sitting) but this should not cause a problem. A criticism is

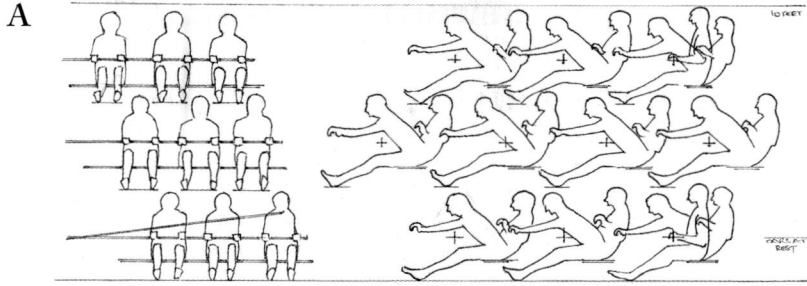

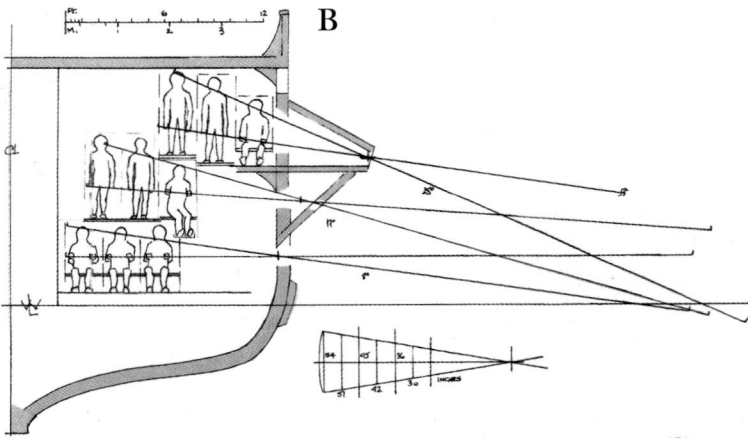

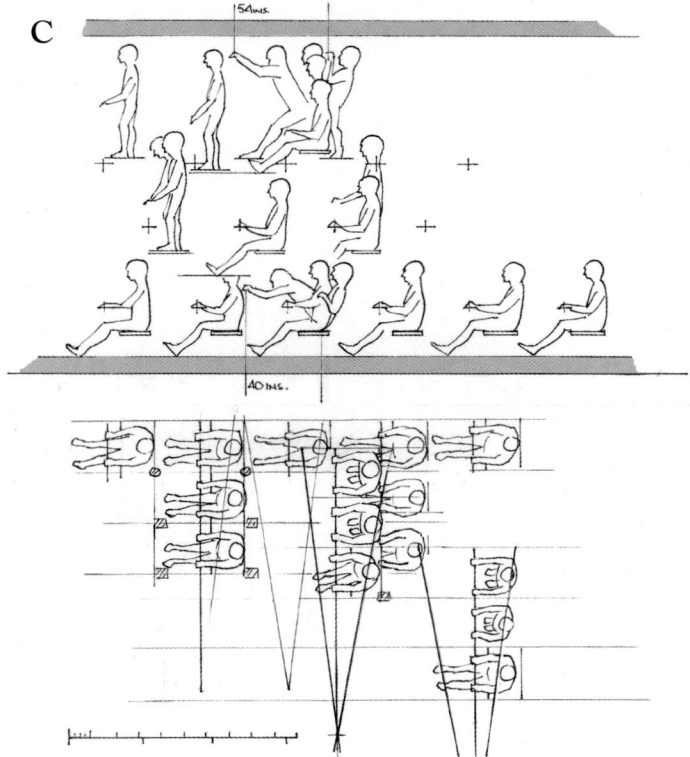

Figures 40A, 40B and 40C. A The nine as a trireme, developed from Figure 39A, B, and C further developed into three dimensions which should work. In A, with only a small degree of roll, the rowers will have difficulties, there being little flexibility in their available vertical movement. Beam overall 44.5 feet/13.6m beam waterline 35 feet /10.6m draft 8 feet /2.4m freeboard 3 feet /0.9m deck above water 16 feet /4.9m interscalmium 4 feet /1.2m oars 38 feet /11.6m gearing 2.9.

that freeboard is only 3 feet /915mm and that with any roll of the hull, the windward thranite oars may be unable to reach the water. The arrangement, viewed from side and above, does give space for the installation of a system of stanchions and thwarts in the building of the hull, as was successfully tried in three dimensions with a scale model and figurines (Figure 41).

Pausanius gives a clue as to the form of a nine, referring to one seen at Delos as 'and had needed the timber equivalent to that needed for approximately fifteen fours to build it'.[4] Although not meaning that the nine was fifteen times the size, it does show that it was bigger, a lot heavier and more massively built than a four.

This leads to another point, applicable also to the other types to a lesser or greater extent, but as we are considering the nine *in extenso*, convenient to be mentioned

Figure 41. Model to prove the rowing system per the text and Figure 40. Top left, the thalamite rowers; top right, a basic structure to position the zygite rowers, view from outboard. Lower left: end view with the thranite rowers added to complete the group. Lower right: view with a dummy ship's side and deck added, together with scale oars shown in the immersed position. NB all of the decks, save the lowest, are shown in frame or nominal form to allow a clearer view of the crew.

here. As a rule of thumb, for stability, a ship should have above the waterline, no more than two-thirds of the distance between the keel and top deck (as demonstrated by Figure 40B). However, it will immediately be seen that all of the rowers are above the waterline, as will be the remainder of the crew with their arms and equipment, as well as the ship's gear (anchors, artillery, rig, etc.). To counteract this, considerable ballasting will be needed which will, of course, add to the mass of the ship which has to be moved.

If we take the estimated displacement of the ship as approximately 1,400 tons/ c.1,425 metric tons,[5] adding 450 rowers plus say 200 marines and twenty or thirty officers and sailors,[6] plus also the artillery, gear, water and rations will add another fifty to fifty-five tons or so. All will have to be counterbalanced to maintain any form of stability in the ship, plus some extra to counteract when for example, if the ship is engaged on one side, most of the marines will go to that side, making the weight uneven. That they were in reality stable is perhaps demonstrated, albeit in a negative way, by the lack of reports of capsizing.

Whether a sailing rig was used in these ships is not known but is likely and any such would have been only carried and raised when needed: a light, dismountable arrangement of square sails on two, perhaps more masts. Again, using the usual rule of thumb,[7] a sail area of 3800 square feet /349 square metres emerges. Not a large amount perhaps for the bulk, but enough in a favourable breeze to give the rowers some respite. With their height, bulk and above-water loading, as well as the low freeboard (the thalamite oars could of course, be withdrawn and their oarports stopped while sailing) it seems very unlikely that these ships would put out to voyage in anything much more than a very calm sea.

The height of the main deck above the waterline, i.e. that immediately above the heads of the rowers, could restrict the internal layout of the hull, a point that will become of increasing importance as the ships continue to have to accommodate more and more rowers. Antonius' biggest ships at Actium in 31 (post Chapter 15) were known to have been tens; the writer Orosius reported their decks as 10 Roman feet (9 feet 8 inches/2.94m) above the waterline. He was however, writing in the fifth century AD, half a millennium after these ships ceased to exist and there is a discrepancy: Roman *quinqueremes* (fives) were known to have decks 10 feet above the waterline and higher than those of a trireme or a four[8] and it would be surprising if the deck of a nine (or ten) were not higher by a substantial margin. Again at Actium, where Octavian had nothing bigger than a six, Antonius' big ships were 'being mounted with towers and high decks they moved along like castles and cities'.[9] Cassius Dio, in the popular ancient tradition of putting heroic pre-battle speeches in to the mouths of antagonists, does have Antonius saying 'the very height of our ships would certainly check them' and Octavius saying 'will they not by their very height and staunchness be more difficult for their rowers to move.'[10] Although these speeches are probably fictitious, there is a common strand running through them, which is that these big ships were high and certainly more so than Octavius' fives and sixes,[11] but ponderous.

As with all of these attempts at reconstruction, there is a caveat: having demonstrated a scheme whereby, in a suggested hull, nine men can operate three oars, it cannot be assumed to be how these ships were in actuality and it may well be, as always, that some fresh evidence may be unearthed to show a nine to have been something totally different.

The Ten

The ten (*dekeres*) was also first built for Antigonos I and Demetrios in about 315 and, together with their nines, was present at Antigonos' siege of Tyre in 314.[12]

Their last appearance was to be at Actium in 31. Whether they were a progression from a nine or a separate line of development (per the suggested comment on the progression of odd and even numbers) may be a matter for conjecture, although there was no eight to follow the six and lead thus to a ten.

By adapting a nine and as a trireme, an additional man could be added at the end of the thalamite or the zygite oar (Figures 42A and 42B). There, he could most easily have the greater headroom needed without raising the deck height and also having to increase the operating angles of the oars. This raises another question, namely what advantage was there in simply adding one more rower (plus his weight) to an already big ship? Perhaps the nine was felt to be underpowered, which could be helped by the addition of an extra rower and achieved with very little alteration to the ship and without needing to design a whole new hull; the nine already posited would seem adequate in this regard. Whether it worked is questioned by the small numbers of tens built as opposed to the greater number of nines, despite their longevity, or should that be survival, in service. Perhaps they were the same and tens were simply 'up-rated nines'.

If the ship were a bireme, with five rowers per oar (Figure 42C) the same arguments apply as to the relative amount of manpower which is exerted through three as opposed to two oars, as examined earlier. A further point is that with these larger ships using multi-manned oars, all of the oar groups must have been the same, i.e. one could not have oars with only a couple of rowers in the bow and stern where the hull narrows, as they would not match the stroke of the big multi-rower oars. Thus, the length of the longest reme of oars determines the length of the maximum beam

A

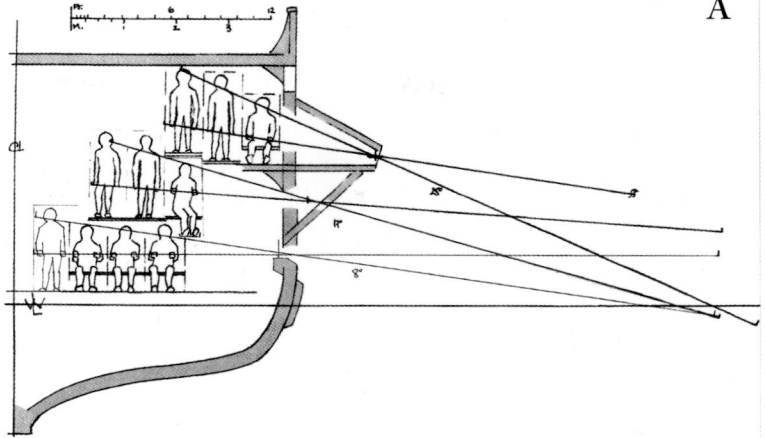

Figures 42A, 42B and 42C. A: The nine converted to a ten by the addition of an extra thalamite rower. The thalamite oar is of 42 feet/12.8m with a gearing of 2.8. The other rowers retain their 40 feet oar/12.2m with the same gearing. The thalamite thole is moved inboard to accommodate the longer oar. B: The same but with the extra rower added to the zygite reme, using the same 42 feet oar; both of these adaptations require only minor modification from the original nine. C: The ten as a bireme with five rowers per oar. The original 40 feet/12.2m oar is retained, with a gearing of 2.8. Waterline beam is 32.5 feet/10.1m. and overall 41 feet /12.5m.

B

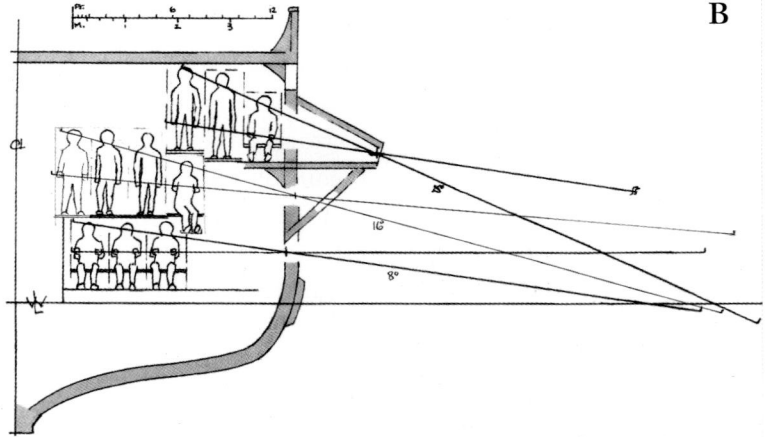

C

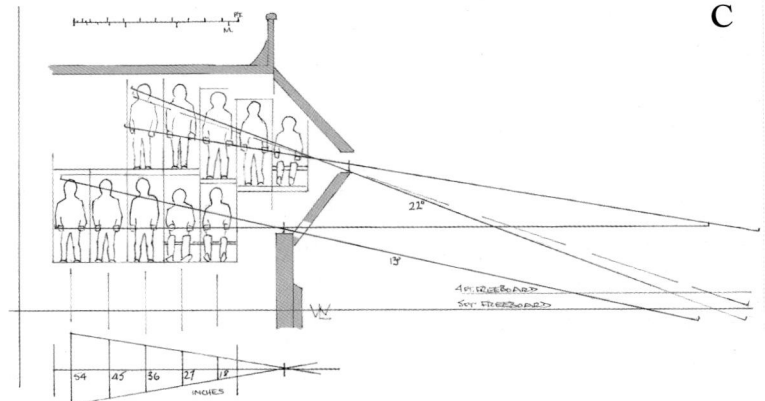

of the hull (in effect in plan a rectangular section containing the 'engine') to which the ship's tapered ends, bow and stern are added.

As to the size of these ships, Antonius' largest ships at Actium were tens and, after the battle, Octavius had rams taken from some of the captured ships and mounted around the rostrum of his victory monument at Nicopolis (see Chapter 15). It would be surprising to say the least, if he did not make a point of mounting rams from the biggest ships that he had taken. Only the sockets remain where these rams were mounted, they having long since been 're-cycled', but the biggest socket still measures some 5 feet/1.51m wide. From this, Morrison[13] has calculated the waterline beam of the ten at 29 feet/8.8m (and 33.5 feet/10.2m overall when adding the oarboxes) and more or less the same as the author's proposed six (which is either too big, or Morrison's proposal is too small); perhaps there was not that much difference in any event. However, in doing so, he has used a formula multiplying the width of the ram by five point nine, the apparent ratio between the Athlit ram[14] and the beam of a reconstruction of a four;[15] this is of course, arbitrary and there is no reason to suppose, even assuming that the ratio proposed for a four is correct (it being only an educated guess at best) that the ten did not have a different ratio; certainly, the proposed beam is rather too little for a ship with perhaps ten men abeam plus the distance between the outboard men and thole on each side and a passageway in the middle; surely about 40 feet/12m is more reasonable (Figures 42 and 43).

Even using Morrison's suggestion, the length can be calculated from such an assumption (for no matter how much one tries to base it in reality, the dearth of hard evidence compels the use of assumptions) and will depend on the length-to-beam ratio of the hull. The trireme *Olympias* was 9.73 to one, very lean and predicated to speed. Taking the argument that the bigger ships were more massive, we could adopt a more reasonable eight to one ratio, which yields a ship 231 feet/70.4m in length; at seven to one, it is 202 feet/61.5m and at a comparatively dumpy six to one, 173 feet/52.8m. Using the middle projection, it is easily possible to have a reme of thirty-five oars, with an interscalmium of 4 feet/1.2m needing 140 feet/42.6m for the length of the hull and leaving 62 feet/18.9m for the 'ends'.

As to rowing crew, as a bireme with five rowers to an oar in an upper reme of thirty oars (150 men) and a lower of twenty-one oars (105 men) totals 510 rowers (Figure 42C); as a trireme, thirty thranite oars manned by three men, twenty-five zygite oars with four men each and twenty thalamite oars, each with three rowers (per Figure 42B) yields a rowing crew of 500, not unreasonable numbers by comparison with other rates. These figures can of course, be varied and are somewhat arbitrary, but within the bounds of what little is known.

Figure 43. Model of a Nine converted to a trireme Ten by the addition of an extra zygite rower as in Figure 42B.

There is corroboration of the ship having been a trireme. At the Battle of Chios in 201 (see Chapter 10) King Philip's flagship was a ten. Polybius[16] relates that it was rammed 'beneath the thranite oars', thranites of course being the topmost reme of rowers of a trireme. Of course, whereas it could be argued that the remes were counted from the top downward so that a bireme would have thranites and zygites only, it could as well have been from the bottom upward, in the same order that the remes were developed and added.

What would be the point of such a ship? Any increase in the propulsive power of the ship was probably marginal and any increase in speed was likely to have been offset by the added weight of the extra rowers, marines and ballast. Perhaps the answer is to be found in added stability as a fighting platform, or perhaps they were just part of a progressive exercise in trying to overawe potential enemies. Their performance in battle could hardly have inspired sufficiently to encourage mass adoption by other powers not wishing to be outclassed, which, as will be seen, they were not. It has been theorized[17] that the ships were evolved to carry out sieges against cities obligingly situated on the coast but that is surely to overlook the reasons for naval warfare and navies and of course, their use in battle.

The *Trihemiolia*

In the late fourth century, a new type of warship was developed as a correspondingly fast counter to fast pirate craft, the *trihemiolia*. It appears to have been developed by Rhodes, as its first appearance in the record is in 304, in use by the Rhodians during the great siege by Demetrios Poliorcetes as a commerce raider against his supply lines.[18] It remained a firm favourite of the Rhodians, who used it with consummate skill as a fighting ship throughout the period of their naval activity, nine for example being listed in their fleet at the Battle of Chios in 201;[19] the last of them seem to have disappeared in 42 with the ending, by Cassius, of Rhodian naval power.

The type was used by others as well, being adopted into the navy of Ptolemy II (283 to 246)[20] and which included the same number of them as of triremes and fours. Athens recorded one in her fleet at about the same time and Pergamum also used them. Some may have been used as support ships for the Roman invasion of Africa in the Third Punic War in 149, but, as they do not otherwise appear in Roman service, were probably allied ships, operating with the Romans.[21]

As to characteristics of the type, comparatively high speed is demonstrated from the outset in their successful operations as commerce raiders as well as later, when they were extremely successful in suppressing piracy; at the same time, they proved to be very agile and capable of engaging in fleet battles. As the *hemioliae*, with their full sailing rig, could outsail a penteconter or trireme, which had only light sailing rigs (intended to be landed when going into action) it seems only logical that the *trihemiolia* also carried a permanent full sailing rig of a more robust type.[22] The frequent and largely successful use of the type in pitched battles, usually against larger ships with greater numbers of marines, indicates that it was better protected than triremes, as well as having more beam, to make it a better sea and sailing boat.

Once more, interpretation of the name of the vessel is a problem; literally, '*trihemiolia*' of course means 'three, half, whole'; (it appears once in the form '*trieremiolia*') but if *hemiolia* is taken to mean 'one and a half,' then *tri-hemiolia* must mean three and a half. But does it mean three plus a half or three less a half? In the former case it could represent an under-powered four and, in the latter, an under-powered trireme. Alternatively, if *hemiolia* means 'one and a half', *TRI-hemiolia* logically means three times a *hemiolia*, which yields four and a half. There is a clue in a tenth century AD. Byzantine lexicon of ancient texts, called the *Souda*, by one Photios: 'the *trihemiolia* is not three times the *hemiolia*, but a *triereis*'; the latter term was used to describe triremes and means 'three fitted' and thus would indicate that the *trihemiolia* was a three level ship. There must be a caveat however: the lexicon was compiled over a thousand years after the type disappeared and successive copyings, by hand, may have distorted the original text; however, it was still a thousand years closer to the real thing than are we.

More recent attempts to decipher the meaning of the term have been made. Rodgers[23] opines that the ship has three remes for only half of its length and is bireme for the rest. It is reasonable and would yield a three, less a half. Morrison[24] basically follows this reasoning and makes a cogent argument that the number relates to the number of fore-and-aft files or rowers on each side (a formula that is then used for a

Figure 44. Silver coin issued by Rhodes, third century, showing one of their warships, possibly a *trihemiolia*. (*Archaeological Museum, Pella*)

proposed reconstruction). However, this layout results in two and a half remes and, as Tilley points out, *tri* means three.[25] It will also result in an under-powered trireme whereas the *trihemiolia* was known to engage in battle after the trireme had ceased to be effective and we must therefore assume it to have been superior.

Figure 45. The Victory of Samothrace prow, suggested as representing a *trihemiolia*. (*Louvre*)

Figure 46. Remains of a naval monument atop the Acropolis at Lindos on Rhodes. The bow is to the right and the top of the base stone is carved to show waves. The projecting oarbox is prominent but no oarports are visible. The stone on top is inscribed with part of the inscription mentioned in the text. Mid third century.

As an authority for the form of a *trihemiolia*, Morrison and Coates have taken the 'Victory of Samothrace' monument[26] (Figure 45) showing the prow of a warship and also a monument at Lindos[27] on Rhodes (Figure 46), showing part of the forward beam of a warship, as well as a relief there (Figure 47) showing a stern (although the former has been argued to have represented a four or a seven).[28] The contention is greatly strengthened in the case of the Lindos monument, by an inscription thereon which lists the names of a commander, two trierarchs and 288 men who served on *trihemioliai*. Morrison[29] interprets this as listing the crews of two such ships (the inscription actually says six) with their squadron commander and a trierarch (captain) and 144 men per ship. He then suggests breaking this down as to thirteen officers and sailors, eleven marines (surely not enough), leaving 120 rowers which have been arranged in his reconstruction[30] as sixty per side in remes of twenty-one thranite, twenty-four zygite and fifteen thalamites in the 'half-reme'. This arrangement places the ship mid-way between a trireme (170 rowers) and a four (160–200 rowers). It

Figure 47. Relief of the stern of a warship, cut into the cliff wall at the entrance to the Acropolis at Lindos on Rhodes. It originally served as the base for a bronze statue. Slightly less than life size, it is most likely to represent a *trihemiolia*. The aft end of the oarbox is shown, but no oarports; the ornate port-side rudder is raised and above it has been interpreted as an open gallery, with the captain's seat on the deck above that; if so, this would mean that the captain and helmsmen would be totally exposed. It is more reasonable, in the real ship, to regard the upper deck as being at the same level as the horizontal rudder post and for the higher line to represent the rail of a surrounding bulwark. Early second century.

thus has seventy per cent of the motive power of a trireme but eighty-five per cent of its weight and yet, being finer, is estimated to be only a half-knot slower.

The system of rowing is different to a trireme in that instead of the three clearly separated remes of oarports, the Samothrace and Lindos monuments show oarports arranged *en échelon* and very close together, emerging from a sponson[31] (see Chapter 10). The 'twin' oarports start from the bow end of the sponson and no lower oarports are represented on the statuary; as the ship is very fine forward, one would not expect there to be room for them in any case and any additional reme would have to start further aft, where the ship had more beam. Thus the thalamite reme would be shorter, conforming to the theory but this still only gives a 'two and a half', so if *'trihemiolia'* means three plus a half, the proposal is wanting.

Further, the structure has a maximum breadth between the tholes of the foremost oarports of only 7 feet 10 inches/2.4m. Obviously this is the bow and the hull would widen as it went aft, but if it is life size, there would not be enough room to install four rowers, pulling one oar each, two per side (if each man took a minimum of 2 feet/610mm in width, plus the space between him and the thole; one would need half as much again at least). Anderson (p.26) suggests the statue is one-third life size, which would make the oarports 3 feet wide by 1 deep /915 by 305mm. This would however, result in a ship some 23.5 feet/7.2m across the front of the oarbox (the trireme was only 16.5 feet/4.9m maximum beam) and suggests a very much larger ship than a *trihemiolia* (perhaps the seven after all). If the statue is magnified by half its size again however, it will in fact conform to the supposed size of a *trihemiolia*, but there again, all of this is surely adjusting the evidence to suit theory, rather than evidence *per se*.

Logically, and following from the *hemiolia,* this author feels that it would have been three plus a half, in effect a trireme with an extra half-reme, doubling the oars at thalamite level[32] thereby keeping their added weight as low as possible in the hull. This would seem to provide an enhanced trireme, retaining all of the manoeuvrability of the type, with the extra oars countering the added weight of the protection and permanent rig.[33] Such a ship would thus fall between the trireme and a four and be superior to a classic trireme in being more able to engage in battle while keeping most of its speed and handiness and at the same time remaining lighter and more swift than the four.

Returning to the crew muster on the Lindos monument, let us suppose that it referred to only one ship's crew; there is no reason not to as the inscription refers to a squadron of six ships and 288 men between them would give a crew of only forty-eight per ship. Clearly the numbers represent less than the total strength of the squadron. The Commander had the two trierarchs as his chief officers (although a trierarch was known to be a ship captain, we have no knowledge of the officer hierarchy in the Rhodian Navy, where the term may have been used differently – perhaps the men had been promoted afterwards) and the other 288 crew can be allocated to suit our larger ship. Deducting the rowing crew of a classic trireme, 170 men, (divided as to sixty-two thranites, fifty-four zygites and fifty-four thalamites)[34] leaves 108 men; further assuming the odd eight men to be the remaining junior officers, there remains enough for an extra half reme of rowers of say thirty men, a marine complement of (a more realistic) thirty-five men and the remaining fifteen men to be the sailing crew, doubling perhaps to operate the onboard artillery.

This interpretation will result in a ship which will look very much like a classic trireme, with slightly more beam amidships (Figure 48) but finer at the bow and

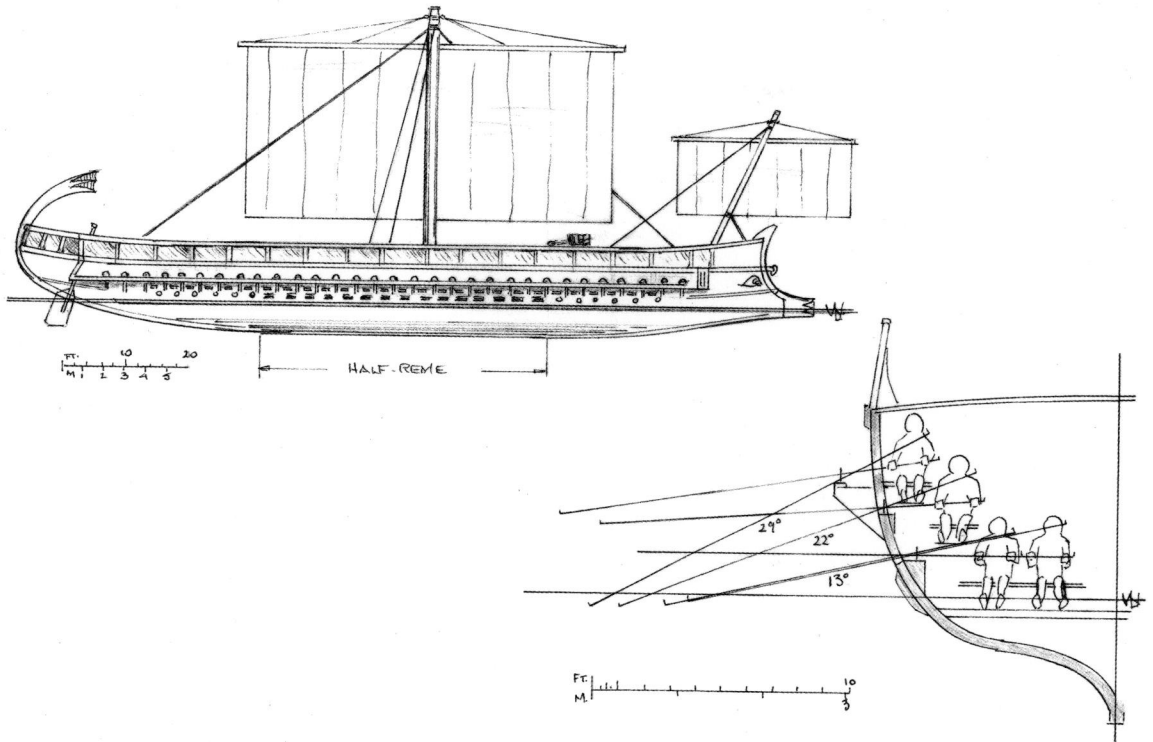

Figure 48. The *Trihemiolia*. The drawing has been developed from the 'classic' trireme (Figure 10) with an extra half-reme of rowers at thalamite level, rowing *alla sensile* and using a 16 feet /4.9m oar, the other rowers all having a 15 feet /4.6m oar. The operating angle of the thranite oar is very near to the maximum possible. Using the 16 feet/4.9m oar would reduce this slightly but increase the gearing of the oar. The hull is much deeper with added deadrise to compensate for the larger sailing rig, now with a sail area of 1940 square feet/164.67 sq.m.

mounting a permanent and more robust complete sailing rig of greater sail area and a deeper draft to enable it to be used effectively. The rowing arrangement is that of the classic trireme, but with an extra half-reme of fifteen or so thalamite oarsmen each side amidships, rowing either a two-man oar, or preferably in an *alla sensile* arrangement. In the latter case, the inboard man's oar need be only a little longer and is more efficient, having more oars in the water and each thalamite contributing his full effort.

PART IV

THE AGE OF THE SUPERGALLEY
310 TO 200 BC

Ornate Macedonian helmet on a stela. Third century. From its location on Samos, possibly that of a seagoing officer (conjecture only). (*Archaeological Museum, Samos*)

Chapter 9

Naval Arms Race

301   After Ipsos, Demetrios retained the troops with which he had escaped and fled to Ephesus to meet with his fleet; from there he went to Corinth, to join with the squadron that he had left there. He still held the Phoenician ports of Tyre and Sidon, some coastal cities in Asia Minor, as well as Cyprus, Corinth and part of the Peloponnese. From this position, he sought to rebuild his power base across the Aegean and to extend his influence across Caria and Ionia and to resurrect his previous 'Hellenic League'. With the ships left in Greece, he could muster nearly 150 warships from the lightest types up to the tens and elevens that he had pioneered. He further strengthened his fleet by having ships built at Athens, Corinth, Chalkis and near to Pella.[1] He started to extend his influence in Greece, opposing the incumbent Cassander. Although the latter had a fleet of perhaps 150 ships, triremes, fours, a few fives and many smaller, many of these were levied from Greek cities, of doubtful loyalty and his fleet was no match for that of Demetrios.

    Demetrios was too weak however to prevent Ptolemy from becoming dominant at sea. Having amassed a fleet of some 200 warships of all rates, augmented by ships taken from Demetrios, he was able to extend his influence deeper into Syria. In Egypt,[2] he founded the port of Arsinoe on the Red Sea coast as a trading centre and as a base from which to protect his Red Sea trade. Alexandria was made the capital and grew, and the famous Pharos was built (c. 280). Ptolemy's expansion continued and by the 280s he had recovered the Phoenician Coast, pushing Seleucos back and removing Demetrios, the latter now having to concentrate on establishing himself in Greece. At the same time, Rhodes built the Colossus, another of the wonders of the Ancient World, reportedly using the materials left behind by Demetrios' forces when they abandoned the siege.

300   In the West, Agathocles, tyrant of Syracuse had increased his navy to some 200 warships and in 300 had invaded mainland Italy to attack the Bruttians. In 299, he ventured into the Southern Adriatic and intervened against Cassander, thwarting the latter's attack on Corcyra (Corfu) which Agathocles occupied. In 295, he made an alliance with Pyrrhus, King of Epirus. Returning to Sicily,

MAP 11—CHANGING FORTUNES 301—200

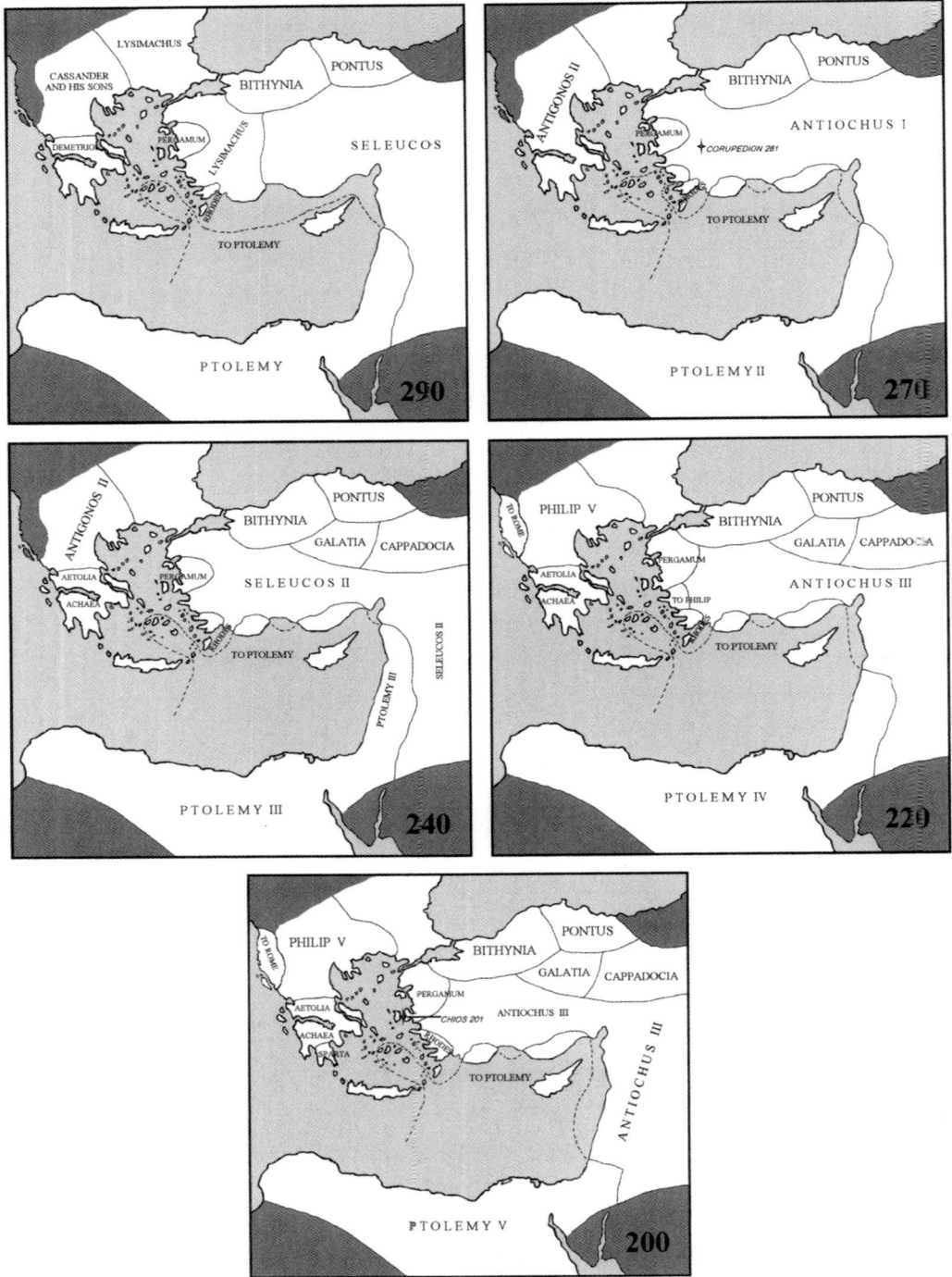

Agathocles took Croton and started to plan an invasion of Carthage, abandoned in 289, when he died.

With the removal of Antigonid power from Asia Minor, a number of independent Hellenistic kingdoms established themselves as the larger powers fought each other to a standstill. Thus was born among them Pontus (302), Bythinia (298) and Pergamum (282) all coastal states that would build and operate navies.

297   King Pyrrhus of Epirus had fought with Antigonos at Ipsos, after which he was sent by Demetrios to Ptolemy as a hostage. In Egypt, he married Ptolemy's daughter and in 297, Ptolemy sent an expedition to return his son-in law to his throne; back in Epirus and loyal now to Ptolemy, he would be a thorn in the side of Cassander in Macedon. Cassander however died in 297, to be succeeded by his three sons, Alexander V (297 to 294), Antipater I (297 to 294) and Philip IV (297). Philip (numbered as Philip III of Macedon) died very shortly after his father, leaving his brothers to squabble over the division of the kingdom. In the confusion following Cassander's death and taking advantage of the sons' disunity, Demetrios, backed by his fleet, mounted an amphibious attack of Athens. He lost a lot of ships in a storm however on the way there and had to return for reinforcements. In 296 he resumed the offensive and blockaded Piraeus. An attempt by a Ptolemaic fleet of 150 ships failed to break the blockade and Athens fell to Demetrios.

296   While he was so occupied, Seleucos seized Demetrios' remaining holdings in Cilicia and Lysimachus took his Ionian ports; Ptolemy recovered Cyprus and the Cyclades. Demetrios meanwhile continued to take advantage of the continuing disunity between Alexander V and Antipater to extend his power in Greece. He had Alexander V assassinated in Athens in 294 and himself proclaimed King of Macedon by the army.[3] His rule and the need for huge sums of money to fund his fleet and army and expansionist plans proved to be increasingly despotic and both Greeks and even Macedonians were on the point of revolt. Demetrios was unable to consolidate his position but he still had a powerful fleet and army which he continued to build up. It was obvious to the others – Lysimachus, Ptolemy and Seleucos – that the return of such a maverick could not be tolerated, especially in view of his obviously expansionist plans. In 289 Lysimachus and Pyrrhus invaded Macedonia from east and west, forcing Demetrios to flee. Undeterred, he rallied his forces and retook most of central Greece and Peloponnese, joining with his fleet once more at Corinth.[4]

287   With Athens in open revolt against him, the threat from Pyrrhus and Lysimachus and Ptolemy's fleet arriving at Piraeus, Demetrios sought peace. He retained

Corinth, Piraeus and Attica and some other ports (but not Athens) leaving
Ptolemy with naval dominance in the Aegean and Eastern Mediterranean.
Leaving his son, Antigonos II Gonatas, in charge of the Greek possessions and
with part of the fleet, Demetrios crossed to Asia Minor in late 287, intending to
take on Lysimachus there.[5] For the expedition, he had some 500 ships available;
this number, if accurate, must include transports for his troops and supplies,
i.e. merchant ships built, hired or impressed into service as well as some of
Cassander's former ships. Of warships alone he could have mustered as many as
200, including his new 'supergalleys', the thirteen, fifteen and sixteen.[6]

He must have been a charismatic and inspirational leader as well as paying
well as he always managed to raise and retain substantial forces, forces who
remained loyal despite his mercurial career. In Asia Minor however, after some
initial successes, he was driven south by Lysimachus against Seleucos. Seleucos
managed to manoeuvre his army between Demetrios' army and fleet and in

Figure 49. Prow of a Hellenistic warship on the grave stela of one Makartos from Delos. Wales are
clearly shown, as is the port-side *epotis* on the front end of the oarbox. There is no *proembolion* and the top
horizontal line would logically suggest the top of the upper deck side screens. The impression is that of a
lighter type of warship, a trireme or four perhaps. Third century. (*Archaeological Museum, Dion*)

Spring 285, the army surrendered to Seleucos and handed Demetrios over to him as a prisoner, which he remained for the rest of his days, living in some opulence in Syria until his death in 283.[7] Ptolemy I Soter (the saviour) died in 282, to be succeeded by his son, Ptolemy II (Philadelphus 282-246).

Without their leader, Demetrios' navy dispersed, many finding re-employment with Ptolemy II, who quickly expanded to fill any maritime power vacuum and became the pre-eminent naval power dominating the eastern Mediterranean and Aegean; he established naval bases on Santorini (Thera) and Samos and formed a naval alliance with Rhodes. They operated together in the supression of piracy, encouraging an increase in maritime trade. Rhodes' wealth depended on trade and it built up a large merchant fleet and, to protect it, had to develop

Figure 50. Grave stela of Heris, son of Menios. Apart from his sword and other equipment, notable is the prow of what appears to be a big warship (presumably on which he served). Compare the relative size of the ram to the hull, with that in Figure 49. (*Archaeological Museum, Istanbul*)

naval power. This navy operated principally to combat endemic regional piracy and developed the fastest ships and tactics to deal with them, becoming a small but extremely efficient force.[8] As a by-product of these changes to the status quo, the centres of trade moved away from Athens and Corinth, to focus on Alexandria and Rhodes, as well as Tyre and Antioch (founded by Seleucos in 300); from these latter, the trade routes ran overland to the rivers of Mesopotamia, to link with Seleucia-on-Tigris and the East.

Antigonos II managed to hold on to most of his possessions in Greece while Lysimachus made himself King of Macedon (killing the last of Cassander's sons, Antipater).[9]

284 After Pyrrhus and Lysimachus had divided Macedonia between them, Lysimachus drove Pyrrhus out, back to Epirus, in 284. Lysimachus, never a 'naval' man, did amass various ships to make a reasonably-sized fleet, mostly to give him dominance over the Hellespont and Bosporus. He does not otherwise seem to have fielded naval forces, despite building the *Leontophoros* (see Chapter 11).

Pyrrhus next turned to Italy and Sicily in 278, going to help Syracuse and raising the Carthaginian siege, he also took over their navy, including their huge *enneres* or nine. He antagonised the Syracusans who refused to support him further and he thus had to leave Sicily in 276. He left with a fleet of 110 warships, most of which he had taken from the Syracusans. This fleet, which had only been used to escort and transport troops, rather than to seek any form of dominance, was caught by a Carthaginian fleet in the Strait of Messina and in the ensuing battle, Pyrrhus lost all but forty of them. He went to Italy, where he was beaten by a Roman army in 275 and was again forced to leave for home (274). Syracusan naval power had been reduced to a nominal level and would never recover to the same extent.

281   Meanwhile, war had erupted between Lysimachus (who had been extending his rule in Asia Minor) and Seleucos, resulting in a battle between them at Corupedion in 281, where Lysimachus was killed. Lysimachus had been joined by Ptolemy Keraunos ('thunderbolt') son of Ptolemy I by his first wife, Euridice (daughter of Antipater). He and his mother had been rejected and disinherited by Ptolemy I when he wished to remarry. Lysimachus had been accepted as King of Macedon and upon his death at Corupedion, Ptolemy Keraunos had been taken prisoner by Seleucos who, by his victory, had extended his rule over much of Asia

Figure 51. THE SELEUCIDS. Top left: Antiochus I (281 to 261). Silver tetradrachm. (*Metropolitan Museum, New York*) Top right: Antiochus II (261 to 246). Silver tetradrachm. (*Altes Museum, Berlin*) Bottom: Antiochus III ('The Great', 223 to 187). Gold octodrachm. (*Altes Museum, Berlin*) Note: in both latter coins, they are styled 'basileos' or king.

Minor and had ambitions to replace Lysimachus on the Macedonian throne. He took Ptolemy Keraunos with him who stabbed Seleucos to death upon their landing in Macedonia. Ptolemy Keraunos rallied Lysimachus' followers and most of his fleet to him and made a claim as Antipater's grandson to the throne, to which he was duly elevated as King of Macedon. He had inherited most of Lysimachus' fleet, including the *Leontophoros* (see later). In 280 with his augmented fleet, he soundly defeated that of Antigonos II when the latter sailed against him, despite Antigonos II using his thirteen and sixteen. Ptolemy Keraunos was however killed in 279 while trying to stop an invasion of Celts.[10]

Seleucos was succeeded by his son, Antiochos I (having given his name to the dynasty that followed him). With the death of Lysimachus, some cities of the Propontis and Black Sea declared independence, Byzantion, Chalcedon and Heraclea Pontica forming a 'Northern League'; Thrace seems to have been left to its own devices, eventually becoming largely occupied by Celtic peoples.

277   After several usurpations and an invasion by Celts, Antigonos II, followed by his fleet, caught and slaughtered the marauding Celts in 277 and was hailed undisputed King of Macedon, extending into Greece and cementing his power base (and dynasty) by 276.

275   In 275, Ptolemy II had the Nile-Red Sea Canal dredged and renovated and sent a fleet, including fours, into the Red Sea to suppress piracy. This canal had first been built by the Pharaoh Necho II in about 670. It followed a course from the easternmost Pelusiac branch of the Nile Delta to Lake Timsah and thence, via the Bitter Lakes, to the Gulf of Suez. It was later refurbished by the Persian King Darius I but was always subject to silting, quickly becoming unusable unless constantly maintained.[11]

After his return to Epirus in 274, Pyrrhus invaded Macedon, forcing Antigonos II to flee to Thessaloniki, where he could be joined and supported by his fleet. Pyrrhus next moved south into Greece, Antigonos II recovered most of his territory and, with his fleet, moved to Corinth. Both armies met at Argos in 272, where Pyrrhus was killed.

274   Between 274 and 271, continuing expansion by Ptolemy II had gained him most of coastal Syria, Cilicia and the South Anatolian coasts, as well as the Ionian city of Miletos; it had however, brought him into a conflict of interests with the Seleucids over Syria and Palestine. Further destabilisation was caused by Celtic tribes which were making ever-deeper incursions into the Hellenistic world. They penetrated into the Aegean, then crossed to Asia Minor, even as far as Syria, weakening the Seleucids. Some stayed and settled in central Asia Minor, giving rise to the area known as Galatia in west-central Anatolia.

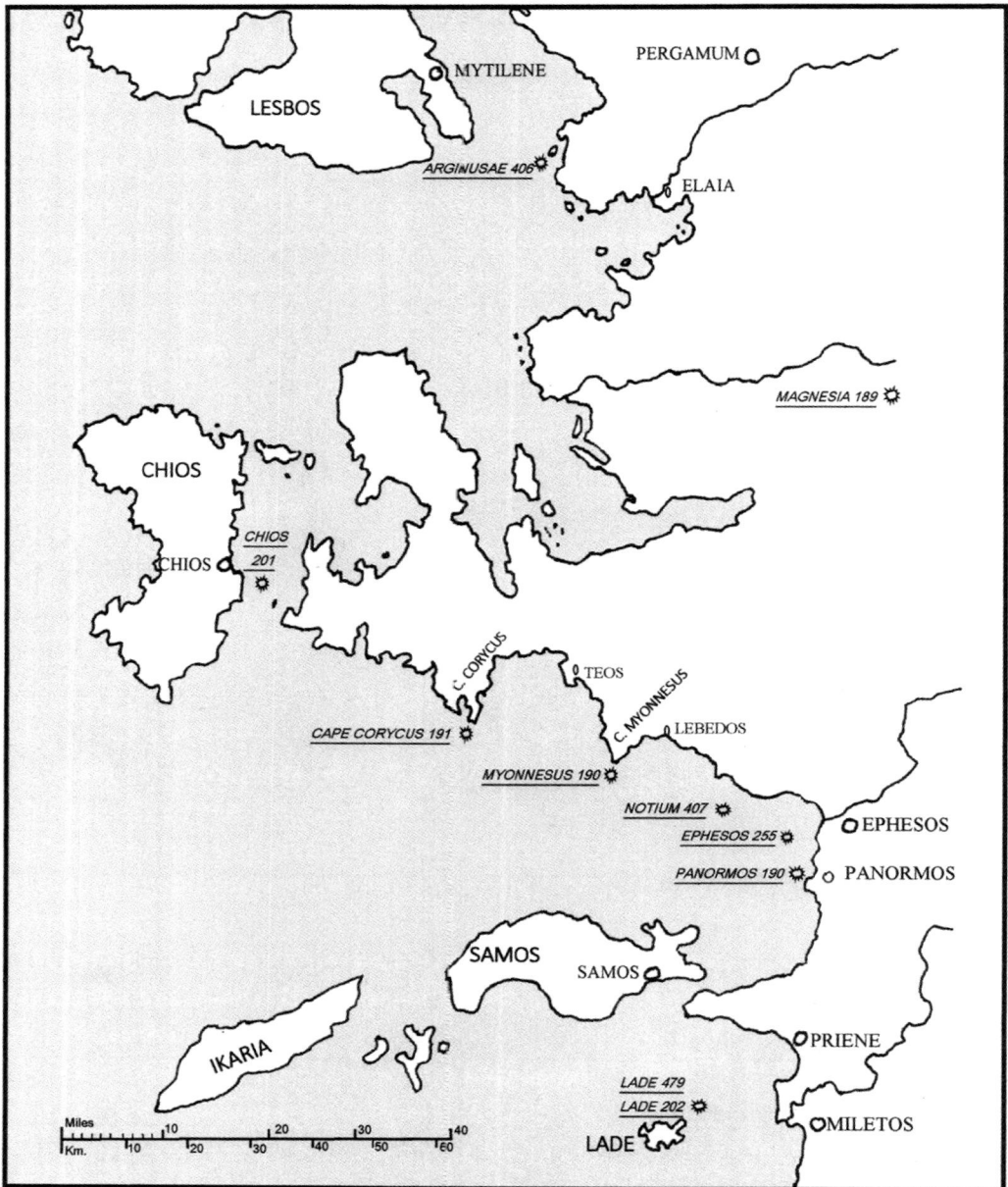

MAP 12. The west coast of Asia Minor. The location of no less than eight naval battles between the fifth and second centuries B.C., from the Persian Wars to the onset of total Roman domination of the Mediterranean basin.

273 In 273, Ptolemy II established diplomatic relations with Rome, which had by now extended its hegemony over most of the Italian peninsula. His diplomacy was also directed towards movements for independence in Sparta and Athens, as a counter to Antigonos II.

270 Syracusan inventiveness and ingenuity had not entirely vanished and between 270 and 265: the tyrant Hieron II had built two huge ships for Ptolemy II. One was a giant merchant ship, possibly over 200 feet /62m long with luxurious passenger accommodation, cabins with mosaic floors, promenades, a gymnasium, library, baths and a small temple. It could carry 2,000 tons of cargo and had three masts, with towers and catapults for self-defence; the other was a giant warship, which Hieron had built in Corinth, a twenty, needing 600 rowers (but see Chapter 12) and having four masts and eight catapults[12] and which was presented or sold to Ptolemy.

264 In the west, war had broken out between Rome and Carthage (the First Punic War 264 to 241) over Sicily. Carthage was the dominant naval power of the central and western Mediterranean and the war would effectively decide which of them would continue as such.[13]

Antigonos II (Gonatas) after re-establishing his family's rule over Macedonia, tried to extend his area of control into the southern Aegean, which duly brought him into conflict with Ptolemy II. The initial contest took place in Greece, where Antigonos II's possession of Corinth and his fleet there, enabled him to defeat Sparta (in 265) and deter Ptolemy II from sending assistance (although he did secure Ephesus).

262 The Greeks had sided with Ptolemy II, but Antigonos II blockaded Athens, which he captured in 262. He next moved his fleet into the Cyclades, going on to systematically take the islands and invaded Samos in 260. His fleet beat Ptolemy's at Cos. Of these fleets there are no details but knowing both antagonists' penchant for big ships, it can be assumed that there were some present, including Demetrios' sixteen.[14]

261 In June 261, Antiochus I died, to be succeeded by his son, Antiochus II. He reached an accord with Antigonos II, intended to drive Ptolemy II out of the Aegean, whereupon Antigonos II set about building up his fleet even more. These two now became locked in an out-and-out struggle which manifested itself in a naval arms race of truly heroic proportions, leading to the age of the 'super galley' as each side strove to outbuild and overawe the other with ever-bigger ships.

Antiochus II campaigned between 260 and 253 and captured Ionia, Lycia, Pamphylia and part of Cilicia; he also took Miletos. Meanwhile, in

258, Antigonos II's fleet ventured into the Dodecanese and there, although outnumbered, defeated Ptolemy II's fleet off the island of Cos. No other details of this battle or of the relative strengths and composition of the fleets survive.[15]

Rhodes had allied itself with Antigonos II and blockaded Ptolemy II's base and fleet at Ephesus. Ptolemy II's fleet came out to break the blockade; the Rhodian admiral, Agathostratos brought his ships into line abreast, i.e. battle formation, then pulled back and returned to his former mooring. Ptolemy II's admiral, Chremonides, thinking that they had refused battle and ceded him the upper hand, returned to his harbour, whereupon Agathostratos quickly returned to the attack

Figure 52. PTOLEMY II. (Euergetes, 246 to 222). Under his aegis, the Ptolemaic fleet grew to its greatest strength and included the biggest of the 'supergalleys'. (*Vatican Museum*)

and caught Chremonides' ships as their crews were disembarking, inflicting a heavy defeat.[16] Ptolemy II sued for peace in 255, accepting Antigonos II's hegemony in the Aegean, but gaining the return of Samos and retaining Thera.

256   Peace was again short-lived before Antigonos II, Ptolemy II and the Seleucids resumed their struggle for supremacy. Ptolemaic naval expansion was again curbed when Antigonos III (Doson) defeated their fleet at the Battle of Andros in 256 and landed occupation forces on the Carian coast. Between 250 and 225, he extended his control of both sides of the southern Aegean. In the east, Antiochus II campaigned against the Parthians, recovering most of Mesopotamia; he also recovered much of Syria and Asia Minor. He sent a naval force into the Persian Gulf, recovering control of the Gulf and its trade. Ptolemy II, smarting from his recent naval defeats and consequent loss of territory, began a massive rebuilding of his navy, adding many new, huge polyremes (including the twenty built at Corinth and continuing on to build two thirties and a forty; these ships were impracticable and never used in battle) with the result that he and his successors were never again to be seriously challenged at sea by the other Hellenistic powers. This did not mean that he could not lose a battle (which he would) but that such a loss could not be enough to seriously weaken his power, let alone threaten its collapse.

All of these wars had served to polarise the post-Alexandrian Hellenistic world even more, with the Antigonids (Antigonos II) in Macedonia and

Greece, the Seleucids (Antiochus II) in Syria and the East and the Ptolemys in Egypt, together with a numer of small, independent kingdoms on the periphery. Curiously perhaps, none of the three 'great' powers sought to conquer these smaller states, concentrating on the greater dangers posed by each other; for their part, the smaller states trod a delicate path between the larger, sometimes allying with one, then the other. For all the constant warring between them, the three larger powers had, apart from exhausting themselves, merely swapped some territory back and forth, but not enough to seriously compromise any of them and leaving a balance of power as the after effect. The constant naval wars had also weakened the powers, allowing Rhodes to operate her small but extremely efficient and effective navy in suppressing piracy and in support and protection of an increasing maritime trade, centred on the island.

252   The navy of Syracuse had remained inactive during the various wars in Sicily and in the early part of the First Punic War, after being briefly allied to Carthage, it changed sides (in 263). The then tyrant, Hieron II remained a staunch ally of Rome until his death in 216. Caught as it then was, between the two warring greater powers, Syracuse could no longer be a leading power itself. In 252, Hieron had sent some ships to join the Roman capture of Lipari and at the end of the war, Syracuse retained its independence when the rest of Sicily became a Roman province. Eventually, the great naval war between Carthage and Rome ended in 241 with a crushing Roman naval victory, leaving Rome as the pre-eminent naval power in the Central and Western Mediterranean.[17] The Carthaginian fleet, although still large, never proved able to recover from the shock of defeat, the naval initiative staying with the Romans.

246   In January 246, Ptolemy II died, followed by Antiochus II in August; the former was succeeded by Ptolemy III (Euergetes, 'benefactor' 246 to 222) and the latter by Seleucos II (246 to 225).[18] Seleucos II only succeeded after the assassination of his half-brother and taking advantage of the uncertainty around the succession, Ptolemy III, using his fleet, sought to extend his coastal holdings in Syria and Anatolia. On his accession, he had inherited a fleet of seventeen fives, five sixes, no less that thirty-seven sevens, thirty nines, fourteen elevens, two twelves, four thirteens, the 'Corinthian' twenty and two thirties, 112 big ships, to which must be added (according to Athenaeus) over twice that number again of lesser rates, triremes, fours, *trihemioliae* and small craft.[19] He occupied Antioch itself between 246 and 242 and won a naval victory off Andros of which, once more, there are no surviving details.

For the rest of the 240s, both Seleucos II and Antigonos II were beset by internal insurrections and conflicts, with parts of their respective realms breaking away and being recovered, matters encouraged by Ptolemy III.

Figure 53. Demetrios I 'Poliorcetes'. Silver tetradrachm, clearly from later in his career when he was attempting to secure the Macedonian Throne, here styling himself as 'King Demetrios'. (*Altes Museum, Berlin*)

Antigonos II Gonatas died in early 239, to be succeeded by his son, Demetrios II (239 to 229). Demetrios II inherited a very unstable situation; although secure in Macedonia, the Greeks had split into two factions, the Achaean League of the Peloponnese and the Aetolian League of central Greece. Their rivalry and open aggression during the 230s resulted in an uneasy alliance against Macedonia. Demetrios II campaigned successfully against them in 233, before being distracted by incursions on his northern border.[20]

229   To the north-west of Greece, the Illyrians of the Dalmatian Coast, under their queen Teuta extended their kingdom to the borders of Epirus. They then proceeded to attack it and stormed Corcyra, defeating a joint Achaean/Aetolian naval force of ten fours and fives by swarming about them with their small, light *lemboi*. Rome

Figure 54. Bronze outer covering of a Hellenistic shield, the centre star device being the symbol of Macedonian kingship. The inscription reads 'of King Demetrios'. (*Metropolitan Museum, New York*)

became involved as a result of Illyrian pirate raids on Southern Italy and the rejection of her envoys to the queen. In 229 a massive Roman fleet of 200 warships, supporting an invasion force of troops, crossed the Adriatic and made short work of the opposition, seizing Corcyra. They imposed peace on Queen Teuta and, more importantly for the future, caused her to cede territory to form a new Roman protectorate in Illyria (approximately contiguous with modern southern Albania).[21] Control of both sides of the Adriatic effectively made it into a Roman lake but more significantly for the Hellenistic world, it brought the growing Roman Republic into direct contact with them, a factor that would see Rome increasingly drawn into Greek affairs.

At some point or points in this period, accounts and details of the huge naval battles of the First Punic War and of the success in battle of the Roman fleets must have reached the Hellenistic and Greek leaders. With the appearance of Roman warships in the Adriatic and Ionian seas, they could see and appreciate these ships and in particular, their fighting towers and we must assume that from then, towers started to appear on Hellenistic warships as well.

229 In the North, Demetrios II was killed in battle. As his son, the future Philip V, was only nine, his cousin became regent as Antigonos III Doson (229 to 221).

226 Rhodes suffered a devastating earthquake in 226 which toppled their famous Colossus and caused widespread damage. Seleucos III gave them ten fives.[22] Presumably some of their ships had been lost in the disaster and the gift of the ships was to enable them to continue to safeguard the sea-lanes, which was in his interest. There is no evidence that the Rhodians operated anything larger than a five, preferring the more agile fours and *trihemioliae*.[23] Fleet strength was maintained at about thirty-five ships,[24] a permanent standing force that could be properly crewed and maintained.

225 Seleucos II died in 225 and was succeeded by his son Seleucos III, who died after three years, the throne passing to his brother, Antiochus III (223 to 187). Athens paid its Macedonian garrison to leave, regaining its independence as a neutral. In Greece, the Leagues and resurgent Sparta were in constant turmoil and frequent warfare, none of which involved naval operations. Antigonos III finally imposed a form of peace upon the warring Greeks when he defeated Sparta in 222. He, however, died in 221 when the young Philip V took the throne (221 to 179). Ptolemy III died in 222 having, despite his naval reverses, retained a strong fleet and far-flung territories; indeed he now held virtually the whole Syrian coast, including the port of Seleucia (the port of Antioch, modern Samandag). His successor, Ptolemy IV Philopator (222 to 205) would prove to be a weaker king.

220 The Roman factor became more manifest when a local tyrant, Demetrios of Pharos, having for some time engaged in piracy along the Greek Adriatic coasts (encouraged by Philip V of Macedon) sought to add part of the Roman protectorate to his own kingdom.[25] He formed a fleet of ninety *lemboi* and sailed to attack Pylos in the Peloponnese. The Romans reacted in 219, sending a fleet and troops, retaking their land and Pharos itself. Demetrios fled to Macedon and his former lands were added to the Roman protectorate. Philip's ambition, via his proxy, had been thwarted for the time being and he had now come into direct contact with Rome.

219 Between 219 and 217, Antiochus III (who became known as 'The Great') recovered Seleucia and captured Tyre, Ptolemais (Acre) and Gaza from Ptolemy IV. He was stopped in 217 when he was beaten in a massive battle against Ptolemy's army at Raphia (to the south-west of Gaza). He had, nevertheless, obtained the seaboard of Syria but Ptolemy managed to retain Coele-Syria and Phoenicia.

218 Philip V saw his next opportunity to redress his recent reverse with the resumption of war between Rome and Carthage (the Second Punic War 218 to 202). An early attempt by him to seize a base in Illyria failed when local people alerted the Romans, who sent a squadron of ten heavy ships to support their allies there. In the next couple of years however, the Romans suffered terrible losses in battle against Hannibal, who was then rampaging in Italy. Philip V greeted Hannibal's envoys with enthusiasm and formed an alliance with him in 216, whereby Philip V would attack the Romans in Illyria and Corcyra while Hannibal kept them busy in Italy.

216 To complete their treaty and arrangements, a squadron of five Macedonian warships, carrying the treaty and plans, with Philip's envoy and some Carthaginian officers were sent to meet Hannibal at a secret rendezvous in the Gulf of Taranto. Before they could land however, they were intercepted by a Roman force of twenty-five warships and, apart from one ship that escaped and returned to Philip, all were captured, together with the treaty and the new allies' war plans. The Romans now fully alerted, were able to deploy another twenty-five ships under Marcus Valerius Laevinus, to bring their fleet in the South Adriatic up to fifty ships thereby preventing Philip and Hannibal from co-operating and co-ordinating their efforts.

215 The first war between Macedon and Rome thus started in 215. The Romans enlisted and supported the Aetolian League of Greek states wishing to be free of Philip and his ambitions and also Rhodes and Pergamum. These latter had powerful fleets of their own and could potentially dominate the Aegean.

Figure 55. The Antagonids of Macedonia. Top: Antigonos II (Gonatas, 283 to 239). Silver tetradrachm. (*Iannina Archaeological Museum*). Bottom: Antigonos III (Doson, 229 to 221). Silver tetradrachm. The reverse shows an almost identical ship image to that of his father and very similar to that of his grandfather. In all cases, the prow of a major warship. (*Altes Museum, Berlin*)

214   Philip chose to strike first in Illyria and in 214 he had amassed a fleet of about 120 light galleys, many built there and thus probably their own traditional *lemboi*, possibly in both mono and bireme versions. Philip and his forces sailed northwards from the Peloponnese to attack Apollonia (near Fier, Albania) and Oricus (Dukat, Albania). The Roman admiral Laevinus sailed from Brundisium (Brindisi) with a fleet of heavier, well-armed ships and transports carrying troops, to Oricus (75 miles/110 km) where he was joined by ten allied Aetolian ships. Philip's fleet was completely outclassed and forced to retreat up a nearby river, until the big ships could follow no further. There they remained helpless

while the Romans recovered their lost territory. Philip was finally forced to burn his boats and retreat overland.

Perhaps Philip had attacked expecting, per his treaty with Hannibal, to be supported by the arrival of a Carthaginian fleet. If so, he waited in vain and without it could not operate effectively in Western Greece or Illyria, let alone hope to link with Hannibal. The war continued on land with Philip, hard-pressed by Rome's Greek allies, maintaining pressure on Illyria, although he did not try to approach the coastal area. Ptolemy IV felt the war ran counter to his interests and sought to mediate. The Romans preferred to keep Philip occupied and persuaded Ptolemy to remain neutral; Rome maintained her fleet in the Adriatic and Aegean in support of her allies preventing any new contacts between Philip V and Hannibal.[26]

212   Syracusan naval power had never recovered from the losses caused by the adventures of Pyrrhus. Nevertheless, Hieron sent twelve ships to intercept a Punic convoy at the outbreak of the Second Punic War (218 to 202) but after his death in 216, the new leaders of Syracuse opposed Rome. The Romans had a fleet of 100 warships in Sicily and apart from a couple of ineffective sallies there was no further activity by Syracusan ships during the ensuing Roman siege of the city and against their overwhelming naval superiority. It eventually fell to the Romans in 212, ending its independence and naval history.

210   In 210, Laevinus' fleet, based on Corcyra, captured Zakinthos and the towns of Oeniadae and Nassus on the Greek mainland from Philip, which was then handed to the Aetolians. His successor in command, Galba, sailed into the Aegean and captured Aegina; he failed to raise Philip's siege of Echinos in Lamia (opposite North Euboea) and returned to the Gulf of Corinth. Philip's fleet was insufficient to challenge the Romans and their allies, but with his Achaean allies, he was more successful on land, recovering Thessaly and driving off an incursion into Greece by Pergamum.

209   The Roman fleet in Illyria raided Macedonian-held shores in the Gulf of Corinth and supported the Aetolians with marines when Philip tried to move south. This happened again in 208, when the Roman fleet landed 4,000 marines in his rear, causing him to lose the ensuing battle. By 207, the focus of the war had moved to the Aegean and half of the Roman ships (twenty-five ships) moved to their base on Aegina and from there to Lemnos; there they were joined by thirty-five ships from Pergamum.

Once again, Philip's fleet was outmatched and kept to its harbours, leaving Macedonia's long Aegean coastline vulnerable. The allies attacked Oreus on Euboea while Philip was unable to cross to the island to defend it in the face of

Figure 56. The Attalids of Pergamum. Top: Eumenes I (262 to 241) second ruler of an independent Pergamum and the first to style himself as king. He built up a compact and powerful navy. The inscription on the coin describes him as 'Philetairos', after his father (283 to 262) who, as Governor of Pergamum established its independence and beat off an attempt by Seleucos I to reconquer it. Silver tetradrachm. (*Altes Museum, Berlin*) Bottom: Attalus I (241 to 197) maintained his independence and navy. Silver tetradrachm. (*Metropolitan Museum, New York*)

the allied naval force. Chalkis did manage to resist and the allies withdrew to their bases. Philip now brought his fleet into the northern gulf between Euboea and the mainland and toured and encouraged his garrisons before returning to Demetrias (Volos). In 207, he advanced into the Aegean but could not face the sixty-ship fleet of Rome and her allies. Conscious of his weakness at sea, Philip ordered the building of 100 warships at his yards in Chalkidiki, which added three fours, seven fives and over twenty smaller ships to his fleet.[27] Attalus, King of Pergamum had to withdraw his fleet to deal with troubles at home and the Roman ships returned to their base in Illyria.

205   The Macedonian War had been lessening in intensity for some time, the antagonists losing enthusiasm and becoming exhausted and the arrival of a Roman fleet of thirty-five ships, together with 35,000 fresh troops at Dyrrhachium (Durazzo, Durres) in 205, proved to be the catalyst to end it.[28] Fifteen of the Roman ships sailed into the Aegean to join their allies but Philip and the Greeks had all had enough and peace was agreed.

202   The Romans finally defeated Hannibal at the Battle of Zama in 202, ending the Second Punic War; Hannibal fled and found sanctuary with Antiochus III, the Seleucid King. Rome was now the only naval power west of Greece: its fleet was large, well founded and trained, experienced and victorious and at the peak of its fighting ability.

202   In 204, Ptolemy IV had died, to be succeeded by his five-year-old son, Ptolemy V. The weakness and internal strife consequent upon this[29] disturbed the precarious balance of power in the Hellenistic world. Undeterred as ever by the constant conflict and his previous setbacks, Philip V of Macedon allied himself with the Seleucid King Antiochus III to drive Ptolemy V out of the Aegean

Figure 57. Mid third century warship prow at Cyrene, Lybia. Much reconstruction work has been done (the pale yellow stone) to position the original remnants in their relative positions. Thus the hull resting forward on a dolphin, rises to a ram, which seems small. Above this is a *proembolion* or secondary ram (which seems too far forward); the lower, main ram is intended to strike at the waterline, whilst the upper strikes the enemy oarbox. The *proembolion* is at the end of wales that sweep beck to the forward end of the ship's oarbox (an original piece). Above can be seen the line of the bulwark around the upper deck, leading to the (missing) stempost; the whole crowned by a statue of Nike. (Compare with the Samothrace prow, Figure 45). (*By kind permission of Mrs. P. Aitcheson*)

and Levant for good. Antiochus advanced upon the Hellespont, invaded Coele Syria and Palestine, while Philip's new fleet moved into the Hellespont and Propontis (Sea of Marmara). This move, if successful would leave Pergamum and Rhodes, both allies of Rome, virtually at the mercy of the allies and isolated. With her allies under threat, Rome sent a diplomatic mission to warn off Philip and seek a settlement between Antiochos III and Ptolemy's Egypt. Antiochus III, at first, paid lip-service to Rome but Philip, perhaps still smarting from his ignominious naval defeat in the Adriatic in 214 and now with his powerful new fleet, was not so swayed. He sent his light ships off on a grand raiding cruise, intercepting ships of the Black Sea trade, and throughout the Aegean and made common cause with the pirates of Crete. In the summer of 201, Philip's Macedonian army advanced into Ionia and attacked Pergamene territory, taking their seaport of Abydos on the Hellespont; his fleet annexed the Cyclades and occupied Samos, capturing ships and defeating a Rhodian fleet off Lade (202).[30]

Philip had made himself 'president' of a Cretan confederacy. Rhodian actions against Cretan pirates was his excuse to become involved and to capture Rhodian outposts in the Propontis and also to capture Miletos. Rhodes and Pergamum supported Athens in its struggle to regain independence and against Philip's invasion of their territory.

Pergamum had built up a compact but potent naval force with thirty or so fours and fives and with at least one *trihemilia* and perhaps a couple of triremes and some smaller.

201   Finally, the combined Rhodian and Pergamene fleets, with ships from Chios and Byzantion, met Philip's fleet off Chios and beat it decisively (see Appendix).[31] This defeat cost Philip half of his fleet and left it unable to seriously challenge the allies again. After the battle, Philip sailed south[32] to the island of Lade. There, he encountered a Rhodian squadron and attacked. One of Philip's ships rammed a Rhodian, stoving in its side and the ship foundered. Another Rhodian ship, seeking to avoid a blow, raised a foresail, whereupon some of the others, thinking to do the same, also raised sail and made for the open sea. The Rhodian admiral, still fighting, with a few of his ships, had to break off and follow. The Rhodians lost two fives to Philip's fleet, who then occupied the camp recently vacated by them.[33] Despite this minor success, Philip had sustained serious losses and if anything, had over-extended himself.

Philip became trapped at Bargylia in Caria and blockaded there for the Winter of 201/200; he managed to escape in the Spring with the remnant of his fleet.[34] On the way, he sent a squadron which captured four Athenian triremes but Rhodian and Pergamene ships pursuing him, forced him to release them [35] Rhodes and Pergamum, to maintain their maritime position and indeed their very existence, appealed to Rome for help.[36] This they had every confidence of receiving in view of their previous operations as allies of and in support of Roman naval forces during the recent war. For her part, Rome continued to be inexorably drawn into Greek and Hellenistic affairs and was already becoming the arbiter of them.

200 Antiochus III, continuing his part of the alliance, once again attacked Ptolemy V's possessions in Phoenicia, destroying the latter's army in battle at Panion (Banias), east of Tyre, but being stopped at Gaza. He then went on to occupy Phoenicia, which became part of the Seleucid realm for the next forty years. Possession of the Levantine ports enabled Antiochus III to build up his naval strength, using the ports, facilities and shipbuilding capability now lost to Ptolemy, who nevertheless still had as many as 200 warships.

Appendix

Battle of Chios 201

Philip V had been unsuccessfully besieging Chios town and found himself blockaded by the joint fleets of Pergamum, under their king Attalus and Rhodes, commanded by their admiral Theophiliscus, together with some allied ships from Byzantion. It is logical to suppose that the allied fleet had gathered at the Pergamene port of Elaia then sailed together, approaching to the north of Chios town and putting into shore there, to start their blockade.

Philip decided to raise the siege and break out, in a surprise move by sea, to his base on Samos to the south. Any hope of surprise was thwarted, however, when his preparations for sea were spotted. Philip put to sea with his fleet ahead of the allies; they in turn put to sea and by hard rowing, managed to catch up with him. The allies were advancing in battle formation and when Philip saw himself being overhauled, he ordered his fleet to turn and form into battle formation to meet them.

Attalus and his Pergamene ships formed the allied right wing, while Theophiliscus and the Rhodians made up the left. The allies had sixty-five heavy ships, plus nine *trihemioliae* and three triremes.

Philip could deploy fifty-three heavy ships, including a ten, at least two eights, a seven and a six, plus four fives and three triremes,[1] together with over 100 or so light open boats (*lemboi* and *hemioliai* which probably included many pirate craft) some of which at least had rams. Philip himself took station on a nearby islet to observe the battle.

Polybius[2] (XVI.2 to 15) wrote an account of this battle only about fifty years after the event and probably with access to eyewitness accounts and to memoirs of actual participants. It goes far to illustrate the violence and chaos of a battle between the giant oared warships of the time and of the effect of ramming.

> The two fleets were in line abreast with Attalus' ships slightly ahead and which came into contact first, ramming a Macedonian eight below the waterline. The marines on its deck kept fighting for a long while, before the ship eventually foundered. The flagship of Philip's fleet, a ten, fell into the enemy's hands in an unexpected fashion. A *trihemiolia* came into its path, which it rammed with a mighty blow amidships, below the topmost oars, the ram however stuck fast

since the commander was not able to keep a check on his ship's impetus. So, with the vessel hanging from it, the mighty ship was in a hopeless situation, utterly unmanageable and unable to move. At that moment, two fives fell upon it, one on each side and wounded it fatally. They destroyed the ship and all aboard including Democrates, Philip's admiral.

We must assume that under these concerted blows from two big ships, the ten started to break up, as, unlike the eight rammed by Attalus, the marines were lost and no further fight was put up, in other words, the ship settled quickly. Polybius continues:

At the same time that this happened, Dionysodorus and Dinocrates, brothers and commanders (*nauarchoi*) on Attalus' side, launched attacks, one on an enemy seven, the other on an eight and suffered strange experiences in their respective combats. In his attack on an eight, Dinocrates' ship received a blow above the waterline, since the opposing vessel had his bows elevated, but in turn struck the enemy below the waterline. At first he was unable to break free, despite repeated attempts at backing water; the Macedonian marines were fighting courageously and boarded his ship, Attalus came to his aid by delivering a blow on the enemy ship, breaking the embrace of the two vessels and Dinocrates' ship was freed. The enemy marines continued to fight courageously but, unable to return to their own ship, they were destroyed and Attalus' men in turn boarded and took over the now undefended eight.

From this, we can of course deduce that the hundreds of rowers below decks were not armed or expected to take any part in combat, nor did they. Again, he continues:

Dionysodorus, charging with great force to deliver a blow, not only missed doing any harm but, being carried on past the enemy, lost his starboard oars and the timbers supporting his towers were shattered. As soon as this happened, enemy vessels surrounded him. Amid shouts and confusion the ship was destroyed with all aboard except for Dionysodorus and two others who managed to swim to a *trihemiolia* that came to their aid.

The battle continued indecisively, the allies superiority in big ships offset by Philip's greater numbers. Eventually, the weight of Attalus' big ships began to prevail and on the other wing, the fast Rhodian ships managed to get around to the rear of the Macedonian line (*periplous*). After some initial successes against them, the Macedonians managed to turn and face the Rhodians, when both sides 'charged'. With their greater numbers, the Macedonians were able to have a second line, so that after the initial charge, the antagonists became mixed in a general melee. The Macedonian marines were very good and preferred to fight hand-to-hand, whereas the Rhodians preferred to rely on their superior speed and ship handling. Thus they used the 'trick' of depressing the bows of their ships, so that any enemy ramming would be above the waterline, whereas their own would be below that of an enemy and thus much more dangerous to it.

Whether this was a particular manoeuvre that they developed, or that they had so ballasted and rigged their ships is not clear, but it rarely succeeded (according to Polybius) and does not seem to have been repeated. The Rhodians favourite ploy was to pass close alongside an enemy, shearing off the oars on that side, then round its stern and ram; this proved very successful and was also a way in which the Rhodian *trihemioliae* could attack their much larger opponents. Their attacks were hampered by the swarms of enemy *lemboi* and small craft which, although incapable of assaulting the bigger ships, could and did crowd their manoeuvrability and of course, shower them with arrows and javelins.

In a further exploit, a Rhodian five rammed an enemy ship, sinking it but in the process, the ram became stuck and was torn off when the ships separated. Taking on water, the five was surrounded by enemy craft (presumably the hordes of light vessels) and was lost. Three more Rhodian fives came too late to rescue the stricken ship, but did manage to ram and sink three enemy boats, before being themselves surrounded and only managed to extricate themselves after a hard fight.

The battle seems to have drifted into two parts, with Philip's right fully engaged against the Rhodians not far from their starting point. Attalus' ships were gradually overpowering Philip's left as it was still trying to retire towards the mainland. One of Attalus' fives was severely damaged by ramming and he went to assist, with two fours. He ventured too far ahead and Philip sped to intercept with four fives and three *hemioliae* and some smaller craft. Cut off, Attalus found himself in the embarrassing position of having to run his ships ashore to effect his escape, the ships being taken by Philip.

After this, and probably with increasing exhaustion, the two sides gradually disengaged, the allies returning to Chios and Philip to Samos. It had been a ferocious fight, Philip having lost against Attalus, a ten (his flagship) a seven and a six, ten other ships and three *trihemioliae,* plus twenty-five of the smaller vessels. Against the Rhodians, he had lost another ten warships and about forty of the small craft. As well

MAP 12
THE BATTLE OF CHIOS -201

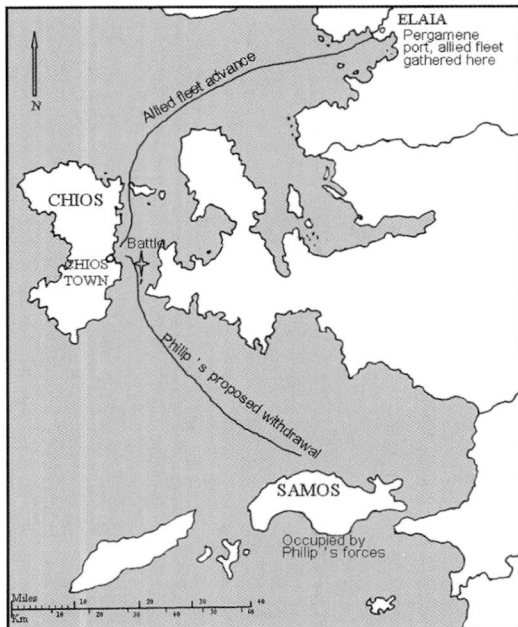

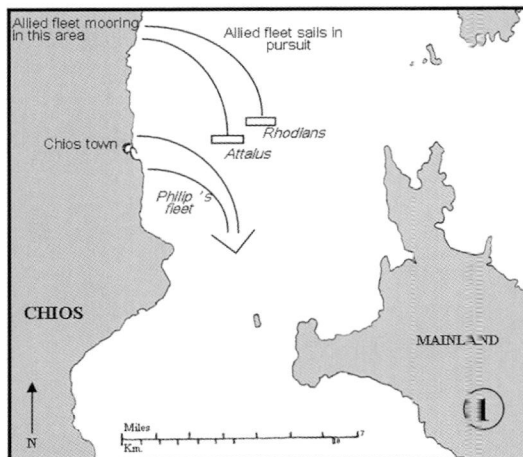

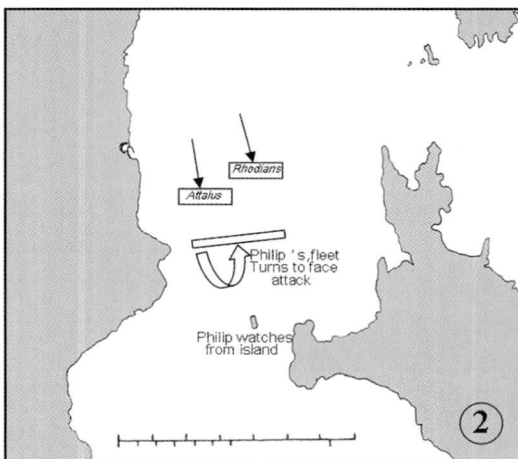

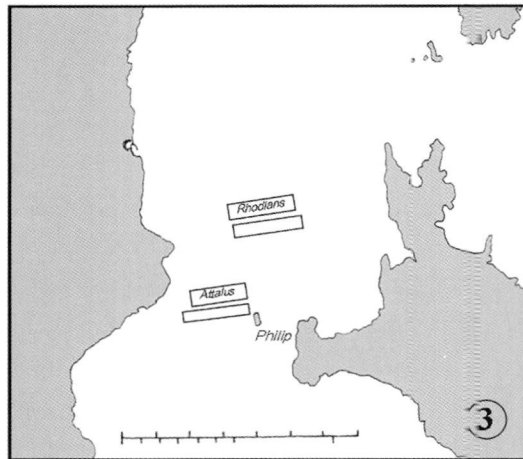

as the ships, his casualties amounted to some 3,000 marines and 6,000 rowers, with another 2,000 taken prisoner; he escaped with only twelve ships and some of the light craft. One can presume that the mercenary/pirate light craft quickly scattered and disappeared. Macedonian seapower had been effectively broken.

On the allied side, Attalus had lost two fives, one *trihemiolia* and the two fours captured by Philip. His casualties were given as only seventy men, plus the 600 men forming the crews of the captured fours. The Rhodians also lost two fives and a trireme, plus only sixty men. Allied casualties seem incredibly low compared to the Macedonian, but it could be suggested that the latter were supplemented by the extra men on board their ships being evacuated from the siege of Chios, so that when a ship was lost, more than the crew went down with it.

Immediately apparent is the lack of any battle plan or the seeking of a tactical advantage: both fleets simply formed up and charged at each other. Both sides relied, initially at least, primarily on the ram as their preferred weapon and the variation in the effect of this weapon, caused by the movement of the ramming ship is notable; the blow could be anywhere between below the waterline (the preferred target) to just below the thranite or uppermost level of oarsmen. Also notable is the differing effect that a blow from a ram could have on its target, the eight that was hit by Attalus' ship must have settled slowly as the marines kept on fighting 'for a long while'. The later occasion when a ship was 'destroyed with all aboard', would indicate that the ship suffered damage that caused it to settle quickly. One of the great ships, even if moving slowly, with its great mass, could inflict a potentially fatal blow, especially on something smaller. Increasing size and ponderousness as well as a larger number of artillery and marines, intent on boarding, made the ram attack a tactic of opportunity rather than design after the initial clash. This appears particularly so in looking at this battle, where the big ships seem increasingly to blunder into each other, whereas the Rhodians maintain their fast-moving and more flexible ramming tactics.

There is no mention of the use of artillery, archers, or indeed of any missiles; one must assume that they were indeed in use but that this did not prove decisive in an encounter. The main reliance appears to be on the ram, with marines in action when ships were in contact and boarding was attempted; on the whole, they did not, unlike as will be seen with the Romans, set out with boarding as the main objective. Finally, there is no mention of the rowing crews of stricken ships joining in the fight (as was seen on Dionysodorus' ship) and presumably they were unarmed and tried to escape and to fend for themselves as best they could, although, from the numbers lost, many were obviously trapped below decks when their ships settled quickly, or escaped only to drown, or were killed by the breaking of their oars or missile shooting, those that were not taken prisoner.

Chapter 10

A New Rowing System

There is a distinct change in the arrangement of oarports between the Lenormant Relief (the classic trireme, Figure 8) and the Samothrace Prow of circa 200 (Figure 45). From being clearly visible as one, two and three distinct, superimposed remes in the former, the oarports appear in the latter, in the ends of a very prominent oarbox, arranged close together *en échelon* and actually overlapping. The ports are both in the same vertical plane and show a thole pin in relief, which presumably means that, to be visible, the pins were not far inboard of the openings. Further, the thole pins are shown in the centre of the ports so presumably the oar could be rigged before or aft of it. Finally, both ports are the same size, indicating that the oars were worked very closely together so that the distance between the two thole pins and the port were very nearly the same (otherwise one oar would need a longer aperture in which to swing).

The same arrangement appears in the Praeneste Relief, the Lindos monument and the Palazzo Spada Relief and can be inferred from the very similar form of the Cyrene Prow as well as the Isola Tiberina Monument in Rome (the only one that may be life-size) (Figures 57 and 59). Both the Praeneste and Palazzo Spada Reliefs indicate long, heavy-type warships with towers, proving that the system was used for big ships. Even allowing for the artists who sculpted the reliefs trying to simplify their work by depicting the oars as closely-spaced (thus only having to cut parallel lines) the Samothrace Prow is the only one to actually show oarports, together with their relative spacing, the others simply having oars emerging through, presumably close-fitting, ports in the hull sides (but see post); in the Praeneste Relief, the oars have protective covers where they emerge.

The problem with a trireme arrangement is that with the ship heeled by more than a few degrees[1] and even a mildly choppy sea, the thalamite oars can become unworkable and have to be shipped; the angle of working the thranite oars also increases, making them less workable as the angle increases while on the weather side, they would barely if at all, be able to reach the water. A bigger ship with multi-manned oars can only multiply the problem.

The 'echelon' system, with only two oars, places them close together both vertically and horizontally so they can be the same length and gearing, minimising any

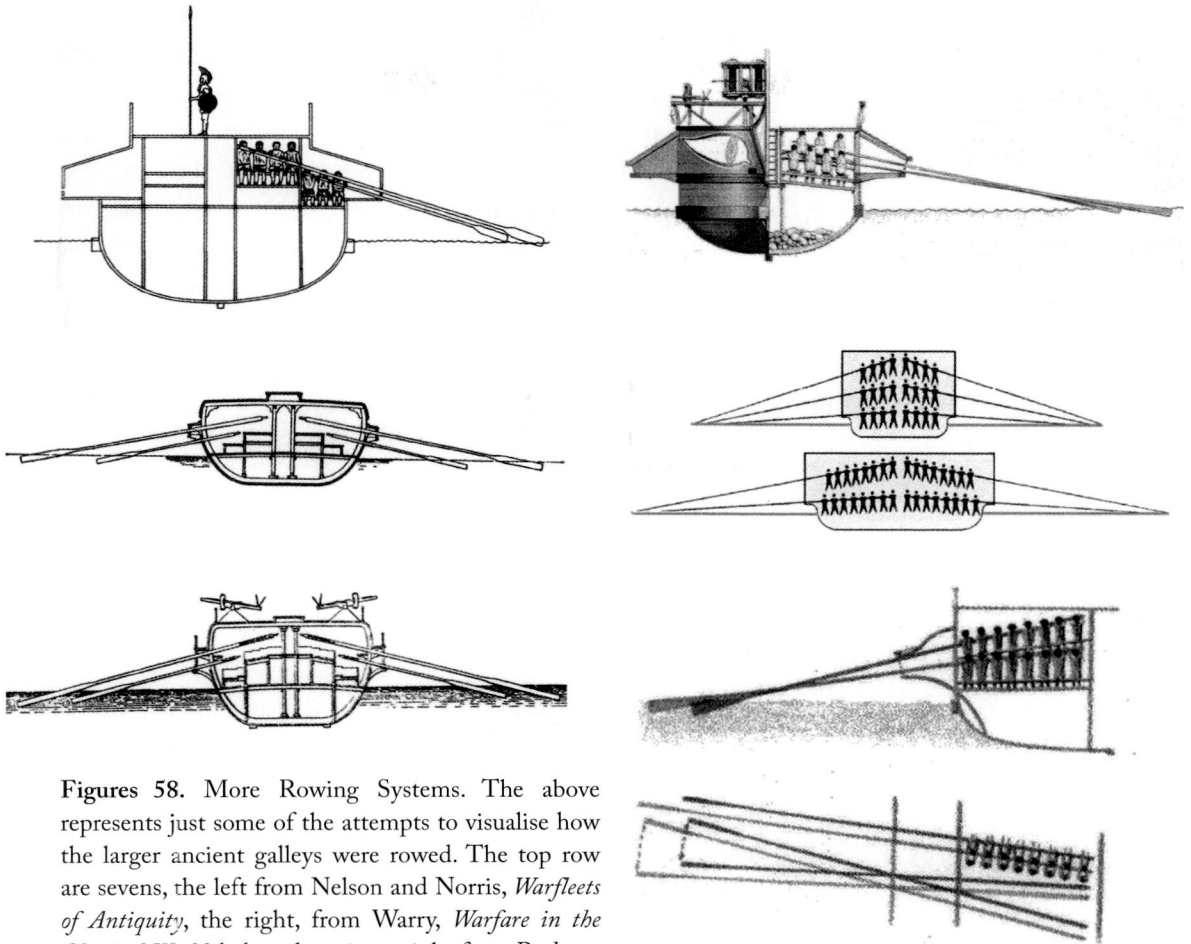

Figures 58. More Rowing Systems. The above represents just some of the attempts to visualise how the larger ancient galleys were rowed. The top row are sevens, the left from Nelson and Norris, *Warfleets of Antiquity*, the right, from Warry, *Warfare in the Classical World*; below them is an eight from Rodgers and middle right, a twelve and a sixteen, from Casson, *SSAW*. In the bottom row, left is a sixteen according to Rodgers and on the right, from Connolly, *The Greek Armies*. Demonstrating varying apparent degrees of practicality, could some or all of them work in three dimensions, with real rowers?

discrepancy in performance between them when they are all affected similarly, or not, by sea conditions. It might also place them higher above the waterline, increasing freeboard and allowing them to continue to be effective in more severe sea conditions. It is also noticeable that the outrigger in this arrangement projects more from the ship's side than that of a trireme. In two of the renditions (Samothrace and Palazzo Spada) the lower port is ahead of the upper, whereas on the Praeneste Relief, the order is reversed. The only conclusion that suggests itself for this apparent anomaly is that the system was the same but perhaps the hull shapes differed.

This seems to represent a fundamental design change, perhaps but not exclusively evolved for use in the new, bigger ships and as an alternative to the existing trireme layout, making the ships effectively a form of 'semi-bireme'.[2] There is no evidence in any of the examples to show that there were any additional oarports in the hulls and it will be convenient to distinguish this new scheme as 'echelon'. The biggest problem is to envisage the internal arrangement for the working of what appear to be two big multi-manned oars working very closely in concert; it could also suggest that it applied to rates of even numbers. Moving inside however, this means that the looms are also parallel and close together, implying that there must be sufficient room between them for the two oar crews to work[3] for a fully synchronised stroke.[4] The rowing crews working in such close proximity, harmony even and without fouling each other, presupposes a very high degree of training and practice.

On both the Praeneste and Palazzo Spada Reliefs, the oars are shown the same length, suggesting a system of identical oars, worked in pairs, each pulled by the same number of rowers, with the alternate oars staggered vertically. If this can be shown to work therefore, we can use the echelon system to reconstruct further Hellenistic warship rates, theoretically at least, up to the sixteen (two oars of eight men in each group).

Returning to Anderson's interpretation of the Samothrace Prow as being a less than life-size model of a large-type ship and which he posits as being one-third life-size,[5] a contention that is supported by the much larger size of the similarly formed Isola Tiberina Monument and also the Palazzo Spada Relief. As mentioned (in Chapter 8), scaling up the monument by three results in oarports 3 feet/915mm wide and 1 foot/305 mm deep or enough to handle a reasonably large, multi-manned oar. The scaled-up beam across the forward oarbox becomes 23.5 feet/7.2m and if we consider that a rower needs a bare minimum width of 2 feet/610mm and there should be perhaps a 3 feet/915mm gangway amidships, plus a distance of perhaps 4 feet/1.2m between the outboard rower and the thole on each side, that beam would (just) permit a three-man oar on each side. The ship's beam would broaden going aft, the increase permitting an incremental addition of rowers per oar. However, this brings in another consideration, namely that more men per oar will necessitate a longer oar and even if this could have the same gearing as the three-man oars, it would have to have the same striking rate, to be able to work in concert. There is no indication that different-sized oarcrews were used in the same ship (although presumably the rating number would refer to the largest) or that different lengths of oars were used in the same ship (undesirable for other reasons – see earlier and as borne out by the illustrations). The larger multi-manned oars have of course, to be significantly greater in girth and thus too large for the rowers to grasp. As in later times, the answer must have been to secure handholds to the face of the oar towards the rower. Another point is that, unlike their unfortunate successors, the ancient rowers, not being chained, could move both feet and bend their arms.

With multi-manned oars so closely spaced, both horizontally and vertically, one might assume that, in order to fit into the necessarily restricted space, both oar crews would, to an extent, have to share the same space without being interspaced (which reduces the pulling stroke of each rower, as discussed in Chapter 8).

As to the width of the ship, as opposed to previous systems, where the rowers in each reme were more or less 'stacked' vertically and could occupy mostly the same width, in the echelon method, every rower of both oars add their own width cumulatively. If we start with the maximum crew per oar of eight men, it should be possible to set a maximum beam for a hull (and of the sixteen, post). Allowing say 2 feet 3 inches/685mm width per rower, times eight, yields 18 feet /5.5m, doubled for the other side of the ship and adding a central gangway of say 4 feet/1.2m plus the distance between the outboard rower and thole pin on each side at a fairly arbitrary 7 feet/2.1m (it could be a little less) there results a waterline beam of say 42 feet/12.8m (allowing a foot /305mm either side for the thickness of the hull) and an overall beam of 54 feet/16.5m.

This in turn, may be used to establish the length of the ship, using a length-to-beam ratio of a modest six to one, resulting in an overall length of 252 feet/77m; at seven to one, this becomes 294 feet/89.6m, sizes that we know they were capable of building.[6]

The next consideration is the spacing of the oars, with their tholes. Returning to Anderson's scaling of the Samothrace Prow by three, the tholes are only about 2 feet /610mm apart horizontally and 1 foot/305mm vertically. This is more or less the same spacing in both planes as that between the thranite and zygite tholes of the trireme *Olympias*, but which of course, only has one rower per oar. With multi-manned oars there is not enough room between them for the lower set of rowers to work whether sitting or standing.

Another observation is that the depictions show an evenly spaced line of oars in each reme, i.e., there is no extra space between the pairs to permit a 'push-pull' arrangement. On the Palazzo Spada Relief however, there are vertical lines shown between each pair of oars, indicating a space before the next pair and allowing extra 'breathing space' between them. The Tiburina Monument shows the same and thus the spacing was greater and enough to allow the crews to operate (the Samothrace Prow only shows one pair of oarports on each side).

If the horizontal measurement of the Samothrace Prow is scaled up by six (instead of Anderson's three), the resultant 4 feet/1.2m space between the oars does allow the

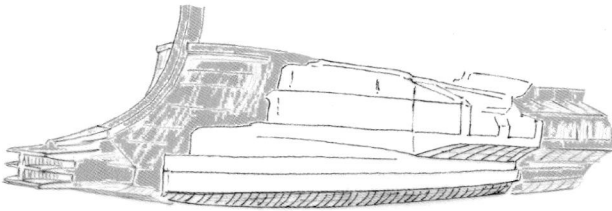

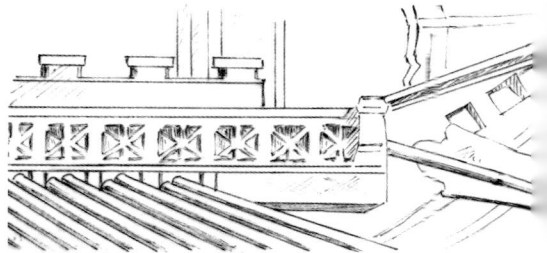

Figures 59. The Echelon System, evidence. Top left, the Samothrace Prow (Figure 45) close-up of the oarports, second century. Top right, the Lindos Monument (Figure 46) detail of the outrigger, mid third century. Centre left, the Isola Tiberina Monument, first century. Centre right, Ship prow atop an altar, end of second century. (*Archaeological Museum, Rhodes*) Bottom left, detail from the Praeneste Relief, first century. Bottom right, sketch detail of the Palazzo Spada Relief, first century (after Anderson).

lower rowers to work; however, scaling the vertical measurement by the same amount results in the lower oarsman colliding with the bench of the upper when pushing his oar to make the stroke. It does work if the vertical spacing is scaled up by three and the horizontal by six (per Figure 60). It may be thought that this is adapting the facts to fit a theory, but it also seems to fail to be workable any other way.

The oarports at that scale would become overlarge (6 feet by 2/1.8m by 610mm) and too easy a target for archers and catapults, quite apart from allowing the possible ingress of water. The Samothrace Prow is the only representation to actually show oarports (and is, of course, very much earlier); in all of the others, oars are shown simply emerging from the oarboxes. It is however exactingly executed and on the face of it we should accept it as accurate but with the size of the oarports exaggerated.

Considering the echelon system and the seeming ease and rapidity with which successive even-numbered rates were introduced, one might wonder if such a formula had been evolved for these ships. Instead, therefore, of having to design a completely new ship *ab initio* with the addition of extra rowers, the formula could be applied and dictate the dimensions of the hull, its constituent parts, components and fittings, to produce a new rate.[7]

This is, of course, pure conjecture but could explain how these ships could follow each other without any intervening experimental or trial pieces (as far as we know)

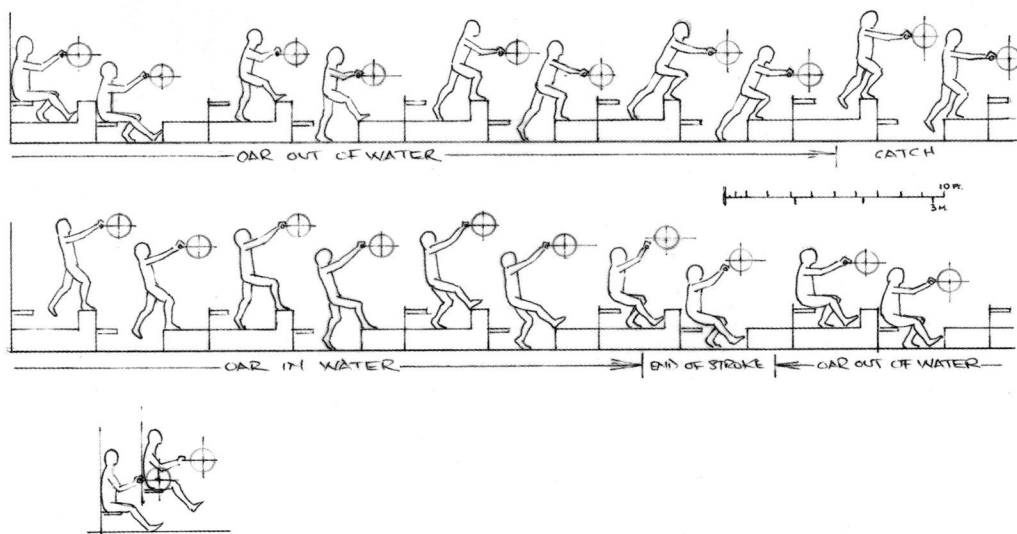

Figure 60. The Echelon System – making it work. At lower left, rowers are spaced per Anderson's scaling of the Samothrace Prow by three; as can be seen, this provides insufficient separation. Above, the vertical scaling remains the same, but the horizontal spacing is increased to six times the original, the extra spacing permitting the rowers to operate.

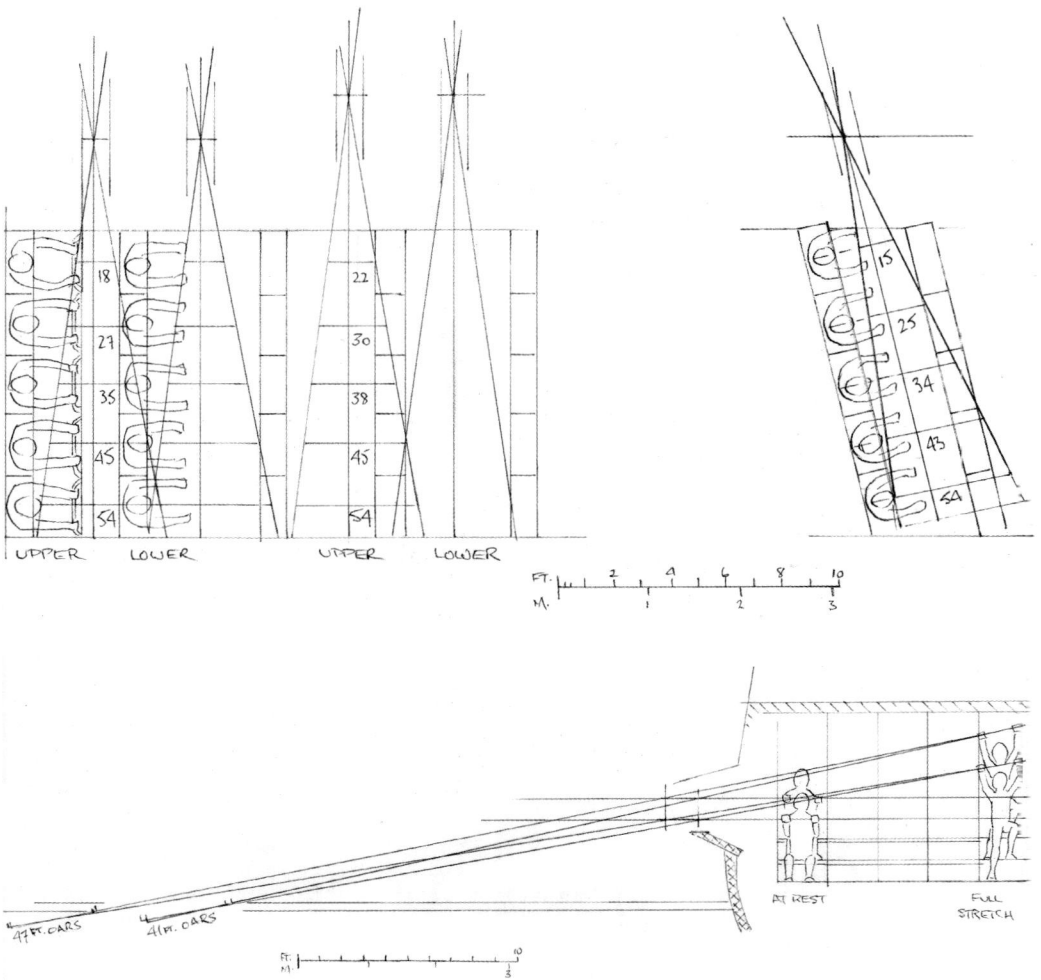

Figures 61. The Ten revisited, the echelon system applied to a ten. Top: plan; lower: cross-section (middle three rowers omitted). Comparison with the rowers' bench perpendicular to the hull (left) and canted (right).

comparatively speedily, in small numbers and thus without the production quantities to iron out the flaws in one, before proceeding to the next.

In Chapter Eight, the ten was examined as a trireme and as a 'conventional' bireme neither of which suggested that it was a notable improvement on its predecessors. However, considering the echelon system and its introduction sometime before 200 (and thus nearly a century after the first appearance of a ten) it could logically have been in response to the need to simplify and improve the performance of the bigger ships and the ten appears as the obvious candidate.

Having established that pairs of rowing crews *en échelon* can operate in elevation (Figure 60) a plan view was constructed for a ten (Figure 61) to prove the concept further. The respective lengths of pull of the rowers is shown (in inches) and for the left pair, the thole pin is quite close at 3.5 feet/1.07m from the outboard man, allowing for a 41 foot/12.5m oar with a gearing of 2.8. The right pair of crews have the thole moved outboard to 5 feet /1.52m and uses a 47 foot oar (14.3m) with the same gearing; the effect is to increase the length of pull of the outboard rowers.

The rowing benches have been arranged perpendicular to the ship centreline. In later, medieval, galleys the benches were canted at about thirteen degrees, but this was done initially from the need to stagger the rowers when rowing *alla sensile*, to allow room for them to operate their individual oars (see Figure 22). This arrangement of benches was retained after the *a scaloccio* system was introduced. Such canting of the benches seems to make little or no difference to the arrangements under consideration here (Figure 61).

As to the arrangement of the cross-section of the ship, Figure 61 (lower) shows how the lower oar has to be operated at a lesser angle; the tholes being in the same vertical plane rules out staggering one of the crews horizontally, therefore reducing the operating angle of the lower oar is the remaining and simplest solution. In the reconstructions, freeboard is little improved from the earlier examples, being only 3.5 feet/1.07m for the shorter oar and 4 feet/1.22m for the longer. Operating angles for both oars are very modest at between ten and twelve degrees and the posited upper deck height of 9.5 to 10 feet/2.88 to 3.05m is realistic.

Chapter 11

The Ultimate Galleys

This century of naval warfare was dominated by the race to build ever-bigger warships and led ultimately to the greatest oar-powered ships ever seen.

After Ipsos, Demetrios I's continued power depended on his fleet and he strove to develop ever-greater ships, intent on achieving naval dominance and was the greatest instigator of the trend. Already in 301, he had built a thirteen, following it with a fifteen and then a sixteen by 288.[1] The sequence was broken by the appearance of the *Leontophoros* in 280 (described as an eight). Demetrios followed with his next monster ship, the *Isthmia*, possibly an eighteen. Ptolemy II then went one further, with his twenty of about 260 and two thirties by 246. On a more practical note, his successor, Ptolemy III produced the twelve in 241 but as the ultimate, his successor in turn, Ptolemy IV capped them all with his forty in about 215.

It will be seen that the numbers of the rates do not always follow sequentially (see Appendix II) there being anomalies (for example the *Leontophoros*) and numbers missing from the sequence (there never was a fourteen). The twelve first appears long after much higher rates and can perhaps be supposed to have been an attempt at a more rational design.[2]

All of the preceding types so far mentioned continued in service, with the addition and adoption into formal naval service of a new type of light craft, the *Lembi*.

Lembi

A type of boat that had originated on the Illyrian Coast, Philip of Macedon impressed a great number into his service. It was a light, seaworthy, open boat, much loved by Illyrian pirates and already well established by the time they were first described by the Romans who came upon them in their Illyrian Wars (from 229). The descriptions do vary in detail: 'a lightly built open galley without a ram, carrying about fifty men and rowed in a single reme';[3] 'Of not more than sixteen oars' (presumably per side)[4] and 'carrying twenty men and two horses plus the crew'.[5] Thus, a smallish, open boat with a fair speed, beamy and capacious, without a ram and in various sizes. Perhaps it was originally an overall style of craft, peculiar to the Illyrian Coast, rather than a fixed design.[6] Later and probably by mid-century and with widespread military use,

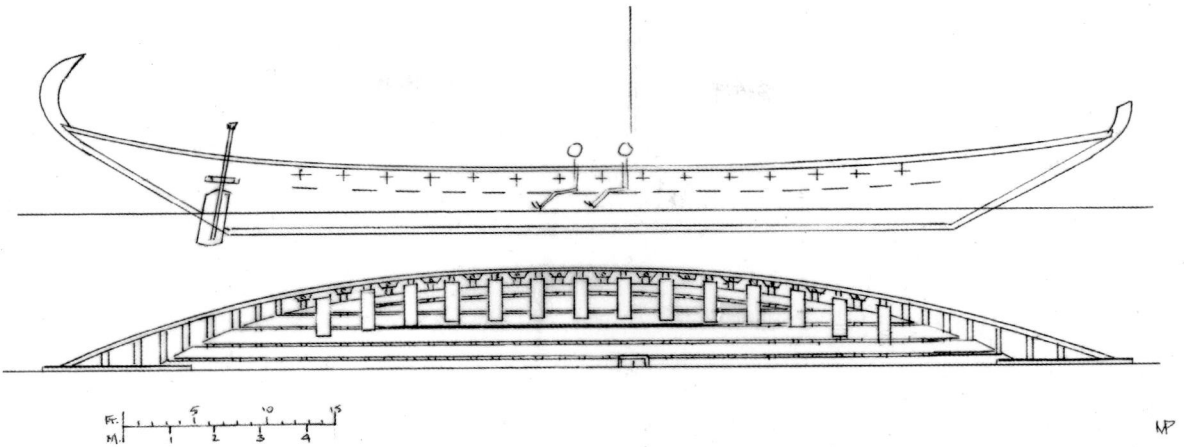

Figure 62. Suggestion for a *Lembi* of thirty oars based on a local-type craft seen at Split in Croatia. There is no reason why the benches should not be longer, to accommodate two rowers per oar, or even canted to allow each rower to have his own oar, as seen with the *hemiolia* (see Chapter 2, Figure 21).

boats still named *lembi* were adapted or built with some decking and protection for the rowers.[7] Further development led to a bireme version, but it is not clear whether this took place before the Romans adopted them.

The Romans captured and took large numbers of these boats into service as a general purpose light warship which they also definitely developed as a bireme version. They adapted and adopted the type in preference to, and to supersede, the long-established conter types, possibly due to their greater carrying capacity, greater beam giving them better seaworthiness and the fact that they were faster. To the Romans, it became the *Liburnian*.

The Eleven

Ironically, the next three rates to be introduced in turn all bore odd numbers and, as previously posited, are assumed not to have employed the échelon system.

For the eleven, the references are few, Plutarch[8] ascribing the type to Demetrios I by 310, relating that the timber for the ship was supplied cut into 75 feet/22.8m lengths.[9] From this it seems that Demetrios only built one of these ships, the next ship of his being referred to as a thirteen.

The next appearance of an eleven is in the list given by Athenaeus[10] of the fleet strength of Ptolemy II (282 to 246) which he relates, included no less than fourteen of them; this is of course, twenty or so years after the appearance of Demetrios' ship. Curiously, perhaps, the fleet list does not include any tens, a relatively popular rate elsewhere. Could it have been that Ptolemy had carried out an upgrade of his tens to re-rate them as elevens, or had built them as such *ab initio*? In any event, the rate does not appear to have been in combat and is not heard of again; that is not to say, of course, that they were not so used, simply not mentioned.

On the assumption that the eleven was a progressive development of the ten, achieved by the installation of an extra standing rower to the zygite and thalamite oars which both then become quadruple-manned. To allow clearance for the extra thalamite, he is on a deck 6 inches/152mm lower than his fellows and the extra zygite is 6 inches/152mm higher than the others. All rowers are using a 42 foot/12.2m oar at a gearing of 2.8. The only major alteration is the need to extend the outrigger so that the thranite thole can be re-mounted to accommodate the longer oar and in which case, the overall beam is increased by 4 feet/1.22m; even this is unnecessary if the thranites continue to use the 40 foot/12.2m oar (Figure 63).

The framework used for and to illustrate the nine and ten (see earlier) can be used, but the extra thalamites are occupying the lowest part of the central gangway, inhibiting access; the same hull, widened by about 5 feet/1.52m would overcome this but, in view of the small number deployed, one wonders if they would have been of new construction or, as said, converted tens.

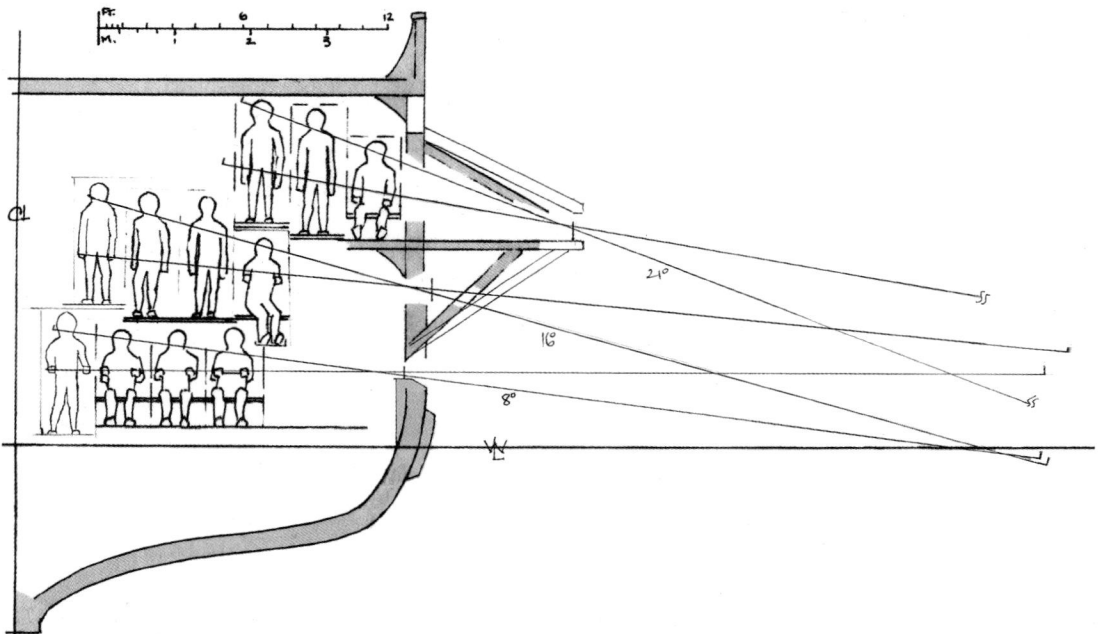

Figure 63. The Eleven as a trireme and a progression from the nine via a trireme ten, adding an extra rower at each stage.

The Thirteen

Once again it is Demetrios I who introduced this next rate, in 301. This particular ship is one of a number that he left at Athens (Piraeus) in that same year, when he went to join his father at Ephesus. Perhaps the ship was so new that it had not yet had its sea trials and awaited a crew to be trained and for the ship to be 'worked-up'; had it been so, he would have been sure to take such a prestigious ship. After Ipsos, the ships, including the thirteen were returned[11] to Demetrios I and he used it as his flagship, even entertaining Seleucos I on board.[12] Four more of the type are included in Athenaeus' list of Ptolemy II's fleet for 246.[13]

As to form, the existing 'rig' which has been used to demonstrate the nine, ten and eleven, cannot be stretched any further and the addition of two more rowers to each group must require a new, larger hull. The odd number of rowers per group dictates that different size crews for the oars in a group and four, four and five seems logical in a trireme layout (Figure 64). If a bireme is envisaged, an even wider hull will be needed to house a crew of six and seven per oar.

With more rowers per oar, the problem remains that an oar is simply a lever and the closer to the fulcrum, the less the arc of movement. As can be seen from Figure 61, the outboard rower pulls through only one third of the pull of the inboard man,

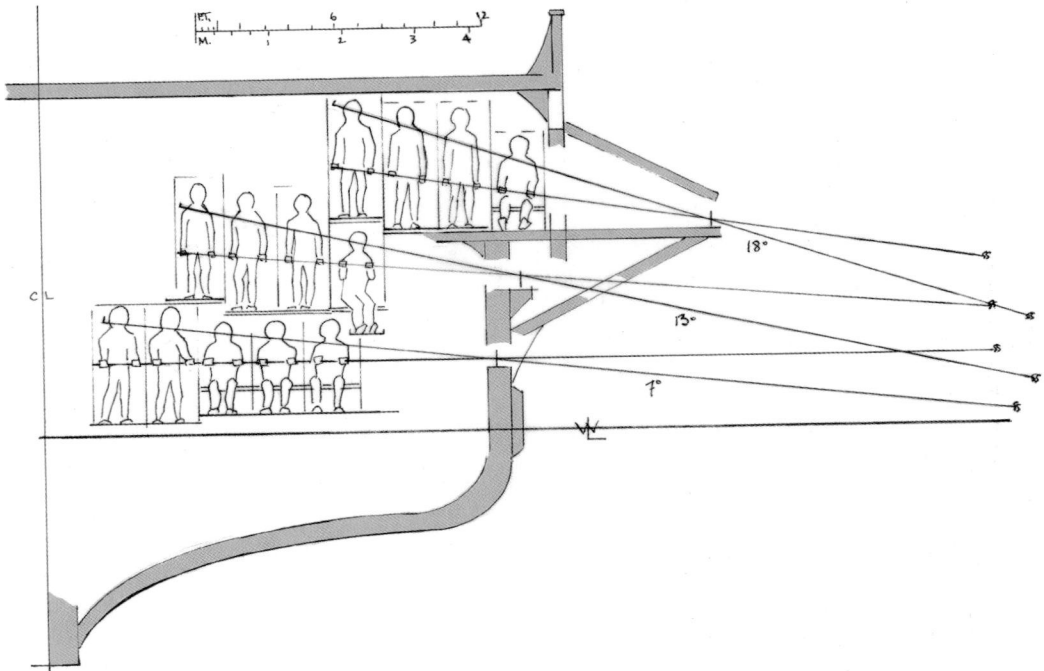

Figure 64. The Thirteen; a wider and deeper development of the eleven.

just enough to be useful. Obviously, any reduction in even this modest amount of work will render the man useless and not worth his added weight to the ship; any extra rowers will thus have to added inboard. As such, they will have to take more than the single step so far examined[14] and of course, to use a longer oar.

Thought has been given to adapting the echelon system to both the eleven and thirteen, although the extra oar length for the eleventh and thirteenth man respectively should not make an insuperable difference. Logically, as said before, this system lends itself to even-numbered crews and there appears to be no point in adding a rower to one oar of a pair without adding one to the other.

Returning to the trireme arrangement used for the eleven, a similar hull, with increased beam, will allow for an extra rower at thalamite and thranite levels, while maintaining balanced oar crews of four, four and five (Figure 64). The ship has been given extra draft to allow for the extra weight, especially on the upper deck, where one can assume the addition of more catapults and marines. The hull is broader and deeper and altogether more massive, but the deck height is unchanged, additions being more in the way of tophamper. The length of the oars must be increased by 2 feet 3 inches/685mm to accommodate the extra rower, for an overall oar length of 50 feet/15.2m. There seems little reason to suspect that the remes were any longer and that the ships therefore remained approximately the same length. This means of course, that the relative length-to-beam ratio decreases to about four-to-one (the same as a merchant ship) making the ships slower and less handy; on the other hand, they are increasingly akin to floating fortresses and probably impervious to ramming except by a similar large ship. The number of rowers required would now be about 714, allowing a thranite reme of thirty oars (30 times 4 men = 120 x 2 =240), a zygite reme of twenty-eight oars (28 times 4 men = 112 x 2 = 224) and a thalamite reme of twenty-five oars (25 times 5 men + 125 x 2 = 250).

The Fifteen

This next rate appears to be a 'one-off' and is only mentioned once in the sources[15] and then only in passing, Plutarch noting ships being built 'with fifteen and sixteen "ranges" of oars'. Built by Demetrios I, probably in the early 280s, it was likely included in the fleet that he took to invade Asia Minor in 287 and which appears to be the ship's only voyage. After the defeat of Demetrios I in 285, this fleet was left on the Anatolian Coast and surrendered to the victors. Some of the ships were taken into Seleucos' service and the fifteen was allocated to Ptolemy[16] in the division of spoils; nothing further is heard of it and it presumably was not retained in service or was converted to something else by Ptolemy as it is absent from the fleet list of 246.

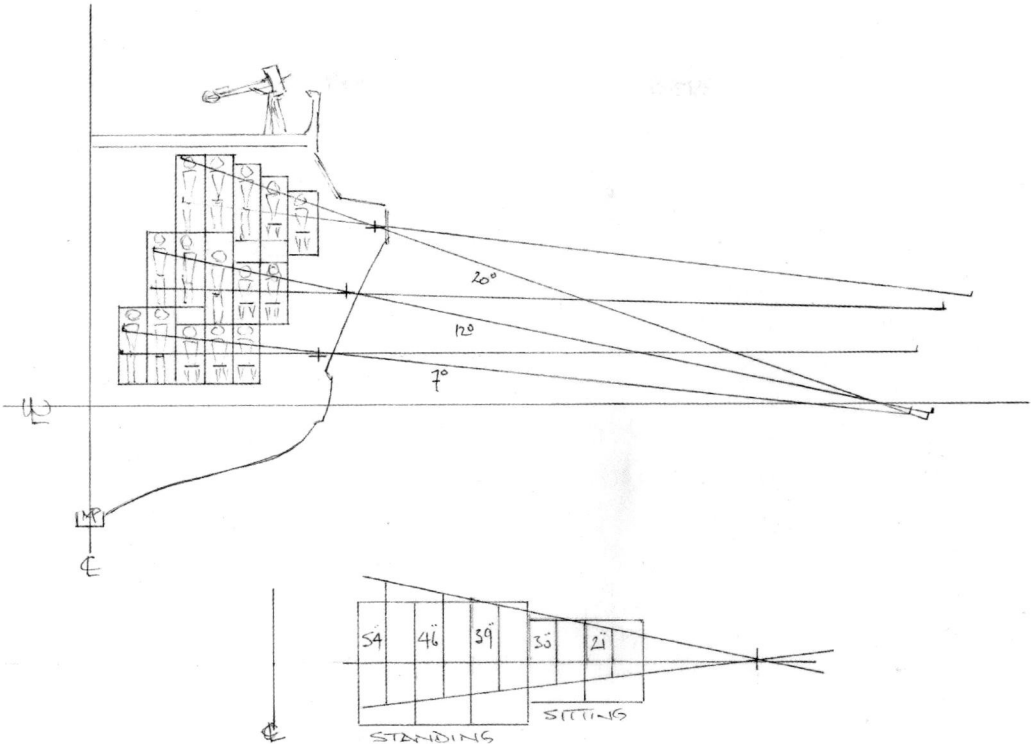

Figure 65. The Fifteen.

The fifteen is not mentioned again and no more seem to have been built, not even by Ptolemy with his predilection for big ships. From this we may deduce that the fifteen was perhaps not a success or worthy of emulation.

The suggested rowing layout (Figure 65) has three remes of five-man oars, pulling oars of 56 feet/17m at a rather high gearing of four. Interscalmium is suggested at 4 feet/1.2m but the width per man is rather too little at 2 feet /610mm; rowing crew must have been 800 men, perhaps even more. To accommodate them, the deck height above waterline is now 19.5 feet /5.9m and the draft shown (of 9 feet/2.7m) would have to have considerable ballast or be deeper, to compensate for the topweight.

The Sixteen

There is no surviving record to suggest that any more than a sole example of the sixteen was built. As such, this ship, unlike its contemporaries, had an extremely long career, spanning some 120 years. Built by Demetrios I in 288,[17] it joined the fleet with which he sailed to Asia Minor in 287. It seems to either have been left at Cos or escaped there after Demetrios' defeat in 285 and the victors allowed it to return to Antigonos II in Greece.

The ship next formed part of Antigonos II's fleet with which he sailed in 280, in an attempt to wrest the Macedonian throne from Ptolemy Keraunos. Antigonos' fleet was soundly beaten (no details of the action survive) and he withdrew.[18]

It remained the flagship after Antigonos II became King of Macedon and throughout the reigns of his successors, although inactive. It was not until the second war against Rome and her allies (200 to 197) that a Macedonian fleet was again active, under Philip V; the fleet with which he fought the battles of Chios (Chapter 9, Appendix) and Miletos, does not however include it, Philip using a ten as his flagship.

With the end of that war in 197, the peace treaty called for 'and the surrender of all his warships with the exception of five light vessels and his huge flagship in which the men rowed eight to an oar'.[19]

Finally, at the end of the third Macedonian War in 167, the occupying Roman troops found this ship. Despite not having been to sea for many years it must have been in remarkably good condition as the Romans sailed it all the way back to Italy and right up the Tiber to Rome, where the Consul was rowed upriver, 'the populace keeping up with the splashing oars as they slowly took the ship along'.[20]

There it was housed in a special shed and was further used in about 149, to house Carthaginian prisoners-of-war.[21]

It says much for the ship and its seakeeping qualities that it was capable of being sailed from the northern Aegean, the length of that sea, around the Peloponnese, across the Ionian Sea and right around the Italian Coast, despite being 120 years old.[22]

As to the form of the ship, did Demetrios somehow add an extra rower to a second fifteen to improve it. Morrison thinks that it was a trireme,[23] which would make sense as, having built the

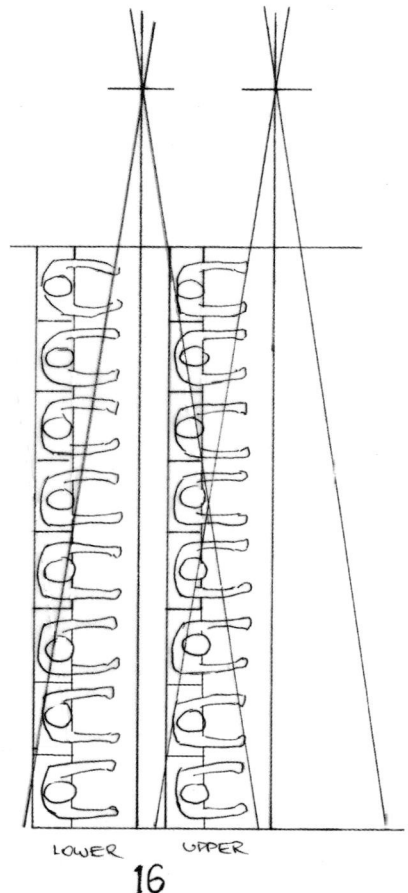

Figure 66. The Sixteen. If the ship had been arranged as a bireme, rowed by the echelon system, it would have been the ultimate expression of that system, twin eight-man oars.

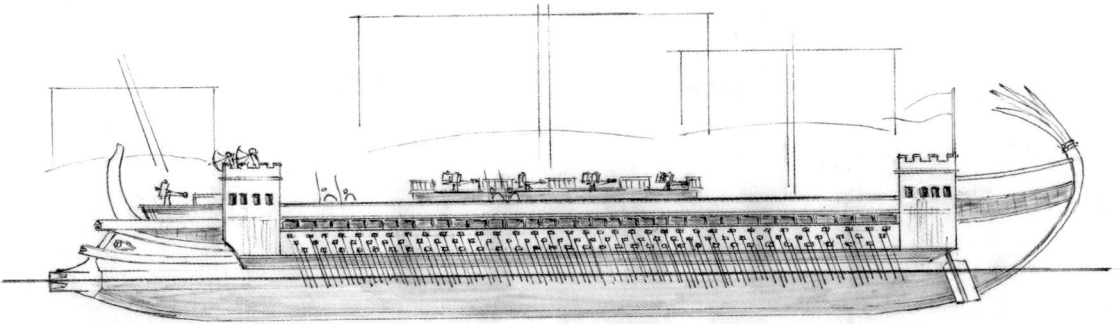

Figure 67. An impression of the Sixteen as a trireme. The sketch is pure conjecture but intended to convey what must have been the sheer size and power of the ship. Towers are jettied out on each side forward and aft of the rowing compartment and raised platforms are mounted forward and amidships to carry the ship's artillery.

fifteen, the laying down of a second to follow it is logical. The ship having proved disappointing, the second ship was modified by the addition of the extra rower. If this were so however, why was the first fifteen not retro-fitted to bring it up to the same standard? Livy describes the ship as 'of almost unmanageable size'. Both Rodgers[24] and Connolly[25] posit the ship as a bireme, Casson posits both.[26]

The only detail known for (reasonably) sure is that, according to Livy[27] it had sixteen files (*versus*) of rowers, that is sixteen lines of rowers from forward to aft.

As a trireme and an 'improved fifteen', the extra rower could most easily be added at zygite level (Figure 65) yielding an improvement that made this ship more satisfactory and justify its long life; an amendment that neither Demetrios nor Ptolemy carried out on the original fifteen.

As a bireme, the ship could employ the echelon system (Figure 66) in its ultimate form, with pairs of eight-man oars. The ship would be of a completely different hull form to the eleven/thirteen/fifteen line of development. A twenty-five oar reme would give a total of a hundred oars, needing 800 rowers, but as it is a different hull, the reme could be expanded to thirty oars, 120 in total.

As to size, if it was an 'upgraded' fifteen, then it would of course, be the same as that ship. As a bireme however, with the thirty-oar reme, it would increase in length to some 230 feet /70m. with a waterline beam of about 40 feet/12.2m and giving a very satisfactory length-to-beam ratio of 6.4. Additionally, it could be less in height above the water, all of which would improve the ship's performance.

Finally, the fifteen and sixteen are lumped together in the all-too-brief source, no other differentiation being made between them, yet this ship sailed all the way to Italy, over open seas and around some very dangerous and notorious coasts.

The *Leontophoros*

In a brief interlude when they were on speaking terms, Lysimachus, having heard of Demetrios' great ships, asked if he might see them. Demetrios agreed and demonstrated his fifteen and sixteen and entertained Lysimachus aboard the thirteen.[28]

To counter these ships, Lysimachus, shortly before 280, had a ship built at Heraclea on the Black Sea, called the *Leontophoros* (Lionbearer) which became 'famous for its size and beauty'.[29]

After Lysimachus' death, Ptolemy Keraunos acquired the ship and it formed part of his fleet with which he defeated Antigonos II in 280. The ship was, perhaps ironically, taken over by Antigonos II when he took the Macedonian throne and was in the fleet with which he defeated Ptolemy II's bigger fleet in 258 at Cos;[30] thereafter it is not heard of again. For its moment of glory therefore, this was a ship that won against Antigonos' and Ptolemy's great ships and can therefore be assumed to have proven superior – unless that is, that it was pure luck that enabled it to prevail on the day and such things do happen.

'In each file 100 men rowed so that there were 800 in each part, 1600 in both; those assigned to fight from the decks totalled 1,200, there were two helmsman.'[31] The problem is that Memnon describes the ship as an '*octereismia e Leontoforos*'[32] i.e. as an eight called *Leontophoros*, implying that it was half the size of its opponent's biggest ship, which it beat. However, the number of rowers that he relates, at 1,600, is roughly twice that of the sixteen. Further, Memnon specifies that there were 800 rowers 'in each part'; does he mean each side of the ship's hull or, as Casson posits,[33] the ship was a catamaran and 'each part' referred to the twin hulls? This of course, calls for two eights, joined by a bridging deck. This solution is ingenious for also answering the question of deck space for the 1,200 marines. The problem is that the eight is not mentioned in the sources until the end of the century, some eighty years later. It is known that a Roman quinqereme (five) had a standard complement of forty marines, to which were added, for battle, a century of troops (sixty to eighty men).[34] This ship had to provide for ten times that number, which once more, Casson posits, could be accommodated on the broad bridging deck between the hulls. Further, he points out that Memnon's description of the ship as an eight would mean a 'double-eight', but he suggests a bireme arrangement of four-man oars with fifty men in each file and fifty oars in each reme; the given file of 100 rowers, one behind the other, is therefore halved by this interpretation.

Morrison[35] retains a monohull some 361 feet/110m long with eight files per side but allows an interscalmium of only 3 feet/980mm to obtain a 'rowing room' 300 feet /98m long, leaving only 40 feet/12m for (very blunt) bow and stern sections and

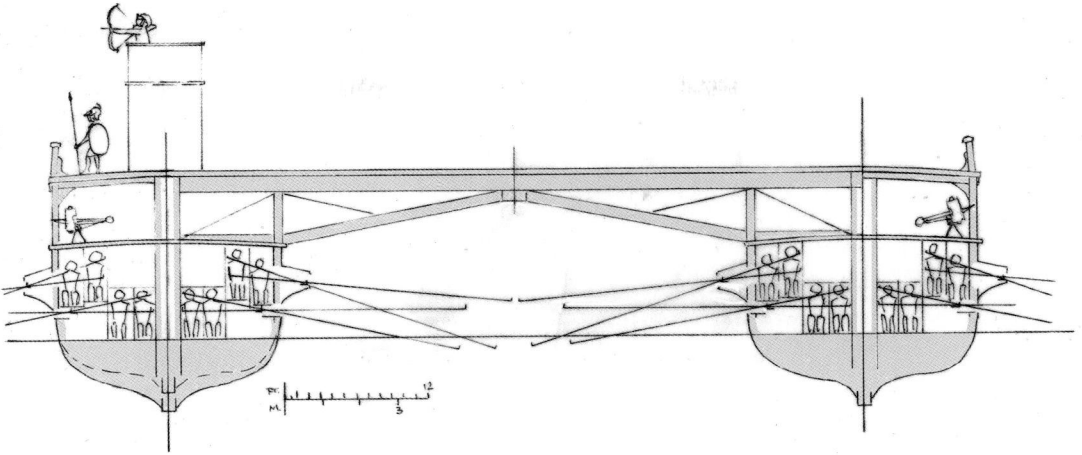

Figure 68. The *Leontophoros* as a 'double-four' catamaran. The left hull shows the original draft of a four; both have the extra deck height added to carry supports and reinforcement for the bridging deck. The extra deck has been utilised as a gallery for the artillery and an outline tower has been shown on the left hull.

being rather too little. As mentioned above, a 4 feet/1.2m. interscalmium is more reasonable for multi-manned oars (and in line with Renaissance practice) which of course, increases the 'rowing room' to 400 feet/122m plus the same for the ends, totalling 440 feet/134m and which seems too long (if we assume that Ptolemy II's forty (see later) was the biggest at 420 feet/128m long).

The problem remains the file of 100 rowers, which is just too many. Imagining the ship as an 'echelon eight', matching the '800 in each part', the length of a thranite (generally the longest) reme in all of the ships so far considered is about thirty oars; given an interscalmium of 4 feet/1.2m. plus say 30 feet/9m for each 'end' yields an average length in the region of 180 feet /55m, the ships having grown in mass rather than length.

If *Leontophoros* was an elongated version of the sixteen, it might have a reme of fifty oars and a resulting overall length of some 260 feet/80m, the extra length and power giving it speed but a slower rate of turn (opening it perhaps to shorter ships being able to turn inside it and ram). This all seems quite reasonable and fits with the known details to date but, once more, it does not amount to a file of 100 rowers.

Finally, perhaps the file had half of the rowers pulling and half pushing the same oar (despite pushing being less efficient); this would also give a reme of fifty oars but as the interscalmium would have to be doubled, we return to the excessive length problem. The problem remains also of how to accommodate the 1,200 marines plus the sailors.

Returning to Casson's suggestion of a catamaran but discounting the 'double-eight' (and as we have no evidence of its existence for another eighty years) we can readily substitute and consider a 'double-four.' The four was already well known (see Chapter 2) and should have been within the capabilities of the shipbuilders of Heraclea, who had not previously, as far as we know built any of the bigger rates. Thus, two fours, joined by a bridging deck would allow for 'eight files in each part.' They would of course, have to be much longer than normal (over twice as long) to accommodate the 100-man files but, as a bireme four, the interscalmium is less at 3.5 feet/1.06m giving a reme of 350 feet/106.6m plus say 50 feet /15.2m and thus an overall ship length of 400 feet/122m. As to beam, using the author's cross-section of a four,[36] a space of 16 feet/4.9m must be allowed for the oars of the inward-facing side of each hull, plus a couple of feet/600mm, more to allow them to operate in clear water and not foul each other, a total of 34 feet/10.4m between the two hulls and to be spanned by the bridging deck. The ship's beam is thus the two fours at 24 feet/7.3m each and the bridge, totalling 82 feet/25m.

A problem with the catamaran could be to ensure sufficient strength of the bridging deck and it having to contend with the movement of two hulls. Bracing to the hull sides for the entire centre section is not possible as it would obstruct the oars; it could be that the covering deck was elevated a deck space above the rowers to give height for bracing (Figure 68). Given the extra weight and to maintain the waterline vis-à-vis the rowers, the hulls would have to be deeper and thus displacement increased for extra buoyancy, beyond that of a normal four.

The above satisfied Memnon's particulars but yields a monster of a ship, 400 feet/122m long and 82 feet/25m. wide carrying nearly 3,000 men. The practicality

Figure 69. Sketch of the *Leontophoros* if it had been composed of two fours linked to form a catamaran.

of this proposal as a real-life floating vessel is perhaps difficult to envisage but if it existed as such, then possibly it inspired Ptolemy II's later huge ships or, possibly, Memnon, writing three centuries later, exaggerated. If so, particularly as to the length of the files of rowers, a practical ship can emerge, with an advantage in battle that it can withdraw the outboard oars and manoeuvre using the centre remes, which would be impervious to attack.

Isthmia

Stung perhaps by his defeat in 280 at the hands of Lysimachus' fleet (which included the *Leontophoros*) Antigonos II built a ship to counter it, the *Isthmia* (named of course, after the Isthmian Games). With this ship in his fleet, he defeated the bigger fleet of Ptolemy II in battle off Cos in 258. Thereafter and in thanks for his victory, Antigonos appears to have dedicated the ship as an offering to Apollo and it was retired from service, by which time it would have been, at most, about twenty years old.

As to the form of the ship, it was said to be '*triarmenos*' and to have 'as many as nine rowers from the decks'[37] and two *katastromata* (upper decks).[38]

Finally, Athenaeus states 'I intentionally pass over the sacred trireme built by Antigonos (II) with which he defeated the Commander of Ptolemy (II) off Leukollos, a city under the dominion of Kos … *omissis* … but it was not one third or perhaps even one quarter of the size of the Syracusan vessel.'[39] By the 'Syracusan Vessel' we must assume that he was referring to Hieron's great merchant ship of over 200 feet (62m) in length and the 'sacred trireme' can only be the *Isthmia*. However, one third of Hierons' ship length would only be 67 feet/20.5m and one quarter a mere 50 feet/15.2m, so it seems that the dimensions are quite wrong and hardly suited to a ship built to outmatch the mighty *Leontophoros*.

The term '*triarmenos*' can mean three-levelled (or decked) or three-masted[40] but having some grouping of nine rowers would logically suggest a trireme arrangement (Athenaeus calls it this).

Having examined the nine as a trireme (Figures 40 and 41) one could posit the *Isthmia* as a catamaran based on two such hulls. However, the overall beam of two such hulls is 89 feet/27.2m and for the 'inboard' oars to work, they would have to be separated by another 60 feet/18.3m or so; the resultant figure appears far too wide to be spanned by a timber bridge. If the inboard oars were not used, the two hulls could be much closer together, joined by a shorter bridging deck. This could yield a ship which although assumed to be shorter than *Leontophoros*, would have mass and be able to turn in a tighter arc; against this is the fact that it only has half of the potential oarpower of each hull.

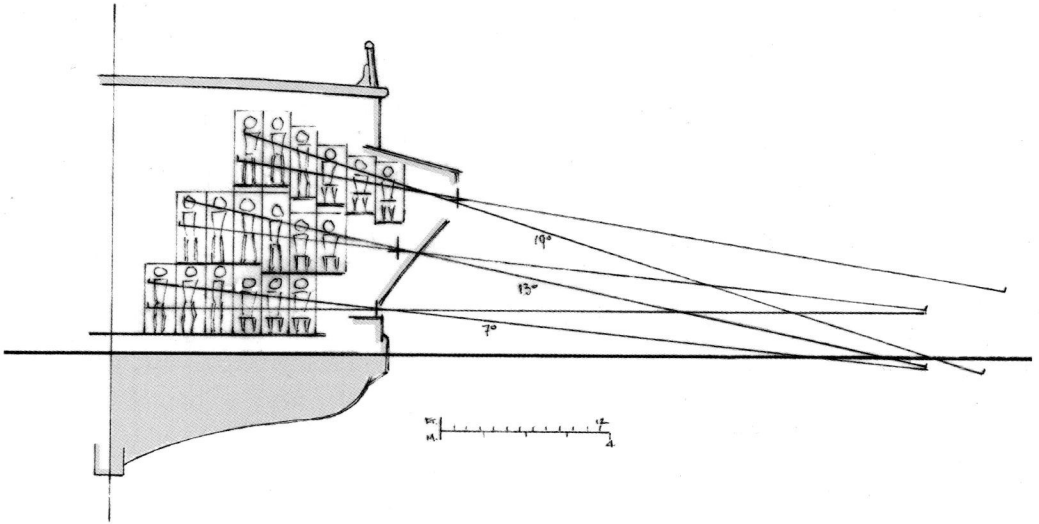

Figure 70. The *Isthmia* as a trireme eighteen. Oars are 58 feet 6 inches/17.8m in length at a gearing of 3.4. Waterline beam is 41 feet 6 inches /12.6m and 52 feet /15.8m overall. At a ratio of 6 to 1, length would be 249 feet /76m.

It has been suggested[41] that the ship was an eighteen and indeed this would seem logical. As a monohull, the ship would be a trireme with each oar manned by six rowers, but this is the double of and at total variance from the only clear detail in the description. However, as has been seen, Athenaeus was wrong in describing the length of the ship so perhaps the reference to nine rowers was also lacking, in which case the ship would indeed have been an eighteen (Figure 70). As such it would also be big and, if we posit a reme of forty-five oars with a 4 feet /1.2m interscalmium and allow 80 feet /24.4m for the ends, overall length is 260 feet /79.2m, length to beam ratio becomes a reasonable 6.26 and a complement of 1,620 rowers is required.

The Twenty and Thirty

These two rates can be conveniently dealt with together for two reasons. Firstly they were unique and were, with one exception, the ultimate expression of the oar-powered ship – nothing approaching them had been tried before, or since. Secondly, their sheer size and manpower requirement made them impracticable – they were never used in action and rarely put to sea or undertook any long voyages (again with one possible exception). By the time that they were built, the Ptolemies had a massively powerful fleet of other rates even without them and no real opposition at that time; they were showpieces and seem to have been little more than *folies de grandeur*.

The Twenty

Only one ship of this rating is known and was built[42] by or for Ptolemy II (282 to 246) in about 260.[43] The ship was said to have had four masts and eight catapults and doubtless inspired Ptolemy to go on to build even bigger ships. If the ship was in fact built at Corinth, then it is the only one of these giants known to have made a sea voyage, from there to Alexandria.

As a catamaran, with two hulls linked by a bridging deck, the ship could be a hybrid of two tens put together. We do not know the beam of this ship, unlike the forty, so need not necessarily be limited by that constraint. However, a trireme ten

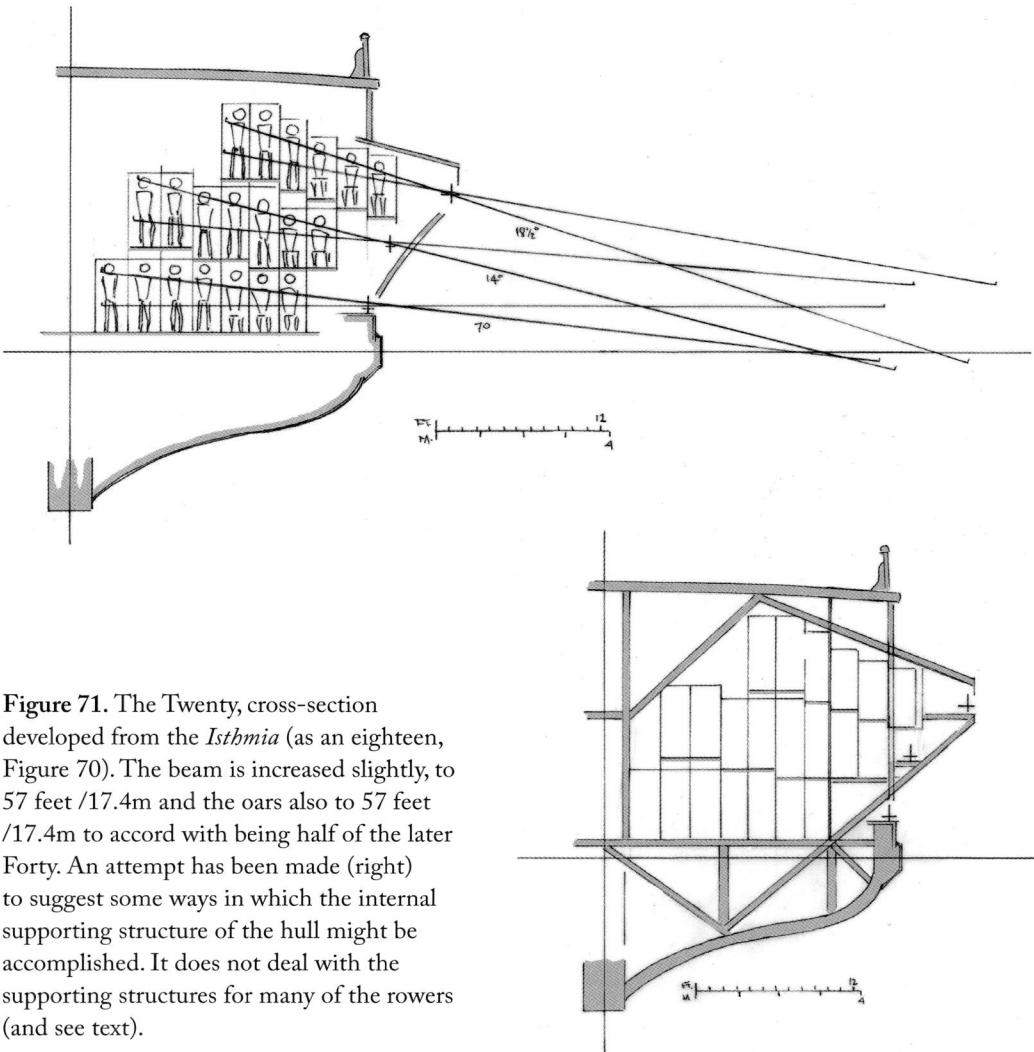

Figure 71. The Twenty, cross-section developed from the *Isthmia* (as an eighteen, Figure 70). The beam is increased slightly, to 57 feet /17.4m and the oars also to 57 feet /17.4m to accord with being half of the later Forty. An attempt has been made (right) to suggest some ways in which the internal supporting structure of the hull might be accomplished. It does not deal with the supporting structures for many of the rowers (and see text).

had an overall beam of about 43 feet/13.1m (Figures 42 and 43) plus a clearance gap between them, which would need to be about 48 feet/14.6m and would give an overall beam in the region of 134 feet/41m or more and a lot more than appears practical. The twenty can however be made to work as a monohull. If it, and the forty, considered later, were a catamaran made up of two twenties, then we have a definite guide in that the hull of the forty was said to be 57 feet/17.4m in the beam, (presumably of each hull, discussed later).

The ship can only be a trireme with any combination of thalamites, zygites and thranites, bearing in mind the previous comments about a maximum of eight rowers per oar and balancing the oarcrews, perhaps seven, seven and six respectively would be best.

Figure 71 is a proposed cross-section of the trireme, monohull twenty and shows how the twenty rowers can be positioned to work. This takes no account of the need for an internal structure to support them or the deck above, let alone the weight of added towers, artillery and hundreds of deck crew, sailors and marines. The inset drawing suggests some ways of bracing the hull and outrigger but does not support the rowers, nor provide vertical support for the upper deck between the centre and outer hull side. As with the model (Figure 43) experimentation and careful positioning of the rowers could suggest positioning of a supporting structure which does not impede their movement.

The Thirty

According to Atheanaeus' list, Ptolemy II had two of these monsters in 246, built shortly after the twenty. Bearing in mind the parameters previously considered (not more than three remes; maximum of eight men per oar) there does not appear to any way in which this ship could be a single hull. The linking of two fifteens as a catamaran would seem a logical solution. Once again, it is the gap between the hulls (about 80 feet /24.4m) to allow the facing remes to work that is the problem, unless of course those remes were not manned and only the outboard oars were used, when it could be much less. Once more, the question of the ship being under-powered arises, but then as they never had to put to sea or be challenged in any way, one can only wonder at the thinking that produced two of them.

The Twelve

In almost a return to more reasonably sized ships, the next rate to be mentioned is the twelve. The only reference to it is once more from Athenaeus[44] in his list of Ptolemy II's naval strength in 246 and in which only two are noted.

There is no record of this rate having been engaged in battle, or indeed, ever again appearing in naval lists. One is tempted to regard these ships as augmented and re-rated elevens, perhaps, rather than examples of a completely new type (Figure 72A).

The alternative is widened bireme tens, rowed *en échelon* by six-man oar crews (Figure 72B). This would seem to be the logical and most straightforward solution, if indeed, they were a new design.

It is always possible that the existence and sole appearance was due to propaganda, some extra men having been drafted aboard a couple of tens for the occasion for

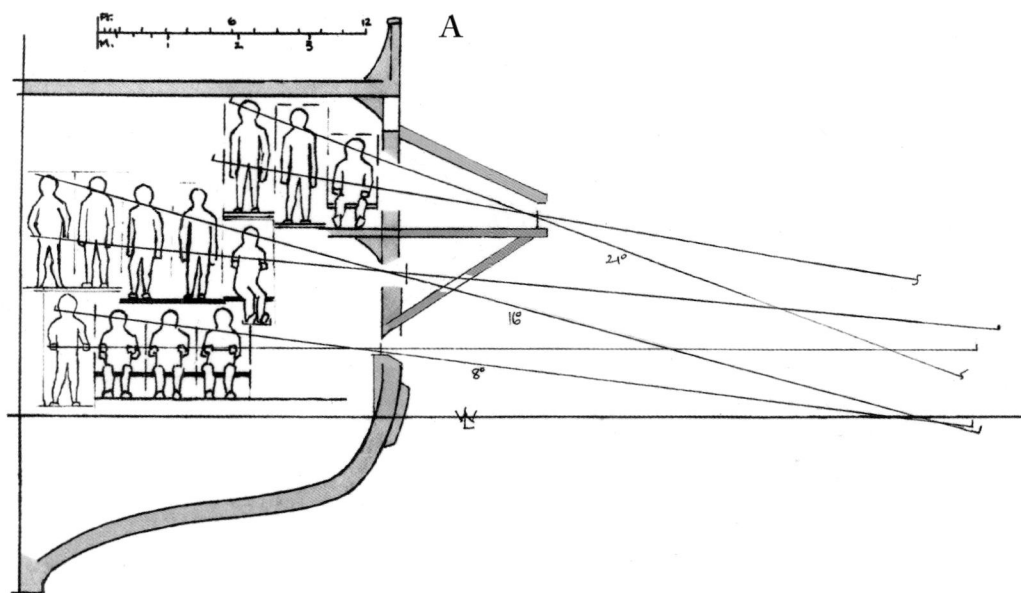

Figures 72A and 72B. The Twelve. A: As a 're-rated' eleven, an extra zygite rower has been added enabling the ship to be re-rated without having to build a new, bigger ship and with only minimal internal alteration. B: As a completely new hull, with rowers using the echelon system; essentially an enlarged echelon ten.

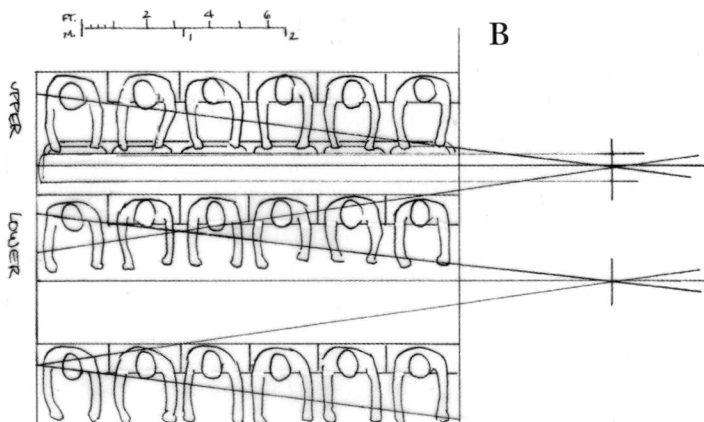

publicity, so that the 'new rate' could be shown and duly recorded; they were never put to the test.

Presumably these two ships continued to serve in the Ptolemaic Fleet, with no notable distinction that has come down to us, eventually being discarded and not repeated.

The Forty

The ultimate in oared ships, the sole example of the forty was built for Ptolemy III in 241. Casson has suggested that for ships larger than a sixteen, a new system of oar arrangement must have been devised.[45] He used the forty as the ship to develop his theory as it is the only one for which the dimensions are actually known and as the logical progression of the series twenty, thirty, forty.[46] Thus, we know that the ship was 420 feet/128m long and 57 feet/17.4m beam and that the thranite oars were also 57 feet/17.4m in length. The fact that they were designated as 'thranite' implies that there were three remes. There were more than 4,000 rowers. Length-to-beam ratio was thus 7.37.

Casson's solution as to how the ship worked is to suggest that it was a catamaran, with two hulls joined by a 'bridging' deck, each hull with its rowing crew working on both sides, i.e. with four lots of oars working together. Ships were known to have been lashed together and decked over (see e.g. the siege ships at Tyre and Rhodes) so an extended deck to give sufficient separation to enable the, now inboard, oars of each hull to work is logical. He suggests eight thranites per oar, seven zygites per oar and five thalamites per oar, giving the group of forty in each hull (although, as has been examined, the oar crews must be more balanced, seven, seven and six being preferable and secondly, that the order should be reversed, with the larger crews manning the lower oars).

There are however, four problems presented by this solution. Firstly, Casson has the inboard oars of each hull working by intermeshing with each other, allowing the hulls to be only 30 feet/9.1m apart, which they have to be within the known beam of the ship; surely (as has been seen in the previous catamaran reconstructions) this could not work in practice, with two sets, six remes, of oars trying to work in the same space; even without taking into account the action of the sea, they must clash. To work with any efficiency, each set of oars must be able to work in their own space and have clear water between the blades of the two sets, necessitating more than twice that clearance between hulls. Even if the oar-sets of the two opposite hulls were staggered, there could only be minimal space between blades trying to work in the same water. A 57 foot/17.4m oar had approximately 37 feet/11.3m of its length outboard when raised;[47] thus, two hulls side by side needed twice that plus a bit between, say 80 feet/24.4m to give clear water for each set of inboard oars. If one adds the beam of each ship, the total becomes far beyond the known beam (at 57 times two, plus 80, equals 194 feet /59m).

Secondly, it is known from later times, that rowing benches were canted at up to twenty degrees and that rowers were allowed about 2 feet 4 inches/700mm in width each; thus, a five-man oar bench would be 11.5 feet/3.5m and an eight-men bench some 18.5 feet/5.6m long.[48] If we allow 17 feet beam for each canted thranite (eight-man) bench, plus say a 4 foot /1.2m. gangway in between and another 4 feet/1.2m each side between the outboard end of the bench and the thole, each hull is forty-six feet beam, twice which, even without the bridging deck, exceeds the known maximum beam. It may be argued that the 57 feet beam was meant for each hull, which would also be in proportion with the hulls of the big ships already considered, however, the remaining dimensions are given as overall for the ship and no differentiation made for the beam measurement.

Thirdly, there is, once more, the strength of the bridging deck to consider, which would need to be in the order of nearly 100 feet/30m overall, including the parts anchored on the two hulls.[49] With about 80 feet/24.4m of unsupported beam and thus more than twice that of the catamaran *Leontophoros* (and about which there are misgivings) the thickness of the timbers, even if laminated must be considerable and heavy and also exert considerable strain on the hull mountings, especially as the hulls will be individually affected by the action of the sea and working against it (the linking of two fifteens, to make up a thirty and two twenties for the forty, brings the same problems).

Finally, there were at least 4,000 rowers in all and as the rate referred to the number of rowers in a group (on one side of the ship) the 2,000 in each hull, divided by the group of forty yields only fifty such groups, each with up to three oars, i.e. three fifty-oar remes. The interscalmium of fifteenth century AD galleys was at most 3 feet 9 inches/1m, so even allowing 4 feet/1.22m, fifty oars only take up 200 feet/61m or less than half of the hull length. The later interscalmium was, of course for monoreme galleys and it has been seen that the trireme system using multi-manned oars required a greater interscalmium. If it were half as much again, it would fit comfortably in the known hull length but power and speed depends on the maximum number of oars being used per given length of hull and, for all of the four thousand men used, the power output of the ship must have been minimal. Perhaps this was, as Plutarch described it, 'the ship was only for show, differing little from buildings fixed to the ground, it moved unsteadily and with difficulty to appear for display, not use.'[50]

A different set of problems arise when trying to envisage the ship as a mono hull. Firstly, the ship is described as being 'double-prowed' and 'double-sterned', indicating a catamaran. Secondly, as a trireme the ship, as has been suggested, would have oars respectively manned by seven thranites, seven zygites and six thalamites, to make up the group of forty rowers. However, in previous rates, the number has related to the total of rowers in a group on each side of the ship, whereas the above suggestions actually give twenty per side.

Taking advantage of the incredible length of the ship,[51] and using a 3 feet 9 inches/1m interscalmium, one can fit a reme of one hundred oars along a side, totalling 350 feet (106.6m), still leaving 70 feet/21.3m for the ends; as a trireme with a six-man oar at thranite level, a seven-man oar at zygite level and a seven-man oar at thalamite level, requiring two thousand rowers a side. Unfortunately, as a monoreme, this brings us back to the fact that the 'forty' cannot apply to one side of this ship, only to the complete crew. Rodgers[52] has a slightly different solution, proposing a ten-man, six-man and four-man combination, but this still only gives two thousand men per side and also does not really address the meaning of 'double-prowed' and 'double-sterned'. The fundamental problem is that if the rate refers to the rowing group on one side, it is impossible to have forty men working three oars.

Logically, Casson's interpretation is the only one that produces a 'forty' and surely the beam measurement given relates to the individual hulls and has become confused over the centuries of copying and translation, but here we are clutching at straws.

This ship was mentioned but only once and never put to sea. It must have existed, even if briefly, for Athenaeus to have been able to leave such an accurate set of its measurements, even going on[53] to describe in detail how it was launched. It appears in isolation some thirty years after the twenty and thirty and at a time when the Ptolemaic navy was not involved in overseas adventures. Perhaps this ultimate rowing ship provided a last hurrah for the giant oared warship and a prototype for Ptolemy III's equally huge river barge that shortly followed it.

The Missing Number, Fourteen

As has been seen, the ten was followed by a twelve, the latter appearing well after many larger types. There was no successive progression from the ten, through the twelve, to fourteen and then on to sixteen, eighteen and so on. The rating fourteen did not appear at all, despite the even-numbered progression and that the fact that it could lend itself to a brace of seven-man oars using the echelon system.

As has been said, the performance and probably the expense of these ships failed to encourage navies to invest in any more than a few of each (and not at all in the west). The numbers built do not compare to the hundreds and hundreds of lesser rates. Their use in battle having failed to prove decisive, presumably as had been hoped, the continued building of even bigger ships can have been solely exercises in prestige and self-aggrandisement.

PART V

THE POWER FROM THE WEST
200 TO 100 BC

Prow of a Roman warship, late first century BC. (*Archaeological Museum, Modena*)

Chapter 12

The Shifting Balance of Power

200 Athens, in the belief that Rome, Rhodes and Pergamum were opposing the expansionist plans of Philip V of Macedon, declared war (too soon) against him; Philip, returning from his adventures in Asia Minor with his forces, duly attacked Athens and ravaged Attica, his Greek allies attacking Sparta. Rome sent envoys to both Philip and to Antiochus III, the Seleucid King, warning them against expansionist moves, which did not however, prevent Antiochus from capturing Sidon. For his part, Philip attacked cities along the Hellespont.[1]

The appeal to Rome by Rhodes and Pergamum for help to oppose this expansionism and Philip's actual attacks, was answered in 200 by the despatch of a Roman war fleet and the start of (for the Romans) the Second Macedonian War (200 to 196). Fresh from their defeat of Carthage, the Romans and their navy were the masters of the central and western Mediterranean and had a very large, well-equipped, efficient and battle-hardened navy, at the peak of its power (despite Livy's comments post). They had over two hundred ships, with battle formations made up principally of fives (*quinqueremes*), together with fours (*quadriremes*) supported by triremes and smaller. The Roman army crossed the Adriatic to Apollonia, escorted by thirty-eight quinqueremes, under Marcus Valerius Laevinus.[2] To support the Athenians, twenty triremes, loaded with 1,000 extra troops were sent to Piraeus, where they were joined by three Rhodian fours. Rhodes was minded to join the Romans as Philip had sent agents to undermine and destroy their fleet by inciting Crete to war against them.[3]

The allied fleet found no opposition and could attack enemy shores at will and, before the end of the year, they captured Chalcis on Euboea.

199 In 199, the Romans increased their fleet to fifty warships,[4] to join the twenty-four Pergamene and twenty Rhodian warships, making up the allied fleet. Philip had only twenty heavy ships remaining and many small ships and could not hope to oppose the allied fleet which proceeded to attack Chalkidiki itself and capture Oreus; the following year they captured Eretria, although an attack on Corinth was repulsed. In November 198, Philip met the Roman and allied commanders near Thermopylae for peace talks, Philip having sailed there by

MAP 14 - CHANGING FORTUNES - 200 TO 100

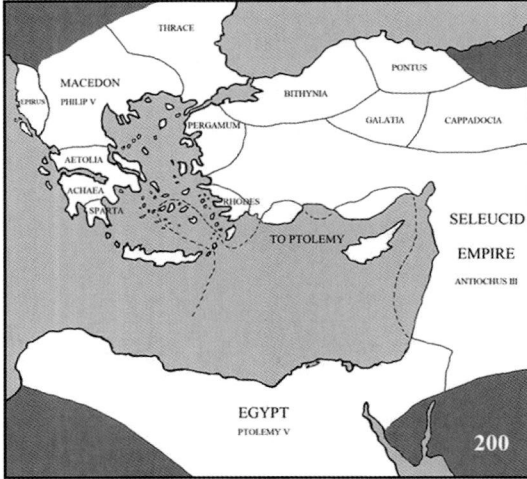

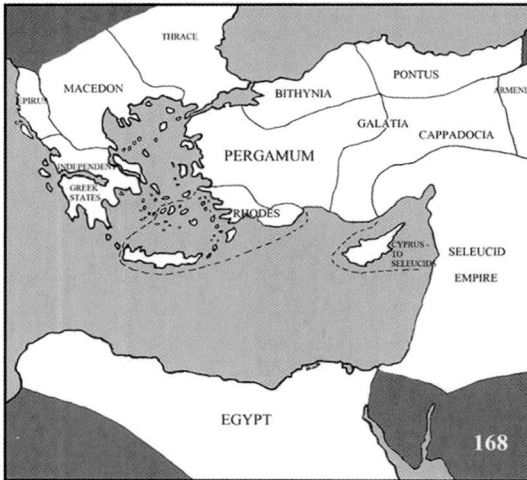

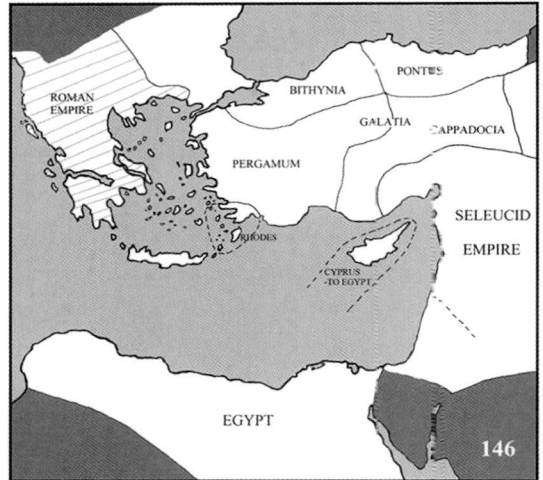

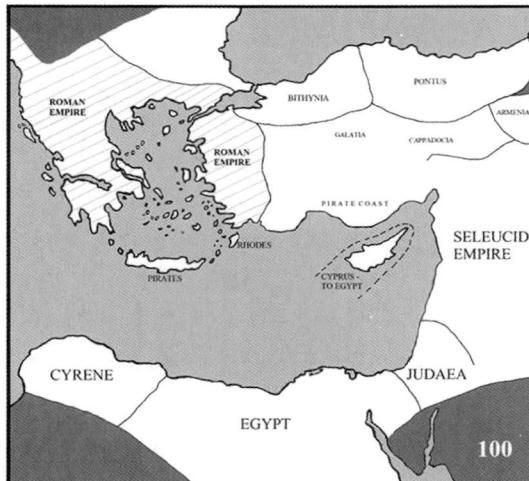

warship, escorted by five others;[5] the talks broke down later. The Roman fleet withdrew to Corcyra for the winter.

The war was ended in 197 by the Romans defeating Philip's army at the Battle of Cynoscephelae. By the peace treaty that followed, the Macedonian fleet had to be surrendered.[6] Philip was permitted to retain only six ships, described by Polybius as "five light vessels and his huge flagship on which the men rowed eight to an oar" – in fact a 'sixteen'[7] (but see Chapter 11). Macedonia had ceased to be an effective naval power. The Romans withdrew from Greece but left a squadron of twenty-five ships in the Aegean, based on the Boeotian and Phocaean coasts.[8]

Antiochus III, the Seleucid King had meanwhile subdued Coele-Syria and was expanding into Asia Minor. He was consolidating his own naval power, having built up a fleet of forty heavy and several light ships (of rates up to and including tens); he also took on as auxiliaries or hired, a number of pirate ships and crews from Crete (long a centre of piracy) giving him a mixed fleet. The pirates, presumably with a promise of plunder, could well have secured some triremes or even larger ships, found laid up and abandoned by the fall of previous antagonists; most would however, have used *hemioliae* or other small types.

With the effective removal of Macedonia and the previous weakening of Egypt, Antiochus saw an opportunity for further expansion. Following his gaining of the Phoenician coast and ports by 200, he put in hand an altogether more ambitious shipbuilding programme, expanding his fleet to some 300 ships.

197/
196
Supported by this fleet, Antiochus' forces were able to overrun Cilicia and advance, carefully avoiding Rhodian territory, across Asia Minor. They took and secured the neutral city of Ephesus as an Aegean naval base and then besieged Smyrna. They attacked Pergamene territory and advanced to and besieged Lampsacus (on the Hellespont) before, in 196, crossing and seizing part of the Thracian coast. Smyrna and Lampsacus had meanwhile appealed to Rome, which had become de facto protector of the Greek states; Rome issued a warning to Antiochus, which he ignored, no doubt encouraged by Hannibal who had found sanctuary in his court and who advised a naval campaign to take distant Corcyra so as to keep the Romans from Greece.[9] Antiochus then signed a peace treaty with Ptolemy V of Egypt and opened a dialogue with the Romans.

194/
193
By 194, the Roman fleet based on Sicily had seventy quinqueremes plus smaller vessels but with increasing tensions in the East, the Senate ordered

the building of another thirty quinqueremes and twenty triremes to augment this.[10] The Achaean Greeks, former allies of Philip of Macedon, were disgruntled by the settlement at the end of the Macedonian War and sought to unite Philip, Nabis the Tyrant of Sparta and Antiochus against the Romans. Philip was not interested after his recent defeat, Antiochus' forces were still too far away and Nabis moved too soon on his own. The allied fleet in the Aegean went into action once more, capturing the Spartan naval base at Gythion and supporting a land campaign

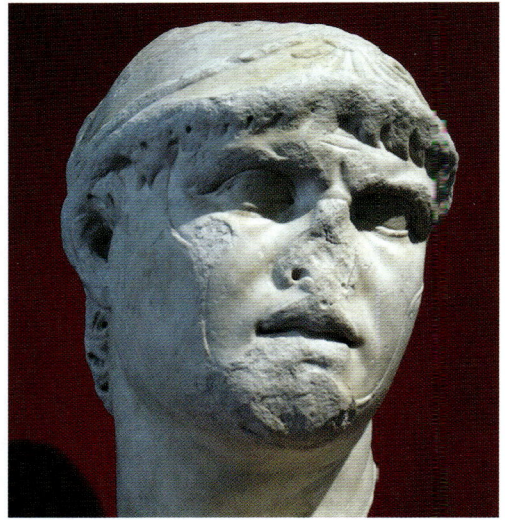

Figure 73. Philip V. King of Macedon, 22? to 179. Note the Argive star motif on his helmet visor. (*Palazzo Massimo Museum, Rome*)

against Nabis.[11] Sparta was defeated and their fleet was surrendered (in 192) and another Greek state ceased to be a naval power.[12]

192   Relations between Antiochus II and Rome did not long remain good and when the Aetolians seized Demetrias (modern Volos) in Thessaly, in the Autumn of 192, he landed troops there; his fleet of forty heavy and sixty light warships covered a convoy of some 200 transports carrying 11,000 troops and twenty-six elephants. The Roman squadron was to the south on the Boeotian Coast when Antiochus attacked Chalcis on Euboea. One of his commanders attacked a Roman detachment on the mainland as it marched to join its ships, leading to war (in October or November).[13]

191   Trading no doubt on the antipathy between Philip V and Antiochus III, the Romans secured Philip's co-operation and that of the Achaean Greeks and in early 191, the Roman Army returned to Greece. With their Greek and Macedonian allies, they quickly drove Antiochus' forces out (beating them at Thermopylae) and back to Asia Minor, their ships capturing one of his large supply convoys near Andros.[14] Pergamum and Rhodes now formally joined as allies of Rome. Before pursuing Antiochus into Asia, mastery of the Aegean had to be obtained in the face of a very powerful Seleucid fleet. A Roman fleet of fifty quinqueremes and triremes under the command of Claudius Livius Salinator was sent to Aegina to join the twenty-five Roman ships already there. Also there was the well-founded Pergamene fleet[15] of twenty-five fours

and fives, with a few triremes, under their king, Eumenes II; Rhodes' fleet had not yet sailed.[16] Antiochus' fleet of seventy ships, under his admiral, the exiled Rhodian Polyxenidas withdrew from the Hellespont (thereby leaving the crossing unguarded) to his base at Ephesus, intending to attack the allies before the Rhodian fleet could join them.[17]

The fleets met off Cape Corycus in September; Livius with the seventy-five Roman ships was in the van with Eumenes and his ships behind. Sailing south, the allies came upon the Seleucid fleet drawn up in line abreast with its starboard flank secured by the shore. As they had been sailing, the Romans slowed to strike sail and stow their rig, they then formed line abreast with a frontage of about thirty ships and allowing Eumenes' ships to work their way to seaward, i.e. to the right of the Romans. Two light ships got well ahead of the Roman line and were promptly attacked by three of the enemy, which raked the side of one, breaking its oars, boarding and capturing it, the other managing to escape.[18]

The two main lines then came into contact and by grappling and boarding the Romans soon got the upper hand. Eumenes' ships joined the attack from seaward in a '*periplous*' outflanking move. Polyxenidas had to break off the engagement and flee to Ephesus, having lost ten of his ships destroyed and another thirteen captured, for the loss of only one allied ship.[19]

The Rhodian fleet of twenty-five arrived the next day[20] and the allied fleet, now in overwhelming numbers, conducted a naval sail-by off Ephesus. Not surprisingly Polyxenidas and his fleet were not tempted to come out. Having little else to do and being late in the season, the Rhodian fleet went home, from where they could cover routes to the south. The Roman and Pergamene fleets took position to the north in a harbour on the strait between Lesbos and Pergamene territory on the mainland. From there they could dominate routes to the Hellespont, remaining on station throughout the winter.

190   For the following year, the Praetor Lucius Aemilius Regillus was sent to command the fleet, bringing with him twenty more warships, a thousand marines and an extra 2,200 troops, bringing the Roman fleet up to ninety-five ships, mostly fives; another two ships joined later. An armistice was brokered with the Aetolian Greeks and Philip of Macedon continued to co-operate as the Roman army marched to the Hellespont. To assure their safe crossing and guarantee their lines of supply however, the threat of intervention by Antiochus' still-powerful fleet had to be neutralised.

For their part, Antiochus' fleet at Ephesus had not been idle, having built no less than forty-three new ships and repaired damaged ones to increase

CORYCUS HARBOUR
(MODERN SIKIA)

25 PERGAMENE SHIPS
UNDER KING ATTALUS

75 ROMAN SHIPS
UNDER CLAUDIUS
LIVIUS SALINATOR

ROMANS FORM A 30-SHIP FRONT-
AGE FOR INTIAL ATTACK, OTHER
SHIPS JOINING AS THEY CAME UP;
FRONTAGE OF APPROX 650
YARDS/594 M.

POLYXENIDAS
PROBABLY FORMED
TWO LINES TO
AVOID A *DIEKPLOUS*
ATTACK; FRONTAGE
OF APPROX 760
YARDS/695 M.

MILES   1/2   1
KM.   1   2

70 SHIPS OF ANTIOCHUS
UNDER POLYXENIDAS

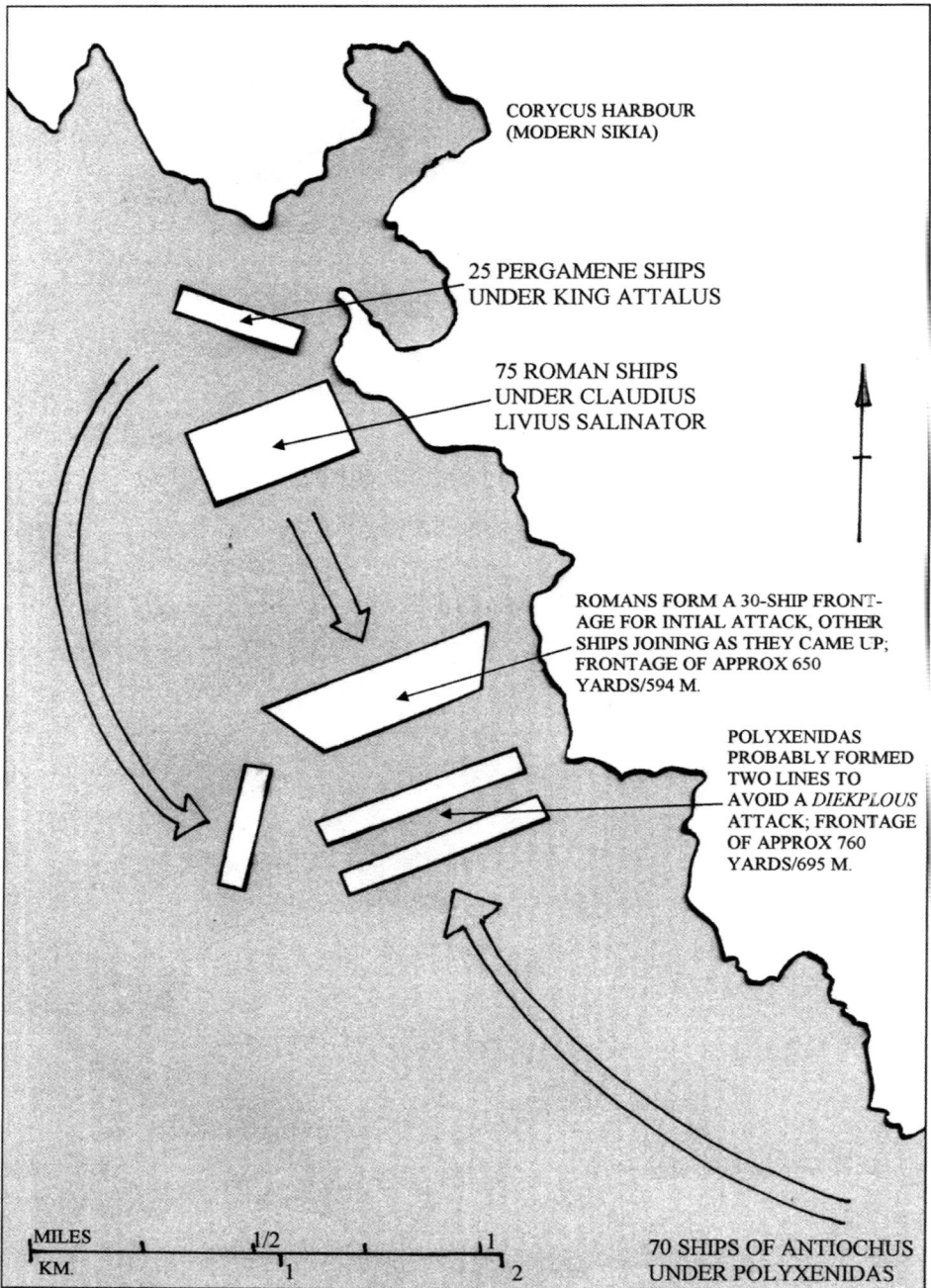

MAP 15 The Battle of Corycus—191

An example of a battle where the *periplous* manoeuvre was successfully used was off Corycus . The Romans used their superior numbers to hold the enemy front while their Pergamene allies worked around the offshore of the enemy line to attack its flank. The allies lost one ship but their enemy lost ten ships destroyed and another thirteen captured

Figure 74. Two second century Hellenistic grave stelae, both very similar, showing a man sat contemplating the stern of a warship. Both have similar inscriptions (in Greek) indicating that these unfortunates were lost at sea perhaps in action. The ship sternposts are identical, the left one also showing a rudder. The left stela says that Prothemo was lost at sea, his body not recovered. (*Archaeological Museum, Avignon, previously Venice, original provenance unknown*) The right, that Archagathos, son of Diodoros died in a shipwreck. (*Museo Lapidario Maffiano, Verona, provenance unknown*)

their numbers to nearly ninety ships, including two 'sevens' and three 'sixes'. Furthermore, Hannibal was raising and equipping a second fleet in Antiochus' Phoenician ports. If the two could unite, they would have a large numerical advantage over the allies.

The allies' problem was that their main fleet, the Roman and Pergamene ships, were committed to keeping Polyxenidas cooped up in Ephesus; if they moved to counter Hannibal, Polyxenidas could emerge to attack them in the rear, or go northward to block the Hellespont. Even without him, hostile ships had appeared in the Hellespont and in March 190, to deal with them, a force of thirty Roman and seven Pergamene ships were detached and sent. They managed to clear the enemy ships, secure the co-operation of local ports and return to the main fleet before Polyxenidas learned of their temporary absence.

In April 190, Polyxenidas managed to take his fleet out of harbour without being seen. A Rhodian squadron of twenty-seven ships was in a harbour south of Ephesus, probably Panormus (approximately modern Kusadasi). The Seleucid fleet landed a strong force of troops which drove the Rhodian crews to their ships. There they had to try to escape through a narrow harbour mouth where the enemy fleet was waiting to pick them off as they emerged. Having previously experimented with the device, some of the Rhodian ships managed to rig braziers of burning material at the end of long spars or booms which they extended out on either side of their bows and which could be dropped onto the deck of any enemy ship that ventured too close.[21] Using this device, seven of the Rhodian ships managed to escape, but the other twenty ships were captured.[22] On hearing of this disaster, the allied main fleet sailed south to renew their close blockade of Ephesus, basing themselves on nearby Samos.[23] As the Rhodians maintained a standing fleet of about thirty-five ships, they must have had a reserve of ships at Rhodes to replace their losses in time to meet Hannibal's fleet (see later).

As only part of the Romans' supplies had reached them, the Roman commander, Aemilius, having learned of a supply convoy bound for Ephesus, sailed south from Samos to intercept. Sailing towards Teos they sighted about fifteen ships, which they assumed to be part of Polyxenidas' fleet but the ships turned out to be pirate boats and galleys on their way home from raiding Chios. The Romans gave chase but were slower than the pirates and by the time they rounded Cape Myonnesus, the pirates had run their ships ashore and taken refuge inland on high ground. There being no profit in going ashore there, the Romans returned to Teos where they landed and ravaged the area until the city gave them the supplies that they needed. The harbour mouth was narrow and when the enemy fleet was sighted at sea, the Romans rapidly put to sea.[24]

The Seleucid fleet being already out, Polyxenidas planned to ambush the allies from behind a suitable promontory, hitting them in the rear as they sailed by. The plan nearly succeeded but when the fleets were in sight of each other, was frustrated by roughening weather which forced both back to harbour.

Reinforcements from Italy had to be stationed at various points on the way to the east to secure the sea route against an upsurge in piracy and only two extra ships joined the allied fleet. A last foray by the fleet under Livius against the Lycian Coast achieved no success, and neither did a further cruise under his successor, Regillus, to Rhodes. Antiochus attacked Pergamum by

Opposite: **Figure 75.** Hellenistic warships under sail and oar. Graffiti scratched into wall plaster at Delos; late third or early second century. Although very roughly drawn, they must represent a more or less accurate overall impression of the ships seen by the 'artist'. Oars have been indicated in a random way but the upper ship has an indication of thirty-eight oars and the lower, of twenty-nine, which suggests that they represent multi-reme ships, but in the absence of any artemon, probably not the great polyremes. (*Delos Archaeological Museum*)

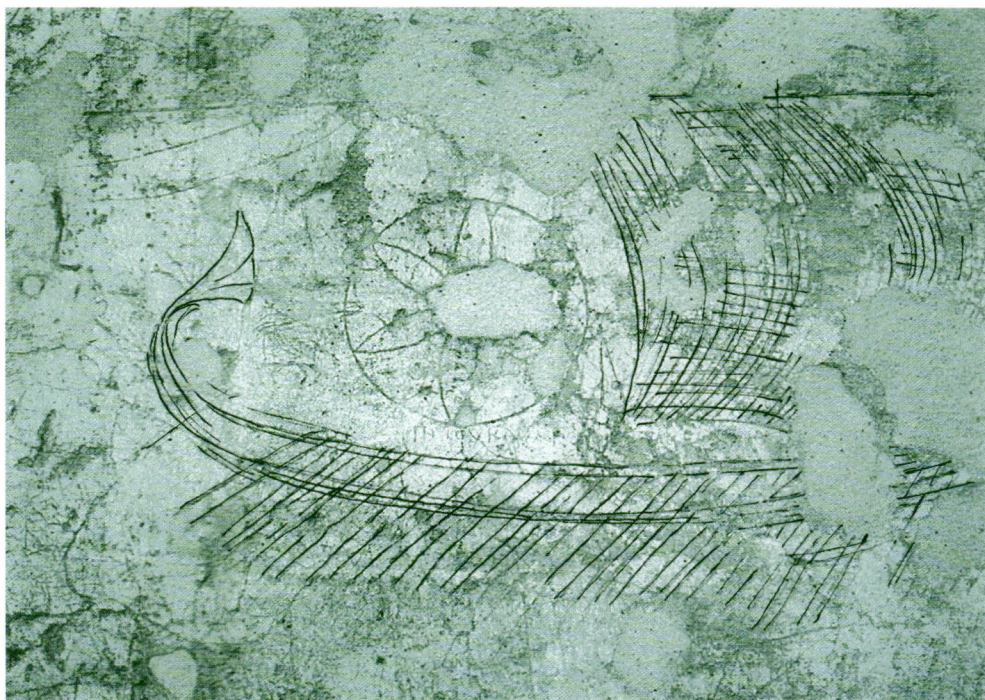

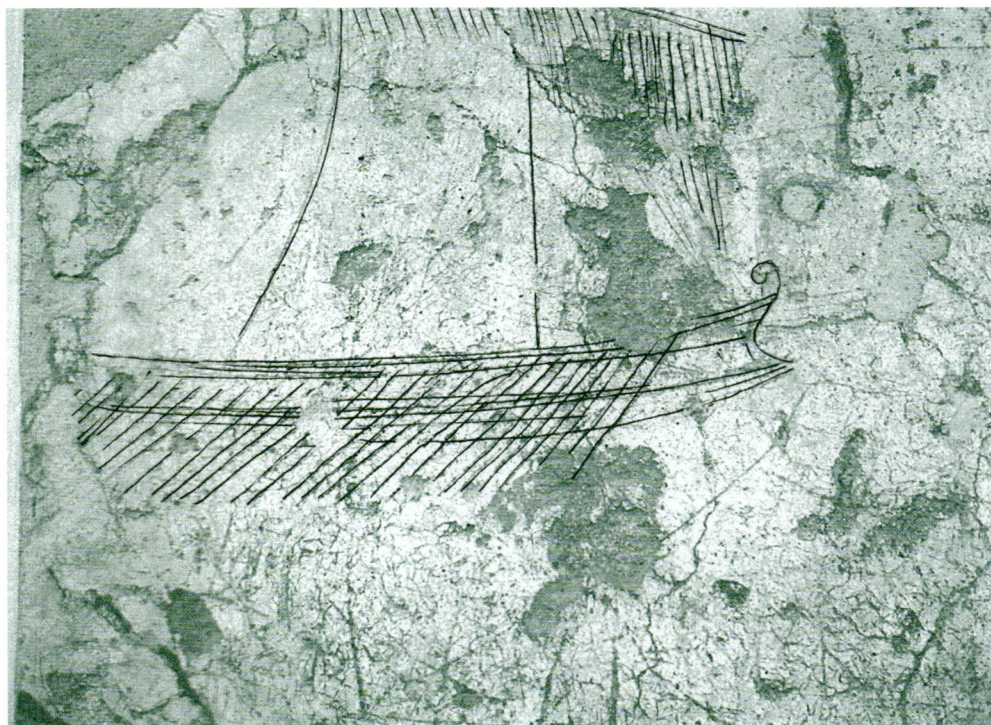

land and their fleet had to be withdrawn to assist in the defence and to ferry allied troops there. The allies agreed that the Rhodian fleet would replace the Pergamene ships in the blockade of Ephesus; as the threat to Pergamum had been averted, their fleet should cover the Roman army, now preparing to cross into Asia.

In June however, the allies learned that Hannibal with a fleet of forty-seven ships, composed of three sevens and four sixes, thirty fours and fives and ten smaller, was sailing westward along the Cilician Coast. The Rhodians under Eudamus, instead of joining the Romans, sailed eastwards to intercept Hannibal with a fleet of only thirty-two 'fours' and four triremes, together with two fives, one from Cnidus and the other from Cos.[25]

The fleets met off Side, Hannibal's ships advancing in line of battle, with their right to shoreward and Hannibal on the left wing, to seaward. The Rhodians advanced in sailing columns and their leading ships under Eudamus deployed to seaward to form for battle. These ships, the Rhodian right, came into action against Hannibal's wing quickly and before the other Rhodian ships could deploy into line abreast. Restricted in their area of manoeuvre and unable to get into line abreast, the Rhodian left formed into short columns of a few ships in line ahead and forced their way between and behind their opposite numbers, effecting in fact, a number of separate *diekplous* attacks.[26]

Despite being greatly outnumbered and their ships being mostly smaller the Rhodian ships were faster and their captains and crews very well trained and practised, a fleet at the peak of its ability. Hannibal's ships were for the most part slower and their crews hastily put together and lacking experience. They had no answer to and could not hope to match the rapid attacks and swift manoeuvring of the Rhodian ships, or the degree of command and control that enabled the Rhodian left, once it had swept away the enemy's right, to respond to a hard-pressed Eudamus' signal and swing to the attack to support him.

Hannibal had lost a 'seven', captured by the Rhodians and about a dozen more ships damaged or disabled. He could see that his fleet was totally outmatched and so broke off the fight and retreated eastward with the survivors. The Rhodians kept twenty ships on the Cilician Coast to guard against any further foray by Hannibal's fleet, which never again ventured forth.[27]

By October 190, the allied fleet had been reduced, some ships having been sent to the Hellespont. Watching Ephesus now were fifty-eight Roman and twenty-two Rhodian ships with about 20,000 men, under Regillus. The

Figure 76. Seleucid Monarchs. Top: Anticchus VI. 145 to 142. Centre: Antiochus VII. 138 to 129. Bottom: Antiochus VIII. 121 to 96. All are silver tetradrachm. (*All, Altes Museum, Berlin*)

and unable to oppose the allied fleet, which was free to take troops to raid enemy coasts and cities. Rhodes did reluctantly contribute six fours for the campaign of 171.[32] There being no opposition, the allied ships were surplus to needs and sent home. The Roman fleet at Chalcis continued to raid enemy coasts, capturing Abdera in Thrace in 170. In 169 the Roman army reached the Aegean coast of Macedon at Heraclaeum. Using this as a new, secure forward base, the Roman fleet, now commanded by Gaius Marcus Figulus, was reinforced by twenty Pergamene and five Bithynian ships.[33] From there, the allied fleet raided Perseus' northern Aegean harbours including Thessaloniki and Cassandeia. The fleet returned to Euboea for the winter, having occupied Skiathos in the Sporades as an observation post. A Roman Senatorial Commission of inspection reported however that, after three years of constant operations, the fleet was in poor condition, as was the army in Greece.

Perseus' navy was not entirely inactive. The six ships that he had inherited had been augmented by the acquisition of several dozen small warships. Although unable to challenge the Romans, a fleet of forty or so warships did operate along the western coasts of Asia Minor, recovering a Macedonian grain convoy from its Pergamene captors and intercepting and capturing a convoy carrying cavalry horses to Greece for its enemies.

His forces in Greece having forced the war to a standstill, Perseus pursued a diplomatic offensive, trying to sow disaffection among Rome's allies and succeeded in bringing the Illyrians into the war against Rome. He also looked for an alliance with the current Seleucid King, Antiochus IV and the appearance of his fleet at sea reinforced this effort. Antiochus, however, was too involved in his latest round of quarrelling with the Ptolemies to respond. For its part, Ptolemaic Egypt still possessed a huge fleet which, in view of the constant aggression afflicting the country's borders, saw virtually no action and was comparatively neglected and deteriorated. When Ptolemy did offer help to Rome, it was in the form of money, rather than addition to the allied fleet; the offer was refused. The fleet is not recorded as being in action even with the rise of Cyrene, to the immediate west, as a centre for piracy. By the end of the period, it can be reasonably estimated that the fleet had halved in numbers and the very largest ships had been discarded, its use being limited to maintaining communication with Cyprus, their sole remaining overseas territory.

168   The Romans reinforced their positions and overcame the Illyrians in a thirty-day campaign. A feint by their Aegean fleet succeeded in persuading Perseus that they were intending to land invasion forces at Heraclaea. Perseus diverted

Figure 78. Perseus. King of Macedon 179 to 168, the last of the Antagonid kings. Top: silver tetradrachm. (*Metropolitan Museum of Art, New York*) Lower: tetradrachm, showing his name on the reverse. (*Altes Museum, Berlin*)

some of his forces to meet this perceived threat and the following day (22 June) his main army met the Romans at Pydna. The Macedonians were totally defeated and Perseus fled. The war ended in the following year and Macedonia was divided into three republics and another Hellenistic power ceased to be.[34]

Unrest continued between Seleucia and Ptolemaic Egypt. Hiding behind the distraction of the Macedonian War, the Seleucid King, Antiochus IV had invaded Egyptian territory. The Roman victory over Macedonia left a Roman army poised there, backed by a treaty of friendship with Ptolemy. Roman insistence, and the latent threat, forced Antiochus to withdraw (168) but not, however, before his fleet had besieged and taken Cyprus from Ptolemy. This did not prevent the continuation of small-scale skirmishing between the two.

In the preceding years, Pergamum had once more expanded its territory by annexing part of Pontus (171–164) and Bithynia (186). As Rome had, since defeating the Seleucids and driving them from Asia Minor, become de facto arbiter of its affairs, they forced the Pergamenes to withdraw and also pressured Antiochus to evacuate the parts of Egypt that he held and to return Cyprus.

Rhodes' less than lukewarm attitudes towards Rome in the recent war, together with its expanding trade in Egyptian grain became the pretext for Rome to order it to vacate Caria and Lycia, which had been entrusted to it twenty years earlier. Military action was not needed for any of these matters.

The Romans handed the island of Delos to Athens in 167, on condition that it became a free port. It quickly boomed as such, causing Rhodes to lose most of its previous maritime trade,[35] upon which its prosperity had depended. With this went her ability to afford and maintain the strong fleet that had been so effective in suppressing piracy. Unfortunately, there were large numbers of personnel who had previously served in the former Macedonian and Seleucid fleets as well as the shipyards that built and repaired the ships of the now non-existent navies, now unemployed. Most likely some warships left in these yards and harbours, not completed or under repair were capable of being used for buccaneering. The men and materials were all available (despite severe restrictions on the trade in 'naval timber')[36] for a rise of piracy, encouraged by the coming of peace and an enormous increase in maritime trade upon seas lacking any policing. With the withdrawal of the Roman fleet homewards and the limited nature of Pergamene and Rhodian efforts, the last constraints upon it, piracy burgeoned across the eastern Mediterranean and Aegean.

167   In 167 a revolt, led by Judas Maccabeus against Seleucid rule progressively removed Judaea and Palestine from their control.[37] Dynastic struggles among the Seleucids weakened successive attempts to recover it. In 163, Rhodes sent a force to recover Calynda in Lycia, no doubt using its fleet; there are no details of the strength or composition of this force.[38]

162   In 162, the Romans sent Gnaeus Octavius to check that Antiochus V was adhering to the Seleucid peace treaty with Rome. He discovered that Antiochus was building a large fleet, which he promptly ordered his men to burn (he was just as promptly assassinated) to prevent any resurgence of Seleucid naval power.[39] The Romans concluded a treaty of friendship in 161 with the state of Israel that had by now emerged. This did not however, prevent Demetrios I, the new Seleucid monarch, from later crushing the rebellious Jews.

155   In 155, Crete, formerly a nest of piracy which had been more or less contained and controlled by Rhodes, fought against its declining power to throw off the former constraint and return to piracy.

154   In 154, in a resumption of his ongoing wars against King Prusias of Bithynia, King Attalus of Pergamum sent a fleet of eighty 'decked ships' commanded by

his son, Athenaeus to the Hellespont. Five of the ships were fours, contributed by Rhodes; it is not clear where the rest came from as the Pergamene fleet, as has been seen, was never more than about thirty ships in strength. On the assumption that the figure is not exaggerated, it may be that the total figure was not entirely of warships but included mercenaries and/or transports.[40]

149   A usurper, Andriscus sought to become king of a re-united Macedon with some initial success. A Roman army quickly ended his career and Macedon, together with Illyria and Epirus became Roman provinces.[41] Widespread unrest broke out all over Greece and in 148 the Romans invaded yet again, this time reducing Greece to a province, initially under the governor of Macedon. The naval ships and crew of the former Greek city-states were officially rated as Roman naval auxiliaries that could be called upon (as would later happen) when needed. In fact, there was little for them to do and many of them could and did turn their idle hands to buccaneering, adding to the pool of ships and men available and indeed with no other incentive or, in many cases, alternative to piracy.

146   In 146 the Third Punic War between Rome and Carthage came to an end with the destruction of Carthage, leaving Rome as the only great power of the Mediterranean world. That year also the Romans sacked Corinth and annexed most of the Balkan peninsula. In 142, the Judaean leader, Simeon established diplomatic relations with Rome. For the Romans, the end of their wars in Spain, the elimination of Carthage, Macedonia and Seleucid naval power, added to their existing friendships with Egypt, Rhodes, Pergamum and Bithynia, meant that they could reduce the burden of their huge military establishment. Their navy's manpower was reduced, older ships were scrapped and surplus ships laid up. The Roman fleet was withdrawn from the eastern Mediterranean to home ports.

134   Antiochus VII failed in a final attempt to recover Judaea for the Seleucids in 134, following which it became independent under Hasmonean kings; it would endure as a buffer between the Ptolemies and Seleucids.[42] In 133 Attalus III, king of Pergamum died without issue and bequeathed his entire kingdom to the Senate and People of Rome. The bequest was taken up and in 130 Pergamum became the Roman province of Asia, its navy coming under the command of the Roman governor and being stood down in the absence of any apparent threat. In the following decades, almost incessant internecine and dynastic squabbling among both the Ptolemies and Seleucids led to clashes between them and encouraged the advance of the new Parthian dynasty and empire in the east, which progressively reduced the Seleucid domains.[43] All of this was played out on land and if anything, reduced naval activity to almost

nothing. Of forthcoming significance would be the accession to power in 112 of King Mithridates VI of Pontus and the progressive expansion of his power and territories in Asia Minor.

102   There remained no check to the rise of piracy and it proliferated exponentially, fed by the disruption of almost endless warfare, the weakening power of the Seleucids, Ptolemies and Rhodes (by now able to keep no more than a dozen or so ships in commission) added to the availability of manpower and ships. Whole fleets of pirate ships and boats could be mustered and they established pirate communities along, and virtually annexed, the Cilician Coast. This area, backed by mountains, has a rocky coast with many inlets and was heavily forested and able to provide timber for shipbuilding. Although driven from the Tyrrhenian Sea, the pirates had the eastern Mediterranean and Aegean virtually to themselves, operating also from Crete and the myriad islands of the Dalmatian Coast.

The availability of ships suited to piracy has already been seen in the shape of the *hemioliae* and *lembi* and the pressing into such service of fishing and other local craft could take place, but it was the availability of actual warships that made the pirates such a force to be reckoned with. It is clear that most island and mainland coastal polities had from one or two to substantial squadrons of types from minor warships, triremes and even fours perhaps, used for local defence and which they contributed to various confederation formations from time to time. As examples, Livy tells us that in 190 Mytilene sent two triremes to join the Romans; two ships from Cos were with the Rhodians at Panormus in 190 and escaped; a pirate chief called Nicander brought five 'decked ships' i.e. warships to join Polyxenidas and some 'undecked' Athenians joined the Romans, together with two fours from Samos.[44]

Whole squadrons of pirate ships operated together, even into the western Mediterranean. They also quickly found that when in such strength, they could attack and sack coastal towns, being in sufficient

Figure 79. Bronze coin of Nicomedia in Pontus, dated to 177 to 192 (the city name is around the top of the coin). A stylised warship is shown under oars, with an artemon but no mainmast rigged. (*Altes Museum, Berlin*)

numbers to overcome any local resistance, or be paid not to do so. Merchant shipping and commerce was reduced to chaos.[45]

102   In 102 the Romans at last made some effort to deal with the problem, sending the Praetor Marcus Antonius (grandfather of the M. Antonius of Antony and Cleopatra fame) with a small naval force to found bases and cruise the coasts of Pamphylia and Cilicia, drawing upon local allied forces as required. He closed the slave markets at Delos, a principal centre for the trade and denying the pirates an outlet for the unfortunates seized by them. He enjoyed some success in suppressing piracy and again when he returned to campaign in 100. When he left however, having left no permanent naval forces behind, the pirates quickly made good the losses inflicted upon them and returned to their previous activities, which proceeded to exceed their prior depredations.

At the end of the century therefore, the naval map of the eastern Mediterranean had changed dramatically. Egypt was the only remaining naval Hellenistic power; Macedon had disappeared and a reduced Seleucia, although still having somewhat nominal control over Phoenicia, was riven with internal dynastic problems and had ceased to have a navy, or at least an effective one. Of the lesser naval powers, Pergamum had become a Roman province and Rhodes was much reduced. Rome was the dominant Mediterranean power and their progressive domination of naval warfare had been gained by their ability and willingness to aggressively deploy powerful forces of the highest quality, with the ability to draw on reserves as needed. At the end of the period, they went home leaving a vacuum by having reduced naval forces to a level well below that necessary to police the seas which, devoid of any other political entity capable or willing to do so, had now in fact become its responsibility.

Appendix

The Battle of Myonnesus – October 190

The two opposing fleets met just north of Cape Myonnesus. The Seleucid fleet, having rounded the Cape, deployed their ninety ships from two sailing columns into battle line abreast, forming two lines, one behind the other, their right or starboard wing close into the shore. Having superior numbers to their opponents, Polyxenidas extended his left, offshore wing to seaward, hoping to envelop his enemy's right in a *periplous* manoeuvre.

The allied fleet of fifty-eight Roman and twenty-two Rhodian ships approached from the north, the Romans forming a line abreast, with the Rhodians in line abreast behind them.

Seeing the enemy line being extended to seaward, Eudamus, in command of the Rhodians, led his ships out from behind the Romans and to seaward to prevent their right from being enveloped.

As the fleets came into contact, Eudamus' swift ships harried and held Polyxenidas' offshore wing while the Romans broke the enemy's centre, smashing their way through with the ram and grappling and boarding as they went.

The battle progressed and developed into two distinct parts. The Rhodians, lighter, faster and more manoeuvrable than their opponents, used these attributes to assail the enemy with rams and missiles and even, possibly, their fire braziers, but avoiding close contact or becoming entangled with enemy ships; the Romans proceeded to systematically grapple and board and take successive opposing ships.

Before long, Polyxenidas' offshore wing, which had been effectively prevented from achieving its intended envelopment, was in disarray and retreat. He had to break off the battle lest he was in turn enveloped and escape with his surviving ships, back to Ephesus.

Livy (XXXVII.29 and 30) tells the story in more detail:

29. When the (allied) fleet was brought round to the city (Teos) and being ignorant of the approach of the enemy, both soldiers and sailors went ashore to divide the provisions and the wine among the ships. At about mid-day a peasant was brought before the Praetor (Regillus) and told him that the enemy fleet was laying off the island of Makris and had been for two days and that short while ago some of the ships were observed to be in motion, as if the fleet were preparing to sail.

Greatly alarmed at this unexpected news, the Praetor ordered the trumpets to sound, to recall those who might have straggled into the country and sent the tribunes into the city to hasten the soldiers and sailors aboard the ships. The confusion was no less than if the city were on fire or taken by an enemy, some running to call out the men, others running to their ships, while the officers' orders were confounded by the irregular shouts, amid which the trumpets raised their din until at length, the crews collected at the ships.

Here, all was confusion, with men trying to make their way through the tumult to their own ships and the disorder would have produced much mischief on land and sea, had Regillus, in the flagship, not sailed out first into the harbour, where upon the arrival of each other ship, he ordered each into its place in the line and formed them into line abreast. Eudamus with the Rhodian fleet, waited at the shore, that the men could be organised without confusion and that each ship might leave the harbour as soon as it was ready. By these means the foremost division formed under the eye of the Praetor, while the rear was brought up by the Rhodians and the whole line, in as regular order as if in sight of the foe, advanced into the open sea.

They were between Myonnesus and the promontory of Corycus when they first sighted the enemy. The King's (Antiochus') fleet, which was coming in a long line with only two vessels abreast, then formed themselves into order of battle, stretching out their left division so far that it might enclose the right of the Romans. When Eudamus, commanding the rear, perceived that the Romans could not form an equal front, but were just on the point of being surrounded, he took his own ships forward. They were Rhodians, by far the fastest sailors of any of the fleet and having filled the deficiency in the extent of the (allied) line, he opposed his own ship to that of the enemy commander, aboard which was Polyxenidas (the enemy admiral).

30. Now the entire fleets in every part were engaged in action. On the side of the Romans, eighty ships were fighting, of which twenty-two were Rhodian. The enemy's fleet consisted of eighty-nine ships and had the largest rates, three of six and two of seven 'banks' (i.e. three Sixes and two Sevens). In the strength of the vessels and valour of the soldiers, the Romans had greatly the advantage of the King's men, as had the Rhodians in the operation of their vessels, the skill of their pilots (helmsmen) and the dexterity of the rowers. However, those which carried fire before them were the greatest terror to the enemy and which was

the sole cause of their preservation when they were surrounded at Panormus, proved here the principal means of victory. When the King's ships, through fear of the fire, had turned aside in order to avoid at the same time encountering the enemy's prow with their own, they could not strike their antagonist with their beaks, but exposed the sides of their ships to his strokes. If any did venture an encounter, it was immediately overspread with fire that was poured in, while the men were more alarmed at the fire than the battle. However, the bravery of the soldiers, as is generally the case, chiefly prevailed in deciding the battle.

For the Romans, having broken through the centre of the enemy's line, they turned and fell upon the rear of the division which was engaged against the Rhodians; in an instant, both Antiochus' centre division and the ships on its left were surrounded and sunk.

The squadron on the right, which was still entire, was terrified rather by the disaster of their friends than any immediate danger threatening themselves; but when they saw the others surrounded and Polyxenidas' ship deserting its associates and sailing away, quickly hoisting their sails, they betook themselves to flight (those steering for Ephesus having a favourable wind).

Having lost forty-two ships in that battle, of which thirteen struck and fell into the hands of the Romans, the rest were burned or sunk. Two Roman ships were shattered and several were much damaged. One Rhodian vessel was taken by an extraordinary casualty for, on its striking a Sidonian ship with its beak, its anchor, thrown out by the force of the shock, caught fast hold of the other's prow with its fluke, as if it were a grappling iron thrown in. Great confusion ensuing, when the Rhodians who wished to disengage themselves from the enemy, pulled back, its cable being dragged forcibly and at the same time, entangled with the oars, swept off one side of them. The very ship which, when struck, had grappled with it, took the Rhodian galley in its weakened state.

The naval battle of Myonnesus was fought principally in this manner.

The Seleucid fleet had lost thirteen ships sunk or burned and another twenty-nine captured, nearly half of its strength. The Romans had lost two ships destroyed and two more damaged, the Rhodians one ship lost.

It was late in the sailing season and it seems that at the outset, neither fleet had expected a battle at that time. Antiochus' fleet had been laying at Makris for a couple of days, close to their base and perhaps hoping for news of their enemy's movements; for their part, the allies had been re-victualling at Teos. It was only a chance sighting that caused the Romans to scramble to put their ships to sea, wary of otherwise

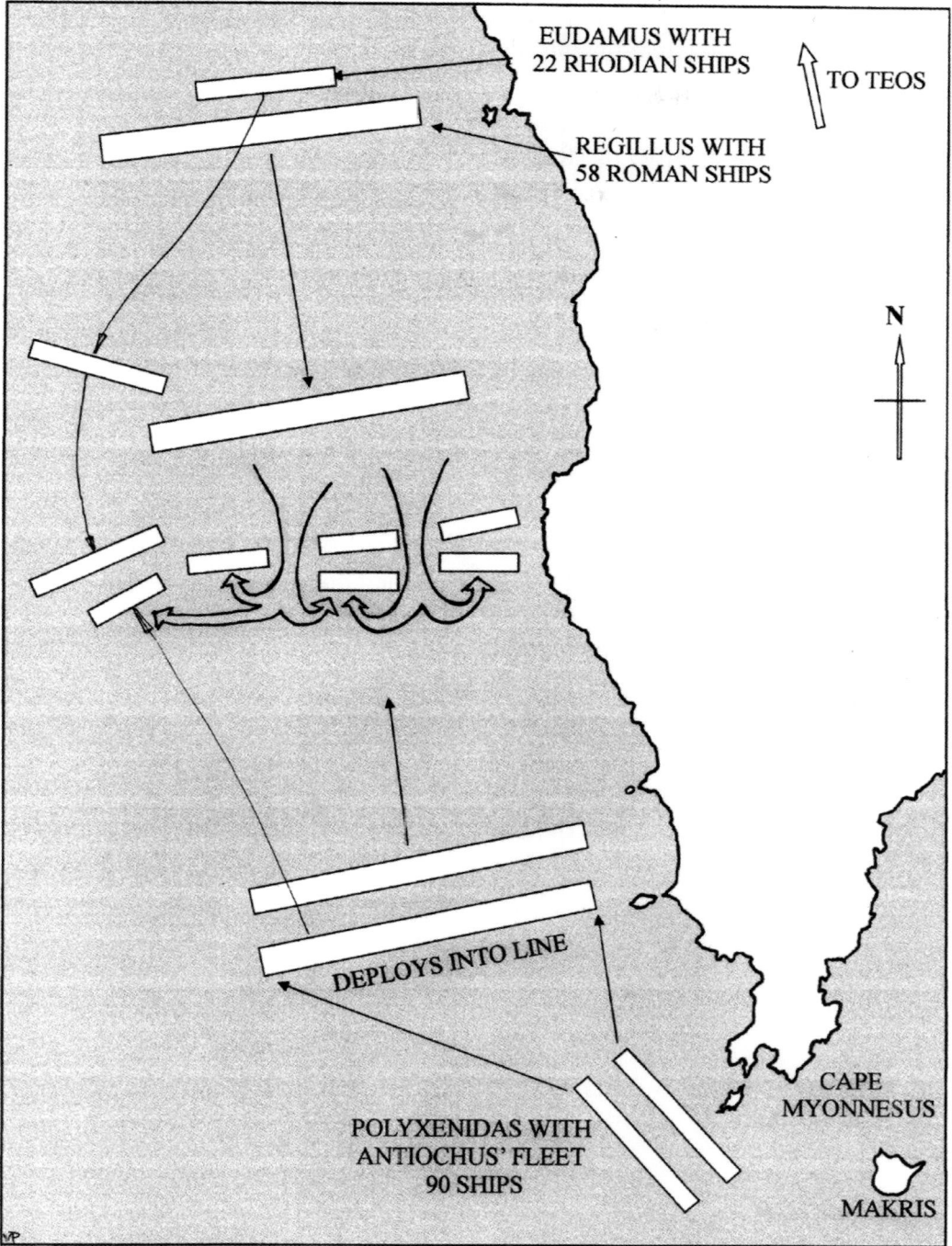

MAP 16. The Battle of Myonnesus —190

being trapped in harbour. They came out in battle order but Polyxenidas' ships were cruising in two columns, presumably under sail as their survivors of the battle hoisted sail to escape. Normally before going into battle, warships would land their sailing rig 'to clear for action' and that Polyxenidas' ships had theirs aboard suggests that they were not expecting a battle; the Romans did not have their rig aboard and so were unable, with their tired rowers, to give chase to the fleeing ships.

The Rhodians once again used their fire baskets, slung outboard on long spars as they had done before; the risk of fire aboard these highly flammable wooden ships was enough for the enemy to turn away, exposing their sides to the Rhodian rams. Fire was of course, anathema to these ships and was not normally used as a weapon aboard them; that the Rhodians still had the fire baskets aboard must have been fortuitous (and effective).

The final incident concerning the only Rhodian ship to be lost is instructive in illustrating the different combat philosophies; whereas Antiochus' fleet and, for that matter, the Romans as well wanted primarily to grapple and board an enemy, relying on missiles and soldiery, for the Rhodians it was the ram. With their smaller ships (no more than a four) they successfully rammed their opponents but when they could not back off to ram again, were overcome by enemy marines.

It was the Romans breaking the enemy line (*diekplous*), allied to the superior fighting abilities of their troops, plus the seamanship of the Rhodians that decided the battle. Antiochus may have had more and bigger ships and a very good admiral but his crews simply did not have the sea-time or experience, or even probably the morale of their opponents.

It had been a virtual re-run of the Battle of Corycus, largely with the same tactics and the same result, but from which Antiochus' naval ambitions would never recover.

Chapter 13

The Ships

The main influence in this period is of course, the appearance in strength of Roman ships in classes evolved, honed and perfected in the great wars against Carthage. Hellenistic innovation was not entirely at an end and saw the introduction of the much more sensible eight at the very beginning of the period.

The Eight

There seem to be only two references to an eight, but they are 170 years apart. The first is by Polybius (XVI.3.2) where, in his description of the Battle of Chios in 201 (see Chapter 9) he refers to the action beginning when the ship of Attalos 'rammed an eight below the waterline and swamping her' and thus the ship was a part of King Philip's fleet. The next time that an eight is mentioned in the sources, is by Plutarch (*Antonius* LXI.1) who relates that Antonius had several 'eights and tens' in his fleet at Actium in 31 (see Chapter 15).

Polybius was born in about the same year as the battle and thus could well have obtained his detailed account of it from veterans who were there, subject to the usual caveat as to translations available to us; we must therefore accept his mention of the eight as accurate.

It is a logical next step, referring for example, to the author's suggested reconstruction of a Roman bireme six (Figure 18) for a similar ship to be propelled by pairs of four-man oars. As a type it is an obvious candidate for the echelon system (see Chapter 10 and Figure 80) although, as with other rates, it would be possible for it to have been a more conventional bireme or even a trireme (Figure 81).

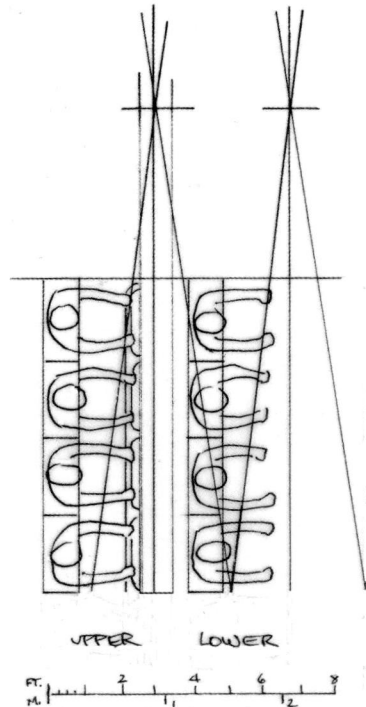

Figure 80. The Eight rowed by the 'echelon' system, with paired four-man oars.

As a 'conventional' bireme (Figure 81A) the eight works reasonably well, using a 40 foot/ 12.2m oar at operating angles of seventeen and nine degrees and a gearing of 3.3; it also allows all of the rowers to be seated and freeboard of 3.5 feet/1.07m.

The trireme arrangement (Figure 81B) is more complex, with extreme overhang of the oarbox and has the thranite oars operating at twenty-three degrees, rather more than ideal. Further, the two thranites have to manage the same 32 foot/9.75m oar as the other two teams, each of three men (at a higher gearing of 3.5). Once more, all of

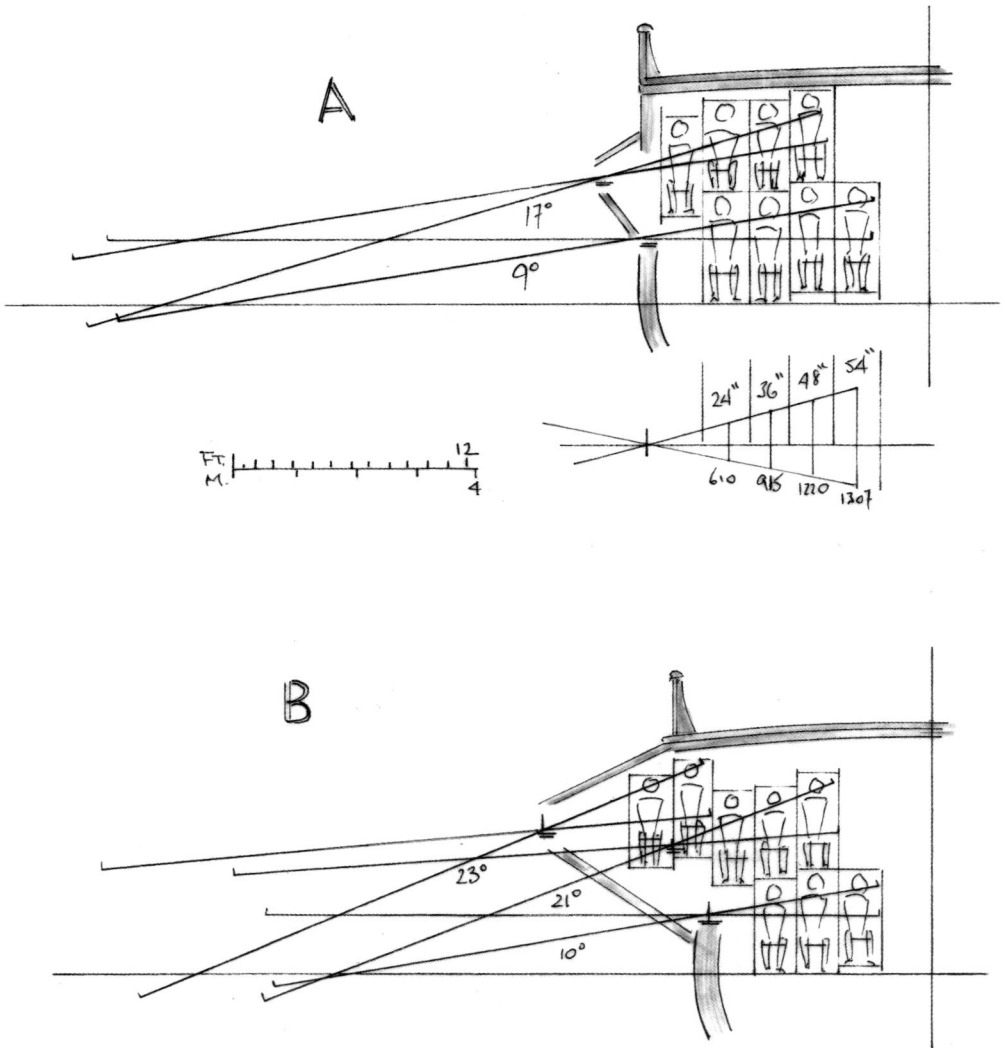

Figure 81. A: The Eight as a 'conventional' bireme per the text; the inset shows the respective pull of each rower. B: As a trireme. The extreme jettying out of the thranite rowers is an unsatisfactory complication. In both cases all the rowers are seated.

the rowers are seated and the advantage is that there are more oars in the water, for the same size crew.

Logic would seem to favour the bireme arrangement, whether by the echelon system or not; it also of course, allows uniform oar crews throughout.

Assuming therefore that it was a bireme and two remes of twenty-eight oars per side, with horizontal spacing between the oar crew as before (see Chapter 10) the remes will extend about 125 feet/38m; allowing say 30 feet/9.14m each for the bow and stern sections. A ship emerges with an overall length of approximately 185 feet/56.4m which appears realistic, as does the total number of rowers, at 224 per side, giving a total oar crew of 448 which is similar to the nine previously considered (see Chapter 8) but in a far less complicated ship.

How widely built or whether it was adopted at the same time by navies other than Philip's is not known but, unless it can be accepted that his eights were, 170 years later, at Actium, then more must have been built perhaps as late as the last half of the first century. In what numbers or by whom such ships were built is not known but, as with the tens and bearing in mind that Antonius controlled them, the shipyards of Phoenicia, with all their previous experience, not forgotten, seem the logical choice. As with the other surviving great ships, after Actium the eights were broken up or burned.

Roman Types

The eight was the last new type to be created by the Hellenistic naval architects; the last and from its apparent longevity in service, a not unsuccessful manifestation of the talent that had produced such an amazing array of warship types and the largest rowed vessels of all time. Henceforth, the ever-increasing and finally overwhelming power and influence of Rome would dictate the form of warships. In the course of the naval wars between Rome and Carthage, both sides had settled on the five or *quinquereme* as the predominant type making up their battle formations. Very small numbers of sixes were built as flagships and rather more fours; triremes were also used but no longer in fleet actions, where they were considerably outmatched.[1] Smaller types continued in use for scouting,[2] communication and even as transports.[3]

These were penteconters, *hemicliae* and the *lembi*. This latter was widely adopted by the Romans, who developed it, firstly into a purely military form, with a ram, as the *Pristis*.

There is evidence from the period of the Carthaginian Wars that the Romans mass-produced warships[4] and one can therefore assume that there was a greater measure of uniformity in the Roman ships of each class.

The *Pristis*

Described as 'a small warship with a ram, of the *liburna* type',[5] it was in service with the Romans between about 170/150 and 30, when it disappears from the record, presumably having been superseded by the evolved liburnians. As early *lembi/liburnae* had no rams, it is suggested (and this can only be conjecture) that this will have been an early adaptation of the Illyrian original to complement it and to give it the same striking ability as the other, previous light warship types.[6]

That the two were contemporary and compatible is evidenced by the way that they were operated together, not only by the Romans, but also by Sparta[7] and by Philip of Macedon.[8] The name appears to relate to a species of shark.[9]

As to form, if we are correct to assume that it was an early development of the original *lembi* (see Chapter 11) then it was a smallish, open boat with a fair speed under oar and sail, despite being quite heavy and capacious (more so than say a penteconter) but with the forefoot adapted and extended to mount a ram. As a *lembi*, enhanced for a more aggressive role, it is not unreasonable to assume that it was the larger, bireme version that was so adapted, with some added screening for the rowers.

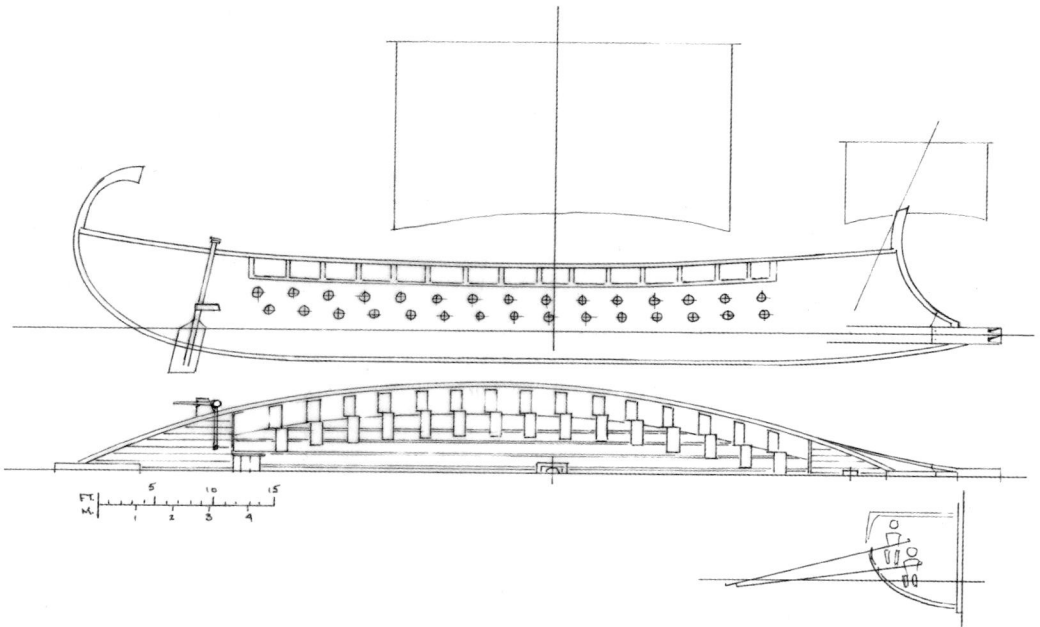

Figure 82. The *Pristis*. Suggested reconstruction, developed from the original *lembi*. The ship is arranged as a bireme, powered by sixty oars. The sides have been extended upward to afford protection for the rowers and they and the cross-frames could be rigged with covers for overhead protection. Raised decks at bow and stern allow for a command and steering position aft and a small fighting platform forward.

Although there is no record of it having had a sailing rig, it would be most surprising if at least a simple, stowable mast, yard and sail were not included.

The example posited in Figure 82 is a bireme of sixty oars with forward and aft raised decks and a beam that allows for reasonable carrying capacity. It is also easy to see that, in the wrong hands, such a vessel would be well-suited for piracy.

Quinquereme

The five, or to the Romans, *quinquereme*, has already been considered (see Chapter 2; Figures 14, 15, 16) but in view of its importance in making up the bulk of the Roman fleets and its inclusion in all the other fleets that were deployed in the Aegean and Eastern Mediterranean, some further examination of the type is warranted. The ships were by this time of a proven and fully evolved type and proved to be capable of taking on and beating the bigger Hellenistic ships that opposed them.[10] The normal Roman military complement of a five was forty marines but, if they knew a battle was imminent, they would embark a century of legionaries or auxiliary troops (approximately eighty men)[11] to augment this and to give them overwhelming superiority in a boarding battle. This certainly was the case in the Punic Wars and presumably, faced with the big Hellenistic ships, they continued the practice.[12]

The ship could have been a trireme or a bireme and as a bireme, would be operated by pairs of oars, two rowers at one and three at the other. The 'Praeneste Relief' (Figure 83) is of the first century and shows a heavy Roman warship.[13] Only two remes of oars are evident, very closely spaced (thirteen pairs survive) suggesting an echelon rowing system (Figure 84A). It makes little sense to use a system logically suited to even numbers and to have oar crews paired that are not the same. It is possible that the rather odd-looking decorative frieze immediately beneath the feet of the marines and above the oars represents a third (thranite) reme of oars which have been withdrawn inboard, but then there is no ventilation course shown and which this would otherwise represent. It does represent a definite projection beyond the hull side (as the men are standing on it) and if so, the relief could be of a trireme five; otherwise, it is a six (and the basis of the reconstruction previously shown).

A tower is positioned diagonally to the centre-line and marines are shown on deck (oversize as seems to have been the convention); they are uniformly equipped, save for the officer[14] in the centre and the two men on the outrigger box are holding javelins or short pikes.[15] There are two different shield motifs suggesting perhaps that one (presumably that with the trident) belongs to one of the ship's marines and the other to embarked soldiers.

Figure 83. The Praeneste Relief. Relief of a large Roman warship from Praeneste (Palestrina), north-east of Rome and now in the Vatican Museum. Large bireme warship with a tower mounted in the bow, diagonally to the ship centreline; the stern section is missing. Marines are shown on deck, their size exaggerated in relation to the ship, as was the convention. There is a crocodile figurehead and a box above it with a head of a god or patron deity; aft of this is a gap in the bulwark for rigging a boarding bridge and aft of this again, a bulwark decorated with disc motifs, not shields, which the men are of course holding. Below this would appear to be a row of louvers for a ventilation course for the rowers. Second half of the first century.

A

B

C

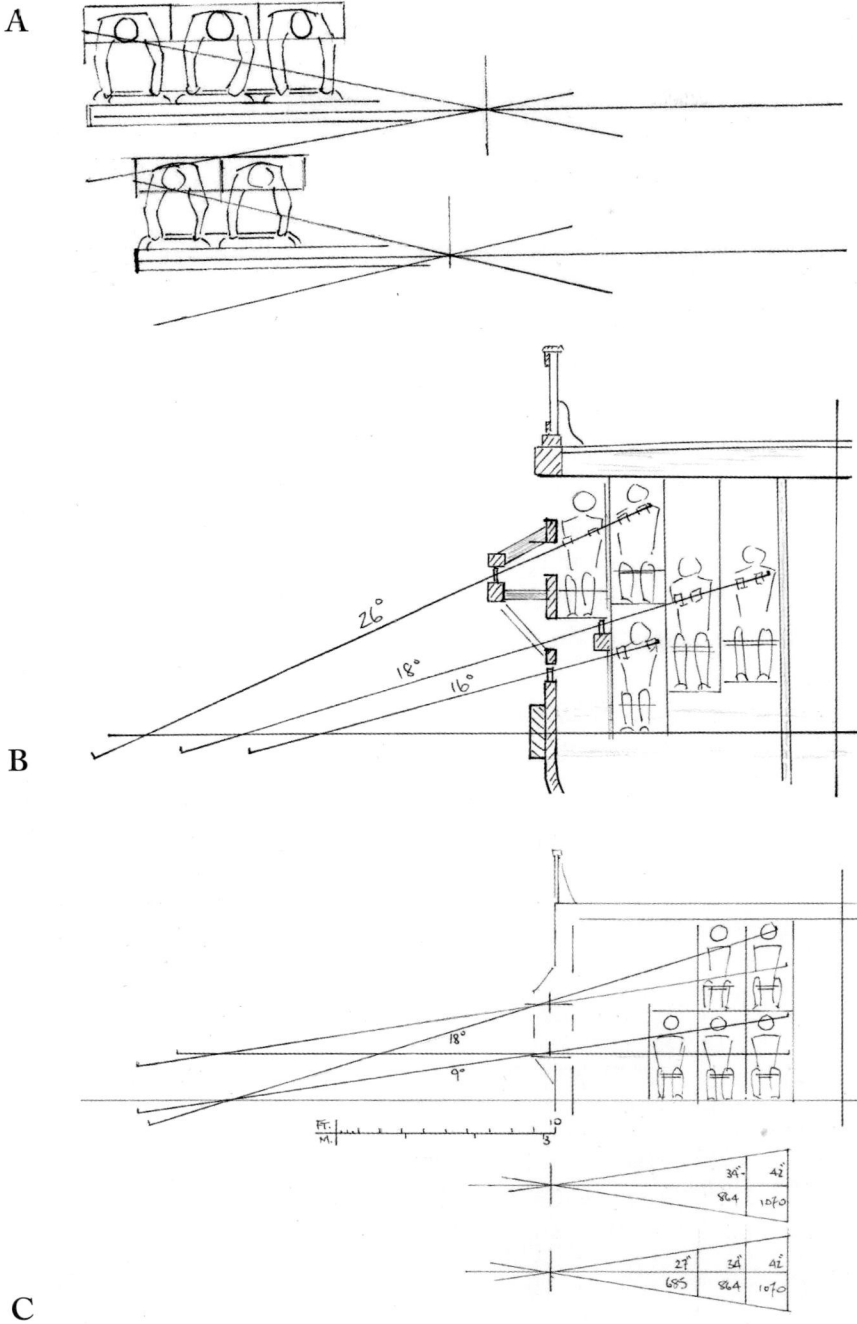

Figures 84A, 84B and 84C. Rowing systems for the Five; A: the echelon system, which seems illogical. B: as a trireme, with the thalamite rower using a shorter oar. C: as a bireme, both crews using a 30 foot /9.14m oar at a gearing of 2.7. Note that here, both thole pins are in the same vertical plane. The relative pulling arcs of the rowers are shown below.

It has been suggested[16] that the crenellations atop the tower represent artillery pieces but no stocks and springs (see Chapter 3) are shown and the faces are decorated to resemble stonework,[17] the mounting of such pieces on towers is unlikely, due to the weight and effect of the recoil of their discharge on what were very lightweight structures;[18] the length of the stocks would prevent traverse and as their missiles only rested in position when loaded they could not shoot downward. The prow bears the figurehead of a crocodile[19] and an artemon (foremast) is mounted without yard and sail.[20]

As a trireme, the ship could be powered by having thranite and zygite oars double-manned and a single thalamite oarsman below (Figure 84B). The problem is that there is an imbalance[21] but perhaps that ship was normally rowed as a bireme four for cruising, the extra reme taking up their oars to add extra power for an engagement. There is of course, a similar imbalance in the bireme version (Figure 84C) where the problem of unequal-length oars and the consequent problem of trying to match stroke is, in this case, obviated and construction is simpler; it could also accord with the Praeneste relief if this in fact showed a bireme.

It is known that the height of the main deck above the waterline was ten (Roman) feet[22] and the ship had an overall length of 160 to 170 feet/51.5m and a waterline beam of about 26 feet /8m. Crew comprised some 300 rowers, thirty officers and seamen and forty marines, a total complement of 370 men, plus on occasion, a century of troops. Apart from the towers, it could mount up to ten artillery pieces, depending on their size.

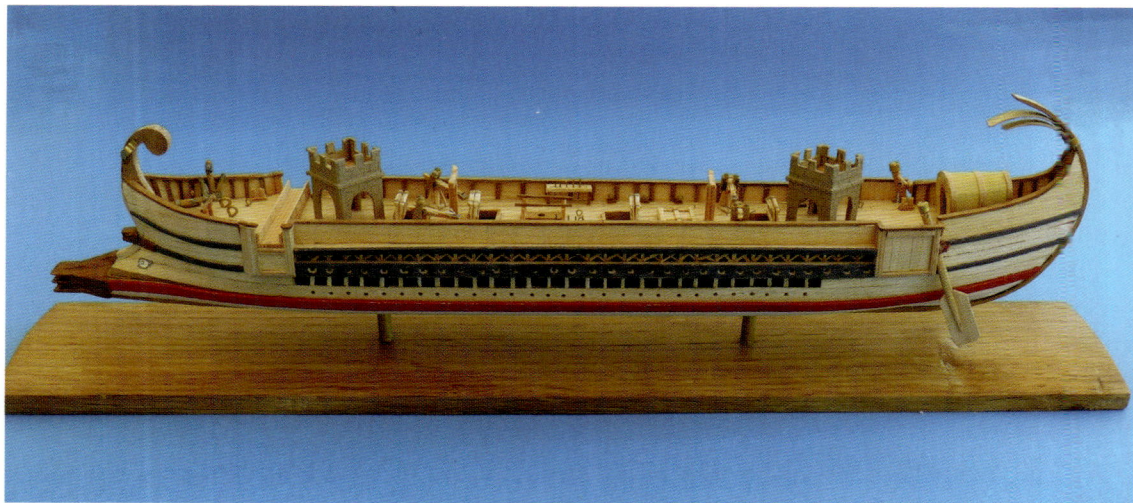

Figure 85. Model of a Roman Quinquereme of the third to first centuries. Scale is 1:192 (1/16 inch) and model length is 10.75 inches/274mm.

Triremes

The Romans deployed a limited number of triremes and could, and no doubt did, make use of Greek and Hellenistic examples that fell into their hands.

It is more than possible that the trireme had undergone development by the Romans during their long naval wars, to make it better suited to their own circumstances in the central and western Mediterranean. Lacking the myriad closely spaced islands of the Aegean and with the greater area of open seas in which they had to operate,

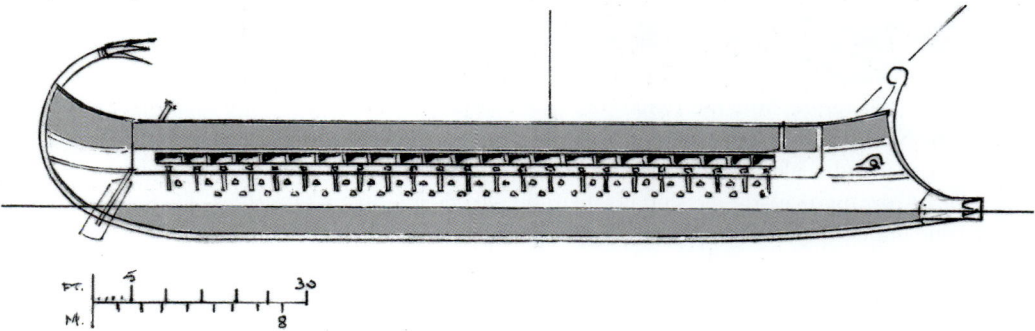

Figure 86. 'Roman-type' Trireme. Although approximately the same size as earlier, Greek examples (127 feet/38.7m overall) the ship is more heavily built and deeper and has fewer rowers but allows more room per man. Crew comprises 132 rowers (46 thranites, 44 zygites and 42 thalamites) with 5 officers, 16 sailors and 20 to 25 marines.

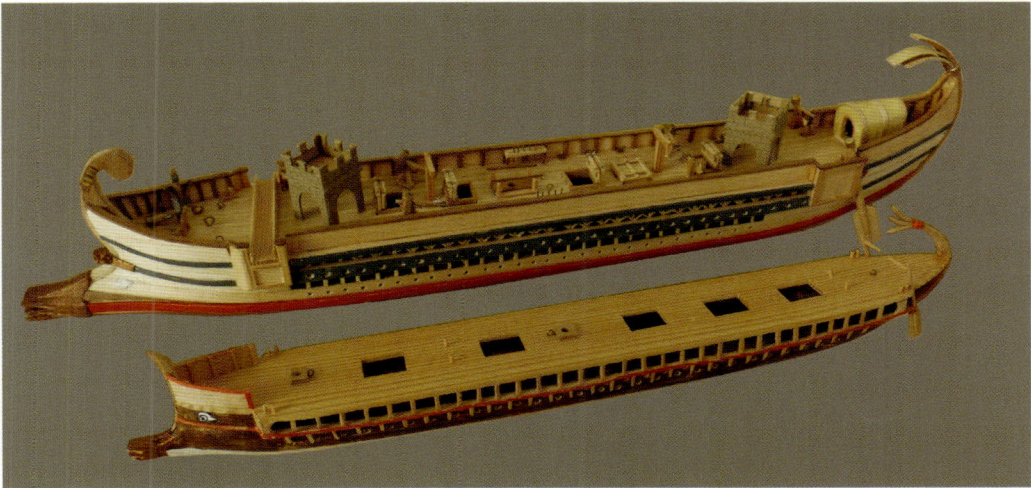

Figure 87. The model quinquereme in Figure 85, alongside a model of a 'classic' trireme to the same scale for comparison. It can be appreciated how the light, sleek trireme was faster, but could not stand against the larger ship in battle.

Figure 88. Wall painting from the Temple of Isis at Pompeii. Late first century to early first century AD. Now in the National Museum, Naples, showing Roman warships. The ships are of similar size, possibly to fit the panel and could depict triremes, liburnians or both. They would appear to have more than one reme of oars, particularly the ship on the right, which appears to have three. They are of course, stylised and impressionistic, being frescoes and thus having had to be quickly painted on to wet plaster.

they were likely to be more heavily built and less 'tender', sacrificing some speed for increased sea-worthiness.

The most prolific source of images that could well include Roman triremes are the many wall paintings from Pompeii (Figure 88) and Herculaneum, together with a relief from Puteoli (Pozzuoli). All of these are admittedly later (no earlier than the very late first century and more probably from the early first century AD) but not so far removed from the period under consideration here to be invalid.

The reconstruction in Figure 86 is arrived at accordingly and shows a ship of 128 feet/39m in length overall and an overall beam, greater than that of the 'classic' trireme, of 21 feet/6.4m and powered by 132 oars.

Liburnae

The Romans were evolving the type as mentioned, and following from the interim *Pristis*, into a general purpose light warship and would continue to do so until it had supplanted all other previous types. Indeed, it became common in later, Imperial times, to refer to warships as 'liburnians' whether they were or not. It would be a mistake however, to assume that, despite some standardisation, they were all alike or of a common design or even class (consider the modern term 'frigate' and all the variations in ships so classified). The problem again is that despite being so often referred to, there survives no accurate description or any illustration that can be definitely attributed. Once more, the most plentiful supply of warship pictures is

Figure 89. Small-scale model of a Roman liburnian at sea (in company with a Six). The sailing rig is stowed on crutches and the ship is under oars alone. The crew has 60 rowers and 2 officers below decks and 4 officers and 6 sailors, together with 6 archers and 10 marines on deck, 88 men in total. Model scale is 1:300 and length is 3.5 inches /88mm.

from the towns buried by the eruption of Mount Vesuvius in AD 79 and although, as mentioned above, later than this period, they do show fairly standardised versions of warships,[23] some of which at least must surely have been of liburnians. It is upon this that the model in Figure 89 is based, which is of a small bireme warship[24] 85 feet /26m in overall length with sixty oars.

PART VI

TWILIGHT OF THE HELLENISTIC NAVIES
100 TO 30 BC

Prow of a Roman warship, late first century BC. (*Archaeological Museum, Modena*)

Chapter 14

Becoming a Roman Lake

100   The anti-piracy campaigns of Marcus Antonius had but a minor and temporary effect on the reign of piracy, many of them having simply avoided or hidden from his forces; some may even have become 'allies' for the duration. He did manage to drive them from most of Cilicia, whence they fled to Crete; once Antonius returned to Rome (to a Triumph) the pirates promptly returned to Cilicia.

96   In 96, Ptolemy Apion (bastard son of Ptolemy VII) who had inherited Cyrene (the north-western part of Egypt and north-eastern part of Libya) died, bequeathing it to the Senate and People of Rome.[1] The Romans accepted the bequest but made no move to take it up and the pirates quickly found it to be a further convenient place from which to operate. The Romans were in fact distracted by internal unrest in Italy (the Social War) which ended in 88, leaving the Dictator Lucius Cornelius Sulla as one of the most powerful men of Rome.

89   The Kingdom of Pontus stretched along the north coast of Asia Minor. It had been a satrapy of the Persian Empire but asserted its independence as that empire weakened, becoming a kingdom under Mithridates I in 337. Although outside of Alexander's empire, it acknowledged his hegemony, re-establishing outright independence upon his death. The king in 89, Mithridates VI (121 to 63) had ambitions to make his realm into a leading Hellenistic power. He had extended his power eastward along the Euxine coast and built up a navy of some 300 vessels, including triremes and some fives, their biggest type.[2] The remainder were mostly smaller types including *hemioliae*[3] and 'a hundred biremes'.[4] In 89 he turned his attentions westward, having designs on the neighbouring kingdoms of Bithynia and Cappadocia, both 'friends' of Rome. Through intrigue and coups he installed his own puppet kings in both; the Romans sent an ex-consul, Manlius Aquillius to restore the original rulers. Mithridates, under threat of military action did so and withdrew. Aquillius, eager for plunder, persuaded the king of Bithynia to attack Pontus. They were duly beaten and a re-invasion by Mithridates proceeded to overrun much of Bithynia and the Roman province of Asia (formerly Pergamum) as well

met by a regular, formed naval force, such as that of Rhodes against whom, despite those numbers, they were unable to obtain a victory.

It was not completely one-sided and, at some point, the Rhodians lost a five, one of their biggest ships. They sent a squadron of six of their fastest ships to recover it and on seeing this, Mithridates sent twenty-five of his ships after them in turn. The Rhodians withdrew towards their harbour and as the sun was beginning to go down, the Ponic ships turned for home; as soon as they did so, the Rhodians turned and attacked, sinking two ships and driving the others towards the Lycian mainland shore, demonstrating again not only

Figure 90. Mithridates VI, King of Pontus 121–66. Fought three wars against Rome, from 88 to 83, again from 74 to 73 and finally, in 66, fled to Crimea where he committed suicide in 63. Silver tetradrachm. (*Metropolitan Museum of Art, New York*)

the swiftness of their ships but their flexibility in reacting to events and the command and control in their officers and crews.[14] On another occasion a convoy of merchant ships, escorted by triremes, bound for Mithridates' forces on Rhodes, found itself blown by an unfavourable wind towards Rhodes (city). The Rhodian fleet attacked, capturing some ships, ramming others and burning yet more, also taking 400 prisoners.[15] Finally, Mithridates ordered a joint land and sea attack on Rhodes; two ships were lashed together and a *sambucus*, a device for permitting troops to be raised to assault the walls, was erected. It was supported by catapults and small assault boats, but the attack was thwarted by the defenders and the *sambucus* collapsed under its own weight. Mithridates thereupon gave up the siege and withdrew.[16] Mithridates was, nonetheless, now virtual master of the Aegean. He had also captured, on Cos, several members of the Ptolemaic family, holding them as hostages and forcing Egyptian neutrality during the war.[17]

Internecine quarrels among the Ptolemies had led to the expulsion of Ptolemy IX in 107, who fled to Cyprus, to be replaced by Ptolemy X.[18] After a decade of misrule, he in turn was forced to flee from Egypt and whereupon he managed to fund and raise a fleet. His attempt to then regain his throne failed when this fleet was beaten, and he was killed in a naval battle off Cyprus. In 83, Ptolemy IX returned to rule Egypt.

Figure 91. The entrance to Mandraki, the military harbour of Rhodes, as it is today. The ancient city was much bigger than the Crusader town and the harbour was wholly within it, with shipyards at the southern end. Although no longer fortified, the narrowness of the entrance demonstrates how gates were mounted to deny entry to the ships of a besieger.

Of these fleets and the battle, there is no surviving account but, since Ptolemy X had taken treasure with him (having sold Alexander the Great's gold coffin) and raised loans, we can presume that he was able to hire a mercenary fleet, ships, supplies and crews from those that would otherwise have been pirates. His opponent on the other hand would be likely to have been the Ptolemaic royal navy, supporting the restored Ptolemy IX. This force comprised over 100 warships in rates up to tens but of these, perhaps only half were kept in commission. Egypt had more ships laid up and plentiful manpower for crews but morale, and therefore effectiveness, had been eroded by the conflict of loyalties arising from the rivalries among the ruling family.

What is notable is the apparent ease with which Ptolemy X could hire not only mercenaries but an entire navy, equipped with warships, presumably of sufficient sizes to be a viable battle fleet and ready for action and to supplement the few royal ships that had presumably remained loyal to him, enabling him to flee and go on a recruiting tour. These same men, ships and equipment and their readiness for adventure, speaks of the resources available for recruitment by both Mithridates and Lucullus (see post) and of course, for piracy, when they operated in squadrons.[19]

It has been seen how, with the demise of Hellenistic navies, hundreds of ships were left strewn in small numbers in harbours around Greece, the Aegean, Asia Minor and Phoenicia. Many must have fallen into disrepair, becoming hulks, rotted or been broken up for timber or burnt; this must have included any survivors of the giant ships as nothing larger than a ten is reported thereafter. Officially of course, these ships became the property of their *poleis*. However, upon becoming a Roman province or being tied to Rome by treaty, local forces were not disarmed but maintained and kept for local defence. They had to be available when called upon, to serve with Roman forces under overall Roman command. This included naval forces (rated as 'Roman Auxiliaries') and coastal provinces were expected to build, equip and man warships. All of which explains the ready availability of warships for hire by such as Ptolemy X and for use by Caesar to punish the pirates who had ransomed him. Doubtless also not a few of these naval forces could do a little freelance buccaneering.[20]

88   In 88 Mithridates invaded Greece, where Athens went over to him and his army advanced until stopped in northern Greece by the Roman garrison. Sulla had meanwhile been given command of five legions with which he crossed to Epirus, advancing to Athens by 87 which, along with Piraeus, he took after a siege and, despite a spirited defence, both were sacked by his troops.[21] The following year, Sulla defeated Mithridates' army at Chaeronea (86 or 85). Mithridates landed another army on Euboea, behind Sulla, which he also defeated. With a third defeat by Sulla near Orchemenas in Boeotia, Mithridates' invasion of Greece was over but as Sulla had no fleet, he could not challenge the Pontic fleet's command of the Northern Aegean or support his troops in the pursuit of Mithridates and the relief of Asia.

The outbreak of the war had demonstrated a glaring difference from the wars of the previous century. Then the Romans had promptly despatched and maintained effective fleets to the east; now Sulla had to campaign without naval support, which severely hampered his operations.

85   Sulla, after taking Athens, sent his deputy, Lucius Licinius Lucullus to gather and organise a fleet from among Rome's remaining allies and those states that had opposed Mithridates, while he took his army on the long route around the north of the Aegean to Thrace.

Sulla, in the meantime, had been declared an outlaw at Rome by his rivals who, in 86, had sent a fleet some thirty to forty strong, mostly fives with some liburnians and certainly powerful enough to better Mithridates' ships if they met. It carried an army, commanded by Lucius Valerius Flaccus, direct to Asia. Flaccus was murdered by his deputy, Caius Flavius Fimbria, under whose command this army marched and beat Mithridates in battle near the Propontis. Lucullus had obtained an escort of three light ships and three Rhodian ships at Athens and with them he sailed to Alexandria via Crete and Cyrene. There, Ptolemy IX, knowing that Sulla had been proscribed and aware of the hostages held by Mithridates, declined to help. Lucullus' tiny fleet narrowly avoided enemy warships near Cyprus but enjoyed more success in recruiting in Rhodes, Greece, Macedonia and Asia, as well as several Greek islands where he managed to hire and cajole a collection of ships and crews to form a fleet which also included ships from Cyprus, Pamphylia and Phoenicia, Lucullus refused to countenance any suspected pirate ships. He raised his flag in a Rhodian five and the fleet sailed to the Propontis, ignoring the 'official' fleet supporting Fimbria. En route it raided enemy-held coasts and skirmished with Pontic ships. When it reached the Northern Aegean, the fleet came up against Mithridates' fleet on two occasions, both times beating it. In one of these battles, at Tenedos, Lucullus' flagship, a Rhodian 'five' came under ram attack from astern; they backed water and suffered no damage when the two ships came into contact, the increased closing speed apparently causing the attacker's ram to slide under the raised stern of Lucullus' ship.[22]

85   Covered by his fleet, Sulla's army crossed into Asia Minor. He met Mithridates at Dardanus, near Troy and agreed to a peace by which Mithridates (whose support among those that he had overrun was failing) was forced to surrender all the territory that he had conquered completely and had to surrender seventy of his ships to Sulla. Sulla's forces then combined with those of Fimbria whereupon Lucullus' scratch fleet was disbanded and sent home; Lucullus then took command of the Roman fleet. Sulla had planned to garrison the Aegean with permanent naval forces at various bases to prevent piracy and using the warships laid up at those ports, presumably those recently used by Lucullus and of course the seventy ex-Pontic ships. Before this scheme could be established, he had to return to Rome; piracy recommenced almost immediately, including a raid on the island of Samothrace while Sulla was still there.

83   Although the main antagonists had left, Sulla to Rome and Mithridates to Pontus, the island of Lesbos, which had sided with Mithridates, refused to return to Roman suzerainty. The new Roman governor of Asia, Marcus Minucius Thermus, had only a few ships, probably some of the ex-Pontic ships with local levies and his own troops. He sent a very young Gaius Julius Caesar to obtain ships from the restored King Nicomedes of Bithynia. With these additional forces, Mytilene, the capital of Lesbos was blockaded and Lesbos brought back under Roman control.

79   By 79, piracy had become so rife that Rome sent the Consul Publius Servilius Vatia with a Roman fleet to scour the Cilician coast for pirates, as Marcus Antonius had done before. In 78, Vatia continued his campaign into Lycia, Pamphylia and Isauria and, in 77, his fleet joined battle against a pirate fleet, which it defeated.

75   By 75, Vatia had driven the surviving pirates to their final refuge in Cilicia and there took Phaselis. As he was about to mount a final attack on the remaining pirates, the war between Mithridates and Rome resumed and Vatia and his fleet had to be recalled. In their absence, the pirates quickly recovered both in Cilicia and Crete. With the ending of Athenian autonomy and the reduction in Rhodian power, there was not sufficient force left to provide any check to their activities. They proliferated and any tacit approval by some merchants (for example for the supply to them of slaves) was quickly lost and they crippled trade. Ranging from the Levant to Sicily, they took to raiding coastal towns and commerce became totally disrupted. They could muster over a thousand boats and ships, many of them warships including large ones.[23]

74   In 74, a Roman military and naval force advanced northward along the western shore of the Euxine (Black) Sea in pursuit of Thracian raiders as far

Figure 92. Wall painting of Roman warships in combat against pirate craft, first century. (*Palazzo Massimo Museum, Rome*)

as the Danube delta, chasing them to the north but leaving no garrisons to deter their return. Also in 74, as part of their anti-piracy policy, the Romans formally annexed Cyrene, occupying it and denying it to pirates. Finally in 74, Nicomedes IV, the last King of Bithynia died, having bequeathed his kingdom to Rome.

Mithridates could not tolerate the Roman acquisition of neighbouring Bithynia and with it, control of the Propontis and Hellespont and thus access to the Aegean. He had rebuilt his military forces and reoccupied Cappadocia; he also now had about 400 ships of all types. At that time, a Roman general, Quintus Sertorius was leading a rebellion in Spain and Mithridates effected a treaty with him, offering forty ships and a large sum of money and got, in return, a military mission to train his forces.[24] A Roman force, hastily sent from Asia, tried to pre-empt him and invade Pontus but was beaten and Mithridates' army invaded and occupied Bithynia, advancing along the southern shore of the Propontis. Once again, the pirates allied themselves with him, contributing *hemioliae, myoparones* (see later) and *dikroter* (biremes) as well as triremes.[25]

73   The Romans countered with a double attack. Lucullus, now a consul, took forces to Asia while the other consul, Gaius Aurelius Cotta, with sixty-eight ships (a total that probably included warships and transports) made to attack Bithynia. Cotta rushed ahead of Lucullus and started operations prematurely; as a result, his ships were beaten by Mithridates' superior numbers, losing a 'four' and six small open ships destroyed[26] and his troops were beaten on land. He was besieged at Chalcedon on the Asiatic Shore of the Hellespont, his fleet being trapped in the harbour there. The fleet was attacked in harbour by

Figure 93. Author's model of a Roman trireme of the first century. Model length is 5.25 inches/133mm.

the enemy fleet, losing two ships burned and two others with many of the rest towed away by Mithridates' ships.

Lucullus meanwhile, advanced overland, driving Mithridates' forces back and relieving Cotta. In the spring, Mithridates had sent his fleet back into the Aegean, encouraging and recruiting pirates as they went. Lucullus sailed with the Roman fleet of sixty-four ships and some Rhodian ships. This was predominantly a Roman fleet as with their recent history, local levies could hardly be relied upon, so many of the Greek states having sided with Mithridates (with the notable exception of Rhodes). He caught and captured thirteen of Mithridates' ships off Tenedos; later Lucullus found another squadron of his ships on the beach at Lemnos and destroyed them. In the face of this onslaught, the remaining Pontic fleet withdrew into the Euxine, where they suffered further losses in a storm, perhaps as many as sixty ships,[27] before they reached home. The Roman fleet fought two more battles against Pontic ships off Heraclea, driving them off and proceeding to blockade the Euxine coast.[28] The fleet, with its (reliable) allies then supported Lucullus' advance along the coasts of Bithynia and Pontus and he took the Pontic capital of Sinope; Mithridates fled to Armenia, ending the war (71).

Once again, apart from some early, surprise success, the rather polyglot nature of Mithridates' naval forces, made up as they were of a significant proportion of freewheeling irregular units, together with their lack of experience as a fleet, meant that for all their numbers they fared badly against a regular fleet under firm, disciplined command. Their problem appeared to be lack of command and control meaning that they could not maintain a sufficient degree of cohesion in battle. An incident perhaps to illustrate this occurred while Mithridates was in his flagship, a five, off Rhodes when one of his allied ships from Chios collided with his ship; he was furious and later punished the Chians.[29]

72   Mithridates had sought the pirates as allies and had encouraged their activities to interfere with Roman supplies and trade. Their strength grew and with the end of the war and withdrawal once more of the Roman fleet, it was totally beyond the capability of a reduced Rhodes to police; for its part, the Ptolemaic navy seemed virtually inactive. Seeking to repeat the anti-piracy campaigns of his father and Vatia, the Roman Senate sent Marcus Antonius (junior) to attack the pirates of Crete. He took a fleet (composition not known) but was badly beaten by a pirate fleet, losing several ships, whose surviving crews were hanged by the pirates.[30]

The pirates were so numerous that they could operate whole fleets of ships which were well manned, trained and with an established chain of command, as if they were a regular navy (which in effect, they became) of an established state. It is probable that they 'borrowed' *trihemioliae*, fours and even fives, operating in squadrons and fleets of as many as a hundred ships at a time, appointing admirals and adopting conventional naval tactics. With such organisation and numbers, they did not have to run before regular fleets (which is how they beat Antonius). They dominated many coasts, coastal towns and cities and could, and did, plunder towns, temples and capture people, the rich for ransom and the poor to be sold as slaves. On

Figure 94. Bust thought to be of the historian Plutarch (c.46 to c.120) whose works, so nearly contemporary, have proved invaluable. (*Acropolis Museum, Athens*)

one occasion they held the daughter of a famous Roman general for ransom and on another, captured two Roman praetors, complete with their staff; the pirates' boldness knew no bounds. Their manpower was plentiful, as has been seen, for men had been recruited to crew the fleets of the various antagonists and generations of them had known no other life; with the demise of those employers, literally thousands of men, experienced only with life at sea and unsuited to anything else, found themselves with nothing to do and no way of making a living.

69   Piracy continued to rage unchecked across the Mediterranean and in 69 they attacked and sacked Delos[31] and even operated in the Strait of Messina, raiding Sicily. Their depredations were such that the vital grain supply to Rome was seriously disrupted and Rome faced starvation. Merchant shipping was at a standstill and coastal towns and villages lived in constant fear of attack. Finally, the Romans were stirred to react and in 69, the consul Quintus Metellus with three legions invaded Crete, one of the pirates' main lairs. In the face of his onslaught, the Cretans surrendered, the pirates were driven out and the island was restored to Ptolemaic rule.

67   The final act that led to all-out war was a daring pirate raid in early 67 upon Ostia, where they captured and destroyed a number of warships in the home harbour of Rome itself.[32] The Romans dealt with the pirate scourge once and

for all by enacting the *Lex Gabinia* in 67, which gave unprecedented power to Gaius Pompeius, one of the most powerful men in Rome. He was given command of the entire Mediterranean and for 50 miles/80km inland from coasts and authorised to raise as many as 120,000 troops, 5,000 cavalry and 500 ships from Rome, its allies and tributaries and to appoint twenty-four legates (the rank to command a legion) as deputies.[33]

Figure 95. Pediment from Pergamum showing a very ornate Hellenistic helmet superimposed on a traditional hoplon shield. (*Altes Museum, Berlin*)

Pompeius raised a fleet of some 200 major warships and seventy lighter ships, gathering every ship that could be found and made seaworthy. There were also ships from Egypt, Phoenicia, Rhodes, Athens and other allies and tributaries in the East. Levies from the provinces helped to crew the ships but the majority of the marines and troops on board were Roman and Roman auxiliaries. Almost the entire resources of the Roman world were concentrated and focused on this one purpose.

For the campaign, Pompeius divided the Mediterranean and Euxine into thirteen areas of operation, each commanded by a Legate with ships and troops.[34] Pompeius held a reserve fleet of sixty ships. He blockaded the Sicilian Narrows to divide the Mediterranean in two and then, starting from the Pillars of Hercules, he systematically swept the western Mediterranean attacking pirates wherever he found them and driving them into the forces of his waiting legates, crushing them between the two. In forty days, the campaign completely eradicated pirates and piracy from the western Mediterranean.

The same process was next repeated for the whole of the eastern Mediterranean, Pompeius sweeping the seas and coasts from Brundisium via Athens and Rhodes, which he used as a forward base, to the pirates' greatest lair, Cilicia. Their greatest and final stronghold was at Coracaesium, a rocky outcrop, separated from the mainland by an isthmus and rising 500 feet/200m above the sea. Pompeius defeated the pirate fleet that came out to defend it in a sea battle and then captured the stronghold itself, taking seventy-one ships and capturing another 300 there.[35] The war had lasted only three months in which Pompeius was said to have captured 600 pirate vessels including ninety warships, killed 10,000 pirates and taken another 20,000 as prisoners.[36] Many of these were resettled, far from the sea, giving them, effectively, a new life and an alternative to buccaneering, the penalty for a return to which was made clear. Piracy was almost totally ended but this time, to ensure that it did not re-emerge the Romans ensured that their naval decline would not recur and that permanent, adequate naval forces would be maintained. Squadrons were established (under Roman control) to patrol the Tyrrhenian and Adriatic Seas, with surplus ships laid up but maintained to keep them seaworthy and available if needed.

66   While Pompeius was still in the east organising naval forces there, Mithridates made what would be his final bid for empire. He had resumed control of his kingdom but, before he could do too much mischief, Pompeius, using the huge numbers of his fleets, placed a naval ring around Asia Minor from the Levant to the Hellespont to prevent any irruption by a renovated Pontic fleet and their former pirate friends. He then marched overland from Cilicia and defeated Mithridates, occupying Pontus. Pompeius moved on to Armenia (which surrendered) and to what is now Georgia, giving Rome control of the entire north coast of Asia Minor. Mithridates fled to the Bosporan Kingdom, where he committed suicide in 63. Pompeius established a naval squadron and garrison at Sinope to cover the Euxine and a permanent naval force at Ephesus, with one squadron to cover the northern half of the Aegean and another for the southern half.[37] The squadrons were composed of local, allied and auxiliary ships and crews; the main Roman fleet again went home.

64   Pompeius moved into Syria and met one of the last claimants to the Seleucid throne, Antiochus XIII; after he was refused support by Pompeius, he was murdered by an associate. The other claimant to the throne, Philip II seems to have disappeared from the record after 63 and the Seleucid throne duly lapsed, Syria and Phoenicia passing by default, to Rome (62).[38]

     Pompeius was still in the Levant when civil war broke out in Judaea between two brothers who were rival claimants to its throne. Pompeius thus marched into Judaea (in 64) and occupied Jerusalem, including the Temple Mount. The kingdom was much reduced and Pompeius' favoured claimant placed on the throne.

63   In the following year, 63, he made Hellenistic coastal cities under Judaean or formal Seleucid suzerainty independent. The effect was to make the whole Levantine Coast subject to Roman hegemony.[39] Crete was annexed in 62.

58   Although (by now only nominally) a domain of the Ptolemies of Egypt, Cyprus had been a major centre of piracy and in 58, Marcus Portius Cato was sent with a naval and military force to annex the island, which was made part of the province of Cyrene.

The Myoparo

The ships involved in this final period were of types already examined, but there was one new type, a type of craft ascribed to pirates namely the *myoparo*, which made a fairly brief appearance in the latter part of the period.

The name first appears in a progressive list of pirate ship types by Appian[40] in use during the Mithridatic Wars (three wars between 86 and 66). He lists *myoparones*, followed by *hemioliae*, then biremes and triremes; the list thus appears to progress from the smallest to the largest types and from which it can be inferred that the *myoparo* was the smallest.

As with so many types, there has come down to us no clear definition or attributable illustration of a *'myoparo'*. Cicero[41] mentions it as a pirate ship and also that another one was provided by Miletus from their fleet, said to have been 'armed' but that does not necessarily mean that it had a ram,[42] which would be little more than an affectation on such a small ship.

Torr[43] interprets the type as a 'fighting ship of no great size,' broader than usual in proportion to its length and thus a better sea-boat. To support this, he quotes Appian[44] and Plutarch[45] referring to an occasion in 37, the last time that the type appears in use as such. They seem to agree that the ship is an interim type, between a 'round' merchant ship and a 'long' warship, powered by a single reme of oars and not intended primarily as a fighting ship; a sailing rig can be assumed. This reference

Figures 96. Civil War antagonists, left, Gnaius Pompeius Magnus (*Louvre*); right, Caius Julius Caesar. (*British Museum*)

appears somewhat late as, by the Roman capture of Coracaesium in 67, the pirates were already giving up their *hemioliae* and *myoparones* and building biremes and triremes.[46] They were briefly pressed into Roman service as captured craft,[47] but not adopted by them as a service type.

There remains a mosaic from Althiburbus (in Tunisia and now in the Bardo Museum, Tunis) purporting to show various ships that all have different names (save numbers 7 and 8, '*tesseraria*': tile carriers), including (number 11) a '*myoparo*' and (number 23) a '*paro*'. This mosaic dates from the third or fourth century AD and thus at least three hundred years after the 'pirate' *myoparo* was last heard of, a considerable break in continuity which need not, of course, obviate this theory. The biggest problem however, is that a comparison of pictures ten, eleven and twelve seem to show the same ship (with slight variations to the stem post) under oars, with its rig being raised and under sail respectively, despite each being differently named. It is similarly difficult to see any difference in type between pictures twenty-two and twenty-three. Perhaps the names simply refer to the names of the ships, rather than to differing types of ship and the mosaic a catalogue of all the vessels owned or operated by a shipping line.[48]

On balance, the term appears to have been briefly coined and used to refer to a small, beamy, monoreme, open galley used for piracy or as a fleet auxiliary with reasonable carrying capacity, appearing and disappearing in the late first century.

Chapter 15

The Last Hellenistic Fleets

There no longer remained any independent Hellenistic or Greek states with a seaboard save for Ptolemaic Egypt (albeit shorn of its former possessions of Cyprus, Cyrene and Phoenicia). The continuing story is of Roman, Greek and former Hellenistic ships and crews (with the sole exception, for a little longer, of Rhodes) being levied or impressed for service only as part of Roman forces and under Roman command. Even the Egyptian fleet, the sole remaining wholly independently raised and organised non-Roman navy, would operate henceforth under Roman aegis.

49   The process that resulted in the breakdown of the Roman Republic had by 49 left two rivals vying for supreme power: Caesar and Pompeius. In January, civil war broke out between them and Pompeius was forced out of Italy to Greece, where he set about building up his forces. The Roman and allied fleets established by Pompeius in the east remained loyal to him and the fleets of the allies, Rhodes and Egypt also supported him. Caesar was left with a much-reduced naval force of twenty-four ships, which he divided between the west coast of Italy and Sicily.

In July, Pompeius sent a force of sixteen warships in an attempt to relieve Massilia (Marseilles) which had sided with him and was besieged by Caesar's men. The attempt failed.[1] The city fell, yielding a further six ships for Caesar.

By the Autumn, Pompeius had gathered a force of some 300 ships,[2] Roman and allied, organised into six fleets under the overall command of Lucius Calpurnius Bibulus. They were the Adriatic, under Marcus Octavius; Aechean (the South Aegean flotilla from Ephesus) under Caius Triarius; Asian (the North Aegean flotilla from Ephesus) under Decimus Laelius; Syrian under Caius Cassius. In addition, there was a Rhodian fleet of sixteen ships, commanded by Caius Marcellus and an Egyptian fleet of fifty ships from the Ptolemaic navy but commanded by Pompeius' elder son, Gnaeus.[3]

The 'Roman' ships, although commanded by Roman officers and probably with a majority of Roman marines, would undoubtedly have the great majority of their crews levied from the provinces and territories of the Eastern Mediterranean, men or whose fore-fathers had manned the fleets of Macedon,

Pergamum and Seleucia and possibly some who had once been pirates. The naval action mostly took place in the Ionian and Adriatic Seas. Bibulus, with a fleet of 110 ships, made his headquarters on Corcyra, with an advance squadron under Laelius at Oricus and another which had previously been sent to the northern Adriatic. Throughout the campaign, Pompeius' superior naval forces were well used and dominated the Adriatic and Ionian Seas, causing Caesar considerable privation by blocking his supplies from Italy.

48   The Pompeian fleets sought to block a crossing by Caesar to Greece but in January 48, during the 'closed' sailing season, he managed to cross and landed with his army in Illyria. To get his army across, Caesar's limited number of ships had to make several crossings. On one return trip, Bibulus managed to intercept Caesar's transports, capturing thirty of them, which he burned at sea, complete

Figure 97. Fragment of a relief, believed to show a naval battle. A helmsman is in the stern of a ship looking at a figure who has fallen into the sea, but still holds his hoplon/shield aloft; however, the rest of the relief could as easily have shown him as on the deck of another ship, which was lower. Second/first century. (*Archaeological Museum, Rhodes*)

with their crews. Caesar appointed Publius Cornelius Dolabella to be his naval commander and his fleet in the Adriatic was built up to forty ships, half of which were fives.

In April the Rhodians were in action when Marcus Antonius, with reinforcements for Caesar, was blown off course and northwards past Dyrrhachium. The Rhodian squadron of sixteen ships there put to sea to intercept but not in time to prevent all but one of Antonius' ships from reaching harbour at Nymphaeum (Shengjin, Albania); the straggler, a transport, was taken by the enemy. A sudden squall arose from the south-west, catching the Rhodians in the port quarter and forcing them onto the nearby rocky shore and where the crews were captured by Antonius' men.[4]

The Egyptian fleet had taken over the blockade of Caesar's forces at Oricus. Caesar's commander sent his ships into the lagoon at the rear of the town and sank a transport as a block-ship in the channel that connected the lagoon with the Bay of Valona. Another transport was adapted to carry a tower and artillery to act as a guard ship. The Egyptian ships attacked and managed to grapple and tow away the block-ship and then attacked the guard ship. Simultaneously, the attackers also seized the neck of the isthmus behind the town and using rollers, hauled four bireme warships across, into the lagoon. With these ships they attacked the garrison's ships moored in the lagoon. At the same time, the other Egyptian ships finally forced the guard ship to be abandoned and passed through the channel into the lagoon and joined the attack on Caesar's ships. They towed four away and burned the rest, isolating the garrison in the town.

In an attempt to interdict Caesar's reinforcements, a Pompeian fleet of fifty ships seized the tiny island of Barra which lies across the entrance to the harbour of Brundisium, using it as a base to raid the coast. Lured into the inlet leading to the harbour by two apparently floundering triremes, five fours gave chase and were attacked in the narrow inlet by many small boats laden with troops, which had been camouflaged, losing one ship. The local commander, Antonius posted cavalry patrols along the coast to prevent landings and as Barra is waterless, the fleet was forced to return to Greece.[5] The Asian Fleet under Laelius were next to attack Brundisium. Learning from their predecessors' mistake, they took water-carrying ships when they seized Barra. The defenders repeated their earlier, successful tactics of fitting out many small boats, hoping to entice Laelius' ships into their trap within the long, narrow channel leading to the port. Laelius fell for their same ruse, sending ships in after a ship which appeared to be (as it was supposed to) in difficulty. He lost a 'five' and two smaller warships, with no room to manoeuvre and overwhelmed by the defenders' boats.[6] The blockade could not prevent Antonius from sailing and despite trying to intercept his merchant ships, the wind freshened, filling their large sails enabling them to out-sail the warships, which only carried light rigs and whose oarpower was reduced by the higher seas.[7]

The Syrian fleet under Cassius meanwhile, made a surprise attack on Sicily where Caesar had a fleet, the main part at Messana and the rest at Hipponium (Vibo Marina, Calabria) to protect the Strait of Messina. The ships at Messina, totally unsuspecting, had failed to post patrols or lookouts and were thus completely surprised when Cassius attacked with pre-prepared fireships, loaded with pitch, resin and other flammable materials. The wind was favourable and all thirty-five of Caesar's ships were burned to the waterline.

Cassius next attacked the Caesarian ships at Hipponium, using another forty fireships. Five of Caesar's ships were lost but the fleet there being more alert, the remainder were quickly manned and counter attacked. They fought with such vigour that they captured Cassius' flagship, a 'five' plus another 'five' and destroyed two of his triremes. Cassius only just escaped by small boat and withdrew from the fight.

In August 48, the two opposing armies met at Pharsalus, where Caesar inflicted a crushing defeat on Pompeius. On hearing the news of battle, Cassius' Syrian and Laelius' Asian fleets broke off operations and sailed east. Pompeius' main fleet tried to concentrate at Corcyra but, their cause in Greece being lost, the Egyptian and other eastern ships went home, their commander, Pompeius' elder son Gnaeus, fleeing to join his father's still loyal supporters in Spain. Most of the remaining ships and the Rhodians went over to Caesar but about fifty-five ships left to join Pompeian forces holding Africa. Pompeius himself fled to Cyprus and thence crossed to Egypt.[8]

In the autumn, Caesar went to Alexandria with troops and about twenty-five Roman warships but also ten Rhodian ships, in pursuit of the fleeing Pompeius, only to learn that he had been murdered on landing there.[9] Although now having some 200 ships, many would have been ex-Pompeian and of doubtful loyalty; the ships he took were 'his own' but the inclusion of the Rhodians is notable. There, Caesar found himself embroiled in a struggle for power in Egypt between Ptolemy XIII and his sister, Cleopatra VII (by their father's will, Rome had been appointed their guardian). He was soon besieged in the royal palace and adjacent Bruchion quarter of the city. His few ships were trapped in the small royal harbour by an Egyptian fleet of seventy-two ships, including fours and fives, in the adjacent eastern harbour.[10] Caesar does not mention in his memoirs any of the bigger ships which remained absent throughout.

47 A surprise attack by Caesar's troops succeeded in setting fire to the Egyptian ships while most of their crews were ashore, destroying twenty-two of the fours, five of their fives and some smaller ships, breaking their hold and sending the survivors into the western harbour. Caesar could then send for reinforcements.

The Egyptian ships sallied to the attack when they espied a supply convoy bound for Caesar, becalmed off the harbour mouth. These ships were having to be towed in by Caesar's warships. Four of the Egyptians attacked the leading Rhodian ship whereupon all of the other Rhodian ships rushed to help their countryman. The Egyptians were beaten off, losing four ships, but did manage to recover Pharos Island and the lighthouse, previously seized by Caesar.

The Egyptians brought reinforcements along the canal from the Nile and refitted as many of their ships as possible to produce a fleet of twenty-two fours, five fives and some smaller. Caesar's reinforcements had brought his fleet up to thirty-four ships, nine Rhodian and twenty-five Roman ships, including five

MAP 18
ALEXANDRIA
IN 48 B.C.
AT THE TIME OF CAESAR

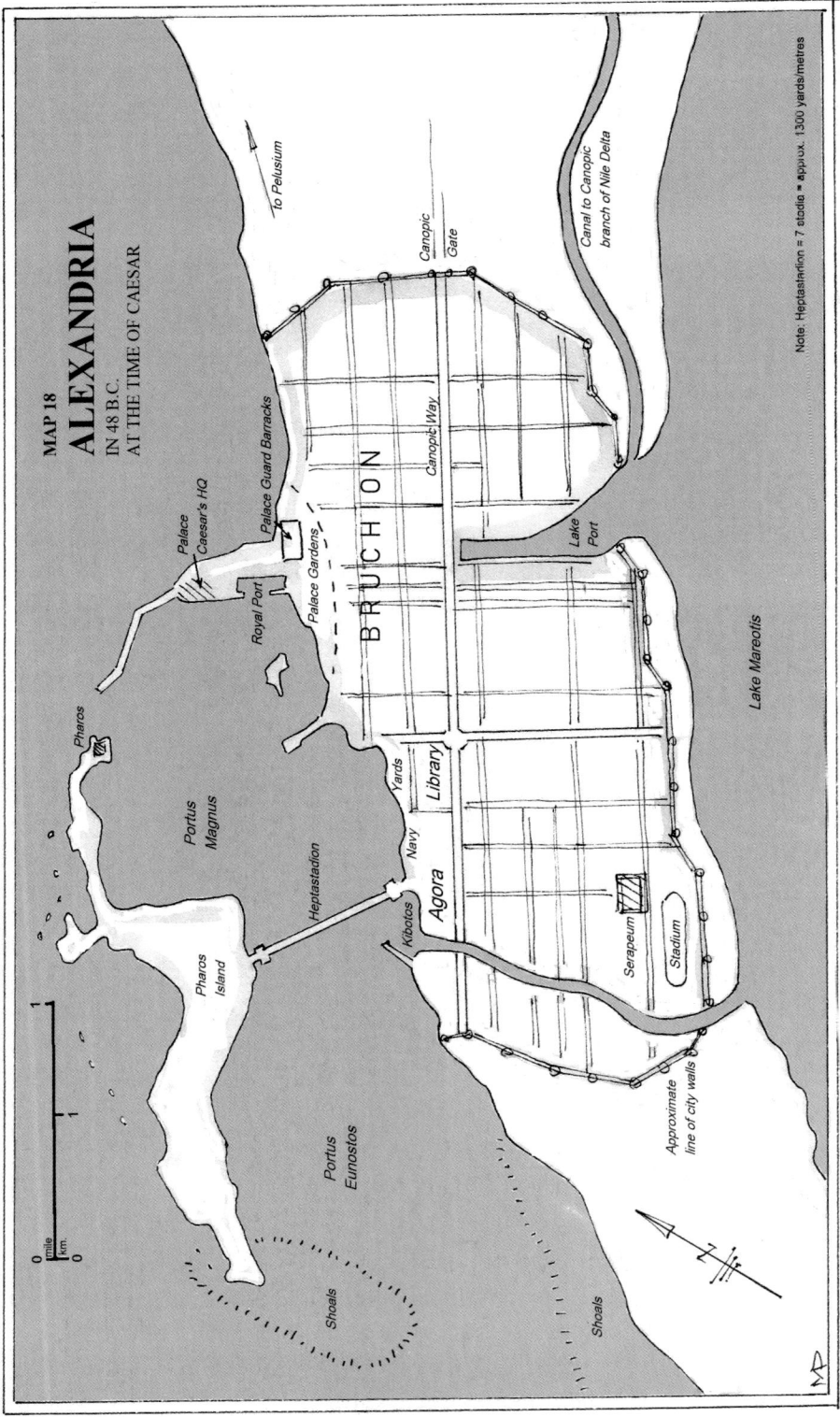

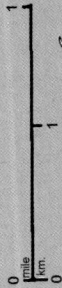

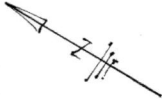

To Pelusium

Canopic Gate

Canopic Way

Canal to Canopic branch of Nile Delta

Note: Heptastadion = 7 stadia = approx. 1300 yards/metres

Palace Caesar's HQ

Palace Guard Barracks

Royal Port

Palace Gardens

BRUCHION

Lake Port

Lake Mareotis

Pharos

Portus Magnus

Heptastadion

Pharos Island

Navy Yards

Library

Agora

Kibotos

Serapeum

Stadium

Portus Eunostos

Shoals

Shoals

Approximate line of city walls

0 mile 1
0 km 1

fives, ten fours, some triremes and smaller, all commanded by Euphranor of Rhodes.

The Egyptians prepared some fireships which they sent through the passages in the Heptastadion, the causeway linking the city and Pharos Island. Caesar's ships managed to avoid them and Euphranor led them to attack the Egyptian fleet in its western harbour. Despite the entrance being restricted by sand bars, which forced them to enter singly, Euphranor's ships gradually pushed in and forced the Egyptian ships away from the entrance. They managed to board and capture and disable several Egyptian ships, the remainder fleeing to the safety of the *Kibotos* or inner harbour.

The Rhodian ships were again in action together with the Roman ships, giving artillery support to Caesar's assault to regain Pharos Island. A similar assault to secure the Heptastadion failed despite the ships' artillery, but the troops did manage to set fire to the Egyptian naval arsenal.

The remaining Egyptian ships next attempted to intercept another of Caesar's reinforcement convoys but were beaten off by its covering fleet in which action, however, Euphranor was killed. Caesar finally sailed with his fleet eastwards to meet his army and another fleet which was approaching Alexandria. Ptolemy's army was defeated and he was killed; Cleopatra remained as ruler, jointly with her younger brother, Ptolemy XIV, backed by a Roman garrison. Caesar left for Judaea and then Rome, pausing en route to defeat an attempt by Mithridates' son to rebuild his father's empire. After campaigns to finish the remaining Pompeians in Africa and Spain, Caesar returned to Rome where he was murdered in 44.

43 In the political turmoil that followed the death of Caesar, his great-nephew and heir, Octavius and his former general Marcus Antonius vied for control of Italy. The Senate meanwhile, appointed two of the authors of the murder of Caesar, Cassius and Brutus to govern in the east. Caesar's fleet commander in Syria, Dolabella with a hastily assembled fleet, tried to stop Cassius from taking over in Syria, but was himself besieged in his base; his ships sailed against Cassius and although both fleets suffered several of their ships disabled, Dolabella did manage to capture five of Cassius' ships.

Rhodes refused to accept Cassius' authority, so he attacked it. Cassius had a fleet of eighty ships but, undeterred, the Rhodian Fleet of only thirty-three ships gave battle near Myndos. Cassius had been educated at Rhodes and was familiar with their naval prowess. He moved his own fleet to Myndos in Caria and prepared and trained it well. When battle was joined, the Rhodians started by using their famous fast-moving ramming tactics. The greater number of heavier Roman ships gradually surrounded and confined the Rhodians, denying them sea-room and their one advantage of swift manoeuvre. The Rhodians lost two ships destroyed and two more captured, before breaking for home. They lost another two ships in a sally against Cassius, who blockaded the rest of their fleet in harbour and prepared to besiege the island, which opened its gates to him, whereupon he sacked it, ending the story of an exceptional naval service.

42   With Rhodes enfeebled, there remained the still-powerful Ptolemaic fleet for Brutus and Cassius to consider. They based a force of sixty warships in the southern Peloponnese to counter any threat from Egypt, but Cleopatra remained resolutely neutral, retaining her fleet as insurance for her independence. As Cassius and Brutus built up their power base, they appointed Lucius Domitius Ahenobarbus to command their fleet. This comprised the Romans' own eastern units, together with such allied ships and crews that could be levied, giving him a total of between 110 and 130 ships of all types.

As there was no threat from Egypt, the ships moved from the Peloponnese to blockade Brundisium, but failed to prevent Octavius and Antonius from moving to Greece with their army. In two battles, they defeated first Cassius and then Brutus at Phillippi. While the armies were engaged, Ahenobarbus intercepted a convoy with reinforcements that had become becalmed. His attack on the convoy drove off its escorts but the transports, loaded with troops, locked themselves together in a tight formation, to provide a fighting platform for the troops. Ahenobarbus' ships attacked using fire arrows and several of the transports were burned, being a sitting target; the rest surrendered, together with the escort of seventeen triremes. After Phillippi, many of the ships deserted, some sailing to join Pompeius' younger son Sextus in Sicily.

Cleopatra VII had been at Caesar's villa near Rome when he was assassinated. She immediately returned to Egypt (with Caesarion, Caesar's son). There, she had her co-regent, Ptolemy XIV killed and sent the four legions in Egypt to join Dolabella (they were later captured by Cassius). She resisted demands from Cassius for ships but did prepare her fleet to join Octavius and Antonius; the fleet was apparently prevented from sailing by a (perhaps convenient) violent storm.[11]

41   By 41 it was apparent where the power now lay and when Antonius summoned her to meet him at Tarsus, she went, displaying all the pomp and splendour of her Ptolemaic forebears. She sailed in a splendid ship, with gilded poop, silver oars and purple sails[12] and an escort of warships. It worked and Antonius had her sister and rival, Arsinoe executed, thus cementing Cleopatra's position as queen.

40   Following their victories, Octavius returned to Italy. Antonius sought to return to and intervene in Italy, backed by Ahenobarbus' fleet, still with seventy ships and

on station in the Adriatic. Before further civil war could break out, Octavius and Antonius met, together with the consul, Marcus Aemilius Lepidus and agreed to rule as a triumvirate – Lepidus in Africa, Octavius in the West and Antonius in the East. Ahenobarbus was made governor of Bithynia and his fleet passed to Antonius (but not before many of their ships had fled to join Sextus Pompeius in Sicily). Octavius was distracted by his struggle against Sextus Pompeius and the war between them over Sicily (38 to 36).

Sextus had set himself up in Sicily, where he attracted many of his father's old crews with their ships, refugees from the defeated Pompeian forces in Africa and Spain. He also

Figure 98. Cleopatra VII, last of the Ptolemaic rulers of Egypt. (*Altes Museum. Berlin*)

attracted some more disgruntled veterans of the civil wars, together with various freebooters and people who, otherwise, would have been pirates. He was able to thus build up a navy of about 130 ships, triremes and a few fours and fives, but mostly lighter types, including *hemioliae*.[13]

39   Judaea again became a problem, this time for Antonius, with widespread unrest leading to civil war. The Romans declared Herod to be king of the Jews and he landed in Judaea with Roman support in 39. He captured Jerusalem in 37, to become undisputed king and a loyal friend of Rome, which he was to remain until his death in 4.[14]

37   Antonius returned to Italy in 37 and the triumvirate was renewed for a further five years. It was agreed that in return for a number of Octavius' legions for use against the Parthians,[15] Antonius would send part of his navy, 120 ships to assist Octavius in his war against Sextus. They were sent and based at Tarentum; of them, about 100 were operational and supported Octavius although they were poorly handled and fared badly in their sole encounter against Sextus' ships, losing thirty or more ships; the rest were returned.

36   With the naval Battle of Naulochus, off Sicily in 36, Sextus was totally defeated and Octavius left supreme in the West, Lepidus having joined him. Sextus fled to Antonius, who had him executed. For his part, Octavius now had a first-class fleet, experienced and battle-hardened and commanded by the ablest of admirals, Marcus Vipsanius Agrippa.

targets. Such attacks would not prove fatal but cumulatively could disable a ship, leaving it unable to manoeuvre.

When it became obvious, after about three hours, that his opponents would not be drawn and as it became more imperative for him to force a battle, Antonius ordered Gellius to advance and attack Agrippa and seek to turn his flank. Agrippa's ships had meanwhile, been gently backing water and increasing the distance between the lines; Gellius' ships had to advance further and as they did so, individually became further apart and began to lose cohesion and the integrity of their 'castle wall'. Sosius on the left also advanced but, as his ships got into more open water and advanced, they also became more extended. With the spreading of the ships, those of Octavius could get between them. At this, Octavius ordered a general engagement and the whole of the lines came into contact.

The fighting was fierce and after an hour or so, despite Antonius' centre (Insteius) and left (Sosius) beginning to fall back, the battle was still far from decided. Antonius' ships managed to grapple and board a few enemy ships and the constant ramming by the smaller ships took the oars off many of the big ones, rendering them immobile. Again as Plutarch[5] relates:

> The two fleets were beginning to come together, they did not drive the ships against, nor strive to crush one another, for Antonius' ships, owing to their weight, were unable to move forwards with any force which would give effect to the blows of their beaks and those of Caesar not only avoided meeting bow to bow, the strong and rough brasswork of the enemy, but did not even try to strike against them on the flank, for their beaks would easily have been broken off by coming into contact with the hulls of the enemy vessels, which were protected by large, square pieces of timber fastened to one another by iron. The battle was therefore like a land fight, or more exactly like the assailing of a fortress; three or four of Caesar's ships at the same time were engaged about one of Antonius' ships, the men fought with light shields, spears, poles and fiery missiles, the soldiers of Antonius assailed them with catapults from wooden towers.

As has been seen, fire was not a weapon deployed in or by ancient warships and in this instance, in an attempt to break the deadlock in the battle, Octavius sent ashore for fire to be brought from his camp.[6] With it, his men tied burning material to javelins and used fire arrows, as well as hurling pots of charcoal, burning pitch and resin (both the latter being materials usually kept for anti-fouling ship hulls). Having done this, the attackers shot fire arrows and pots of burning pitch and charcoal from

Figure 102. Nicopolis. Part of the surviving base of the great victory monument built by Octavius/ Augustus, erected close to where his headquarters were for the campaign and battle of Actium. The indentations in the wall are the sockets where some of the rams taken from Antonius' ships, including some of the largest, were mounted. The bottom picture is a view of one such socket, the largest measure nearly 6 feet/1.83m in width and height, indicating a ram at least twice that in length, made, as far as we know, from a single bronze casting.

their catapults.[7] The ships so assailed 'quickly defied the efforts of their crews and commenced to burn furiously'.[8] This is the only time that the use of such missiles in a sea battle is mentioned in the sources.

Cleopatra's fleet, which had not been engaged, then formed into columns and advanced between the divisions of the fleets that were locked in combat, emerging to the rear or seaward of Octavius. The moment was critical, Octavius had no reserves, all of his fleet being committed; if Cleopatra, as she was free to do, had caused her fleet to turn and fall upon the rear of any of Octavius' squadrons, they would have been annihilated, a process that could then have progressed along his entire line; an attack from seaward would trap Octavius' ships, pushing them onto the rams and grapples of Antonius' floating castles. Antonius and Cleopatra would have had a crushing victory.

Instead, Cleopatra's ships hoisted sail and with the wind now blowing favourably, ran to the south.[9] Antonius saw this and, managing to extricate about fifty of his ships, followed her. Octavius managed to detach some liburnians in pursuit and which caught and overcame one large ship that turned to meet them, enabling the others to escape; having no sails aboard, the tired liburnian crews could do no more. The rest of the fleet continued fighting but as the word of Antonius abandoning them reached them, they surrendered or returned to their anchorage. A week later, these remaining ships together with the remnant of Antonius' army also surrendered.

Later, Octavius returned to the site and raised a great victory monument on the site of his headquarters tent in his original camp, which he grandiosely named *Nikopolis*. Around the base of the edifice, he had mounted some of the rams taken from the great ships that had been captured, the sockets for which are still to be seen (Figure 102).

Chapter 16

The Great Ships and Hellenistic Naval Warfare

We know that threes (triremes), fours and fives were widely built in great numbers, forming the mainstay of all the fleets of the centuries that have been examined. It is informative to compare, in summary, the numbers built of the larger and ever-more esoteric types that have been encountered.

The Six

These first appeared at Syracuse in the mid-fourth century and ten of them are included in Demetrios I's fleet at Salamis in 306. The Romans had two as flagships in 264 and Ptolemy II had five of his own by about 260. Philip of Macedon arrived with one six at Chios in 201 (which he lost) and Hannibal brought four from Syria in 190; Cato took a six to Rome in 56 and which may have been the same as that used by Brutus at Massalia in 49. Pergamum fielded a couple in 190 and Sextus Pompeius had one in 36. Both sides at Actium in 31 had a few sixes, perhaps three each (although this figure is purely conjectural). Finally, the *Ops* was flagship of the newly formed Roman Imperial Fleet at Misenum in 22, the last of the type, by which time it was only a showpiece. Some of these ships may be the same (the *Ops* was doubtless a veteran of Actium) but even allowing all of them to be different ships, the total built over the 325 years or so of their existence, was at most, about thirty-four.

The Seven

Designed shortly before Alexander's death in 323, the first did not appear until 315, in the fleet of Antigonos I and Demetrios I, in which they had seven. The next example that we find is the flagship of the Carthaginian Fleet at Mylae in 260. Ptolemy III inherited no less than thirty-seven of them in 246 and Hannibal's fleet of 190, included three. Finally, there was one in Antonius' fleet at Actium in 31. It is of course, Ptolemy's totals that tend to distort things but, even granting them to be accurate, a total of fifty-two of these ships would have been built.

The Nine

Another product of Antigonos and his Son's naval programme of 315/314, they built three of this rate. Ptolemy's naval list of 246 includes no less than thirty more. King Pyrrhus of Epirus took one apparently from Syracuse when he acquired their ships in 278, although this account does not seem too secure. The last of which we know appeared in Philip of Macedon's fleet at the Battle of Chios in 201. The total that we can trace of the nine is thus thirty-five.

The Ten

Once again, the type first appeared in Antigonos and Demetrios' naval lists for 315/314. They seem to have built an example of all the various designs, perhaps to assess which might emerge as the best; if so, they were not convinced as further types were to emerge later. They did however build ten of this rate and presumably therefore may have intended this to be a standard for their fleet. Although Ptolemy may have built or acquired one sometime after 306, it does not appear in his successor's naval inventory of 246. Philip of Macedon had one as his flagship at the Battle of Chios in 201 and their last appearance was in the fleet of Antonius and Cleopatra at Actium in 31 (although Orosius claims that they were nines). As they were referred to in the plural, let us estimate that they had four of them. The total built of this rate is thus only sixteen ships in nearly three centuries.

The Eleven

The eleven made its first appearance in 301 in the fleet of Demetrios I. The only other appearance is in the fleet list of Ptolemy in 246, which boasted no less than fourteen of the rate. Assuming the Demetrios only built one, the total built (or adapted) is fifteen.

The Thirteen

The first example of the thirteen was once more that of Demetrios I, who had one in 301, being one of the ships that he had left at Piraeus and which were returned after Ipsos. He used it as his flagship and even entertained Seleucos I on board. Ptolemy II built four of them, which were included in his naval inventory of 246. Five of the type can be thus accounted for.

The Fifteen

Only one ship of this rating is known, built for Demetrios I in 288 and which was acquired by Ptolemy II either in 285 when Demetrios was captured by Seleucos, or was captured by him when he beat Antigonos II Gonatas at Cos in 280. Thereafter the ship disappears from the record.

The Sixteen

This was also built for Demetrios I in 288, and also passed to Ptolemy II. It was re-captured by Antigonos II when he in turn, beat Ptolemy II at Cos in 258. His successor, Philip V also boasted a sixteen as his flagship, possibly the same ship and the one subsequently taken to Rome. An almost unbelievably long-lived ship but there is no evidence to suggest that any others were built.

The Twelve

This rating appears but once, when two are listed in Ptolemy's naval inventory of 246.

Ptolemy's Giants and Other Rates

There were of course other 'one-offs', the *Leontophoros* and *Isthmia* and of course, Ptolemy III's twenty and two thirties and Ptolemy IV's forty.

Eight

This rate is only referred to twice and although examples of it were included in fleets and took part at Actium, there is no indication as to how many may have been built
In summary therefore, the totals are:

Six	34
Seven	52
Nine	35
Ten	16
Eleven	15
Thirteen	5
Fifteen	1
Sixteen	1
Twelve	2

Figure 103. An 'official' end to the last Hellenistic state. Egyptian obelisk brought to Rome by Octavius and raised in 23, the plinth upon which it stands declaring '*Aegupto in potestate*' – Egypt in his power. The cartouche on the obelisk is of Pharaoh Psamtik (595 to 589). Now in Piazza Montecitorio, Rome.

Twenty	1
Thirty	2
Forty	1
Eight	not known
Total	165

The totals are those that can be gleaned from the accounts; it is based on the assumption that each of the ships mentioned was a 'new-build' and does not consider whether any were conversions from other rates (e.g. as has been suggested for the series nine – ten – eleven and twelve). It may well be for example, that some of the tens were upgraded to elevens, but as tens appear at Actium, well after the (supposed) demise of the eleven, either the latter were returned to the ten configuration (especially as they mostly appear in Ptolemaic fleets) or some were indeed built as such. The same suggestion can be offered for most of the other rates but, without better contemporary information, it is impossible to say, only that, obviously, if such conversions (and re-conversions) took place, then the figures suggested must be reduced.

With the end of the Hellenistic navies came the end of the vast oared warships with their huge crews of rowers. Trireme warships of more modest size continued in use, probably in decreasing numbers into the fourth century AD and the bireme layout, in its last manifestation in the *dromons* of the continuing Eastern Roman Empire (Byzantine) into the ninth century AD. In the next great age of rowing warships, from late medieval times to the eighteenth century AD, only monoremes were built. Interestingly, a ship with three men to an oar was then called a 'trireme' and so on, but bore absolutely no relationship to its classical namesake, the coincidence of its name being the only link.

As has been said, the performance of these ships failed to encourage navies to invest in any more than a few of each (and hardly at all in the west). The numbers built over the three centuries of the era do not compare with the hundreds and hundreds of triremes, fours and especially fives built; the Romans built over 500 fives during the First Punic War alone, during the course of which the Romans and Carthaginians between them lost over 1,000 warships of those rates. The use of the giants in battle failed to prove decisive, presumably disappointing the hopes of their patrons and failing to justify the enormous expense of building and the huge demands upon manpower that they made. Nevertheless, the continued building of even bigger ships can only have been exercises in imagined prestige and self-aggrandisement, or, as Plutarch had it, 'were meant quite as much for fighting as for looking at…'[1]

Throughout the three centuries or so that have been considered, all of the antagonists, without exception, poured vast investment into warfleets. Wars were fought and won or lost on land but it was the sea that was the focus of much of their endeavour, over which their rivalries were played out and which largely influenced the course of their operations on land. The contested lands largely form a natural amphitheatre and the sea (whose name says it all) the only arena across which they faced each other and across which alliances and adversaries could be pursued.

Their attitude was perhaps further focused by the tradition, even a mindset, that came from the earliest Aegean history. Thus it was that the Myceneans crossed by sea to the siege of Troy in the twelfth century and later the same century, the Sea Peoples invaded Egypt, to be defeated in a naval battle. According to Herodotus,[2] one Polycrates, tyrant of Samos in the reign of the Persian king Cambyses (529 to 522) was the first Greek to conceive a maritime empire of the Aegean islands and adjacent coastal lands of Ionia, building up a powerful navy.[3] A century later, Thucydides[4] averred that 'those who applied their energies to the sea acquired the greatest strength from revenues and empire.' He later[5] recounted that the Corinthians warned that the sea was vital even for those who lived inland off the main trade routes.[6]

Sea trade can be loosely defined perhaps as an exercise in taking things to people who need or want them in exchange for things of value to others. This can refer to anything from the exotic such as fine bronze sculptures,[7] to the mundane such as bulk metal or grain. The common thread is that water transport was (and is) faster and cheaper and could move bulk infinitely better than a lumbering oxcart. Despite being basically agrarian societies, for millennia before the period here considered, maritime trade had been pursued with an intensity that grew with the growth of populations and the increase in centres of population.

'Command of the sea' (arguably still not possible) perhaps better expressed as domination of the seaways, requires that warships 'keep the sea' i.e. that they remain at sea for extensive periods, being supplied at sea and holding their station to dominate a sea area, denying it to an enemy; ancient warships could not do this. Their inability to operate in all but relatively calm seas and whenever possible a preference therefore to keep to coastal waters rendered command of the sea impossible but domination of trade routes, most of which also were coastal, certainly was. As has been seen, in many cases the ability to conduct land warfare depended on sea lanes, fleets transporting and shadowing armies advancing along a littoral, protecting the flank and allowing supplies to be brought. Due to its geography, no invasion of Egypt was possible without an accompanying fleet to keep lines of supply open and against which the Ptolemies had to have a fleet. Fleets could be used against seaward flanks of besieged coastal cities, such as at Tyre and Rhodes and could also enable a defeated general such as Demetrios to escape and rebuild his power, or they could interdict supplies such as the interruption of Athenian grain ships, to force a submission.

Conversely the lack of a fleet would have prevented the Ptolemies from being able to export their agricultural surpluses and import the timber they lacked and severely adversely affect their economy; similarly Rhodes could never have become prosperous as an international trading centre. No-one from Alexander to Pompeius could cross to Asia Minor without a fleet and Philip V's ambitions were thwarted once he had lost his. Fleets were faster than armies and the threat of raids could tie down a disproportionate amount of an enemy's forces, as the allies did against Macedon. However, a well-defended shore could thwart a fleet with no nearby haven as happened to Demetrios' attempted invasion of Egypt.

The importance of naval domination was not at first learned by the Romans who, having failed to provide for the neutralising of the Carthaginian navy at the end of the First Punic War, made a point in every subsequent peace treaty of requiring the surrender of all but a nominal number of ships from each defeated power, systematically eradicating all navies but their own. The lesson had been well-learned, as Cicero said 'the master of the sea must inevitably be master of the Empire',[8] which would of course be proved at Actium.

There were great armies and campaigns on land (six wars between the Ptolemies and Seleucids alone) which used pre-existing weaponry, formations and tactics, at least until the Romans arrived. Inventiveness and innovation by comparison, was poured into the design and building of ships that became the showpieces of power of their day.

All routes coalesced in the Aegean and eastern Mediterranean and domination of the seaways there protected on the one hand, one's own supplies and trade, as well as coastal towns, farms and fisheries; on the other hand it could deny that of an enemy and threaten their coasts as well as allowing the party enjoying dominance and the initiative in the conduct of a war.[9] A point well illustrated by Antigonos and his son Demetrios, who consistently put a very great effort into the building and maintaining of a powerful fleet; Ptolemy and the others were moved to do likewise as a reaction to this policy.

Domination of the routes of supply of materials, foodstuffs and goods, both luxury and mundane and the relative geographical position of each of the rivals played a major part in determining the antagonists' policies. Thus Athens and much of Greece depended on grain from the Black Sea, but Lysimachus in Thrace sat astride the route and amassed a reasonably-sized fleet to give him dominance of the Hellespont and Bosporos. Exotic goods from India and the east had to pass through Seleucos' lands but Ptolemy controlled most of the Phoenician ports at the end of those routes. He could also operate down the Red Sea and trade with the Arab and Indian merchants there, partly by-passing Seleucos. He also needed to retain Cyprus for the timber and his enclaves on the south and western Anatolian coasts to satisfy Egypt's needs and also to give him a platform from which to interfere and sometimes intervene in greater Aegean politics. He always had a large population from which to draw crews for his ships, although levies from farm folk with little or no training often showed in the comparatively poor performance of his fleets in battle.

Philip V of Macedon, with all the expansionist zeal of his forbears, must have felt himself increasingly hemmed in by Lysimachus to the east, wild Balkan tribes to the north and all the other powers to the south. His attempt at expansion into Illyria was thwarted by a Roman fleet, which enabled them to establish themselves there and gradually push him out. He then looked to the richer, more sophisticated south for expansion and to counter the Ptolemies' increasing acquisition of territory in Asia Minor, despite a warning that 'the Romans are masters of the sea, whatever lands they come to they at once subdue.'[10]

Seleucos had held the greater part of Alexander's Asian empire but he was nonetheless a Macedonian with a natural empathy towards the west and Aegean, especially as the rise of the Parthians in the east would begin to erode his empire. Expansion into the Levant and Asia Minor countered losses in the east and also brought a seaboard and the perceived need for a navy.

For Rhodes a navy was essential and protected them against threats from pirates and Philip V; they maintained good relations with the Ptolemies and acquired considerable lands on the adjacent mainland, to which the Seleucids would later pose a threat. Pergamum's navy was seen as an important organ of the state and its use, albeit alongside allied forces ensured their support in due turn. Although its foreign adventures were not so successful, having it gave the country a prominence denied perhaps to other minor Anatolian states.

For all of their limitations, having a fleet of ancient warships was a deciding factor in the schemes of the antagonists, as indeed they had to be, as all of them were focused towards the sea that formed the hub of their world. The costs of building, equipping, raising and paying crews and victualling the ships was enormous, but one to which they were willing to subscribe.[11]

The existence of these fleets exerted a great influence on the unfolding of events. Thus Alexander, who could not hope to overcome the Persian fleets yet could not depart for the interior, leaving his homeland open to invasion, adopted the solution of taking all of their ports, the taking of Tyre being the tipping point beyond which the Persians could not recover at sea. That he was able to do so was aided by their being in a single overall polity, something that did not recur after his death (until the Romans). The course of his invasion of the Persian Empire was thus determined by the need to first neutralise their fleet and secure the sea lanes.

It has been contended[12] that 'not until the sixteenth century AD did naval conflicts such as Lepanto and the Spanish Armada have significant consequences' which is clearly nonsense. As only three examples, sea power decided that the heirs of Antigonos would be the last kings of Macedon; Roman mastery at sea in the Second Punic War meant that Hannibal could not win and that much of Europe would speak Latin-based languages instead of Phoenician and finally, Actium determined the manner of the future of the Roman world and thus of modern western civilisation.

The projection of influence and power by sea and its influence on the varying fortunes of the antagonists has been illustrated by the maps indicating 'changing fortunes'. In some cases this has occurred through seizing opportunity, accident or in others by deliberate planning; it is difficult to see any 'grand strategy' beyond a wish by the *diadochoi* to overcome their fellows and by their respective successors to grab as much as they could before they were themselves edged out. It was the constantly perceived threat from the others together with their instability that compelled each of them to pursue aggressive policies, with the sea as their cockpit, and which ultimately led to their destruction.

APPENDICES

Marble oculus, possibly from a trireme. (*Piraeus Archaeological Museum*)

190	Side	(June) Rhodes v. Hannibal. Hannibal's Syrian Fleet defeated
190	Myonnesus	(Oct.) Seleucid Fleet v. Rome & Rhodes. Allies defeat Syrian Fleet
85	Tenedos	Rome v. Mithridates VI of Pontus. Romans beat Pontic Fleet in two battles
73	Chalcedon	Rome v. Pontus. Over-extended Roman Fleet beaten
73	Lemnos	Rome v. Pontus. Romans destroy Pontic squadron
73	Tenedos	Rome v. Pontus. Romans capture Pontic squadron and burn another on the beach
73	Heraclea	Rome v. Pontus. Romans beat Pontic Fleet in two battles
67	Coracaesium	Pompeius v. Pirates. Pirates eradicated
48	Messina	Roman Civil Wars. Eastern Fleet destroys Caesar's squadron
48	Hipponium	Roman Civil Wars. Caesar's fleet beat off Eastern Fleet
48	Brindisi	Pompeius' squadron beaten in harbour approaches
47	Alexandria	Caesar v. Ptolemy. Roman & Rhodian ships prevail in three actions against Egyptian Fleet
43	Myndos	Cassius v. Rhodes. Rhodian seapower destroyed
36	Naulochus	Agrippa defeats Sextus Pompeius
31	Actium	Octavius v. Antonius & Cleopatra. Octavius victorius when Antonius & Cleopatra flee
30	Alexandria	Octavius v. Egyptian Ptolemaic Fleet. Cleopatra's fleet come out but then surrender

Appendix II

Order in Which the Ship Types Appeared

Part I	20–30–50 Conters	pre- 8th century
	Bireme	c. 700 Phoenicia
	Trireme	600–500 Corinth
	Four	399 Carthage
	Five	398 Syracuse
	Six	post 367 Syracuse
	Hemiolia	c. 350 South Anatolian Coast
Part II	Seven	323/315 Alexander / Antigonos
Part III	Nine	315 Demetrios I
	Ten	315 Demetrios I
	Trihemiolia	304 Rhodes
Part IV	Eleven	301 Demetrios I
	Thirteen	301 Demetrios I
	Fifteen	288 Demetrios I
	Sixteen	288 Demetrios I
	Leontophoros	280 Lysimachus, Heraclea
	Isthmia (Eighteen)	258 Antigonos II
	Twenty	post 260 Corinth
	Thirty	by 246 Ptolemy II
	Twelve	241 Ptolemy III
	Lembi	229 Illyrian Coast
	Forty	c. 215 Ptolemy IV
Part V	Eight	c. 200 Philip V
	Pristis	c.200 Roman type
	Liburnian	c.200 Roman type
Part VI	Myoparo	c.86 Pontus

Appendix III

Suggested Total Rowers Per Rate

Trireme	170	(170 oars)	Athenian trireme
Trihemiolia	200		ante Chapter 9
Fours	200		*Roman Warships* p.105; ante Chapter 3
Fives	296	(180 oars)	*Roman Warships* p.97; ante Chapter 3
Six	360		*Roman Warships* p.95; ante Chapter 3
Seven	370		*GROW* p.345; ante Chapter 6
Eight	448		
Nine	450		
Ten	510		six rates between
Eleven	550		c.390 and 800 rowers
Twelve	600		estimates per text
Thirteen	714		
Fifteen	c.800		
Sixteen	880		Rodgers p.258
Leontophoros	1600		Memnon
Isthmia	1620		
Twenty	2000		based on the known number for the Forty
Thirty	3000		halfway between the Twenty and Forty
Forty	4000+		Athenaeas V.37

Appendix IV

Index of Characters

AGATHOCLES	Tyrant of Syracuse; died 289
AGESILAOS	Brother of King Agis of Sparta
AGIS III	King of Sparta 338 – 331
AGRIPPA, M. VIPSANIUS	Octavius' close friend and admiral.
ALEXANDER IV	Son of Alexander the Great by Roxana. Killed by Cassander in 310
ALEXANDER OF PHERAE	Pirate/privateer leader 362-361
ALEXANDER THE GREAT	King of Macedon 336 – 323
ALEXANDER V	Son of Cassander, joint ruler of Macedon 297 to294
AMPHEDOROS	Macedonian fleet commander
AMYNTAS	Admiral of Rhodes
ANDRISCUS	Pretender to the throne of Macedon
ANTIGONOS I	Monopthalmos (one-eye) took Lycia, Pamphylia and Phrygia. Killed at the Battle of Ipsos in 301
ANTIGONOS II	(Gonatos) Son of Demetrios I, King of Macedon 283 to 229
ANTIGONOS III	(Doson) Son of Antigonos II, king of Macedon 229 to 221
ANTIOCHUS I	(Soter) second Seleucid king, 281 to 261
ANTIOCHUS II	(Theos) Seleucid king 261 to 246
ANTIOCHUS III	(The Great) Seleucid king 223 to 187
ANTIOCHUS IV	Seleucid King, 175 to 164
ANTIOCHUS VII	Seleucid King, 138 to 129
ANTIOCHUS XIII	Seleucid King 69 to 64
ANTIPATER I	Son of Cassander, joint ruler of Macedon 297 to 294
ANTIPATER	Regent in Macedonia and Greece, died in 319
ANTIPATER	Macedonian general
ANTONIUS, M. (III)	Triumvir, opposed Octavius for supreme power. Paramour of Cleopatra VII
ANTONIUS, M. (junior)	Commanded anti-piracy operations. Father of M. Antonius III
ANTONIUS, MARCUS (Senior)	Praetor, commander of anti-piracy campaign
ARCHELAOS	Mithridates' admiral
ARRUNTIUS, L.	One of Octavius' fleet commanders at Actium
ARTAXERXES III	Persian King 359-338
ATHENAEUS	son of Attalus III of Pergamum

ATTALUS I	(Soter) Second king of Pergamum, 241 to 197
ATTALUS III	King of Pergamum, 139 to 133
AUTOPHRADATES	Persian admiral
BIBULUS, L. CALPURNIUS	Pompeius' overall fleet commander
BRUTUS, M. IUNIUS	One of Caesar's murderers. Sent to govern the East with Cassius. Beaten in battle by triumvirs
CAESAR, G. JULIUS	Triumvir, general and Dictator
CAESARION (PTOLEMY XV)	Cleopatra VII's son by Caesar. 44 to 30
CASSANDER	Son of Antipater, succeeded him as ruler of Macedon; died 282
CASSIUS, CAIUS	Commander of Pompeius' Syrian fleet
CASSIUS, C. LONGINUS	One of Caesar's murderers. Sent to govern the East, sacked Rhodes; beaten in battle by triumvirs
CLEITUS	Macedonian Admiral
CLEOPATRA VII	Queen of Egypt 51 to 30, the last Ptolemaic ruler
COTTA, G. AURELIUS	Consul, defeated by Mithridates
CRATEROS	General, killed in Battle by Eumenes 321
DARIUS I	Persian King (521 to 486) occupied Egypt, refurbished Red Sea Canal
DARIUS III	Persian King 336-331
DEMETRIOS I	Seleucid King, 162 to 150
DEMETRIOS I	Poliorcetes (The Besieger) son of Antigonos I; captured by Seleucos I; died 283
DEMETRIOS II	Antigonid king of Macedon 239 to 229
DEMETRIOS OF PHAROS	Tyrant, ruler of a semi-piratical state on the Adriatic coast of north of Epirus, part of Illyria
DIONYSIUS I	Tyrant of Syracuse 404-367
DOLABELLA, P. CORNELIUS	Caesar's admiral
DOMITIUS AHENOBARBUS, L.	Commander of Cassius and Brutus' fleet
EUDAMUS	commander of Rhodian fleet at Side
EUETION	Athenian admiral
EUMENES II	King of Pergamum, 197 to 160
EUMENES	Took Paphlagonia and Pontus. Killed by Antigonos in 316
EUPHRANOR	Rhodian admiral, with Caesar at Alexandria
FIGULUS, G. MARCUS	Roman fleet commander
FIMBRIA, C.FLAVIUS	Flaccus' deputy and murderer
FLACCUS, L VALERIUS	General appointed by Senate to oppose Mithridates
GALBA, P. SULPICIUS	Successor to Laevinus as commander of Roman forces
GELON	Tyrant of Syracuse 485-478. Built first triremes for Syracuse
HANNIBAL	Carthaginian general. Invaded Italy and won victories against the Romans, campaigned there for 16 years. Defeated at Zama in 202. Suicide 183

PERSEUS	Last King of Macedon, 179 to 167
PHILIP ARRHIDEOS	Alexander's elder half-brother. Proclaimed Philip III, murdered by Alexander's Mother in 317
PHILIP II	King of Macedon 359-336. Father of Alexander the Great
PHILIP II	The last Seleucid King 65 to 64
PHILIP IV	Son of Cassander, died 297
PHILIP V	Son of Antigonos II, King of Macedon, 221 to 179
POLYPERCHON	Regent in Macedonia, driven out in 318
POLYXENIDAS	Commander of Seleucid fleet
POMPEIUS, G. (Junior)	Eldest son of Pompeius the Great. Commanded Egyptian fleet, later led Pompeian forces in Spain, killed there
POMPEIUS, G.	Admiral and general, named 'The Great'
POMPEIUS, S.	Younger son of Pompeius the Great. Set up semi-pirate realm in Sicily. Defeated at Naulochus in 36
POROS	King of the lands around the upper Indus
PRUSIAS I	King of Bithynia, c.230 to183
PTOLEMY APION	Bastard son of Ptolemy VII, inherited Cyrene; died 96
PTOLEMY I	Soter (founder) seized and made himself ruler of Egypt; died 282
PTOLEMY II	(Philadelphus) 282, died 246; second of the dynasty to rule Egypt
PTOLEMY III	(Euergetes I) Ruler of Egypt 246 to 222
PTOLEMY IV	(Philopator) Ruler (Pharoah) of Egypt 222 to 205
PTOLEMY V	(Epiphanes) Ruled Egypt, 204 to 180
PTOLEMY VI	King of Egypt, 180 to 145
PTOLEMY IX	King of Egypt 88 to 81
PTOLEMY X	King of Egypt 101 to 88
PTOLEMY XIII	King of Egypt 51 to 47
PTOLEMY XIV	King of Egypt 47 to 44
PTOLEMY KERAUNOS	Son of Ptolemy I; disinherited, made himself King of Macedon in 281, killed 279.
PUBLICOLA, GELLIUS	One of Antonius' fleet commanders at Actium
PYRRHUS	King of Epirus, killed in 272
REGILLUS, L. AEMILIUS	Praetor of Roman fleet in 191
SALINATOR, C. LIVIUS	Praetor of the Roman fleet in 191
SELEUCOS I	Took Syria, Persia and Mesopotamia; died 281
SELEUCOS II	(Callinicus) Seleucid king 246 to 225
SELEUCOS III	(Soter) Seleucid king 225 to 223
SERTORIUS, Q.	Roman General, led rebellion in Spain
SIMEON	leader of Judaea
SOSIUS, G.	One of Antonius' fleet commanders at Actium
SULLA, L. CORNELIUS	Roman Dictator

Appendix V

Dynasties

Macedon

Argead Dynasty

Philip II	359 – assassinated 336
Alexander III (the Great)	336 – 323
Philip Arrhideous (Philip III)	
Alexander's elder half-brother	323 – murdered by Alexander's Mother 317
Alexander IV	
Son of Alexander the Great,	
born posthumously	323 – executed by Cassander 310
Regency of Cassander	311–306
Cassander	306–296
Sons of Cassander	296–294

Antigonid Dynasty

Antigonos I (Monopthalmos)	306 – killed at Ipsos 301
Demetrios I (Poliorcetes)	294–287
Lysimachus, Pyrrhus, Ptolemy	
Keraunos and other claimants	287–277
Antigonos II (Gonatos)	
Son of Demetrios I	276–239
Demetrios II	
Son of Antigonos II	239–229
Antigonos III (Doson)	
Half-brother of Gonatos	229–221
Philip V	
Son of Demetrios II	221–179
Perseus	
Son of Philip V	179–168 (Pydna)

Syria, the Seleucids

Seleucos I	312 – 281
Antiochus I	281 – 261
Antiochus II	261 – 246
Seleucos II	246 – 225
Antiochus III (the Great)	223 – 187
Seleucos IV	187 – 175
Antiochus IV	175 – 164

Antiochus V	164 – 162
Demetrios I	162 – 150
Alexander Balas	150 – 145
Demetrios II	145 – 140
Antiochus VI	145 – 142
Antiochus VII	138 – 129
Demetrios II (again)	129 – 125
Antiochus VIII	125 – 96
Antiochus IX	115 – 95

From 95 to 69, there were six overlapping reigns; Seleucos VI, 96 – 95; Demetrios III, 95 – 88; Antiochus X, 95 – 83; Antiochus XI, 95; Philip I, 94 – 83 and Antiochus XIII, 87 – 69

Antiochus XIII	69 – 64	
Philip II	66 – 63	Monarchy lapsed

Egypt, the Ptolemies

Ptolemy I	323 – 282
Ptolemy II	282 – 246
Ptolemy III	246 – 222
Ptolemy IV	222 – 205
Ptolemy V	205 – 181
Ptolemy VI	181 – 146
Ptolemy VII	146 – 144
Ptolemy VIII	145 – 116
Cleopatra III and Ptolemy IX	116 – 107
Cleopatra III and Ptolemy X	107 – 101
Ptolemy X and Cleopatra Berenike	101 – 88
Ptolemy IX (again)	88 – 81
Cleopatra Berenike and Ptolemy XI	80
Ptolemy XII	80 – 58
Berenike IV	58 – 55
Ptolemy XII (again)	58 – 51
Cleopatra VII and Ptolemy XIII	51 – 47
Cleopatra VII and Ptolemy XIV	47 – 44
Cleopatra VII and Ptolemy XV (Caesarion)	44 – 30

Pergamum

Philetairos	c.283 – 263
Eumenes I	263 – 241
Attalus I	241 – 197
Eumenes II	197 – 160
Attalus II	160 – 139
Attalus III	139 – 133
To Rome	

Gazeteer

ABDERA	town on the north Aegean Coast in Thrace, near to Thasos
ABYDOS	near modern Canakkale on the Asian shore of the Dardanelles
ACARNANIA	area of western Greece on the Adriatic, south of Epirus
ACHAEA	area of and league of northern Peloponnesian city-states
ACRAGAS	now Agrigento in Sicily
ACTIUM	village at the entrance to the Gulf of Ambracia, battle in 31
ADRIATIC SEA	
AEGEAN SEA	
AEGINA	island in the Saronic Gulf near Athens
AETOLIA	area of and league of southern mainland Greek city-states
ALEXANDRIA	founded by Alexander in 332, Egypt, became Ptolemaic capital
AMBRACIA	Gulf of, on the west coast of mainland Greece
AMORGOS	city on the Hellespont Battle 322
ANATOLIA	now approximately per Turkey in Asia
ANDROS	island of the Cyclades, battle in 242
ANTIOCH	in north-west Syria, founded by Antiochus I
ANTIUM	now Anzio, south of Rome
APOLLONIA	seaport near Fier, Albania
ARADOS	city of northern Phoenicia
ARCADIA	area of the central Peloponnese
ARGOS	originally a Mycenean city, gives its name to surrounding area
ARMENIA	kingdom to the south-east of the Black Sea
ARSINOE	port on the Red Sea coast of Egypt
ASIA	Roman province, formerly Kingdom of Pergamum
ASIA MINOR	now Turkey in Asia
ASIA MINOR/ANATOLIA	now Turkey in Asia
ASPENDOS	near modern Antalya
ATHENS/PIRAEUS	still the Greek capital and its port

ATTICA	the region forming Athens immediate territory
BABYLON	ancient city on the Euphrates
BALKAN PENINSULA	
BARGYLIA	port in western Caria
BARRA	small island at the entrance to the inlet to Brindisi harbour, battle in 48
BITHYNIA	kingdom on the southern shore of the Propontis
BLACK SEA	Euxine to the ancients
BOEOTIA	region of mainland Greece, adjacent to north-west Attica
BOSPORAN KINGDOM	Greek-founded realm of the Crimean peninsula and surrounding mainland area
BOSPOROS	the strait from Istanbul to the Black Sea
BRUNDISIUM	now Brindisi, Italy
BRUTTIUM	now the province of Reggio Calabria, Italy
BYBLOS	city-state of Phoenicia
BYZANTION	later Constantinople Now Istanbul
CALYNDA	in Lycia, coastal town west of modern Antalya
CANOPIC NILE	westernmost branch of the Nile Delta, no longer extant
CAPE CORYCUS	battle in191; on the west coast of Asia Minor
CAPE GRECO	the south-eastern point of Cyprus
CAPE MYONNESUS	battle in 190; on the west coast of Asia Minor, north-west of Ephesus
CAPE SARPEDONIUM	on the coast of Cilicia, now south-east Turkey
CAPPADOCIA	central-eastern Turkey
CARIA	part of south-western Anatolia
CARTHAGE	city now in Tunisia, head of an ancient empire
CASPIAN SEA	
CASSANDEIA	port on the Macedonian Coast
CEPHALLENIA	island in the Ionia Sea, opposite the Gulf of Patras
CHAERONEA	battle site 338 and 86
CHALCEDON	on the asian shore, opposite Byzantion
CHALKIDIKI	peninsula of the North Aegean, also Halkidiki
CHALKIS	on Euboea at the narrows
CHIOS	island of the southern Sporades battles in 357, 356 and 201
CILICIA	coastal area of south-eastern Turkey
CLAZOMENA	coastal town of Pergamum
COELE-SYRIA	central-western Syria
CORACAESIUM	former pirate capital of Cilicia
CORCYRA	now Corfu
CORINTH	city on the Isthmus separating the Peloponnese from the mainland

CORUPEDION	battle 281, east of Pergamum
COS	island of the Dodecanese
CRANNON	Battle 322, in central Thessaly
CRETE	
CRIMEA	
CROTON	coastal city of southern Bruttium
CYCLADES	island group in the south central Aegean
CYNOSCEPHALAE	battle in 197; in Thessaly, near modern Larisa
CYPRUS	
CYRENE	now eastern Libya
CYTHNOS	island in the Cyclades
CYZICUS	city on the Sea of Marmara
DALMATIA	coastal region of the north-east Adriatic
DARDANOS	town on the southern shore of the Hellespont
DELOS	island in the mid-Cyclades
DEMETRIOS	now Volos in eastern Greece
DYRRHACHIUM	now Durres, Albania
ECBATANA	in southern Iran
ECHINOS IN LAMIA	on the mainland opposite Euboea
EGYPT	
EPHESUS	port city of the central west-Asia Minor Coast, now Efes
EPIRUS	kingdom of (now) north-west Greece
ERETRIA	south of Chalkis on the island of Euboea
EUBOEA	now Evvia
EUPHRATES, RIVER	
EUXINE	ancient name for the Black Sea
FAMAGUSTA BAY	gulf of south-eastern Cyprus
GALATIA	area of central Asia Minor settled by Gauls (Celtic peoples)
GAZA	fortress city of southern Palestine, at this time the eastern border city of Egypt
GRANICUS	battle site 334
GULF OF CORINTH	eastern half of the gulf separating the Peloponnese from the mainland
GULF OF TARANTO	the 'instep' of Italy
GYTHION	port of Sparta in southern Peloponnese
HALIKARNASSOS	now Bodrum
HALKIDIKI	peninsula complex of the North Aegean
HELLESPONT	now called the Dardanelles
HERACLEA PONTICA	port on the Black sea, near modern Zonguldak
HERACLEA	port on the south Macedonian Coast
HIERON ORIS	anchorage in Propontis

HIPPONIUM	now Vibo Maritima, Calabria, Italy
HYDASPES	battle site 326
HYDASPES, RIVER	now the River Jhelum
IASSOS	island near Rhodes
ILLYRIA	coastal lands of the eastern Adriatic, north of Epirus
INDUS, RIVER	
IONIA	coastal region of Western Anatolia settled by Greeks
IONIAN SEA	sea area west of Greece and south of Italy
IPSOS	battle 301, in west-central Anatolia
ISAURIA	region inland of the Cilician coast
ISSUS	battle site 333
ITALY	
ITHSMUS	narrow strip of land joining Peloponnese to the mainland
JERUSALEM	capital of Judaea
JUDAEA/PALESTINE/ISRAEL	
KITION	near modern Larnaca on Cyprus
KOS	island in the Dodecanese
LADE	small island near Miletos in Caria; battle 202
LAMIA IN THESSALY	strategic city on the coast of Thessaly
LAMPSACUS	port city on the Hellespont
LARNACA BAY	on the south coast of Cyprus
LEMNOS	island in the northern Aegean
LESBOS	large island of the north-east Aegean
LEUCAS/ LEUCTRA	one of the Ionian islands, now Levkas
LEVANT	littoral part of the East Mediterranean bounded by the coasts of Egypt, Phoenicia and Southern Anatolia
LIPARI	islands off the north coast of Sicily
LYCIA	region of south-west Turkey, west of Antalya
MACEDON	kingdom of north-east Greece
MAGNESIA	battle in 189; south-east of Ephesus
MANTINEA	battle site 362
MASSILIA	now Marseilles, France
MEGARA	city-state west of Athens
MEMPHIS	once capital of Egypt
MESOPOTAMIA	area of the lower rivers Euphrates and Tigris
MESSANA	now Messina in Sicily
MESSENE	the south-west part of the Peloponnese
METHONE	seaport of the south-west Peloponnese
MILETOS	coastal city south of Ephesus
MOTYA	town in a lagoon in the west of Sicily, North of modern Marsala
MYCALE	on the coast between Ephesus and Miletos

MYNDOS	in Caria, battle in 43
MYONNESUS	cape on the Turkish coast, due north of Samos
MYTILENE	city on the east coast of Lesbos
NAFPLION	Gulf of, in the eastern Peloponnese
NASSUS	coastal town opposite Corcyra
NAULOCHUS	on the north coast of Sicily, battle in 36
NAXOS	island in the central Cyclades, battle site 376
NILE – RED SEA CANAL	cut under the Pharoah Necho II in about 610
NILE DELTA	
NYMPHAEUM	now Shengjin, Albania
OENIDAE	coastal town opposite Corcyra
ORCHOMENOS	in Boeotia, battle in 86
OREUS	town of northern Euboea, now Istiala
ORICUS	now Dukat, Albania
OSTIA	ancient seaport of Rome, at the mouth of the River Tiber
PALESTINE	
PAMPHYLIA	province on the Gulf of Antalya in southern Turkey
PANION	battle 200, now Banion east of Tyre
PANORMUS	sea port just south of Ephesus in western Turkey
PAPHLAGONIA	on the north coast of Turkey
PAPHOS	city of western Cyprus
PARTHIA	the empire that succeeded the Seleucids in the East
PATRAS	Gulf of, the western part of the gulf separating Greece from the Peloponnese
PATTALA	town of the Indus Delta
PELOPONNESE	the great peninsula of the southern part of Greece
PELUSIAC NILE	easternmost branch of the Nile Delta, no longer extant
PELUSIUM	fortress guarding the coast road into Egypt
PERGAMUM	kingdom and city, near modern Bergama in western Turkey
PERSIA	south-west Iran
PERSIAN EMPIRE	
PERSIAN GULF	
PETRA	ancient trading city, now in southern Jordan
PHAROS IN PYLOS	town on the coast of southern Illyria
PHARSALUS	in central Thessaly, battle in 48
PHASELIS	town in Cilicia
PHOCAEA	port near Smyrna, modern Foca
PHOENICIA	a collection of city-states on the coast of Syria, Lebanon and Israel
PHRYGIA	central-western Turkey
PILLARS OF HERCULES	the Rocks of Gibraltar and Ceuta either side of the strait

PIRAEUS	the port of Athens
PONTUS	kingdom of northern Asia Minor, on the Black Sea
PRIENE	ancient seaport, south of Ephesos
PROPONTIS	now the Sea of Marmara
PTOLEMAIS	later Acre, now Akko, Israel
PYDNA	battle in 168; near the coast of north-east Macedon
RAPHIA	battle 217, south-west of Gaza
RHEGIUM	now Reggio Calabria, Italy
RHODES	largest of the Dodecanese islands; republic
ROME	
SALAMIS, CYPRUS	city of eastern Cyprus
SAMOS	in the Southern Sporades islands of the south-eastern Aegean
SAMOTHRACE	island of the northern Sporades, in the north-east Aegean
SARDIS	city east of Izmir (Smyrna)
SELEUCIA	port of Antioch, now Samandag, Turkey
SELEUCIA-ON-TIGRIS	port town created by Seleucos I
SICILY	
SIDE	city just east of modern Antalya in Turkey
SIDON	city-state of Phoenicia
SINOPE	now Sinop, capital of Pontus on the south coast of the Black Sea
SIPHNOS	island in the Cyclades
SKIATHOS	island of the northern Sporades
SMYRNA	modern Izmir in Turkey
SPARTA	city-state in the Peloponnese
SPORADES	island chain in the central and south-east Aegean
STRAIT OF MESSINA	separating Sicily from mainland Italy
SYRACUSE	city-state of eastern Sicily
SYRIA	
TARAS	Tarentum, now Taranto
TARSUS	city in Cilicia
TENEDOS	island of the north-east Aegean
TEOS	coastal city between Capes Corycus and Myonnesus
THEBES	capital city of Boeotia
THERA/SANTORINI	island of the southern Cyclades
THERMOPYLAE	battle in 191; famous pass adjacent to North Euboea
THESSALONIKI	Port city of northern Greece
THESSALY	area of eastern-central Greece
THRACE	that part of Europe forming modern Bulgaria, European Turkey and north-east Greece
THRACIAN CHERSONESUS	now the Bosporus, narrow strait separating Europe from Asia between Istanbul and the Black Sea

TIGRIS, RIVER
TRIPOLIS   city-state of Phoenicia
TROY   Ilium of legend
TYRE   ancient sea port, now in Lebanon city-state of Phoenicia
TYRRHENIAN SEA
VALONA   on the coast of Albania
VERGINA   in Macedon, burial place of their Kings
ZAKINTHOS   one of the Ionian islands
ZAMA   in central Tunisia, battle 202

Notes

Chapter 1

1. Burn, *The Pelican History of Greece* p.326
2. Demosthenes LI.13
3. Hale p.95 et seq.
4. Ormerod p.109
5. Thucydides IV.8/9; Ormerod p.110
6. Ormerod p.113
7. Xenophon, *Hellenica* VI.4; Diodorus XV.95; Ormerod p.116
8. Demosthenes XVIII.145
9. Ormerod p.118
10. Demosthenes VIII. 25/26
11. Diodorus XVI.7
12. Ormerod pp. 116/7
13. Demosthenes XXIII.166
14. Ormerod p.117
15. Berthold p.31
16. Diodorus XVI.74 & XVI.77
17. A young Alexander led the decisive cavalry charge of the battle.
18. Champion, *The Tyrants of Syracuse*, Vol. I
19. The Syracusan fleet had totalled some 200 warships in 398, probably its largest muster.
20. Diodorus XIV.41
21. Diodorus XIV.42.5 says that he built over 200 ships in addition to the 110 that he already had; this is surely an exaggeration as Dionysius never seems to have had more than 180 in all, of which most were triremes.
22. Diodorus XIV.42.2
23. Mott L. V. In *War at Sea in the Middle Ages and Renaissance* p.111
24. Gabrielson, *The Athenian Navy in the Fourth Century BC, in Age of the Galley* p.234 et seq.
25. For example, in 325/24, the fleet sent to the Adriatic included four triaconters
26. Hale p.272
27. Demosthenes XIV.14-30
28. Barker, *Alexander the Great's Campaigns* p.57
29. Berthold pp.20-27
30. Berthold p.29
31. *Navies of Rome* p.20; Liyy VIII.14
32. Diodorus XIV.41
33. Diodorus XIV.44.6

Chapter 2

1. The first record of a sea battle was found on clay tablets, relating a battle between the Hittites and Cypriots in 1210. Pemsel, *Atlas of Naval Warfare* p.11. Although Homer in the Iliad details the Greek fleet used in the Trojan War (probably eleventh century), no naval battles are related.
2. Such a battle was that between the Egyptian fleet of Pharoah Rameses III and that of the 'Sea Peoples' in c.1176, illustrated in relief at Medinet Habu. Apart from the clear difference in style between the ships

of the antagonists, there is little that might classify them as 'warships'. For an illustrated examination see *Age of the Galley*, pp28-33; also Murnane W.J. *The Penguin Guide to Ancient Egypt.*

3. See, for a listing, the *Navis Online Database of Ancient Shipwrecks.*
4. The concept and practice of rowing, as opposed to paddling is very old, e.g. illustrated by a tomb painting from Saqqara of c. 2500.
5. Homer, *Iliad* I.308
6. The earliest incontestable representation of a ram appears on a bronze fibula or brooch from Athens dated to c.850 BC
7. Thucydides II.93
8. Homer, *Iliad* I.308/9
9. Herodotus IV.148
10. Herodotus I.152; Homer, *Iliad* I.402/09, 509/10, *Odyssey* I.280
11. 'conter' Anglicised version of the Greek *kontos* or number
12. Xenophon, *Economica* VIII.8; Thucydides III.9; Xenophon, *Hellenica* VI.2
13. *SSAW* p97
14. Wall relief from Ninevah showing Phoenician biremes, 702 BC
15. Homer, *Iliad* II.719/20, mentions a 118-man warship, a bireme with 58 lower and 60 upper level rowers; such is not known to have existed during the time he was writing about (the Trojan War, probably in the eleventh century) and must relate to a ship of his own time (eighth century). Anderson, *Oared Fighting Ships* p.5, refers to painted Greek pottery showing 20 thranite and 19 zygite oars per side, i.e. 76 oars in total.
16. Herodotus, II.159 states that the Pharoah of Egypt built Threes, c. 600 Thucydides I.13 as to the first three built in Corinth.
17. The oars were light in weight and rowers could make a forced march carrying them, Thucydides II.95
18. Hale p.256
19. *Age of the Galley* p.234
20. It has been posited that the Phoenicians developed their own form of trireme that did not use an outrigger for the thranite oars. Morrison et al. *GROW/Greek Oared Ships*
21. Battle of Hellespont AD 324, the last time that triremes were recorded in battle
22. Morrison, Coates and Rankov, *The Athenian Trireme* p.25 et seq.
23. Tilley, *Seafaring on the Ancient Mediterranean* p11 et seq.
24. There is still dissent, see Tilley, *Seafaring on the Ancient Mediterranean*
25. For full particulars of the building, see Welsh, *Building the Trireme* and Morrison, Coates and Rankov, *The Athenian Trireme;* for the sea trials and conclusions therefrom, see Rankov, *Trireme Olympias, the Final Report*
26. *Roman Warships* p. 18; *GROW* p.1
27. Morrison, Coates and Rankov, *The Athenian Trireme* p.1
28. Pliny, *Natural History* VII.297, quoting Aristotle (384 to 322)
29. *Navies of Rome* p.17
30. There is some disagreement in the ancient sources as to who invented what. Diodorus for example (XIV.41/42/44) says that the four was invented in Syracuse; Thyucidides (*Nat. Hist.* VII.257) that it appeared first at Sidon, Aristotle says Carthage. The balance of the evidence favours it having been a Carthaginian introduction.
31. Arrian II.21.9
32. *Roman Warships* p.103
33. *Navies of Rome* p.19; Diodorus XIV.41/42; (as quoted in Torr, *Ancient Ships*)
34. *Navies of Rome* p.72; *R. Navy* p.26
35. Diodorus XVI.44
36. Barker, *Alexander the Great's Campaigns* posits the Five as a bireme with three rowers per upper oar and two for each lower oar in a ship of only 120 feet/36.5m by fourteen feet/(4.3m, twenty feet/6m across the outrigger
37. Polybius I.20, I.59
38. *GROW* p.290

39. *Roman Warships* p.100
40. *GROW* p.330
41. Aelian, *Var, History* VI.12; Pliny, *Natural History* VII.207
42. *Roman Warships* pp.90-95, for a consideration of the type
43. *Roman Warships* as above
44. *GROW* p.308
45. Zosimus V.20
46. Johnston, *Ship and Boat Models in Ancient Greece*; Torr, *Ancient Ships*, p15; Theophrastus XXV.5; Diodorus Siculus XVI.61.4, notes them in service (in 346/45) under a Phocian commander
47. Torr, *Ancient Ships*, pp 14 & 41 says the term actually means 'a whole and half'
48. Ormerod p29; Diodorus Siculus XIX.65; Theophrastus, *Characters* XXV.5; Appian, *Roman History* XII.9; Arrian, *Anabasis* III.2.3
49. In the same way that the modern term 'ketch' is used to describe any sailing yacht with two masts, steered from abaft the rearmost and irrespective of size, shape, purpose or any other attribute.
50. *Age of the Galley* p.75
51. *SSAW* p.128
52. Meijer p142; Casson, *Ancient Mariners* p.78
53. The problem is that the vase is dated to the sixth century, there is no mention of the *hemiolia* before about 350 and the pirate ship is shown as a full bireme.
54. Diodorus Siculus XIX.65 once more
55. Arrian III.2; Polybius XVI.7.4
56. Xenophon, *History of Greece* XXI.30
57. Meijer p.203
58. *Age of the Galley* pp.73/75
59. *Age of the Galley* p.139; *GROW* pp.317/318, 345
60. Per Ormerod, Torr, *Ancient Ships*, *SSAW*, Meijer, *GROW*; although none of the ancient authors say as much or allude to the arrangement of rowers in the hull.
61. Torr, *Ancient Ships*, p.15
62. Casson, *Ancient Mariners* p.139
63. Ormerod, p.29
64. Casson, *Ancient Mariners* pp.78, 139
65. *The Athenian Trireme* op.cit pp.105 n6
66. But see *GROW* pp.317-21; *Age of the Galley* pp.39/40
67. Nelson, *Warfleets of Antiquity* p.19
68. Meijer p.141
69. *Age of the Galley* op.cit pp.73-75
70. *Age of the Galley* pp.139/140
71. *GROW* pp.317/318
72. Tilley, *Seafaring in the Ancient Mediterranean* p.52. This author cannot agree with the contention that it was 'a respectable warship, big enough to engage a flagship' as on the occasion referred to, the flagship was attacked by no less than four Fives, the three *hemioliae* involved merely lending support with their extra men.
73. Xenophon, *History of Greece* II.1.30; Barker, *Alexander the Great's Campaigns* p.56 also proposes the craft to be seventy feet (21.3m) long and ten feet (3m) beam, with a crew of sixty-two and capable of ten knots under oar and sail.
74. Tilley, *Seafaring in the Ancient Mediterranean* pp.26/27, who posits this arrangement as a Four.
75. Casson, *Ancient Mariners* p.180; the last record of them being in service, with Cilician pirates in the first century BC.
76. Diodorus XIX.65; Champion, *The Tyrants of Syracuse* Vol.II *p.84.*

Chapter 3
1. *GROW* p.346
2. Thyucidides VII.24

3. Polybius VIII.4
4. Livy XXXVII.23
5. Polybius XVI.3
6. Athenaos V.208
7. *GROW* pp.207-214
8. According to Pliny XXXII
9. Marsden, *Greek and Roman Artillery;* Wilkins, *Roman Artillery*
10. The development of the high explosive shell provided the first such weapon.
11. As at Actium
12. Arrian, *Indica* 24.7
13. Caesar, *The Alexandrine War* XIX.3
14. Marsden, *Greek and Roman Artillery*
15. Livy XXVI.26
16. For example, Caesar, *Civil War* II.1.6
17. Appian, *Civil Wars* V.118/119
18. Appian, *Civil Wars* VII.8
19. One of the worst examples being the disaster that struck a Roman fleet in 255. *Navies of Rome* p.64
20. Thucydides I.48, notes that a Corinthian fleet off Corfu in 432, carried three days' food.
21. For a fuller discussion, see *inter alia, Roman Navy* pp.110 to 114; Guilmartin, *Galleons and Galleys*
22. Polybius XVI.3 and Thucydides II.84
23. Thucydides, *The Peloponnesian Wars*

Chapter 4
1. Arrian, *Anabasis* I.3.3-4
2. Ormerod p.115
3. Rodgers p.219; Arrian, *Anabasis* I.11.6
4. Barker, *Alexander the Great's Campaigns* p.154
5. Rodgers p.221; Reynolds, *Command of the Sea* p.44. Warry, *Warfare in the Classical World* p.75 says 200 ships, mostly from Greeks but includes transports in this total. Hale p.298 says 160 (including 20 Athenian) but that this total was at the Hellespont. Arrian I.17.6 says 160 triremes and 'a good number' of freighters.
6. Diodorus XVII.7; XXII.5;XXIX.2
7. Diodorus XVI.89.5 & 17
8. Arrian, *Anabasis* I.18.4-6
9. Arrian, *Anabasis* I.18.4-6
10. Arrian, *Anabasis* I.19.4-6
11. Ormerod p.120
12. Arrian, *Anabasis* I.18.6
13. Arrian, *Anabasis* I.19
14. Arrian, *Anabasis* I.20
15. Hale p.301
16. Arrian, *Anabasis* II.1&2
17. Arrian, *Anabasis* II.7.2
18. Southworth, *The Ancient Fleets* pp.153-154
19. Herodotus II.44; it had reputedly been founded c.2755 B.C.
20. Arrian, *Anabasis* III.2.4
21. And see Arrian, *Anabasis* III.17
22. Arrian, *Anabasis* III.1-3; Plutarch XXVI.5
23. Rodgers p.223
24. Hale p.302
25. Hale p.305; Rodgers p.203. There is a dispute about the actual numbers in any particular year. The figure of fifty fours is consistent but the number of fives varies between two and seven. The figure of

360 triremes seems excessive unless one includes old ships, the transports and unseaworthy ships still in the lists.

26. Ormerod p.122; Q. Curtius IV.8.15
27. Arrian, *Anabasis* V.3.5
28. Arrian, *Anabasis* VI.1.6
29. Arrian, *Anabasis* V.8.5 and V.12.4
30. Arrian, *Anabasis* VI.1.1
31. Perhaps an exaggeration, the accounts vary between 800 and 2,000
32. Arrian, *Indica* XX to XLI recounts this voyage
33. Arrian, *Anabasis* VII.16.1/2
34. Arrian VII.14, *Anabasis*
35. Arrian, *Anabasis* VII.16.3
36. According to Arrian, *Anabasis* VII.19.3; *SSAW* p.136
37. Curtius, *History of Alexander* X.1.17-19
38. Herodotus II.158
39. Arrian, *Anabasis* VII.20
40. Reynolds, *Command of the Sea* 9.45
41. Diodorus XVIII.4

Chapter 4: Appendix

1. For Map 4, the author has relied upon the maps in Harden, *The Phoenicians* p.29 and Frost, *Under the Mediterranean* pp.74/75, which relate to the underwater surveys of Poidebard (1935 to 1939).
2. Berthold p.34
3. Arrian, *Anabasis* II.23.3; Diodorus Sic. XVII.43.4
4. Arrian, *Anabasis* II.23.6

Chapter 5

1. Reynolds, *Command of the Sea* p.46
2. Pliny, *Natural History* VII.57
3. Curtius, *History of Alexander* X.1.17-19
4. *Age of the Galley* p.184
5. *GROW* p.306:Coates' drawing of a seven does exactly this, the lower oar being two feet /610mm longer.
6. Thucydides II.93.2
7. *Roman Warships* p.32; Murnane, *The Penguin Guide to Ancient Egypt* p.222
8. Polybius I.23
9. Quoted in *GROW* p.272
10. Contrast Morrison, *GROW* p.272 and *Navies of Rome* p.57
11. *Roman Warships* p.17
12. *GROW* pp.305/306
13. *GROW* p.309
14. I have previously suggested (*Roman Warships* p.95) an overall length of some 186 feet /56.7m for a six; *GROW* p.345 suggests a length overall for the seven as 154 feet/47m but this is with a much shorter interscalmium.
15. Barker, *Alexander the Great's Campaigns* p.56
16. Barker, *Alexander the Great's Campaigns* p.56
17. *GROW* p.272
18. Arrian, *Anabasis* VII.21.1
19. Arrian, *Anabasis* VI.1.1; also Diodorus XVII.86.3
20. Herodotus IV.148
21. *SSAW* 125
22. By the Peace of Apamea in 188, Antiochus III had a limit imposed as to his maximum warship size, namely 30-oared ships. Polybius XXI.43; Livy XXXVII.38

23. Meijer, p.14 suggests 75.5 feet/23m which he admits is too much ('unmanageable' as he puts it).
24. Depictions of monoreme conters rarely if ever show convenient round numbers of oars (20, 30, 50 – there is no Greek term for a 60-oar ship) so oar numbers could be a few more or less than 30; the ship was still classified as such.
25. Anderson *Oared Fighting Ships* p.8

Chapter 6
1. Berthold, *Rhodes in the Hellenistic Age* p.36
2. Hale p.309
3. *SSAW* p.97
4. Diodorus XVIII.10 claims Athens had no less than 315 triremes and 50 fours, presumably including the old unseaworthy ships previously noted; in any case shortage of manpower limited the numbers.
5. Hale p.317
6. Chugg, *The Lost Tomb of Alexander the Great* p.42 et seq.
7. Diodorus XVIII.72
8. Diadorus XVIII.51
9. Appian *Bello Civilis* II.89, records Caesar's fleet sailing from Rhodes to Alexandria in three days (post Chapter 17) a distance of 374 miles (601km).
10. Ormerod, *Piracy in the Ancient World* p.116
11. Plutarch, *Demetrios* 29; Diodorus XXIX.8; Rodgers p.236
12. Reynolds, *Command of the Sea* p.48
13. Diodorus XIX.69
14. Marlowe, *The Golden Age of Alexandria* p.35
15. Green p.29
16. Green p.687
17. Plutarch, *Demetrios* 8
18. Plutarch, *Demetrios* 10
19. Berthold; Polybius XXX.5.8
20. Rodgers p.246
21. Siege: Diodorus XX.81.8; XX.91.100; Plutarch, *Demetrios* XXI.2
22. Diodorus XXI.1; Plutarch, *Demetrios* 28–30

Chapter 6: Appendix
1. Plutarch, *Demetrios* XVI.2
2. Diodorus XX.49.2/XX.50.2; Plutarch, *Demetrios* XXXI.1/XXXII.2; Rodgers p.246; *SSAW* p.137 says however, that Demetrios had ten sixes, seven sevens, etc.
3. Diodorus XX.47.1
4. Plutarch, *Demetrios* XVI.2; Nelson, *Warfleets of Antiquity* p.77
5. Murray, *The Age of Titans* p.107 suggests that Demetrios formed his line parallel to the shore. Clearly he would not have done this as it would leave them without searoom and liable to be pushed ashore by Ptolemy's attack. Also, when Ptolemy rounded the Cape, he would have been confronted by Demetrios' completely open right flank, composed of his weakest ships; an attack would quickly roll up the line, leaving his strongest ships at the other end, unable to intervene. Finally, fleets drawn up parallel to a shore, lose (eg. Drepanum 249; the Punic fleet at Ebro 217; Octavius at Cumae and again at Pelorus in 38).
6. Nelson, *Warfleets of Antiquity* p.77, avers that Demetrios used and manned transports, albeit military and probably obsolete warships, to fill out his centre; Morrison *GROW* p.25 thinks they were triremes.
7. Diodorus XX.49–53
8. Compare that in *GROW* p.29/30, to that in Rodgers p.241/242
9. Also see Rodgers p239 et seq.; *GROW* pp.24–30

Chapter 7
1. *SSAW* p.98
2. Guilmartin, *Galleons and Galleys* p.110; *Roman Warships* p.32

3. Rodgers, *Naval Warfare under Oars* p.230
4. Morrison, Coates & Rankov, *The Athenian Trireme* pp.136/240
5. The probable average height of a man of the time and place.
6. Less than the author has used for his example in *Roman Warships* p.30, but hopefully more realistic for the age; the principle remains sound.
7. *GROW* p.305
8. *Age of the Galley* p.198
9. Barras de la Penne, *La Science des Galeres* 1697; he was the captain of Louis XIV's galley fleet.
10. Anderson, *Oared Fighting Ships* pp.25 & 29; Rodgers p.254. Conversely, see Tilley, *Seafaring in the Ancient Mediterranean* p.83 describing the Portuguese *Saveiro*, rowed by both pushing and pulling.
11. *SSAW* p.106
12. Rodgers p. 29 et seq.
13. Rodgers p.258; SSAW p. 107.; Anderson, *Oared Fighting Ships* p.27
14. *Age of the Galley* pp.173 to 205, for a detailed analysis of the two rowing methods.
15. Such as that in tomb of Mereruka, c.2330, *Roman Warships* p.32 and Figure 37.
16. Lucan III.542.43; quoted in *SSAW*
17. As examples, Guilmartin, *Gunpowder and Galleys*; Morison & Gardner *The Age of the Galley*
18. *Age of the Galley* p.171; *SSAW* p.106
19. Morrison, Coates and Rankov, *The Athenian Trireme* p.137. The midships oars were very slightly longer to compensate for the curvature of the hull.
20. Anderson, *Oared Fighting Ships* p.22. Presumably the short trireme oars were for the thalamite position in a trireme five.
21. *SSAW* p.109
22. Although they were about the same length as the longest Renaissance oars (*SSAW* p.109), as the ancients could build bigger ships, presumably they could also make longer oars.
23. *Roman Warships* pp. 87,106, 100 &95 respectively
24. Athenaos V.206
25. Donato, *Mare Nostrum, The Roman Sea* p.49; Navis Online Database of Ancient Shipwrecks
26. *Age of the Galley* p.194

Chapter 8
1. *GROW* p.346
2. *SSAW* p.106, suggests a bireme with 5 thranites and 4 zygites
3. Whereas the thalamites in Figure 40A can operate easily with a 25 feet/7.6m. oar, the zygites will need a 48 feet/ 14.6m. oar and the thranites a 49.25 feet/ 15.1m. oar; as seen from the table at the end of Chapter 7, a 47 feet / 14.3m. oar was intended for a seven-man crew in later times.
4. Pausanius (mid-second century AD) I.29.1, quoted in Murray, *Age of Titans* p.276
5. Waterline length multiplied by waterline beam multiplied by draft multiplied by 62.4 (weight in pounds of a cubic foot of water) divided by 2240 = displacement in tons (imperial).
6. Allowing a rower at 150 lbs., an armed marine at 180 lbs. and the rest at 165 lbs.
7. Waterline length multiplied by waterline beam multiplied by two-fifths.
8. *Navies of Rome* p.45; Polybius XV.2; Livy XXVIII.30
9. Florus IV.11
10. Cassius Dio, *Roman History* L.29
11. *Roman Warships* p.94. The author has put the deck of a six as 12 feet (3.7m) above waterline.
12. Diodorus XIX.62.7
13. *GROW* p.346, also has a table of the socket sizes.
14. A complete second century ram recovered from the sea off Athlit in Israel, thought to have been from a four. Casson & Steffy, *The Athlit Ram*
15. *GROW* p.294
16. Polybius XVI.3
17. Murray, *Age of Titans*
18. Diodorus XX.93.3

19. Polybius XVI.2
20. Athenaeus V.203; Appian, *Roman History* preface
21. *GROW*, p.113
22. Also *SSAW* p.129/31
23. *GROW* p.380
24. Morrison in *The Age of the Galley*, pp.75/76
25. Tilley, *Seafaring on the Ancient Mediterranean*, pp.52/53
26. *GROW*, p.219; Johnston, *Ship and Boat Models in Ancient Greece*, pp.102/103
27. *GROW* p.203; Johnston, *Ship and Boat Models in Ancient Greece*, pp.100/102
28. *SSAW* p.102 says the prow was erected by Rhodes c.200-180 and as they mostly used the four, it is this that is represented, rowed by 2 two-man oars through the ports shown; the Palazzo Spada and Palestrina mosaics show the same arrangement. Anderson (p.25) says it was believed erected for Demetrios for his victory at Salamis in 306 and thus represents his flagship, a seven; alternatively it is by his son Gonatas for his victory at Kos in 258, where his flagship was the *Isthmia* (see later chapters). The problem with these arguments is that Samothrace is nowhere near Rhodes, Salamis or Kos, so why should either of them put it there anyway?
29. *GROW*, pp.205, 266, although he is surely altering the facts to suit the theory.
30. *Age of the Galley*, p.139; *GROW* pp.319/321
31. Also see the 'Palazzo Spada' relief, *Roman Warships* p.33
32. *Navies of Rome* p.29
33. *Roman Warships* p.134
34. *Roman Warships* p.84

Chapter 9

1. Using timber from the forests of Cyprus, which he still controlled. Plutarch, *Demetrios* XLIII
2. Marlow, *The Golden Age of Alexandria* p.36
3. Green p.26; Plutarch, *Demetrios* 41–42
4. Plutarch, *Pyrrhus* 12
5. Green p.129
6. Plutarch, *Demetrios* XXXI.1
7. Plutarch, *Demetrios* 52
8. As an example, there survives an inscribed stela from this time, commemorating a naval expedition to Aigila (Antikythera) in pursuit of a band of pirates from Tarsus in Cilicia (a notorious lair of pirates). First half third century, seen by the author in the archaeological exhibition of the Palace of the Grand Master, Rhodes (photography not permitted).
9. Green p.131
10. Green pp.131 to 133
11. *Navies of Rome* p.4
12. *SSAW* p.191; *Navies of Rome* p.37; Athenaeus, *Deipnosophists* 5.40-44
13. *Navies of Rome* p.51
14. Polybius XIV.44
15. Plutarch, *Moralia* XXI.16 refers to 'a sea fight off Cos' where one of his friends said to Antigonos II "see you not how many more ships the enemy have got than we have." Athenaeus, *Deipnosophists* 44 refers to a 'sacred trireme' built by Antigonos which defeated 'commanders of Ptolemy II off Leucolla, a city under the dominion of Cos'.
16. Polyaenos V.18, quoted in *GROW* p.55
17. *Navies of Rome* p.77
18. Bickerman, *Chronology of the Ancient World* pp.128-129
19. Athenaeus V.36; Pliny VII.57; *SSAW* p.140
20. Green p.253
21. Polybius II.11 & 12
22. Polybius V.89

23. In the tablet referred to in note 8 above, the force is specified as a number of fours. Polybius IV.46 and 47 refers to Rhodes being honoured at the shrine of Delos for its anti-piracy work.
24. Berthold p.239
25. Polybius III.16
26. *Navies of Rome* p.95
27. *Navies of Rome* p.106
28. Livy XXIX.12
29. Green p.304
30. Polybius XVI.10
31. Polybius XVI.3
32. Polybius XVI.10
33. Polybius XVI.15
34. Polybius XVI.3
35. Livy XXXI.15.5
36. Livy XXXI.2

Chapter 9: Appendix
1. Polybius XVI.6 and XVI.7
2. Polybius XVI. 2 to 15

Chapter 10
1. Coates in *GROW* in his reconstruction drawings allows only a 3 degree angle of heel and assumes a smooth sea. Also see Rankov, *Trireme Olympias, the Final Report* for reports of actual sea trials.
2. The author preferred a bireme for his interpretation of the Roman six, *RomWar* p.90; Morrison *GROW* p.274 prefers the bireme for big ships but, in making his case for the Samothrace Prow as a *trihemiolia*, has to assume the existence of additional oarports in the hull, below the outrigger; there are none such on the statue, but as it is only of the very bow and as he says, any such would appear further aft. Unfortunately there are also none on any of the other examples either.
3. *RomWar* pp.31/33 the author has given some initial consideration to this problem and has even considers if the oars were worked in an 'X' fashion, giving enough room between them for the crews but impossible because a) the oars would clash with neighbouring oars, b) greater distance would be needed between the oarports than shown and c) the sources all show the oars together.
4. Unlike Coates' reconstruction of a five *GROW* p.314, where operating angles are too acute and differing oar lengths are used.
5. Anderson, *Oared Fighting Ships* p.26
6. For the purpose of exhausting possibilities, consideration has even been given to a scheme, for which it must be emphasised, there is no supporting evidence, whereby the two oars of a pair are linked or connected inboard and both operated by one oar-crew. The advantage is that all crew members are contributing maximum effort while doubling the number of blades in the water. It fails because the problem of excessive beam remains and also because each oar loom will describe a different path, requiring a flexible coupling, which makes it unworkable as direct effort cannot be applied. Surely the only answer must be that each oar had its own crew, returning us to the problem of fitting them into the available working space.
7. A similar solution to the formula evolved to calculate the size of artillery pieces and their components (see Chapter 3)

Chapter 11
1. Plutarch, *Demetrios* XXXI.20.4 and XLIII.4.5; Meijer p.136; Warry, *Warfare in the Classical World* p.94
2. Different sources sometimes give different dates for the appearance of some rates e.g. Athenaos V.203 claims that Ptolemy III had elevens as well as twelves in 246.
3. Appian, *The Illyrian Wars* III
4. Livy XXIV.35